War, Peace and International Relatio

War, Peace and International Relations is an introduction to the strategic history of the past two centuries, years which were shaped and reshaped by wars. The book shows that war is not only about warfare – the military conduct of war – but is crucial to the political, social and cultural behaviour of states.

Written by leading strategist Professor Colin Gray, this textbook provides students with a good grounding in the contribution of war to the development of the modern world, from the pre-industrial era to the post-industrial age of international terrorism and smart weapons.

War, Peace and International Relations:

- is the first one-volume strategic history textbook on the market
- covers all the major wars of the past two centuries
- is up to date and comprehensive, including chapters on irregular warfare and terrorism
- includes summary points, boxed sections, student questions and further reading.

Colin S. Gray is Professor of International Politics and Strategic Studies at the University of Reading, UK and a professional strategic theorist and defence analyst. His twenty-one books include *Modern Strategy* (1999) and *Another Bloody Century* (2005).

War, Peace and International Relations

An Introduction to Strategic History

Colin S. Gray

Routledge
Taylor & Francis Group

LONDON AND NEW YORK

First published 2007
by Routledge
2 Park Square, Milton Park, Abingdon, Oxon, OX14 4RN

Simultaneously published in the USA and Canada
by Routledge
270 Madison Ave, New York, NY 10016

Routledge is an imprint of the Taylor & Francis Group, an informa business

© 2007 Colin S. Gray

Transferred to Digital Printing 2008

Typeset in Times New Roman by
Keystroke, 28 High Street, Tettenhall, Wolverhampton
Printed and bound in Great Britain by
Cpod, Trowbridge, Wiltshire

British Library Cataloguing in Publication Data
A catalogue record for this book is available from the British Library

Library of Congress Cataloging in Publication Data
Gray, Colin S.
War, peace and international relations : an introduction to strategic history /
Colin S. Gray
p. cm.
Includes bibliographical references.
ISBN 978–0–415–38638–8 (hardback : alk. paper) –
ISBN 978–0–415–38639–5 (pbk. : alk. paper)
1. War. 2. Military policy. 3. Strategy. 4. International relations.
5. Military history, Modern–19th century. 6. Military history, Modern–20th century.
I. Title
U21.2.G673 2007
355.0209–dc22
2006034566

ISBN 10: 0–415–38638–1 (hbk)
ISBN 10: 0–415–38639–X (pbk)
ISBN 10: 0–203–08899–9 (ebk)

ISBN 13: 978–0–415–38638–8 (hbk)
ISBN 13: 978–0–415–38639–5 (pbk)
ISBN 13: 978–0–203–08899–9 (ebk)

To the memory of John Erickson, an inspiring teacher,
a wise mentor and a good friend

Contents

Maps

Boxes and tables

Boxes

Tables

Preface

I have long been convinced that students of strategic studies know too little history, while students of history and international relations are inclined to short-change the strategic dimension to their subjects. This book attempts to provide a coherent narrative and analysis of the past two centuries, keyed to the strategic perspective.

A textbook should explain what happened, not advance the author's beliefs. Truth and error should be accorded equal space by the author, so that students can judge for themselves where the balance of probability lies. All I can say in self-defence is that I have tried earnestly to be neutral on the more controversial topics, but the assertive habits of a professional lifetime cannot easily be set aside. The result is a compromise. My personal opinion probably intrudes into this work more than it should. But it appears less than I would have liked.

This book has benefited greatly from what I have learnt teaching the course on which it is based, both in Britain and in the United States. I know from experience – the students' experience, that is – that this melding of modern history, international relations and strategic studies works well. I am in the debt of my students at the University of Reading in Britain and at Missouri State University in Washington, DC.

For most of my career I have been a professional defence analyst and theorist, to which activity of recent years I have added university teaching. It follows that I had need of some expert help in preparing this work, since textbook writing requires a skill set all its own. My principal debt is to the excellent Andrew Humphrys, my editor at Routledge/Taylor and Francis. I have been amazed by his patience with an opinionated strategist who does not count brevity among his virtues. Andrew's advice invariably has been sound, even though I tried to resist some of it initially. Also I have learnt a lot from friends who truly are artists in the writing and illustrating of textbooks. Most especially, I must thank Jeremy Black, the extraordinary quantity of whose output is matched only by its high quality. Jeremy probably will not approve of my liking for a 'master narrative', but he may be won around when he realizes that that narrative is only 'strategic history' and not a particular storyline. In addition, I would like to thank my friend John Baylis, now at the University of Wales, Swansea, a scholar whose superior textbooking talents are approaching legendary status.

This book has been possible only because of the support I have received from the School of Sociology, Politics and International Relations at the University of Reading in England. In particular, I am grateful for the assistance provided by Dr Robert McKeever, the erstwhile Head of School. As usual, I am entirely dependent upon the outstanding skill and dedication of my manuscript preparation person, Barbara Watts, who truly is an inspiration. Her speed on the keyboard, her ability to read my handwriting and her readiness to meet unreasonable deadlines are beyond praise.

Last, but not least, my ever-suffering family deserve the most sincere thanks for tolerating, usually with good humour, my protracted distraction with the challenges of book creation. Valerie and TJ, I could not have done it without you. That may serve to share some of the blame!

Colin S. Gray
Wokingham, UK
September 2006

Introduction
Strategic history

Reader's guide: The meaning, importance and value of strategic history

War and the fear of war have been by far the most powerful among the influences that have shaped the course of international relations over the past two centuries. It is the central thesis of this book that the history of the use and threat of force enables us to make sense of the main currents of events. What is strategic history? It is the history of the influence of the use and threat of force. Strategy, and strategic, sometimes is a contested concept, and the term is widely misused (Gray, 1999: 17). This text adapts and adheres strictly to a slightly amended version of the definition given by the Prussian soldier Carl von Clausewitz (1780–1831), whose ideas and significance are explained in Chapter 2. Strategy refers to the use made of force and the threat of force for the ends of policy (Clausewitz, 1976: 177). This book is not a military history. The strategic focus ensures that our prime concern will be on the instrumentality of military power. Furthermore, notwithstanding the primacy of the strategic, the mission here does not comprise a reductionist effort to conflate the rich and interweaving strands of history into a single mould. The analysis is heavily political throughout, because it is only the political context that gives war its meaning.

The term 'strategy' frequently is employed in such a way that it is not clear whether the author means military strategy or grand strategy. The latter embraces all the instruments of statecraft, including the military. In that perspective, discussion and interpretation necessarily lose any special focus upon force. The high relevance of the concerns of grand strategy is recognized in the treatment of war's contexts in Chapter 2. The book could hardly be more explicit in that regard. But this analysis maintains as its primary focus the influence of force, and the threat of force, upon the course of history. That is the plot.

The history of the international relations of the past two centuries lends itself all too easily to understanding within the framework provided by military strategy. The strategic perspective does not explain everything, but it does capture the major currents of change and continuity, provides for a unity of interpretation, and certainly offers by far the most persuasive explanation of what happened, why and with what consequences. War has made the modern world more than has any other influence. That claim needs amendment by another: the modern world has been *unmade* several times by war. Each of the great conflicts of 1792–1815, 1914–18, 1939–45 and 1947–89 had transformative effects upon international relations. One author, Geoffrey Perret, tells us that 'Since 1775 no nation on Earth has had as much experience of war as the United States: nine major wars in nine generations' (Perret, 1990: 558). He warns that states are both made and unmade by strategic histories that record excessive defence preparation or war-making. At the time of his writing in the late 1980s, the theory of imperial overstretch was politically fashionable (Kennedy, 1987). Ironically, it was seized upon by those critical of American policy, but it showed its potency as a theory in the precipitate decline and definitive fall of the Soviet empire. The point most worthy of note is that it is hard to find countries that have not been made by war. Inevitably, some of them have been unmade by the very same agent. Nearly all countries were created through a process of greater or lesser violence. There are a few exceptions, but they are so minor as to prove the authority of the general rule. As late as the 1740s, England was still enforcing its union with Scotland against Jacobite challenge by force of arms, while the Irish dimension to the United Kingdom continues to occasion some violence. Peace may have broken out in Northern Ireland, but it remains fragile.

Because war, and its conduct in warfare, is no more than an instrument of political decisions, or policy, one might argue that strategic history can make no sense apart from political history. That is true, which is why this narrative and analysis attach such high importance to several of war's most vital contexts, pre-eminent among which is the political. Those contexts are identified and discussed in Chapter 1. But while granting the sovereignty of the political, the past 200 years have revealed that warlike outcomes are consistent with a bewildering array of specific causes, general conditions and particular triggers. Politics and the other sources of contextual fuel for conflict yielded an irregular, but always repeated, urge to fight during those two centuries. War was ever available as a live policy option. On balance, it has been a relatively stable agent of politics, while its political and other parents have served up a veritable feast of historically particular motives. Just as the very concept of strategic history provides, indeed reflects, a unified understanding of the course of events over 200 years, so also does a fundamental view of why communities are prepared to fight. In that latter regard, Thucydides wrote for all time when he identified 'fear, honor, and interest' as the strongest and most enduring of motives (Strassler, 1996: 43). Particular wars may be prevented, or tamed and rapidly concluded, by the settlement of specific political differences. But war itself, war as a human social institution of great antiquity, will never be eradicated until people discover definitive remedies for the maladies, even pathologies, that are the anxieties conflated by Thucydides into his deadly triad of motives.

Some historians warn against the grand narrative, the explanatory framework that threatens to explain too much (Black, 2004: 1). Braving such perils, this book is constructed around the grand narrative that strategic history provides a valid and essential way of understanding the course of events. Also, this theory holds that the strategic history of the past 200 years serves well enough to enable one to make sense of the ebb and flow of events. Most major developments in international relations from 1800 to the present can be accommodated, even in many cases explained, with reference to strategic criteria. Of course there is far more to history than war and peace but, to repeat the thesis, the strategic dimension to international relations has been by far the most significant of the influences shaping events.

As the title suggests, this work is a somewhat experimental exercise in what military analysts would call 'combined arms'. Specifically, the following chapters express an endeavour to combine the strengths of international relations, history and strategic studies. The result is a strategic history of the modern world. The book can be approached both as a historically grounded introduction to strategic studies and as a strategically grounded introduction to modern international relations.

The core of the book comprises a body of historical chapters, fifteen to be precise, which explain the course of history in strategic perspective from the late eighteenth century to the present. Those chapters are supplemented by four others, which: (1) identify themes and specify contexts; (2) outline the enduring theory of war; (3) treat irregular warfare and terrorism as fairly distinctive phenomena; and (4) consider the record of new world orders over the past two centuries, as well as the meaning and challenge of peace.

Overall, as the title claims, this is a venture in explaining the strategic perspective upon modern history, its ever-dynamic content and its often bloody consequences.

Key points

1. War is the most powerful influence on international relations.
2. Strategy can refer to grand strategy or to military strategy. The former includes the latter.
3. Nearly every country has been made by war.
4. The motives for war have been stable through the ages: fear, honour and interest.
5. Strategic history provides a grand narrative that serves well enough to explain the course of events.

Questions

1. **What is strategic history?**
2. **What are the benefits of a strategic perspective?**
3. **What are the potential dangers in adopting a strategic perspective upon history?**
4. **Why are some scholars sceptical of 'grand narratives'?**

1   Themes and contexts of strategic history

Reader's guide: Themes and contexts. The themes are: historical continuity and discontinuity; the relationship between politics and war; the relationship between war and warfare; the relationship between politicians and soldiers; the interdependence of war and society; and the relations between war and peace, and peace and war. The contexts of strategic history are the political; socio-cultural; economic; technological; military-technological; geographical; and historical.

Introduction: a binding framework

The historical narrative and its analysis here are held together by the organizing thesis that modern international relations can be understood within the framework of strategic history. Furthermore, that framework, partial though it is, provides a tolerably reliable guide to the course of international relations globally. However, as grand theory, the strategic historical postulate is minimal almost to a fault. What other ideas might bind this long period of modern history for better comprehension? What other aids to analytical coherence can be identified and exploited? This chapter provides and discusses answers to those questions in the forms of themes and contexts. Six major themes are identified which run through the whole of the text. These vital six are relevant to every period in the two centuries, and to all matters having to do with war and peace. Next, the principal contexts are presented. In total, they constitute the variable conditions within which war and peace occur in international relations. Again, in common with the themes, these contexts are as permanent in their existence and generic significance as they are vastly diverse in content and relative influence. This discussion of themes and contexts leads to formal confrontation with the following question: is there some master plot, some truly grand design, which can be employed to unlock the major mysteries of why and how modern strategic history took the frequently bloody course that it did? But first it is necessary to register an important caveat.

One needs to be aware of what deserves to be called the historian's curse: the curse of unavoidable foreknowledge or hindsight. The historian knows, broadly at least, what happened, though not necessarily why. Blessed or cursed with this godlike wisdom, it is tempting to explain the past in terms of its consequences. This phenomenon is especially prevalent in the field of strategic history, since major wars all but demand to be interpreted as the necessary consequence of a host of preceding conditions, trends and events. The idea that great wars are uniquely potent in their ability to shape international relations for decades to come, a persuasive idea indeed, can march in step with the notion that, in some inescapable sense, anticipation of those great wars dominated their antecedent periods. This is an unsafe assumption. To illustrate the point, Chapter 1 of *The Second World War* by Spencer C. Tucker bears the title 'The Road to War, 1931–1939' (Tucker, 2004). With the benefit of hindsight, one can hardly object to such a description of the 1930s. But does it aid understanding to approach the international relations and strategic history of that decade almost solely with reference to its explosive conclusion? Most of the statesmen and soldiers of the 1930s, certainly prior to Germany's illegal reoccupation of the Rhineland on 7 March 1936, did not believe that they were on 'the road to war'. Indeed, approached historically, which is to say from prior to after, it is not entirely self-evident that the 1930s were 'the road to war', at least up to a certain date. As earth-shaking events, the great conflicts of the past two centuries easily can seem to have been overdetermined. One needs to beware of the approach which reads backwards from the facts of wars to the causes that are presumed to have been responsible for them. Similarly, one has to be on guard against the complementary view that strategic history proceeds purposively towards some preordained, if only temporary and partial, conclusion.

Themes

The first and most general theme is the rich interplay between strategic historical continuity and discontinuity. What changes and what does not? Although these pages tell a tale punctuated by many revolutions of several kinds, the continuities also are impressive. Chapter 2 demonstrates that war, the subject which comprises the core of this story, has a nature that is as unchanging as its character is highly variable. With some exceptions granted, the atomic discovery for example, strategic history more often moves by evolution than by revolution. Moreover, there are factors that always matter deeply, even when discontinuity is unarguable, say as between the military styles, the tactical 'ways of war', of the German and British armies in 1918, as contrasted with 1914. Morale is by far the most important component of fighting power, while discipline and training are eternal necessities. Vociferous defenders of traditional values are apt to receive rough treatment by the prophets for novelty, but the last 200 years have registered many a claim for dramatic discontinuity in strategic and international political affairs which seriously overreached the bounds of the possible. Time after time in the twentieth century, the conclusion of a great war was expected, or at least hoped, to herald a brave new world characterized by a pattern of international cooperation for which a new institutional framework was optimistically provided. Later chapters will comment critically upon both the League of Nations and its successor, the United Nations Organization (UN), as vehicles for the continuities and anticipated discontinuities in international relations. A most important question is why strategic history, for all its obvious dynamism, has enduring features which on balance are destructive of international political stability. 'Fear, honour and interest' comprise a powerful compound source of continuity.

Box 1.1 Themes in strategic history

1. Continuity and discontinuity in strategic history.
2. The relationship between politics and war.
3. The relationship between war and warfare.
4. The relationship between politicians and soldiers.
5. The dependence of war on society.
6. The relations between war and peace, and between peace and war.

The next theme is the relationship between politics and war. Strategic history is all about the threat or use of organized violence carried on by political units against each other for political motives (Bull, 1977: 184). '[F]or political motives' has been added to Bull's definition. War is political behaviour using the agency of force. In strategic history, politics are sovereign. In the 1790s, as today, strategic history moved to the beat of political passions and calculations. The entire sad story told and analysed here is, at root, a political one. War has no meaning beyond the political, at least it should not, though it certainly has multidimensional consequences. It ought not to be waged for its own sake, though at times that reversal of the proper order of things can appear to occur. It should not be conducted for entertainment, regarded as a spectator sport (McInnes, 2002), or resorted to for the psychological satisfaction of mentally disturbed leaders, to cite but a few possible pathologies. Some societies, the American being a prominent case, draw a sharp distinction between politics and war. They have a tradition of civil–military relations which insists upon a rigorously apolitical professional military. Such societies are apt to suffer severely from the malady that one could call the strategy deficit. After all, strategy is the bridge between military power and political purpose. Since war should only be waged for political ends, who ensures that the organized violence is directed to the ends that are politically intended? And just how do the distinctive professions of soldier and politician–policy-maker conduct the 'unequal dialogue' that is so essential if strategy is to be devised, pursued and, when necessary, revised (Cohen, 2002)? It is one thing to assert, accurately, that war is a political instrument; it can be quite another to wage war in such a manner that it privileges one's political objectives. Strategic history is chock full of examples of wars waged in ways that were politically, if not militarily, self-destructive. For an extreme example, today, fortunately the historical jury is still out on the questions of whether nuclear weapons are really weapons, and whether nuclear strategy is a contradiction in terms. Can nuclear war be regarded as an instrument of policy?

The third theme is the relationship, and often the tension, between war and warfare. All too often the two are simply conflated by careless or ignorant commentators. War is a legal concept, a social institution, and is a compound idea that embraces the total relationship between belligerents. In contrast, warfare refers to the actual conduct of war in its military dimension. Warfare bears the characteristic, even defining, stamp of violence. States and other political communities wage warfare in order to prosecute their wars. However, the two concepts are vitally different, as the past 200 years reveal with startling clarity. Historical illustration provides the clearest explanation of the distinction.

George Washington was not overly gifted as a military commander in the conduct of warfare, but he was truly outstanding at waging war. History records a verdict in favour of the American Revolution which makes the point unambiguously.

For some negative examples, Clausewitz claimed that Napoleon was the 'God of War' (Clausewitz, 1976: 583), but it is more accurate to see the Emperor as the god of war*fare*. Somehow, time after time, his battlefield successes did not lead to victories sufficiently politically decisive as to lay the foundation for a peace that would last. Two yet more compelling historical cases are provided by the German Army, which was the finest fighting machine in the world during both world wars, yet Germany lost both. To be good, even excellent, at fighting – that is to say, at warfare – is not necessarily to be proficient in the conduct of war. This distinction is not an abstruse academic point. It expresses a difficulty that some states and other political units face when attempting to employ force, organized violence, for the strategic effect necessary if victory is to be secured. What is lacking is skill in strategy. War is not about fighting. The fighting is essential, but it can only be a tool, a means to a political end. Again, as Clausewitz advises, the object in war is not military victory; rather, it is to bend the enemy to one's will (Clausewitz, 1976: 75). No more warfare should be waged than is necessary for that end.

The fourth theme is the often troubled relationship between politicians and soldiers. Military violence and its political consequences comprise two different currencies, and it is difficult to convert one into the other by strategy. So, also, military and political professionals have different values, skills, perspectives and responsibilities. In addition, soldiers and politicians are likely to be drawn from different kinds of personalities. On the one hand, soldiers favour an ideal type who is decisive, determined, honest, loyal and a person of action. Politicians, on the other hand, favour compromise as a high virtue, regard expediency as a necessary mode of operation, are apt to think little of being economical with the truth, hold to an honour code that would not pass muster in a military context, and their careers rise and fall with words, the tools of their trade. One exaggerates deliberately, but there can be no doubt that there is a wide cultural divide between the two professions. From the difficulties that Wellington in the Iberian Peninsula had with civilian politicians in London (Rathbone, 1984), to the nightmarish troubles suffered by American general Wesley Clark – SACEUR (NATO's Supreme Allied Commander, Europe) in 1999 – as he strove to conduct a militarily rational air campaign against Serbia over Kosovo, the story is essentially unchanged (Clark, 2002). The conflict and tension in civil–military relations are neatly captured in a pair of rival maxims: first, 'war is too important to be left to the generals'; and second, 'war is too important to be left to the politicians'.

Strategic history is amply populated with cases of soldiers being given impossible tasks by policy-makers, and of soldiers compelled to operate in the absence of clear political guidance. Clausewitz insists that politicians must understand the military instrument that they intend to use, but in historical practice that has been an exceptional condition, not the norm. Needless to say, different states and societies have different traditions governing the relations between soldiers and civilians. Soldiers can believe that they, and they alone, represent the best interests of their country, and that they serve the state rather than the government of the day. For an extreme example, on 22 April 1961 elite units of the French Armée d'Afrique, led by the parachute regiments of the Foreign Legion, staged a coup in Algeria and planned and began to execute a parachute drop on

Paris itself. The purpose was to save France from what the soldiers saw as Charles de Gaulle's betrayal of French Algeria. The abstractions of policy and military power, and the often fraught and always challenging connection between the two, translate in historical reality into the flesh and blood of people with distinctive professional cultures and responsibilities attempting to reconcile what may appear to be irreconcilable. It is necessary to emphasize just how difficult it is, and has always been, to function well as a strategist. Politicians and soldiers have to cooperate to generate positive strategic effectiveness. This need, and the hindrances to its efficient achievement, is a thread that runs through all of strategic history.

The next theme is the dependence of war on society. War is a social institution and it is waged by societies, not only by states. Because of war's myriad varieties and contexts, wars do not have anything resembling a standard social impact. World War II was literally a total struggle for Germany, the Soviet Union and Britain. It was a conflict that required the complete mobilization of those countries' assets. Most wars are not of that kind, at least not for both sides. Until the end of the Cold War, however, modern history did see a fairly steady rise in the involvement, as well as the active participation, of society at large, in both decisions for war and in the actual conduct of hostilities. In the mid-nineteenth century the slow but inexorable growth of literate electorates was fed with real-time news of distant events by the new profession of war correspondents exploiting the recent invention of the electric telegraph. Suddenly, policy on war and peace had to consider public opinion as a significant factor. Foreign policy and the resort to force were no longer what they had been, almost strictly matters for executive discretion. The age of industrial mass warfare, with its requirement for wholesale social commitment, closed in 1945 – or perhaps at the very latest in 1991. But the revolution in communications technologies effected in the last quarter of the twentieth century has meant that societies today are informed, and misinformed, instantly by live 'feeds' via satellite of strategic history in the making half a world away. Paradoxically, war's social dimension is as powerful in the 2000s as its actual intrusiveness is minimal by modern historical standards in most cases. A potent contemporary exception to this claim may be the so-called 'war on terror' – although, even in this case, barring the possible use of weapons of mass destruction (WMD), terrorists comprise an enemy that can be opposed without the mobilization of whole societies.

The final theme to be highlighted concerns the complex reciprocal relationships that exist between peace and war. Analysis of the strategic history of the past two centuries must examine the war–peace nexus from both perspectives. First, one must consider the consequences of wars for the peace and order–disorder that follow. Second, and no less important, one has to understand the consequences of periods of peace for the succeeding wars.

War is not a sporting event; it is not waged for the purpose of winning. Victory, or a tolerable stalemate, is sought for political reasons. It is inherently difficult to craft the desired condition of peace with order out of war. Perhaps order with peace is the proper way to express the relationship, because, following Clausewitz, one knows that war supremely is the realm of chance and uncertainty. Moreover, it can be so challenging to succeed militarily and strategically in war that the immediate demands of warfare easily become all-consuming of available creative energy and scarce effort. However, the way that a war is waged – and, for example, the deals that are made with allies – will be important, even crucial, for shaping what, after all, the fighting is about. Why is one fighting? Unless the war is strictly a desperate exercise in self-defence triggered by an invasion, the purpose of the whole bloody enterprise ought to be 'to attain a better peace', as British strategic theorist Basil Liddell Hart has written (Liddell Hart, 1967: 366). That notion should be understood to include a condition of international order which is better than the one which preceded the war in question. Understandably, soldiers tend to be unsympathetic to orders and other guidance from politicians which, if followed faithfully, would restrict their ability to fight in the most effective manner. Not all politicians comprehend the fact that warfare is a blunt instrument. It is not a scalpel to be applied with surgical skill for precise military and then strategic, and consequential political, effect. Among a host of difficulties, it is in the nature of war for there to be an enemy with an independent mind and will who is committed with variable skill, determination and capability to thwarting you. Undue fascination with our military behaviour and its anticipated strategic returns is ever likely to be shaken rudely by the inconvenience of an uncooperative foe. As Winston Churchill warned, 'However absorbed a commander may be in the elaboration of his own thoughts, it is sometimes necessary to take the enemy into account' (quoted in Heinl, 1966: 102).

As peace follows war, so war follows peace, though not with any temporal regularity. Strategic history is distressingly cyclical, notwithstanding the fact that the cycles can be long or short. Over the past 200 years, wars great and small have erupted, or have been planned and purposefully unleashed, out of conditions of peace. It follows that one has to be interested in the provenance of wars in the periods preceding active hostilities. In particular, one would like to know whether some arrangements for international order have proven to be more peace-friendly than others. Within the historical domain of this enquiry there were four great wars: French Revolutionary and Napoleonic, otherwise known as the Great War with France (1792–1815); World War I (1914–18); World War II (1939–45); and the virtual war, but all too real conflict, that was the Soviet–American, East–West, Cold War (1947–89). Were there common elements among the origins, causes and triggering events of these four mighty episodes? Most probably there were. In particular, attention must be drawn to the persisting significance of the concept and practice of the balance of power and, yet again, to the enduring validity of Thucydides' fatal triptych of fear, honour and interest. Throughout the whole course of strategic history, the challenge has never been simply to master the periods of war. Instead, the real demand for skill in statecraft and strategy derives from the necessity to make effective provision for peace with tolerable security. The qualification is as essential as, ultimately, to date, it has proved unduly difficult to achieve on a truly lasting basis to the general satisfaction of all of the essential – which is to say the major state and other – players. In addition to the four great wars just cited, since 11 September 2001 a global conflict has erupted between violent Islamic fundamentalists and their enemies, which some commentators speculate may be 'the Third World War' (Freedman, 2001).

Contexts

Because wars do not occur for reasons internal to themselves, context is literally vital to their understanding. Historian Jeremy Black explains, 'War had an enormous impact on the historical process, but as Napoleon noted, it was not alone at work. Throughout, an understanding of war requires contextualization. Military history exists in a context of other histories' (Black, 2004: 243).

Context is so significant that it can overwhelm the scholar, with the unhappy result that a strategic history may be all context and scarcely any war or warfare. One must not make that mistake. However, strategic history proceeds on its erratic, sometimes non-linear, way, in context (in fact, in multiple contexts). For clarity in analysis this discussion treats the principal contexts of war separately, but strategic history moves holistically, with everything influencing everything else simultaneously. The contexts discussed here are always in play. Every event, episode or process that later chapters consider as a note-worthy happening in strategic history occurred subject to the influence of contemporary detail in the contexts identified here.

Box 1.2 Contexts of strategic history

1. Political
2. Socio-cultural
3. Economic
4. Technological
5. Military-strategic
6. Geographical
7. Historical

With some compression and many exclusions, the winning shortlist of the contexts of war comprises the political; the socio-cultural; the economic; the technological; the military-strategic; the geographical; and the historical. Some of these may be less than fully self-explanatory, so it is necessary to probe a little beneath the bare labels on the concepts. There are two purposes to this exercise. First, strategic history makes no sense if it comprises the story of force bereft of context. Second, because it will be necessary to make frequent references to one context or another throughout the historical discussion in this text, it is essential that there should be no vagueness as to their meaning.

The political context provides the lion's share of the fuel for the strategic strand in history. It is what war is about, by and large at least. It is where war and peace come from. Decisions to fight, or not, are the products of a political process. Armies and their military behaviour are, or should be, the servants of a political context. Needless to add, perhaps, even when a state has a tradition of strict separation of civilian from soldier, the armed forces are not only an instrument of policy, but a part of the society they are pledged to protect. To a highly variable degree, soldiers are the agents of a political context and they themselves are an integral part of that context.

Next, strategic history is made within a socio-cultural context. Strategic performance typically bears a label with its maker's name. States and their societies approach strategic issues, and behave militarily, in ways shaped by their prevalent values and beliefs. Those values and beliefs will evolve over time, but they provide a definite socio-cultural context within which policy and strategy must be made. The socio-cultural context is by no means necessarily a potent constraint upon decision for action. Not only may a state command the services of a quasi-religious ideology, as did Nazi Germany and Soviet Russia, but in some countries – indeed in most countries occasionally – civil society can, and will, voice demands for war.

Strategic history is an economic story, among others. There is always an economic context to the record of war, peace and order. Optimistic peace theorists used to argue, persuasively one must admit, that modern economies and their financing were so internationally interdependent that war had become impracticable and unprofitable (Angell, 1911, 1938). Unfortunately, the optimists were proved partially wrong, repeatedly. Where they were correct was in their argument that war did not pay, a claim of less than critical significance because in modern times by and large states have not fought for economic gain. Governments found ways to finance warfare on credit, rather than through taxation, by official controls and by currency devaluation, and they bequeathed to the future the dire consequences of spending grossly beyond their societies' current means. Long gone were the days when war could be so conducted that it paid for itself. The last successful practitioner of profitable predation by war was Napoleon. This is not to deny that Adolf Hitler made aggression pay in peace and war, but he did so only for a while: 1938–41 to be precise. The economic context to strategic history is always important; indeed, it is a potential showstopper, no less. Defence preparation and actual warfare are exercises in economic choice, in affordability, as well as in military judgement. Furthermore, as Germany and then the Soviet Union demonstrated, a major competitive economic shortfall ultimately will prove strategically fatal, assuming that the enemy is tolerably militarily competent.

War is waged with the products of technology. At any point in the two centuries covered here there was a particular technological context. That context was dynamic. It contained many artefacts from earlier contexts, as well as many prototypes of immature products that were not quite ready for military prime time. But, at any date from 1800 until today, statesmen and soldiers inhabited a world with definite technological opportunities and limitations. In the face of baffling military problems which had grim strategic implications, technological advance would be accelerated. Sometimes the technological context evolved with scant influence from the realm of government. It was moved by strictly commercial or scientific motors. But there is no denying that in the age of total war in particular, which is to say in the twentieth century, the strategic path in history played a huge, if not dominant, role in spurring technological innovation.

Next, at all times there is a military-strategic context to policy decisions that may have consequences for war and peace. This context refers to the contemporary state of the art in military affairs, what Clausewitz meant by his 'grammar' of war (Clausewitz, 1976: 606). When married to an assessment of the strategic meaning of the balance of military prowess among relevant state, and other, players, one arrives at this useful concept of the military-strategic context. Some theorists believe that a military-strategic context wherein offensive capabilities appear to enjoy a significant combat advantage over the defensive is perilous for peace (Van Evera, 1999). But other theorists find it unpersuasive to argue that countries go to war when the military context appears to privilege a bold offence. Politicians are able to persuade themselves that victory is certain, or at least probable, for a variety of reasons that seem good to them at the time. Warfare is far too complex an enterprise to be corralled for reliable calculation according to the net objective, and abstract, advantage of offence relative to defence. Nevertheless, a belief in the superiority of the offence can hardly help but offer support to arguments that urge the taking of the military initiative.

'Geography is destiny' is an overstatement of an enduring truth that has pervasive strategic meaning. All strategic history has a geographical context. We humans live in geography, are attached to our home geography, and sometimes covet other people's geography. Especially in its political and strategic connections, geography plays a major role in the story told and analysed here. The geopolitical context, which is to say the political meaning of spatial relationships, could not help but provide a fairly stable context for the strategic history of the past two centuries. The geographical location of political units, the identity and characteristics of neighbours and neighbours-but-one, and the political implications of the natural arrangement of land and sea have had far more than a marginal influence on events. Consider the strategic consequences of Germany's position in the centre of Europe, or of America's effectively insular location an ocean removed from both Asia and Europe. Every strategic matter has, and must have, a geopolitical context of some consequence.

Finally, it is important to recognize the salience of the historical context *per se*. In other words, while many historians prefer to write and teach their history thematically, there is no escaping the fact, even the tyranny, of chronology. Every event, episode, process and trend discussed here occurred at a specific date and, necessarily, happened in the stream of time. That stream and its implications play momentous roles in strategic history. The human actors discussed in this book played out their roles on a stage that was set in good part by great impersonal forces, or even by structures, but human agency is always important. This book is about human behaviour – strategic behaviour admittedly, but still human. The people in this strategic history were moulded by the times in which they lived, the societies of which they were a part, and of course by the ideas that were fashionable and sometimes authoritative. In other words, in order to understand how and why people behaved strategically as they did, it is essential that we locate them historically.

For example, it is necessary to remember that nearly all of the politicians and soldiers of 1914 had no hands-on understanding of modern warfare. Arguable exceptions included the British experience against the Boers in South Africa (1899–1902), and the Russians and the Japanese in their struggle for Manchuria and Korea (1904–5). In sharp contrast with 1914, in 1939 the human players in all the countries entangled in the European crisis had had almost too much personal experience of modern warfare. Most of the politicians and all of the senior soldiers of 1939 were among the survivors of World War I. Their attitudes were shaped by their experience of total war and its consequences. As a general rule, policy-makers are too busy in office to add significantly to the intellectual capital with which they began their duties. That capital is the product of their period of education, which may have been brief, and especially of some defining experience. For every individual and his or her contribution to strategic history, there is a historical context keyed to a definite chronology.

These seven contexts must have a constant relevance to our analysis. Strategic history is nested within them, and is shaped and driven by them. Their presence will be noticed throughout this tale.

Conclusion

The literature on strategic history is thin. There is an abundance of military history, as there is also of political, diplomatic, economic and social history; yet, strangely, strategic history is largely missing. Perhaps it is not so strange, though, because both scholarly and popular understanding of strategy and its vital function are in short supply (Strachan, 2005b). Strategy is difficult to comprehend, and even more difficult to do well. It is the somewhat mysterious bridge between the military instrument and political objectives, the meaning of both of which is simple to grasp. It is unfortunate that so few scholars grapple seriously with the challenges and dilemmas of strategy, because it can provide by far the sharpest tool for analysing the course of modern history. Our modern world has been made, unmade and remade pre-eminently by the threat and use of organized force. Although strategic history cannot possibly capture the whole story of modern times, it does offer a superior guide to what happened, and why, in international relations. The binding thesis of this text holds that strategic history provides the best navigation aids to explain and understand the relations among polities.

To put flesh on the bare bones of a general commitment to the strategic perspective, six themes which permeate this analysis have been identified. These are: the relationship between stability and change, or continuity and discontinuity; the crucial nexus between war and the politics which alone renders belligerency purposeful and meaningful; the ill-understood distinction between war and its conduct in warfare; the frequently tension-fraught relations between politicians and soldiers; the connections between war and the societies that wage it; and, finally, the oddly underexplored, yet surely critical, agencies and agents that connect war with peace and peace with war.

Strategic history always is nested in, and is shaped and driven by, multiple contexts. The contexts specified here were: first and foremost, the political; the socio-cultural; the economic; the technological; the military–strategic; the geographical; and the historical, or chronological. To understand the contexts of war is to grasp a great deal. It is not, however, to understand everything. This book does not offer a structural interpretation of events, a story bereft of the inconvenient variability of human performance. The history of war and peace in international relations is a big story that shows the engagement of mighty forces and powerful contexts. Nevertheless, strategic history has to be done by individual human agents. This, emphatically, is not a history without individuals of importance.

There is an essential unity to the strategic history of modern times, regardless of the cumulatively radical changes in contexts. The next chapter makes explicit that which was largely left implicit here. It presents the theory of war and strategy, predominantly with reference to the writings of the most influential of all strategic theorists, Prussian major general Carl Philipp Gottlieb von Clausewitz.

Key points

1. Major themes run through strategic history: continuity and discontinuity; the relationship between politics and war; the relationship between war and

continued

warfare; the relationship between politicians and soldiers; the dependence of war on society; and the relations between war and peace, and peace and war.
2.   The principal contexts of strategic history are: political; socio-cultural; economic; technological; military–strategic; geographical; and historical. These contexts are always in play.
3.   'Fear, honour and interest' provide historical continuity of motivation for conflict and war.
4.   Because war is waged for political goals, there needs to be a continuous dialogue between politicians and soldiers, albeit a dialogue weighted in favour of the former.
5.   To be good at waging warfare is not necessarily to be competent at the conduct of war.
6.   Societies and people with their values and beliefs make war, not just states.

Questions

1.   **What is the difference between war and warfare, and why does it matter?**
2.   **Can the contexts of strategic history be rank-ordered in importance?**
3.   **Is it persuasive to argue that Thucydides said all that needs to be said at a general level when he identified 'fear, honour and interest' as the principal motives for war?**
4.   **What factors can inhibit dialogue between politicians and soldiers?**

Further reading

J. Black *Warfare in the Western World, 1882–1975* (Chesham: Acumen, 2002).
—— *Introduction to Global Military History: 1775 to the Present Day* (London: Routledge, 2005).
B. Bond *The Pursuit of Victory: From Napoleon to Saddam Hussein* (Oxford: Oxford University Press, 1996).
P. Browning *The Changing Nature of Warfare: The Development of Land Warfare from 1792 to 1945* (Cambridge: Cambridge University Press, 2002).
P. Hirst *War and Power in the 21st Century: The State, Military Conflict and the International System* (Cambridge: Polity Press, 2001).
J. S. Nye, Jr *Understanding International Conflicts: An Introduction to Theory and History*, 6th edn (New York: Pearson Longman, 2007).
C. Townshend (ed.) *The Oxford History of Modern War* (Oxford: Oxford University Press, 2005).
J. J. Weltman *World Politics and the Evolution of War* (Baltimore: Johns Hopkins University Press, 1995).

2 Carl von Clausewitz and the theory of war

Reader's guide: The importance of strategic ideas. Jomini and Clausewitz compared. The superiority of Clausewitz's theory of war. The major elements of his theory.

Introduction: theory for all seasons

Strategic history offers a catalogue of horrors of the utmost diversity, but those grisly events are all, without exception, explicable according to a single theory of war and strategy. The theory available to us is largely the product of the Prussian soldier Carl von Clausewitz (1780–1831). Of course, one can find some individual elements characteristic of his thinking in the writings of earlier theorists, but the total edifice of ideas that he constructed was monumentally original. In his unfinished work *On War*, Clausewitz explained the essential nature of war, how it endures through time and circumstance, even as its character is ever changing. He emphasized the effective, logical unity between politics and war, and he laid stress upon war's moral dimension. Clausewitz insisted that war has to be a duel between competing wills, that it is subject to the many frustrations of what he termed, collectively, 'friction'; and he insisted that war was the realm of chance, risk and uncertainty. He is not beyond criticism, naturally, but most scholars and soldiers agree that his great achievement was to draft a general theory of war and strategy that was good enough to be both highly plausible and superior to the theories of all his rivals.

Clausewitz's writing is an essential and central element in this study of modern strategic history, as it has to be. He explained for all time the nature of the strategic dimension to history. His most mature work of theory, *On War*, provides a framework that enables understanding of all the strategic phenomena in the lengthy period covered by this text. *On War* is not infallible, and it might well have been improved had the author lived longer than his fifty-one years, or had he viewed technology and industry, and perhaps sea power, with a friendlier eye. But the test of perfection is irrelevant. A distinguished modern American strategist, Bernard Brodie, wrote of *On War* that 'His is not simply the greatest but the only truly great book on war' (in Clausewitz, 1976: 53).

It will seem strange, even implausible, to some people that an incomplete book written in the 1820s can be as relevant to the twenty-first century as it was to the nineteenth and the twentieth. Surely, one could ask, the price paid for such enduring validity must be a level of generality that robs the theory of much of its utility? The high esteem in which Clausewitz is widely held is by no means a universal opinion today (Van Creveld, 1997; Keegan, 1998b: 41–3). The batting order now opens with a discussion of the importance of strategic ideas and their connection to strategic behaviour. Next, a relatively kind opinion is offered on the work of Clausewitz's contemporary and rival, Baron Antoine Henri de Jomini. Then the theory of war and strategy to be found in *On War* is outlined and analysed.

Strategic ideas and strategic behaviour

Political scientist Richard Betts has asserted boldly that Clausewitz 'is worth a busload of most other theorists', but that judgement has not always seemed persuasive to people who had strategic dilemmas to resolve (Betts, 1997: 29). Clausewitz sought to educate the mind of the soldier so that he would be adequately equipped intellectually to solve his problems. Unsurprisingly, soldiers in all periods, while sometimes valuing a deep understanding of the nature of war and strategy, have been rather more interested in finding answers to the strategic difficulties of the moment. Clausewitz, it must be said, provided brilliant answers to questions that few, if any, people even ask. Soldiers and their political masters need to know how to win, or at least how to avoid losing too badly. Their active interest in the nature of war typically is not high. This is the principal reason why Clausewitz's contemporary, and much longer-lived, more prolific rival, the Baron Antoine Henri de Jomini (1779–1869), was so popular in the nineteenth century, and why his influence persists to this day (Jomini, 1992). He provided soldiers with the conceptual tools for victory, or so he claimed. By the 1870s, however, Jomini's reputation came to be eclipsed by that of Clausewitz. In part that was because Field Marshal Helmuth Graf von Moltke, the military victor in the latter two of the three wars of German unification (1864, 1866 and 1870–1), paid tribute to Clausewitz as a vital contributor to his success. In fact, Moltke either disagreed with or misunderstood the most important arguments in *On War*, but no matter. As the most successful and therefore most respected soldier of the age, Moltke's blessing was authoritative (Hughes, 1993). Deliberately, Clausewitz did not seek to write a strategy 'cookbook', a step-by-step, how-to manual for victory. The strategist, hopefully armed with the logic and the insights he should have gleaned from *On War*, is quintessentially a man of action, not a scholar. A powerful intellect is usually an advantage for a general, though not if it harbours an overactive imagination, but the qualities he needs are by no means restricted to those of an intellectual kind (Clausewitz, 1976: 100–12). A fine intellect may be governed by an irresolute will. A general theory of war and strategy, no matter how brilliant, does not, indeed cannot, cut to the chase for the world of applied violence.

Strategic ideas really matter. Frequently, though not invariably, they are not mere intellectual decoration on behaviour already conducted, and neither are they simply fashionable notions that are bandied about in more or less lively debate. People invent, rediscover and refine strategic ideas because there is a demand for them from the realm of strategic behaviour. No one has stated this condition more clearly than the French sociologist Raymond Aron. He claimed persuasively that 'Strategic thought draws its inspiration each century, or rather at each moment of history, from the problems which events themselves pose' (Aron, 1970: 25). Consistent with, and obedient to, the general theory of war supplied in *On War*, the past two centuries have yielded a multitude of particular problems that demanded more or less innovative responses in strategic thought. Bernard Brodie stated the matter with a directness, and from a wealth of personal experience, that forecloses on the possibility of misunderstanding:

> Strategic thinking, or 'theory' if one prefers, is nothing if not pragmatic. Strategy is a 'how to do it' study, a guide to accomplishing something and doing it efficiently. As in many other branches of politics, the question that matters in strategy is: will the idea work? More important, will it be likely to work under the special circumstances under which it will next be tested?
>
> (Brodie, 1973: 452)

Soldiers and statesmen should be so educated by Clausewitz's general theory of war that they understand how war must serve politics, as well as how the nature of war can frustrate strategic intentions. But, well educated or not in such general theory, every generation of soldiers and policy-makers has had to find solutions – practical solutions, that is – to the problems of the day to which Aron and Brodie refer. The strategic thinking that is nearly always in demand has the character specified by Brodie. Officials, military and civilian, are in need of strategic answers that work well enough. The whole of strategic history shows a common hunt for the strategic ideas that should solve or alleviate the strategic problems of the day. In time of war, the need is urgent; and the pace of experiment and willingness to take large risks with innovative equipment and ideas for its employment are greatly accelerated. The popular belief that militaries are hidebound and so conservative that in peacetime they resist change and only feel comfortable preparing for the last war is, by and large, a serious fallacy. The evidence of bold peacetime military innovation is overwhelming (Rosen, 1991). The challenge in peacetime is to guess just how well or poorly novel ideas on tactics and new equipment, and their meaning for operations, will perform in the only test that counts, on the battlefield. Until experience of combat provides education, one is strictly in the realm of speculative theory. Soldiers know that they themselves will be testing the new ideas and machines under fire, and that their performance in combat could well translate into victory or defeat for the country they are sworn to serve. It is hardly surprising, therefore, that unproven devices and strange notions should be regarded with healthy scepticism by their prospective users.

Both Aron and Brodie are devotees of Clausewitzian theory, but the strategic thinking to which they referred in the quotations above was not the kind of thought that they admire so much in *On War*, at least not directly (Aron, 1983; Brodie, 1976). Policy-makers and soldiers do not demand strategic philosophy, vital though that is to their intellectual preparation. Instead, they demand pragmatic answers to such questions as: what are the strategic implications of railways? What is the strategic meaning of steam propulsion and screw propellers for warships? In the face of far more lethal small arms and automatic weapons, how can infantry cross 'the killing ground'? Indeed, can soldiers still take the offensive in the teeth of modern firepower? What is the strategic promise in mechanized land warfare? Can air power win the next great war on its own? And so forth. The list of questions, each of enormous significance at a particular time, is of quite inordinate length. This book cannot possibly deal with all of them, but it does treat the most important in every period in its historical context. The succession of strategic questions of the period and the variety of answers provided all share an essential unity, notwithstanding their apparent diversity. They all are governed by the higher lore of war and strategy that was developed by Clausewitz.

There is scope for argument over the extent to which Clausewitz managed in his writings to transcend the imprint of his times, his personal experience and his culture and circumstances. *On War* is a book written by a Continental-minded army officer devoted to the security of his native Prussia. He abhorred, yet deeply admired, Napoleon and France, and he was very much influenced by the German Romantic movement of the era. That was by way of some contrast to the more rational focus of the Enlightenment thought that had dominated the theory of war in the eighteenth century. He was also much shaken by the trauma of national defeat at the Battle of Jena–Auerstädt on 14 October 1806. His subsequent labours on behalf of the reform of the Prussian Army as an assistant to the brilliant and energetic Gerd von Scharnhorst reflected his recognition of the necessity for radical change. No book on the theory of war, not even *On War*, can help but bear some stamp of its author and his life and times. However, to date at least, the occasional claim that Clausewitz's theory is unduly culture-specific, and hence of limited domain, has not been advanced convincingly. *On War* is far from perfect, as the author himself was the first to recognize: not all of its more intriguing ideas are well thought through, for example. But the test for greatness, for true classic status, is not the impossible standard of perfection. It is sufficient that Clausewitz would seem to have been right, or right enough, about the major issues that bear upon the nature and changing character of war.

In sharp contrast to *On War*, the huge library of writings over the past 200 years that one might categorize generously as strategic thinking bears more than merely the stamp of contemporaneity. Recalling what Aron and Brodie had to say about the stimulus of events to strategic thought, strategic ideas, and, more accurately, the military ideas that had strategic implications, have followed the sound of the guns. While there have been occasional exceptions, as always, as a general rule strategic thought is a reactive, not an anticipatory, activity. The early theorists of air power probably are a valid example of just such an exception. But it is highly unusual for a body of advanced strategic thinkers to develop ideas that stimulate strategic behaviour in the forms of weapon development and notions for the proper use of new weapons. Instead, as Aron claimed, strategic ideas are invented, or perhaps dusted off and refurbished, when the world of political and military decision and action is in need of answers that might work well enough to enable security communities to cope with novel strategic challenges. In the mid-nineteenth century, dramatic improvements in the range and accuracy, and hence the lethality, of infantry small arms caused a tactical crisis. In World War I the latest version of that tactical crisis imposed a tactical and operational paralysis that, again, begged for practicable solutions. And in the Cold War era the atomic (then the hydrogen) bomb, soon to be empowered as an instrument of swift mass destruction by long-range ballistic missiles, again demanded intellectual control by strategic ideas that would work well enough as policy and as doctrine.

This analysis makes constant reference to strategic ideas at two different yet connected levels. On the higher plane there is a general theory of war and strategy authoritative for all kinds of warfare, by all character of belligerents, using all manner of weaponry and tactics, in all historical periods. But this general theory, of which Clausewitz's *On War* is the exemplar by a country mile and more, does not address the specific concerns of actual policy-makers and soldiers. That is not a weakness. Had Clausewitz written the best manual of strategic advice of which he was capable, his work would have been instantly dated. His advice would have been useful only in the military context of his time. On the lower plane, in contrast, chapter after chapter of this discussion shows both how well and how poorly historical players managed to cope with the challenges of revolutionary changes in the contexts and the character of war. Clausewitz is brilliant and invaluable, but how does one succeed in land warfare against an entrenched enemy who has no flanks, which was the situation on the Western Front from 1916 to 1918? Or, with the British Army expelled ignominiously from continental Europe in May–June 1940, just how should, or could, Britain continue to prosecute the war, let alone hope to win? By and large, in fact near exclusively, the historical strategic questions and answers that occupy the attention of most of this analysis are not of an elevated philosophical nature; rather, they are eminently, even desperately, practical.

The historical record shows beyond any reasonable doubt that strategic thinking is vital to the shaping of strategic behaviour. But the record also shows that that thinking has been stimulated all but invariably by the pragmatic needs of policy-makers and soldiers who are more or less baffled by new strategic problems and opportunities. Paul Hirst asserts that 'War is driven by ideas about how to use weapons and military systems almost as much as it is by technical and organizational changes themselves. Ideas are thus crucial' (Hirst, 2001: 9). But one should not interpret Hirst's claim as meaning anything other than that the development of strategic ideas is driven by the actual challenges revealed in warfare, or in preparation for it. Strategic ideas do not occupy the driving seat of strategic history. That place is reserved for politics.

Jomini and Clausewitz

Clausewitz has no plausible rival in his articulation of the nature of war and strategy. Indeed, his reputation as the most penetrating theorist of war is unchallenged by serious criticism. However, the actual influence of the Prussian theorist almost certainly has been a great deal less than it deserved. The reasons are not hard to locate. Clausewitz aimed to educate the mind, not to advise directly for action. Many of the politicians and soldiers who have been familiar with Clausewitz's theory either failed to grasp its key elements or chose to 'cherry-pick' those ideas, lifted out of intellectual context, which best fitted their preferences. *On War* is a work of educational intent, not a practical guide to behaviour. In Clausewitz's words (1976: 141), 'Theory should be study, not doctrine.' The trouble is that many of the minds that must grapple with strategic challenges are uneducable. For a leading example, none other than the great Elder Moltke, cited already as the leading nineteenth-century propellant of Clausewitz's reputation, held a view of strategy and of the effective autonomy of military operations which was directly anti-thetical to the argument in *On War*. Moltke bequeathed to his successors on the Great General Staff these deadly nostrums: 'The demands of strategy grow silent in the face of a tactical victory and adapt themselves to the newly created situation. Strategy is a system of expedients' (Hughes, 1993: 47). That lethal reversal of the proper relationship between strategy and tactics was to be a signature feature of German military behaviour in both of the world wars, with predictable consequences.

Before outlining the essential elements in Clausewitz's theory of war, it is useful to pause briefly to offer a not unfriendly judgement upon the theorizing of his rival, Antoine Henri de Jomini. The latter's reputation was eclipsed by that of Clausewitz, and has never staged a solid recovery, but, paradoxically perhaps, 'Jomini is the most influential theorist of modern times,' in the view of historian Daniel Moran. That view extends to the claim that 'the practical impact of Jomini's ideas can hardly be overstated' (Moran, 2002: 25). Moran's judgement on Jomini's theory of strategy will not be to everyone's taste, but it is at least interesting, if not wholly convincing. So what did Jomini offer that soldiers from early in the nineteenth century until today allegedly have found so irresistible?

Unlike Clausewitz, Jomini promised to instruct soldiers in how to win. Also unlike the Prussian, he effectively abstracted military science, or the art of war, from its political context. His theory was advanced as timeless professional guidance, supposedly immune to changing political conditions. Based on his study and observation of Napoleon's campaigns, he advanced a set of rules, presented as principles, which he claimed would lead to victory if followed. This was what soldiers wanted, and indeed still want, to know: how do we win? Jomini 'proposed to show that there is one great principle underlying all the operations of war – a principle which must be followed in all good combinations' (Jomini, 1992: 70). His one great principle held that a general should endeavour to throw the mass of his army against a fraction of the enemy's forces at 'the decisive point and at the proper times and with energy'. This was good advice. Jomini was the most influential author of a set of principles of war for which he claimed universal authority. These principles have been much vilified for their ambiguity, even their near banality, and yet they live on into the twenty-first century, notwithstanding controversy over their utility (Alger, 1982; Mc Ivor, 2005). Moran points out that Jomini, unlike Clausewitz, lived long enough to have to deal with the implications for his theory of the new technologies produced by the Industrial Revolution; and the world developed a great deal between 1831 and 1869.

> Yet he remained insistent that the basic principles of war exemplified by Napoleon, and codified by Jomini himself, would survive all technological change – a point of view that has been thoroughly vindicated by events. All good armies today profess to base their doctrine and operational methods upon 'principles of war' similar to those Jomini identified.
>
> (Moran, 2002: 24)

Jomini has received a worse press than he deserves. What are these allegedly universal principles of war? According to the most recent listing by the US Army in its *Field Manual FM3-0, Operations*, they comprise mass; objective; offensive; surprise; economy of force; manoeuvre; unity of command; security; and simplicity (see Box 2.1). They are sensible, if not especially helpful. It is worth noting that Clausewitz was by no means wholly averse to venturing into the terrain of principles, despite his expressed disdain for sets of rules for warfare. Usually he regarded war as a realm wherein genius and chance jousted creatively. But in Chapter 11 of Book 3 of *On War*, Clausewitz sounds distinctly Jominian:

> The best strategy is always *to be very strong*; first in general, and then at the decisive point. Apart from the effort needed to create military strength, which does not always emanate from the general, there is no higher and simpler law of strategy than that of *keeping one's forces concentrated*. No force should ever be detached from the main body unless the need is definite and *urgent*. We hold fast to this principle, and regard it as a reliable guide.
>
> (Clausewitz, 1976: 204; emphasis in original)

Box 2.1 **The principles of war**

Principle	*Definition*
Mass	Concentrate combat power at the decisive place and time.
Objective	Direct every military operation towards a clearly defined, decisive and attainable objective.
Offensive	Seize, retain and exploit the initiative.
Surprise	Strike the enemy at a time, at a place or in a manner for which he is unprepared.
Economy of force	Allocate minimum essential combat power to secondary efforts.
Manoeuvre	Place the enemy in a position of disadvantage through the flexible application of combat power.
Unity of command	For every objective, ensure unity of effort under one responsible commander.
Security	Never permit the enemy to acquire an unexpected advantage.
Simplicity	Prepare clear, uncomplicated plans and clear, concise orders to ensure thorough understanding.

Source: US Army, *Field Manual FM3-0, Operations* (2001)

Sad to say, much as many of Clausewitz's critics over the years have seized upon isolated sentences and paragraphs, quite out of their context in *On War*, in order to support their views, so Jomini also has been, and continues to be, considerably misrepresented. Although Clausewitz stands head and shoulders higher in theoretical merit than Jomini, there are many similarities between their writings. Indeed, one can extend the point to assert that in addition to there being elements common to Clausewitz and Jomini, one finds strategic ideas in Sun-tzu's *Art of War*, written in China around 400 BC, compatible with those of the nineteenth-century theorists (Sun-tzu, 1994). The most careful scholarly comparison extant of the writings of Clausewitz, Jomini and

Sun-tzu, by Michael I. Handel, claims boldly that 'Jomini has traditionally been assumed to represent the positivistic if not mechanical approach to the study of warfare, but a careful comparison of Jomini's work with those of Sun Tzu and Clausewitz indicates that these three strategists are mostly in agreement on the fundamental issues' (Handel, 2001: 3).

Clausewitz's theory of war is considered here from two broad perspectives: what he has to say about the relationship between politics and war; and then on the nature of war itself. It may be important at this juncture to restate exactly why a book on the strategic history of the past two centuries requires a discussion of strategic theory. The tersest explanation is that everything strategic in the history of those 200 years was governed by Clausewitz's theory. That is a highly imperial, perhaps hegemonic, claim. To a degree not even approached by any other theorist, Clausewitz unravelled the complexities of war and strategy. He provided the soundest education available to anyone who wished to understand how and why those activities function. It is probably true to argue that without a firm grasp of Clausewitzian theory one cannot analyse strategic behaviour properly. The strategic history in this book is not simply a narrative – an exercise that may tell the story well enough but would yield little understanding of the reasons for, or the consequences of, strategic events. In short, Clausewitz rules all of strategic history: the past, the present and the future.

The first perspective to be probed is the Clausewitzian dictum on the indissoluble link between politics, meaning policy, and war. He insists that 'the only source of war is politics' and that 'war is simply a continuation of political intercourse, with the addition of other means', then argues that 'policy converts the overwhelmingly destructive element of war into a mere instrument' and that 'If war is part of policy, policy will determine its character' (Clausewitz 1976: 605–6). Clausewitz was not confused about the nature of war, at the heart of which lies the distinguishing feature of organized violence. In some contrast to the modern theory of strategic coercion that envisages a 'diplomacy of violence' (Schelling, 1966), Clausewitz demands that war's unique nature be treated with respect. War may be a political instrument, first and last, but, in his word, it has its own 'grammar'. He warns clearly enough that although politics must always hold sovereign sway over warfare, 'That, however, does not imply that the political aim is a tyrant'. He proceeds to explain that:

> It [the political aim] must adapt itself to its chosen means, a process which can radically change it; yet the political aim remains the first consideration. Policy, thus, will permeate all military operations, and in so far as their violent nature will admit, it will have a continuous influence on them.
>
> (Clausewitz, 1976: 87)

There are potent caveats in that passage. Having declared that war is a 'continuation of political activity by other means', Clausewitz goes on to argue that 'War in general, and the commander in any specific instance, is entitled to require that the trend and design of policy shall not be inconsistent with these means'. He allows that 'That, of course, is no small demand; but however much it may affect political aims in a given case, it will never do more than modify them' (p. 87). Lest his point remains obscure to some readers, he resorts to the most direct language in order to preclude misunderstanding, or so he must have hoped. He concluded the passage with this sentence: 'The political object is the goal, war is the means of reaching it, and means can never be considered in isolation from their purpose'. At least, that is how strategic history ought to work. In his theory, 'The political object – the original motive for the war – will determine both the military objective to be reached and the amount of effort it requires' (p. 81). Being a sophisticated theorist, as well as a person deeply experienced in the historical realities of war and its contexts, Clausewitz goes on to warn that although the scale of the political objective should determine the scope of the military aim, in practice the pursuit even of a modest military aim may trigger a disproportionate enemy response.

Integral to his essentially political theory of war is the insistence, on the first page of *On War*, that 'War is nothing but a duel on a larger scale'. Furthermore, for a truly vital and ill-understood point, he maintains that its purpose has to be 'to impose our will on the enemy'. In a war for an unlimited political objective – the unconditional surrender of Nazi Germany, for example – 'we must render the enemy powerless' (p. 75). But in a war for far more limited political goals, the military objective is not to effect the military ruin of the foe, but rather to coerce him, to affect his will decisively.

The historical domain of this text provides ample negative illustration of the wisdom in the Clausewitzian explanation of the proper connection between politics and war. For example, in great war after great war Germany effectively lost the political plot. It waged warfare more as an end in itself than for reasonable and plausibly attainable political objectives. In the great Pacific War of 1941–5, Imperial Japan provided a masterclass for all time in how not to wage war for limited, albeit ambitious, political goals. The attack upon American forces in Hawaii and the Philippines proved to be errors of stunning magnitude. Those preventive actions intended to facilitate the violent seizure of the resource-rich British and Dutch colonies of South East Asia had the unexpected consequence of condemning Japan to the waging of an unlimited and therefore unwinnable war. Recall Clausewitz's claim that war is a duel, and his subsequent comment that the strength of the enemy's will is far more difficult to gauge than is the strength of his military forces (p. 77). Strategic history is abundantly studded with cases of belligerents underestimating the strength of their intended opponent, most especially of his will to resist. Clausewitzian theory maintains sensibly, though perhaps as a forlorn hope, that 'a certain grasp of military affairs is vital for those in charge of general policy' (p. 608). Very few policy-makers today, world-wide, could meet that Clausewitzian standard.

The nature of war is the second compound category for the appreciation of Clausewitzian theory. This is a rare instance where it is useful to be more definite and clearer in argument than was the theorist himself. It so happened that Clausewitz suffered an acute intellectual crisis when the manuscript for *On War* was already well advanced towards completion. On 10 July 1827, to be precise, he penned a note which stated a sudden new intention to revise the whole of the work to reflect two critically important organizing ideas. The ideas were, first, that war comes in two variants – all-out and limited – and, second, that war is a continuation of policy by other means (Gat, 1989: 199). In the few years of life left to him, around his military duties Clausewitz achieved only a partial revision of his text. This fact helps account for some of the inconsistencies, real and apparent, and the incomplete analysis of elements vital to the political dimension of warfare. The resulting manuscript, with different books in *On War* revised in varying degrees, leaves ample scope for scholars to debate what the author 'really meant'.

Clausewitz asserts that war has two natures: objective and subjective. The former comprises those qualities common to all warfare in all periods. He states unequivocally that 'all wars are things of the same nature' (p. 606). Furthermore, he explains that 'war, though conditioned by the particular characteristics of states and their armed forces, must contain some more general – indeed, a universal – element with which every theorist ought above all to be concerned' (p. 593). In contrast to its objective or universal and eternal nature, war also has a subjective nature, comprising the actual, dynamically changeable, highly variable detail of historical warfare. In the language of today, Clausewitz's objective nature of war translates simply enough to mean what it says: the very nature of war. But his second nature of war, the subjective, translates into what now is called the *character* of war. So, following the Prussian, the strategic history of the past 200 years has encompassed war of many kinds, but with a nature that is constant in its essential features. In addition, those years have recorded wars of nearly every imaginable kind whose characters have been more or less unique, as well as sometimes radically distinctive from previous strategic experience.

The preceding paragraph might appear to focus on an unimportant distinction, but in truth the difference between war's enduring nature and its dynamic character is vital. Clausewitz sometimes comes close to suggesting that even war's objective nature is variable (pp. 87–8). However, to interpret him in that way would be an error. Nevertheless, often he does emphasize war's variability and diversity rather than its constancy. That fact, though, does not alter the authority of the theory which outlines the key constituents of war's permanent nature. What are those enduring constituents?

A useful way to grasp Clausewitz's theory of war's permanent nature is to approach the matter as he did, which is to say holistically (pp. 75, 607). The most important of his ideas about the nature of war are the remarkable (or paradoxical) trinity of violence, enmity and passion, chance and opportunity, and reason (p. 89); the climate of war, comprising 'danger, exertion, uncertainty, and chance' (p. 104); and friction, which accounts for the difference between 'real war' and 'war on paper' (p. 119). To these central pillars of his theory – the trinity, the climate of war and friction – one should add his ideas on the fog of war (pp. 101, 140); on the importance of moral qualities in military leaders (pp. 103–4); on the thesis that belligerents have a centre of gravity (p. 595); and on the distinctions between, yet interdependence of, the policy logic and the grammar of war (p. 606).

The heart of Clausewitz's theory is his proposition that all war is driven by the ever-changing unstable relations among the trinity of passion and enmity, chance and creativity, and policy reason. Famously, he wrote, 'Our task therefore is to develop a theory that maintains a balance between these three tendencies, like an object suspended between three magnets' (p. 89). Clausewitz did not exactly equate passion with the people, chance and creativity with the army and its commander, and reason with the government, but he did grant that the three aspects of war did, respectively, mainly concern those agencies. While noting the logic of the Clausewitzian trinity, it is necessary to avoid an inflexible and mutually exclusive understanding of their relations. For example, policy may be the responsibility of the government, but in the modern world it is likely to be influenced by a public opinion that could prove volatile. Also, policy can be moved by the military commanders who are shaping strategy, in a process of dialogue with politicians.

Clausewitz's trinity has been much misunderstood. Some recent commentators have proclaimed that we now inhabit a post-Clausewitzian era, because, allegedly, war is no longer largely an enterprise conducted by governments with armies on behalf of their societies (Van Creveld, 1991; Honig, 1997). Instead, so the argument goes, the state is in decline and much, probably most, of contemporary warfare is waged by non-state entities for purposes that do not lend themselves to national interest analysis. That view does not seem to be supported by the text of *On War*. A careful reading of what Clausewitz wrote reveals that his trinity, certainly his primary trinity, comprised passion, chance and reason. The people, the army and its commander, and the government were cited as what should be understood as a secondary trinity, one by no means strictly essential to his meaning. The primary trinity will be busily at work in warfare of all kinds, between adversaries of every character who are fighting for any set of purposes that has political significance.

In addition to the 'remarkable trinity', Clausewitz's theory of war offers the powerful ideas that war has a permanent and unique 'climate', and that all of warfare is troubled by 'friction'. Again, as with all of the theses and ideas introduced already from *On War*, the climate of war and friction permeate the whole of strategic history. They are vital elements in every bloody episode in the past two centuries. Recall that Clausewitz's climate of war is the product of danger, exertion, uncertainty and chance. Uniquely among strategic theorists, Clausewitz emphasizes that war is 'the realm of chance' (p. 101). This is valuable, albeit seemingly obvious, because many a war or campaign has been launched in the false confidence that chance has been eliminated by careful planning. In addition, the uncertainties of war stressed by Clausewitz are liable to be ignored or understated by policy-makers whose capacity to confuse their wishes with what is feasible can be astounding. There is a term which describes an extreme, almost euphoric, condition of strategic overconfidence: the 'victory disease'. Both Germany and Japan suffered from this malady in 1940–2, while the United States showed symptoms of its presence in the mid-1960s over Vietnam, and in 2003 with respect to Iraq.

'Friction' is among the most potent concepts in the strategist's lexicon, yet it is among the most difficult to apply pragmatically. The idea holds that things go wrong in war. Not only do enemies behave in unexpected ways, but mistakes are made by flawed, tired or overstressed soldiers. Moreover, nature is always likely to intervene to harass human grand designs. As usual, with friction Clausewitz serves up a concept that defies direct operational application, yet which should function educationally as a warning of the utmost significance. Many have been the war-waging disasters that descended upon politicians and soldiers who did not anticipate the serious possibility of friction on such a scale that operations could be endangered or even rendered impractical. Napoleon's invasion of Russia in 1812, and Hitler's emulation of that disaster in 1941, offer especially rich pickings for those who treasure deadly examples of friction at work. Among the general theorists of war, only in Clausewitz's writing is heavy emphasis placed upon what can go wrong and how sovereign chance may prove to be. It should be noted, however, that Thucydides also recognized the importance of chance in war (Strassler, 1996: 44). As a general rule, theorists strive to sell their ideas as a certain source of strategic benefit. They do not see advantage in pointing out how great are the risks in war.

As well as such central pillars of his theory as the trinity, the climate of war and friction, there is a long list of powerful, or at least intriguing, ideas. Clausewitz introduced the metaphor of the fog of war, referring to the 'uncertainty of all information' (p. 140). Modern technology may seem to overwhelm the commander with information, but more often than not that information will not be of the most useful kind. For example, the Clausewitzian 'fog' is especially prevalent in war waged against irregular enemies. How well are we doing? When will victory be secured? Is victory possible? These questions have been posed, and have defied confident answer, in war after war, both regular and irregular. Despite the wonders of the information revolution, it is no easier to answer these questions in the twenty-first century than it was a hundred years ago.

Among his many important ideas, true to the intellectual climate in Germany of his time Clausewitz laid emphasis upon what he called the moral qualities in war. He stressed the significance of the will and of character as contrasted with sheer intellect. This is especially relevant as a caveat to countries whose defence establishments have a preference for technological, at least material, solutions to strategic problems. Also, he warns against cleverness as a sufficient qualification for high command. Brain power and robustness (or stability) of character are by no means synonymous.

An idea he advanced which has prompted seemingly endless debate is the notion of the 'center of gravity . . . the hub of all power and movement, on which everything depends' (pp. 595–6). This is an idea that, unlike so much else in *On War*, soldiers find directly useful. Whether they employ the concept as Clausewitz intended is, of course, another matter. The hypothesis of the centre of gravity lends itself to over-simple attempts at real-world application. Clausewitz appears to offer exactly what a military planner, even a grand strategist, needs. By popular interpretation, every belligerent has a centre of gravity which, if destroyed, severely damaged, paralysed, captured or credibly threatened – whichever condition is appropriate to its particular character – must mean his defeat. Despite the many problems with this concept, not least the fact that in wars for limited objectives one should be careful not to menace the enemy's centre of gravity, the idea does have merit. As an aid to strategic historical understanding, the concept has some value. In World War I, for example, the centre of gravity of the Central Powers was the German Army on the Western Front; in World War II it was the person of Adolf Hitler. In order to reach Hitler, though, the Allies first had to defeat the German Army, and most of that army was deployed on the Eastern Front.

The last of the ideas on the nature of war to be cited from the Clausewitzian canon is the distinction he draws between the policy logic and the grammar of war (p. 605). With this distinction he insists that even though warfare must be subordinate to the political purposes that caused, launched and ultimately direct it, organized violence in any period has a military integrity of its own. When a policy-maker orders 'go', the military machine must fight in the only ways that it is able, subject, naturally, to interference from the enemy. What Clausewitz is saying is that although warfare is, and has to be, a political instrument, it is still warfare and it has a 'grammar', a technical and human character unique to itself and particular to a time and place. Politicians have been known to forget that. They can believe, fallaciously, that warfare is a precise instrument for the infliction of surgical-style damage in the interest of political goals. They are wrong. Warfare is a very blunt instrument, even in an age when the most modern military establishments pride themselves on their claimed ability to use force in so exact a manner that unwanted 'collateral damage' is all but eliminated. When war against irregulars is waged 'amongst the people', as General Rupert Smith puts it, some of those people are certain to suffer (Smith, 2005).

Conclusion

Despite the diversity of its events and the changes in its contexts, all of strategic history is explained adequately by a common theory of war and strategy. Revolutions in warfare come and go, new technologies rise, age and generally are replaced, and public attitudes to war alter. But war remains war and the inevitable changes in its character matter not at all for the authority of the general theory bequeathed by Carl von Clausewitz. When augmented by Sun-tzu, Thucydides and even the much underrated contemporary of the Prussian, Jomini, Clausewitz's *On War* serves as a tool kit good enough, perhaps more, to prise open the doors that might hide understanding of strategic history. Clausewitz wrote to educate, not to instruct directly with advice on behaviour. *On War* educates understanding of what war is about, how it functions, and why it can, and frequently does, go terribly wrong.

Strategic ideas are important: they move people and machines, and they have been known to persuade, and mislead, policy-makers. However, strategic thought is not a strictly intellectual, let alone philosophical, pursuit. It does not seek objective truth as an endeavour that is self-validating. Instead, such thought is a pragmatic effort, even though it is often deemed unhelpfully abstract by soldiers. Typically, it is spurred by the excitement and anxiety caused by the need to understand new strategic conditions and to develop recommendations for strategic action. Every topic in the mainstream of modern strategic theory – deterrence, limited war, arms control, crisis management, counter-insurgency, for some examples – has been pursued because of its importance to contemporary security.

Inevitably and inescapably, this analysis has had to focus upon the unfinished writings of Clausewitz. His ideas were explained as falling into two categories: those on the relationship between politics and war; and those on the nature of war itself. After probing and discussing his pre-eminent dictum that war must be an instrument of policy, this chapter proceeded to outline and consider his view of war's permanent nature, and presented his ideas of the trinity of, and unstable relations among, passion, chance and reason; of war's persistent climate of danger, exertion, uncertainty and chance; and of the friction which is liable to thwart even the best laid of cunning plans. In addition, attention was drawn to his important concept of the fog of war, his emphasis on such moral qualities as courage and determination or will, and his essential idea of the centre of gravity. Finally, the chapter commented upon Clausewitz's vital insistence that both policy-maker and warrior needed to respect the contemporary realities of each other's realms of behaviour and competence, notwithstanding the undoubted ultimate authority of the political. It is necessary to understand what Clausewitz's theory of war did not cover explicitly, as well as what it did. In that regard, Box 2.2 identifies some of the more notable absentees from *On War*.

Box 2.2* Important subjects deliberately omitted from or treated only briefly in *On War

Time and again in the text, attention is drawn to the range and power of Clausewitz's general theory of war and strategy. In some contrast, here I present some important matters that *On War* does not discuss adequately; or, in one case at least (sea power), at all. There were good reasons why Clausewitz chose not to dwell on these subjects – good reasons to him, that is. However, as the history chapters that follow this one explain, such neglect would not always have benign consequences. Contrary to appearances, perhaps, these points are not raised as criticism of *On War*, but rather simply to draw attention to topics on which Clausewitz's theory could benefit from some augmentation. (Matters which Clausewitz could not possibly have anticipated – for example, the effect on war of a globalized electronic mass media – are omitted from the list.)

1. *Grand strategy: On War* presents a general theory of war and military strategy, but it does not attempt to deal with the non-military aspects of strategy and war-making. Given the significance of the economic warfare waged between Britain and France during the Napoleonic Wars, this is a notable, and arguably damaging, certainly limiting, omission.
2. *Logistics:* Chapters 14 and 15 of Book 5 discuss supply and movement, as do the other chapters of that book in passing. But logistics is not accorded high significance in the theory of war. For two centuries the Prussian–German 'way of war' privileged the operational concept over questions of logistical feasibility.
3. *Raising an army: On War* simply assumes that armies are raised. Clausewitz himself likened that activity to the art of sword-making, and commented that his book was about the use of the sword.
4. *Sea power:* There are only two references to sea power in *On War* (pp. 220, 634), neither of them substantive. This may not matter, given that the book provides a general theory of war. Necessarily, it also lacks discussion of air power and nuclear weapons! However, given the profound significance of British sea power in the warfare of 1793–1815, it is at least possible that Clausewitz might have devised a somewhat different theory of war, had he been educated in maritime topics.
5. *Technology: On War* does not discuss technology; certainly, it does not even hint at the possibility that technological change might be significant. Dying in 1831, Clausewitz narrowly missed the onset of the Industrial Revolution on the Continent. His theory of war is protected from instant obsolescence by this silence on technology, but readers of *On War* need to be alert to the absence of this subject.
6. *Intelligence:* Clausewitz, in some contrast to Napoleon, was fairly disdainful of intelligence. In his experience, it tended to be contradictory, false, or missing when needed. In common with logistics, intelligence would prove to be a persisting weakness in the German way of war.

7. *Friction:* The definition, explanation and examples of friction provided in *On War* are brilliant and highly original. Unfortunately, the discussion is confined to one very short chapter (Book 1, ch. 7). Clausewitz has little to say on the subject of how soldiers and policy-makers might cope with friction.

8. *The policy logic and the grammar of war: On War* makes plain the properly dominant role of policy logic, but it also draws attention to the integrity of the contemporary character of warfare – its grammar, to use Clausewitz's term (p. 605). But how does one deal with an emerging mismatch between policy and warfare? *On War* is silent on this crucial matter.

9. *Military understanding by policy-makers:* '[A] certain grasp of military affairs is vital for those in charge of general policy' (p. 608). Clausewitz is surely correct, but what is to be done when those in charge of general policy do not have a grasp of military affairs? The strategic history of the past two centuries, up to and including the present day, was well peopled with politicians who were all but entirely ignorant of the grammar of war. *On War* simply tells us how things ought to be.

10. *Ethics: On War* contains no ethical discussion of war. Clausewitz's general theory of war is entirely bereft of an ethical dimension. This omission, which is a little strange, given the theorist's interest in contemporary philosophy, was of course deliberate. To Clausewitz, war was existential. It was a permanent fact of history, and it was not formally proscribed by international law until the Pact of Paris in 1928 (the Kellogg–Briand Pact). *On War*, of necessity, culturally, was a book of its time.

Now, well educated with a grasp of the meaning of strategic history, equipped with themes, aware of context, and suitably armed with Clausewitz's theory of war, this book moves on to explain and understand the strategic history of the past two centuries.

Key points

1. *On War* is a philosophical treatise, designed to educate, not to provide practical solutions.
2. Typically, strategic thought is triggered by the pragmatic needs of the moment.
3. Clausewitz insists that war has two natures: an 'objective' nature that cannot alter; and a 'subjective' nature, or character, that is always changing.
4. War is political activity by violent means.
5. The core of Clausewitz's theory of war is his postulate of the trinity of passion and enmity, chance and creativity, and policy reason; and the unstable, ever-changing relations among them.
6. The difference between the conduct of warfare on paper, in plans, and in reality is explained in good part by the compound concept of 'friction'. The axiom that 'what can go wrong will go wrong' captures the spirit of this idea.

Questions

1. Why is Clausewitz's *On War* widely regarded as the best book ever written on the theory of war?
2. Does Clausewitz's theory of war apply only to conflict between states?
3. How do policy-makers and soldiers try to cope with 'friction'?
4. To what extent is war 'the realm of chance'?

Further reading

A. Gat *The Origins of Military Thought: From the Enlightenment to Clausewitz* (Oxford: Oxford University Press, 1989).

C. Gray 'Clausewitz, History, and the Future Strategic World', in W. Murray and R. H. Sinnreich (eds), *The Past as Prologue: The Importance of History to the Military Profession* (Cambridge: Cambridge University Press, 2006).

M. I. Handel *Masters of War: Classical Strategic Thought*, 3rd edn (London: Frank Cass, 2001).

—— (ed.) *Clausewitz and Modern Strategy* (London: Frank Cass, 1986).

B. Heuser *Reading Clausewitz* (London: Pimlico, 2002).

M. Howard *Clausewitz* (Oxford: Oxford University Press, 1983).

P. Paret *Clausewitz and the State* (New York: Oxford University Press, 1976).

—— *Understanding War: Essays on Clausewitz and the History of Military Power* (Princeton, NJ: Princeton University Press, 1992).

—— (ed.) *Makers of Modern Strategy: From Machiavelli to the Nuclear Age* (Princeton, NJ: Princeton University Press, 1986).

H. Smith *On Clausewitz: A Study of Military and Political Ideas* (Basingstoke: Palgrave Macmillan, 2005).

3 From limited war to national war

The French Revolution and the Napoleonic way of war

Reader's guide: Eighteenth-century wars contrasted with the wars of the French Revolution and Napoleon. The transformation of war in the 1790s. The Napoleonic art of war and its problems. The strategic and political failure of Napoleonic France.

Introduction: two transformations

In its contribution to strategic history, the era of the wars launched by, and against, revolutionary and Napoleonic France witnessed two profound transformations, at least so it is argued by many. First, the political context of international relations, its norms, rules and procedures, allegedly was transformed from its condition of near-permanent great power hostilities in the eighteenth century to a very different milieu, with radically distinctive, more benign modalities governing great power behaviour in the nineteenth (Schroeder, 1994). Second, the wars of the period 1792–1815 revealed the actuality of a strategic transformation, because French armies were wielded as would-be agents of radical political change. Warfare in pre-revolutionary Europe had not had implications for the structure of the political context. It was paradoxical, though probably predictable, that the extraordinary violence of the Napoleonic Wars should trigger political innovation in the approach of the great powers to the maintenance of order and the management of their differences.

One can argue that the relative lack of great power conflict in the nineteenth century was in part a consequence of lessons learnt from the wars against France. This is not entirely convincing. Nevertheless, there is no doubt both that the scale and aims of warfare were transformed between 1792 and 1815, and that the statecraft of international order in the nineteenth century was markedly different in character from that of the eighteenth. As was emphasized in Chapter 1, continuity and change is a major theme in this exploration of modern strategic history. The relationship between the two repeatedly comes to the boil over claims, contemporary and subsequent, for and against transformation. Each of these historical chapters presents evidence for political and strategic transformation, typically, though not invariably, keyed to allegedly transformative technologies, civil and military. It so happens that in this, the first of the historical

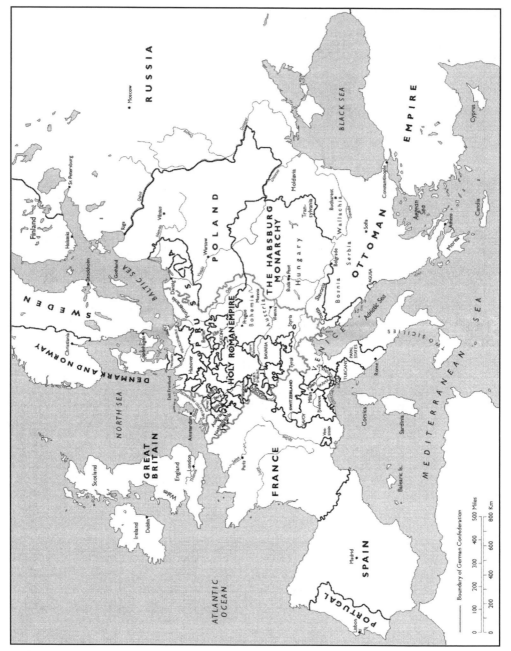

Map 3.1 Europe in 1789

chapters, technological change was unimportant for the conduct of war on land or at sea. But Britain's substantial technological lead in its industrialization was the foundation of an export-led wealth created by manufacturing that was crucial to the financing of the seven coalitions that were required to humble Napoleon definitively.

In explaining the strategic transformation tripped by the French Revolution and then exploited and perfected by Napoleon, this analysis re-emphasizes the dominant significance of the changing political context. Also, two arguments are introduced that will reappear repeatedly in later chapters. First, the rise and fall of Napoleonic France illustrates the perennial strategic truth that enemies learn from each other. In a highly competitive international system, one wherein states with many similarities struggle for advantage, any strategic transformation is certain to be copied and adopted and adapted to local circumstances. No state is able to achieve and then sustain a long strategic lead over its rivals. Second, the history of Napoleon may be a story of genius, but it is also a cautionary tale about the particular limits and vulnerabilities that flow from the egotism, ambitions and illusions that accompany genius.

Limited war and great war

This chapter is about the strategic history of a Europe that was at war, with only minor breaks, from 20 April 1792, when France declared war on Austria, until 20 November 1815, the date of the Second Peace of Paris. This protracted warfare was the greatest strategic episode for a century in either direction, past and future. Although the eighteenth century was anything but peaceful, Europe had not ended a lengthy general war among its great powers since the conclusion to the War of Spanish Succession, 1701–14. That conflict was pursued with a ruthless and bloody determination to resist an aspiring hegemon, the France of Louis XIV. Somewhat closer to the period of concern here, the years 1740 to 1763 witnessed virtually continuous warfare among the great powers, in Europe, Asia and America, with states changing sides as opportunity beckoned. As Jeremy Black has argued, the extensive warfare of the middle decades of the eighteenth century was important for what it revealed about the limitations of contemporary armies and navies. Much of the military reform of which revolutionary and Napoleonic France would be the prime initial beneficiary stemmed from lessons learnt in the 1740s, 1750s and 1760s (Black, 2001: 23).

Moving forward from 1815, the next general European war, which was also a world war because of the colonial possessions of the belligerents, did not occur until 1914. It is true that there was a strategically active period from 1854 until 1871, but the wars of those years were distinctly limited in purpose and restricted in participants.

It would be difficult to exaggerate the multidimensional impact of the wars of 1792–1815 upon the course of strategic history. Britain, for example, was at war with France from 1793 until 1815, save for a fourteen-month break in 1802–3 (the Peace of Amiens, 27 March 1802–16 May 1803), and the eleven-month gap between Napoleon's first abdication and exile to Elba (11 April 1814) and his subsequent return on 1 March 1815. The shock, trauma even, of the eruption of these wars can be gauged with the help of a contemporary authority. No less a person than Britain's Prime Minister William Pitt (the Younger) offered a sunny prospect while presenting his budget to the House of Commons on 17 February 1792. He advised that 'unquestionably there never was a time in the history of this country when, from the situation of Europe, we might more reasonably expect fifteen years of peace, than we may at the present moment (Pitt, 1915: 16). Instead of fifteen years of peace, Britain was to endure twenty-two years of war.

The wars with France cast a giant shadow forward over the first half of the nineteenth century and even beyond. As a strategic event those linked wars were a potent source of reputations, memories, myths and legends throughout Europe. After all, the Napoleonic style of statecraft and strategy was nothing if not geopolitically inclusive. Napoleon's strategic behaviour reached out and touched people from the River Tagus to the River Moskva, not to mention the unfortunates who crossed his path in Egypt and the Levant in 1798–9. Culture – popular, strategic and military – in many lands was heavily permeated by tales about the Great War against (or for) France. Of course, the memories faded, the veterans expired and new contexts emerged. But some legends grew rather than faded over time, especially if strategic history provided no evidence to suggest that a legend should not be treated as a historical, or even divine, verdict on national worthiness. For example, Britain's Royal Navy, the premier symbol of and instrument to protect its great power status, did not wage a fleet battle from 21 October 1805 (Trafalgar) until 31 May 1916 (Jutland). The burden of Trafalgar was one of exalted national expectations. For a century, Britons believed that the outcome there was the proper, even inevitable, result when the Royal Navy met enemies in main force at sea.

Until 1914, by far the greatest strategic episode in modern times was that which soaked Europe in blood between 1792 and 1815. If that reads like purple prose, inappropriate to a serious work of strategic history, consider the estimated facts on casualties. In the wars of 1792–1815 some 1.4 million Frenchmen died, albeit principally from the hardships of military life and, above all, from disease (Browning, 2002: 45). For a telling comparison, of French males born between 1790 and 1795, 38 per cent died in the wars. That figure compares unfavourably with the death rate for French males born between 1891 and 1895, of whom some 14 per cent fell in World War I (Gates, 2001: 55). Also, the death rate for British soldiers from 1794 to 1815 was proportionately higher than from 1914 to 1918. British fatalities in these French wars were 240,000, with 27,000 of those falling in battle. Military life, its hardships and many risks, carried a high promise of death or incapacity.

Throughout the nineteenth century, people looked back to the Great War with France, and to its dominant figure, Napoleon Bonaparte, for inspiration, for instruction, as a warning, and simply because it was the last general European, hence 'world', conflict. Intellectually, notwithstanding the galloping material progress of the nineteenth century, the leading theories of war were, and remained, decidedly Napoleonic. Both Clausewitz and, especially, Jomini were inspired by Napoleon's behaviour as the exemplar of the war-maker. Clausewitz transcended his contemporary historical context and the often raw emotions occasioned by his varied personal experience. Jomini too was successful in that he set out to explain both how Napoleon triumphed as a general and how those triumphs could be attributed in good part to the Emperor's adherence to certain rules and enduring principles. It is scarcely surprising that Napoleon's reputation and methods, puffed vigorously and even rigorously by Jomini, should dominate the military thought, and some of the military practice, of most of the century. After all, Napoleon fought no fewer than fifty-five battles between the time of his first independent command in 1796 and his nemesis at Waterloo in 1815. Of those fifty-five, only eight (some people argue for just six) were not victories. By any standard, that is a remarkable military record. So formidable was revolutionary and then Napoleonic France that it took seven coalitions twenty-three years to bring it down.

Here we should look back, briefly, to note the contrasts as well as the continuities with the warfare of the preceding century. The contexts of war are vitally important, although they cannot be all-important, because the mystery of combat performance is by no means entirely the product of contextual factors but rather is driven in part by influences integral to warfare itself. In other words, ultimately soldiers need to perform in battle. Nevertheless, the political and socio-cultural contexts play a determinative role in defining the character of war in a particular period. It is a general truth that societies wage war according to their natures and for the kinds of political goal that express their views of the world.

Dynastic Europe in the eighteenth century inhabited an 'Age of Reason', the era of the Enlightenment, when rationality and reform were intellectually fashionable. Such a Europe by and large waged its wars in what contemporaries regarded as a reasonable manner. At least, such was the broad intention. There were exceptions, but then there always are and always will be. It can be tempting – following Clausewitz, one must add – to exaggerate the limited character of eighteenth-century warfare. Some historians have suggested or implied that European wars in that period tended to take the form of an elaborate and sedately paced game of move and counter-move, with little effort expended to seek decisive victory. This is one of those frequent cases of a sound argument becoming unsound through exaggeration. The sound argument holds that after 1792 there was indeed a transformation in the purposes for which wars were waged, and in the ways in which they were conducted. The unsound argument proceeds to present a substantially fictitious picture of eighteenth-century warfare. That warfare was exceedingly bloody, with battlefield death rates entirely compatible with Napoleonic practice. That point scarcely requires much explanation. Little imagination is needed to grasp the character of the sharp end of war in the eighteenth century, when well-drilled ranks of professional soldiers exchanged volleys from smooth-bore muskets at close or even point-blank range (from 200 down to 80 yards or so). Such warfare was no game to the soldiers who had to do it. However, provided one is alert to the errors of exaggeration, it is not difficult to present a fair characterization of the warfare of the era which highlights its differences from what was to follow in the 1790s and, for a while, thereafter.

As a general rule, wars were waged for reasons of state and they did not impact heavily upon civil society. Enemy society certainly was not generally regarded as a legitimate target. Needless to say, though, there was no shortage of exceptions. To cite but two, the British Army treated Scottish Highland clan society as a foe, and it found itself obliged to regard a sizable percentage of the populace in the American colonies – perhaps one-third – as more or less actively hostile. Warfare against irregular enemies was not unknown in the eighteenth century, especially to those who had soldiered in the Americas or the Balkans, but, by and large, belligerents waged war against foes of broadly like character to themselves. In the language of today they waged symmetrical warfare. In this period armies were professional, expensive to train and maintain, and therefore modest in size. Politics, strategy and the army are interdependent. States generally did not wage their frequent wars in a half-hearted fashion, as sometimes seemed to be the case, but rather as vigorously as their military instrument and the contemporary 'grammar' of war permitted (Clausewitz, 1976: 605). The enterprise was governed by the crucial political context.

To curb desertion, soldiers were required to move together under tight control. They could not be trusted to forage for themselves, a practice which was generally forbidden anyway because of its potential to harm civilians. It followed that the movement of armies was tied to magazines, supply depots, and as a consequence tended to be ponderous. A slow tempo of military movement, one driven by logistic realities, translated as an opportunity for the enemy to evade battle, should it so choose. Eighteenth-century armies were not instruments of swift decision. They could not move rapidly. Moreover, they certainly could not turn a battlefield success into a decisive victory, because they lacked the ability to rout and destroy a beaten enemy. In general, with soldiers relatively scarce, expensive and hard to replace, and with political goals generally modest, commanders, while not necessarily battle-shy, assuredly were inclined to regard battle as a last resort and not as their dominant operational intention. Warfare was characterized more by siege and manoeuvre than by a ruthless quest for decision by blood. Again, one must cite an exception. Because of a geopolitical vulnerability unique among the greater powers, Prussia was obliged to seek decisive battle. The relatively weak Prussia of Frederick the Great (1712–86; reigned 1740–86) could not afford lengthy, indecisive campaigns. Its central European geographical position and lack of natural frontiers meant that it lacked the depth of territory to withstand and recover from severe military misfortune.

Warfare was not waged in the winter, it had little impact upon civilian society, and its recruited soldiers were all 'volunteers' who were motivated by almost everything except for any approximation to patriotic sentiment. Soldiers joined up because of poverty, for drink, to escape the noose, because they were stupid and, in a few cases, because they were romantically attracted to the lies they had heard about the soldierly life. That said, from such unpromising human material every European army managed to drill its volunteers into a coherent body of semi-automatons who would, and did, stand heroically to face massed musket-fire at point-blank range. Warfare was extensive, frequent and indeed a normal activity of state, but rarely was it other than behaviour conducted for limited political goals. The reason was the eminently practical one that was noted above: eighteenth-century armies were not capable of being wielded as instruments of rapid decision. Strategy reflected the reasonable ambitions of the political context of the century as well as the character of the military agent. Strategy is nothing if not pragmatic.

The eighteenth century had an intellectual and cultural climate that favoured reason, proportion and rationality. States accepted each other's political legitimacy – albeit with the notable exception of Poland, which suffered three, ultimately terminal, partitions (1772, 1793, 1795) – and they knew that no gains or losses were likely to be final. The outcome of warfare today would be contested again in warfare's inevitable next round. An important, even critical, factor to add to those already cited in explanation of the limited character of eighteenth-century warfare was the fundamental matter of cost. States in that period, with the lonely exception of Britain, simply lacked the ability to pay for long, expensive wars. State financial institutions were rudimentary, or altogether absent. Officials lacked the authority or the means to collect taxes reliably and in great amounts. States that cannot tax effectively cannot raise credit. This is an appropriate point at which to shift focus from pre-Revolutionary Europe to the new age that was triggered by – what else? – the financial crisis of the French state brought on by its inability to meet the debts it had incurred in aiding the American colonists from 1778 to 1783.

The Revolution and its warfare

If ever there was an unambiguous demonstration of the power of the political context to drive strategic history, it was provided by the French Revolution. The transformation in warfare effected by French commanders, Napoleon in particular, owed next to nothing to radical advances in military science or equipment. The new potency of French arms was entirely the product of political and human forces. There is a cautionary lesson here of which twenty-first-century technophiles would do well to take note.

There is a dynamic to political revolutions which typically, indeed all but invariably, escapes control by the original revolutionaries. Time after time, in country after country, those who begin a revolution with fairly modest goals focused upon reform and generally better governance discover that they have unleashed a tiger that cannot be returned to its cage. So it was in France in the 1790s, as it was to prove in Russia in 1917 also. The French Revolution of 1789 began with competing visions of constitutional monarchy or a liberal republic. By 1799, in the form of Napoleon Bonaparte's *coup d'état*, the visions had transmogrified into the reality of a military dictatorship. Napoleon made himself First Consul in 1799, First Consul for Life in 1802 and Emperor in 1804. This text concentrates on the political, military and strategic dimensions of events, but the social and economic contexts are always significant, too. In the case of France in the late eighteenth century, behind the noisy politicians and the ambitious soldiers was the social reality of a demographic explosion which had flooded Paris with unemployed, and unemployable, young men. These were internal refugees from a countryside whose family farms could not support them. They were to be prominent among the rioters and the soldiers of the Revolution. It is worth mentioning that a large surplus of unemployed young men nearly always provides fuel for extreme political behaviour, from France in the 1790s to Iraq and elsewhere in the Arab world in the 2000s.

The Revolution transformed the political and social contexts for war and peace. Although the dramatic military events of the warfare of the period tend to attract most attention, the real story is political. The Revolution made the defence of France a national concern, a patriotic duty of 'citizens' for the first time. The new revolutionary France was a deadly menace to dynastic order and its legitimacy everywhere. King Louis XVI was executed on 21 January 1793, with the National Convention having voted for his execution by 683 to 38. The new republic was ideologically aggressive and it had many sympathizers abroad among those well-meaning and progressive people who were attracted to the heady ideals of liberty, fraternity and equality. In the twentieth century, communist and fascist regimes held similar attractions to naïve foreign idealists.

Austria and Prussia formed an alliance (7 February 1792) which grew into the First Coalition (26 June 1792–17 October 1797), for the purposes of stifling the Revolution in France before its radical poison could infect other lands, and of restoring Louis XVI to his throne. Their decidedly credible military threat was seen off in some style by a hybrid French Army at Valmy, near Reims, on 20 September 1792. The French won with a combination of superior artillery, regulars from the former royal army, and a rabble in arms of enthusiastic volunteers. All in all, they were fortunate. Valmy was not the harbinger of a superior new way in warfare. Notwithstanding the political hindrances to military effectiveness in 1792–3, the new armies of the Republic did inherit the finest artillery park in Europe, as well as the most modern drill book, which is to say manual of tactical doctrine. Eighteenth-century military drill was direct preparation for tactical movement and discipline on the battlefield.

As so often is the case for the armies of revolutionary regimes, French commanders in the years of high peril from abroad, 1792–4, were in more danger from their own political masters than they were from the enemy. As a grim precedent for what was to become Soviet practice in the twentieth century, political commissars from Paris were attached to the new armies. Those men were vigilant in the extreme in sniffing out signs of treason to the current regime. Failure in battle often was taken as prima facie evidence of disloyalty. Some eighty generals and other senior officers were executed in 1793–4, providing Stalin with a model to copy in his period of desperation in 1941–2. Foreign perception of the new France as constituting a fundamental threat to the existing European order was correct. As the tide of war turned generally in the French favour by 1794, especially following their victory over the Austrians at Fleurus on 26 June that year, aggressive French strategic behaviour made clear beyond any room for doubt that a truly revolutionary force was on the loose in Europe. French armies in those early years were the revolutionary instrument of an ever more extreme republican regime in Paris.

The strategic story of the early years of the Republic is quickly summarized in its essentials. What was new about the French way of war was the scale of its armies and, initially, on balance, their lack of professionalism. But France possessed the world's finest artillery and had Europe's most advanced manual in the form of the Army Ordinance of 1791, and its raw volunteers and draftees were leavened substantially by the remnants of what had been a more than competent royal army. These were considerable assets. The combination of enthusiastic volunteers and former royalist regulars just, but only just, sufficed to keep France's enemies at bay from 1792 to 1794. It was a close-run thing, however. One should resist being overimpressed by an alleged high potency to a new French way of war in the early revolutionary years. The *levée en masse* of 23 August 1793, which was a startling proclamation of commitment to total war, in theory conscripted for the army all single men between the ages of eighteen and twenty-five. The *levée* had dramatic political effect, but pragmatically it reflected the grim reality that the voluntary principle had failed to produce sufficient soldiers for the Republic's armies. Notwithstanding their limited advantages, the armies of the new Republic were taking on some worthy enemies. The Prussians, and especially the Austrians, may have lacked revolutionary *élan* and generally been challenged in numbers, but they were skilled military professionals, led by some fine generals. As a result, French arms did not sweep all before them in the early and mid-1790s. In addition, it is important to remember that revolutionary regimes have to combat enemies both without and within. France needed unusually large armies in those years not only to compensate for their amateurishness, but to suppress serious royalist insurgencies at home, most particularly in the Vendée and in Brittany in the west.

Why did revolutionary France survive its years of maximum peril? Because of luck, because of the incompetence of its enemies – a quality never to be discounted, even though one dare not rely on it – and, above all else, because the enemy was a coalition of divergent interests. In such a political context, the substitution of men and enthusiasm for professional skill proved just sufficient to keep out the enemies. Tactics typically were crude, but effective. This is a point with relevance throughout the historical domain of this book. Successful strategy is strategy that works well enough. There is no requirement from some Law of Strategy that one must win elegantly. It is sufficient simply to win. Some professionally disadvantaged armies can find ways to offset their lack of skill. Moreover, the longer a war lasts, the more even become the skills of the rival belligerents.

The political context for the strategic history of the early and mid-1790s could not endure. Regime succeeded regime in Paris, each more extreme than its predecessor. The liberal dream of liberty, equality and fraternity turned into the nightmare of the Jacobin Terror. In a dark hour of national strategic peril, the Jacobins conducted 'the Reign of Terror' from September 1793 to June 1794, organized by Maximilien Robespierre on behalf of the menacingly titled Committee of Public Safety. The Reign of Terror claimed 40,000 lives, and it was in that atmosphere that the *levée en masse* was first introduced, on 23 August 1793 as already mentioned. It produced 300,000 men and allowed for the creation of eleven armies.

The political context just described, one characterized by chaos, panic, extremism and genuine foreign and domestic threats, provided the perfect launch pad for the opportunistic adventurer. If he was extraordinarily competent, that was a bonus, while he needed to be lucky in order to survive the lethal uncertainties of revolutionary politics. The rise, and further rise, of the Corsican Napoleon Bonaparte was the product of revolutionary chaos, but he might well have gone to the guillotine had luck not been with him. As it was, he survived the fall of patrons and a period of imprisonment (August–September 1794). Nevertheless, Napoleon took full advantage of the unique opportunities for self-advancement which a revolutionary political context offered. He prospered because the government of the Directory (1795–9) repeatedly needed him. Politicians in distress need the aid of a strong, utterly ruthless and competent military hand. Napoleon was more than willing to oblige. Just as Stalin was made by the Russian Revolution, which was enabled only by World War I, while Hitler as Führer is inconceivable except in the context of a Germany transformed politically by that same conflict, so Napoleon was the product of the French Revolution.

Napoleon's art of war

If this were a military, rather than a strategic, history, it would be obliged to devote extensive attention to Napoleon's dazzling achievements in warfare. It is true that those achievements were by no means unblemished by error, but a record of close to fifty battlefield victories still speaks for itself. The size of his reputation, and the indisputable fact that he has the truly rare distinction of lending his name to an era, also attest to Napoleon's stature in public consciousness, if not always public esteem. But, as a strategic historian, one might argue that Napoleon was not only strategically incompetent but grossly and murderously strategically irresponsible. Napoleon's art of war was indeed impressive, but what was it for? What was the plot? Since war should not serve itself, to what end, with what political consequences, was the Emperor's military genius applied? That is the plot, and it is a plot with a story arc and conclusion of ultimate, and almost certainly inevitable, failure. Strategic history is a tale of means and ends. All too often, writers allow themselves to lose the strategic plot in their enthusiasm for the colour and dash of the means. However, this analysis cannot leap over the military story, since, with a vital caveat, it is the necessary partner to the negative strategic judgement already suggested. The caveat is that the details of Napoleon's extraordinary military career really do not much matter strategically.

In common with Hitler's Third Reich, Napoleonic France was condemned by the character of its leader to eventual, comprehensive and irrecoverable defeat. Napoleon's great military and administrative skills postponed France's fatal meeting with destiny, but it could only be a postponement. In similar fashion, the superior fighting qualities of the German Wehrmacht in World War II could only delay the date of inevitable catastrophe. There is no avoiding a feeling of some unease with an argument for strategic historical inevitability. Napoleon's military and political gifts, though extraordinary, were lethally inadequate to meet the monumental challenges to statecraft and strategy that the exercise of those gifts themselves created. But, first, what was the Napoleonic way in warfare?

In order to understand that way, its strengths and its weaknesses, it is essential to be clear as to the meanings of, and distinctions among, three key terms: tactics, operations and strategy. Box 3.1 provides the necessary clarification.

Box 3.1 Tactics, operations and strategy

- *Tactics* refers to the actual use of armed forces, primarily, though not exclusively, in combat. In essence, tactics are about how to fight, about military behaviour itself.
- *Operations* refers to the use made of tactics for the conduct of a military campaign.
- *Operational art* is the skill with which forces are manoeuvred so that they are well positioned for tactical advantage. But it refers also to the ability to know when to accept or decline combat, with a view to advancing campaign-wide goals. Operational art uses the threat and the actuality of battle to win a campaign.
- *Strategy* refers to the use made of operations for their impact upon the course and outcome of a war. Strategy is the bridge between military power and policy.

Napoleon imposed a distinctive style of warfare on Europe, but, in detail, he was not a great innovator. His military modus operandi was a classic example of the total effect being far greater than the sum of its fairly familiar parts. Although he was certainly a well-educated soldier in the Royal Artillery, his genius lay in the practical realm of action. Not for nothing did Clausewitz emphasize the vital role of the *coup d'oeil* to genius at work, the ability to sum up a dynamic situation almost at a glance (Clausewitz, 1976: 102). Napoleon's superior mental gifts generally enabled him to make swift decisions, act boldly and exploit fleeting opportunities. A key to his ability to manufacture victory thus was his personal ability to grasp the essentials of a highly fluid situation. Another key was his 'joined-up' approach to warfare, which, unusually among his contemporaries, enabled him to campaign for decisive battle, rather than to move and manoeuvre and then consider whether battle might be forced on favourable terms. Napoleon always moved for the purpose of forcing battle on the enemy. He marched to fight.

Napoleon's strictly military innovations were modest, although in one instance highly important. He innovated with the battlefield formation of the division square – as contrasted with the usual battalion square – in Egypt in 1798, in order to repulse Mameluke cavalry. Of far greater moment, however, was his innovation of the wholesale introduction of corps organization to the army. The idea was not his, but its comprehensive introduction and employment in 1800 was. Each of his *corps d'armée*, of which he created seven initially, comprised three or four divisions, of eight to ten thousand men each, providing a balanced all-arms force of infantry, cavalry and artillery – a mini-army, in effect. The corps, unlike the division, which had been introduced into the pre-revolutionary army in 1787–8, was strong enough to stand alone against a large enemy force pending relief and assistance. Also, an army organized by corps, each thirty to forty thousand men strong, could be much larger than a single unarticulated force because of the delegation of command that it mandated. Until the introduction of the corps, a general could aspire to command not many more than 70,000 men. It was an elementary matter of the physical limits of personal command. Corps organization also enabled the army to move more swiftly and flexibly on parallel roads and tracks, and to live off the land where that was possible. The operative principle was that the army, subdivided into all-arms corps, should march divided but fight united. One need hardly emphasize the vulnerability of this excellent principle both to the variable quality of corps commanders and to the evil machinations of those ubiquitous hindrances covered by Clausewitz's compound concept of 'friction' (Clausewitz, 1976: 119–21). However, the military potency of an isolated Napoleonic army corps may be gauged from the fact that with a single such corps, totalling only 28,000 men, Marshal Davout defeated the main body of the Prussian Army at Auerstädt on 14 October 1806. Napoleon, fifteen miles away at Jena, in command of most of the Grande Armée, was mortified to discover that he had faced no more than a wing of the Prussian forces.

Napoleon's army, as noted already, adopted state-of-the-art tactics but only insofar as the skill and experience of the soldiers and their officers permitted. Although the years of warfare necessarily produced a highly professional cadre of veterans, the mass of his armies tended to comprise volunteers and, increasingly, raw conscripts. Between 1800 and 1811 he conscripted and mobilized 1 million soldiers, while in 1812–13 alone he conscripted a further 1.4 million. It is well to remember that, aside from Russia, France, with 29 million people, was by far the most populous country in Europe in this period. (For comparison, the British census of 1801 revealed a population total of 8.3 million.) Also, French armies of the Napoleonic period always included a healthy wad of contingents from allied and subject states (the two were typically indistinguishable). As a general rule, maintaining a ready flow of manpower was not Napoleon's dominant military problem. Far more challenging was the need to field armies sufficiently skilled in the trade of war. Constant campaigning and frequent battles wrought appalling attrition upon the troops. The veterans suffered least, especially if they were husbanded as the imperial reserve in the elite Imperial Guard, a force that would grow to be 60,000 strong, but still they suffered. The Emperor was obliged to adapt his tactics to suit the variable quality of his military instrument.

It is probably fair to comment that Napoleon's Grande Armée, so titled in 1803, although one of history's most effective military forces, was not especially strong in tactical skills. The reasons are not hard to identify. The Emperor, while an inspired battlefield general, was not a great tactician, especially for the infantry. He was an educated artilleryman who, unlike Wellington for example, had not benefited from early experience of infantry command in battle. The Emperor's excellence was primarily operational rather than tactical, let alone strategic. Moreover, careful study of his military method shows clearly that despite his vast experience of command in warfare between 1796 and 1815, he neither improved nor adapted and adjusted his military methods significantly as the military and strategic contexts changed. The exception to that generalization was his substitution of more artillery to take up the slack caused by the shortage of experienced infantry.

Napoleon did not effect a battlefield revolution. As in all periods, the challenge was to achieve an effective and mutually supporting balance among fire, movement and shock. He inherited an army that typically attacked in battalion, or occasionally division, columns. The column was a terrifying formation for assault which should redeploy into line as it closed with a linear enemy in order to bring its thus far masked firepower to bear. In practice, attack columns frequently would achieve so complete a moral ascendancy by their seemingly inexorable advance that there would be no need to shift into line to exchange musket-fire. Against steady, professional infantry, the head and flanks of a column would take such a beating that it would be driven to retreat in bloody confusion, not redeploy in good order into a thin firing line. It is well to remember the rawness of much of the French Army throughout this lengthy period. Inexperience in the ranks was the inevitable product of the high wastage of experienced troops from disease and other hazards of military life, in addition to death and injury in battle. Because of the high percentage of novice soldiers in the French Army, it is understandable that the relatively unsophisticated tactic of the assault column battering ram never lost its appeal. Indeed, the last hurrah for the nerve-testing columnular assault was provided by no less a body than the Emperor's Old Guard at Waterloo. When that failed against a steady and well-handled allied line, the game truly was up for Napoleon.

Weapons technology was stable from 1792 to 1815; in fact, it had barely changed in a hundred years. The standard infantry weapon was the muzzle-loading flintlock musket, smooth bore, approximately 1.75cm in calibre, and firing soft lead balls propelled by black powder. The musket could kill at up to 300 yards, but in practice its effective lethal range was little better than point blank, say 80–100 yards. Muskets were equipped with a detachable socket bayonet, a great innovation over the former 'plug' bayonet at the end of the seventeenth century, which enabled infantry to defend themselves from cavalry (the pike, and therefore pikemen, consequently became obsolete). Musket and bayonet comprised a weapon that combined firepower and the shock value of cold steel. Napoleon, however, was never greatly interested in the weapons of his soldiers. His style of battle did not depend upon the securing of fire superiority, but rather of decisive manoeuvre and shock for the unhingeing of the mind and the destruction of the spirit of the enemy.

With respect to artillery, again little had altered technically for many decades. But the mobility of French guns was enhanced by a reduction in weight, and a useful standardization of calibres had been effected. The guns fired principally solid iron roundshot which killed by bouncing along the ground; grapeshot, which killed by dispersing pieces of scrap metal; and case-shot, which killed by spreading musket balls from a canister which disintegrated on firing. The range of Napoleon's artillery was not much greater than 1,000 yards, but the Emperor, himself a former artilleryman of course, came to rely ever more heavily on his artillery train. A hallmark of his battlefield style was to assemble and employ a 'grand battery' of 100-plus guns. The effect of a cannonade from such an assemblage could be both physically and morally devastating.

Napoleon also inherited the late eighteenth-century innovation of light infantry units. These troops would be employed as skirmishers to protect the attack columns and especially to keep the enemy's skirmishers at a respectful distance, as well as to harass and shake the confidence of soldiers in the firing line. Unlike the British Army, with its excellent, if slow to load, Baker rifle, French skirmishers, the voltigeurs, were not issued with rifles. To repeat, Napoleon had little interest in the small arms of his army and, indeed, he represented a point of view which held that a dependence by infantry upon their firepower could harm their will and determination to close with the enemy.

As for his cavalry, the arm which because of its aristocratic connections had suffered most in the upheavals of the early 1790s, Napoleon employed it principally for reconnaissance, to screen and hide the direction of his army's march, and as the instrument of destruction to annihilate a routed foe.

So much for the military instrument that Napoleon inherited. What did he do with it? Wherein lay his military genius? What follows is a terse summary of the key features of the Emperor's military style.

Box 3.2 The Napoleonic way of warfare

1. The corps would march independently for speed and ease of self-supply, but fight united. Napoleon's army thus moved faster than the enemy, and typically much faster than the enemy expected.
2. Each corps was commanded by a trusted marshal or general (the marshalate comprised a wide range of talent, though the average was certainly high).
3. Ideally, army corps would march in a rough 'box' or a diamond formation, so that each corps could support the rest and the entire formation could change direction easily.
4. Napoleon did not simply manoeuvre; rather, he always manoeuvred for battle. He fused operational art and tactics.
5. He would seek to outflank his enemy and threaten its line of communications and retreat. This was known as the *manoeuvre sur les derrières*, a tactic he employed no fewer than thirty times between 1796 and 1815.
6. Sometimes Napoleon would use the outflanking threat to induce an enemy fearful for his communications to weaken his front. This enabled the French to strike straight for the centre of the enemy's army and achieve a decisive

penetration. This was the tactic that won the Battle of Austerlitz against the Austrians and Russians on 2 December 1805.

7.   On the rare occasions when the French were badly outnumbered, Napoleon favoured the strategy of the central position. He would strive to place his army in the middle of the array of his enemies' forces, exploit his shorter interior lines of communication, and beat his foes one at a time.

8.   Finally, the Emperor always sought decisive battle with the main body of the enemy's forces. He strove to achieve swift and complete victory.

Napoleon's military genius did not lie in any unique understanding of warfare and how to succeed at it. He did not know things about war that were mysteries to other professionals. Rather, his genius lay in the ability actually to do what the general wisdom recognized should be done. Recall that strategy – or, in Napoleon's case, largely operations – is an eminently practical undertaking. He had an outstanding *coup d'oeil* on the battlefield. He was a brilliant practitioner, by any historical standard, of operational manoeuvre for battle. He was a genius at inspiring his men; his charisma was extraordinary. Since morale is by far the most important quality contributing to the fighting power of an army, it is clear that Napoleon's persona was an asset of almost priceless value. A further benefit of his charisma was that he enjoyed a reputation which intimidated his enemies. Robert E. Lee and Erwin Rommel exercised a similar, if briefer, hold over the minds of their foes. In the later years of the Empire, the wiser among his enemies strove hard to avoid confronting troops commanded by the Emperor himself, sensibly preferring to cross swords with his marshals instead.

This description of the Napoleonic way in warfare will close with an appreciation from the Israeli military historian Martin Van Creveld. Commenting on Napoleon's work habits while 'in the field', Van Creveld has this to say:

> Frequently dictating to four different secretaries on four different topics at one time, Napoleon would send off up to sixty missives a day. Commanding eight corps in the field in 1805, he still found time to write to his stepson in Italy two or three times every day, going into the greatest detail as to what was to be done, where, and how. Reading these letters and appreciating the enormous powers of concentration and of memory behind them is to experience at first hand the most competent human being who ever lived.
>
> (Van Creveld, 1985: 64)

High praise indeed, but there were problems. As usual in strategic affairs, a new difficulty arises to harass every solution.

Problems with the Napoleonic way of war and warfare

First, because Napoleon's armies became too large to be commanded efficiently in real time by one brain, and because the communications of the period were slow and unreliable, he was obliged to depend upon trusted subordinates to command his corps, or even whole armies. Some of the marshals were men of only modest talent (Chandler, 1998): prominent among the marshalate were men of outstanding bravery who, alas, were tactically, let alone operationally, profoundly unsubtle. Marshal Ney is a name that springs to mind. He was the commander of the rearguard in the retreat from Moscow, and the very last man among the 25,000 who survived from the central body of the army (which had been 450,000 strong) to recross the River Niemen. Also, though, 'the bravest of the brave' was the man who single-handedly contrived to lose the Battle of Waterloo, where he neglected to observe the most basic of rules for the conduct of a combined-arms battle: specifically, neither infantry nor cavalry should attack unsupported by the other. Of course, the ultimate fault lay with the Emperor, who should never have delegated overall battlefield command to a man whose qualities, or lack thereof, were so well known to him. Indeed, it is a severe indictment of Napoleon that he declined to train his marshals in the fine art of high command, except by example. Not all were ineducable.

Second, Napoleon's style of war, with its requirement for rapid movement by detached corps, was shot through with the potential for lethal difficulties, or friction on a grand scale. The principle of marching divided for speed but then uniting to fight was an ideal rather than standard practice. Many times, especially in the opening weeks in Russia in 1812, and fatally in the Ligny–Waterloo campaign in 1815, articulated corps-sized pieces of his army were not united when and where the Emperor needed them to be. Also, his continuation of the innovative habit of the armies of the Revolution of living off the land translated in practice into stealing from, looting and generally abusing the unfortunate peasantry and townsfolk on the line of march. This practice may have contributed vitally to the swiftness of French military movement, but it could not help but be disastrous in its political consequences. When the territory traversed could yield little sustenance to French foragers, the consequence was that the army went hungry. Over time, the poor diet imposed by Napoleon's haphazard logistics contributed to high wastage among men and animals.

Third, France's enemies copied, selectively adopted and adapted, and sometimes improved upon the practices of the French military market leader. In a protracted period of warfare, Napoleon inadvertently trained his enemies. They could not emulate his individual genius, but they did not need to do so. Although the Grande Armée was probably close to unbeatable when it was at its peak in 1805–6, the armies of France's foes were far from rabbles in arms. Aside from the personal worth of its charismatic leader, France did not enjoy an extensive lead in military effectiveness. Moreover, in practice there were no ways in which Napoleon could prevent his enemies from closing the military effectiveness gap, since he proved incapable of forcing any of them off the gaming table definitively.

Fourth, by 1808 and thereafter, although Napoleon still won battles, his enemies were improving, while his own army was deteriorating in quality. The grim exigencies of supply compelled him to move his troops rapidly and seek decisive battle. That necessity naturally was reflected in crude battlefield tactics which entailed the suffering of high casualties. Also, the practice of living off the land greatly facilitated desertion in most regions, though admittedly not in Russia, and contributed to a significant loss of discipline.

Fifth, Napoleon's way of war proved ineffective against a maritime enemy. His endeavours to defeat Britain, the most persistent of his enemies, tripped him into the commission of fatal errors. Once he had grasped the unwelcome fact that he had no naval answer to the Royal Navy, and to the wealth that flowed from the trade protected by that navy, he was compelled to seek a continental solution to his British strategic problem. The invasions of Spain and Portugal in 1808, the subsequent expensive six years of Iberian misery, then the invasion of Russia in 1812 were all motivated in large part by the Emperor's determination to close the coasts of Europe to British trade. Alas, his Continental System of British exclusion foundered on the self-interest of continental demand for the products of the 'workshop of the world', as well as on national pride. Napoleon developed an obsession with the British menace which clouded his judgement.

Sixth, a problem endemic to the predatory imperialism practised by French arms at the expense of almost everybody else was that it could hardly fail to stimulate a patriotic response among some of its victims. The misbehaviour of French troops, from Iberia to Russia, fuelled anger and resentment among all classes and estates. The Grande Armée was not the bearer of liberty, good government and modernity, or at least not only of those desiderata. More often it brought impoverishment, famine, murder, rapine, theft and military impressment. The new French nationalism, actually aggressive chauvinism, all but obliged other societies to discover, or rediscover, themselves politically in response. This was not feasible for the multinational empire of the Habsburgs, but it was eminently practicable for Prussians and other Germans, as well as for Spaniards, Portuguese and Russians. Political revolution in France, the basis of the Napoleonic way of war, triggered national feelings abroad which laid the groundwork for more effective resistance to French aggression.

Seventh and finally, Napoleon's was an intensely personal way of waging war. Nevertheless, his system of delegated command was necessitated by the Europe-wide scope of his war-making and by the sheer size of his army. That necessity meant that even if the Emperor was at the peak of his powers, large fractions of France's army were commanded by people whom no one would confuse with military geniuses. A one-man system of war direction must have the vices of its virtues. Unfortunately for France, though contrary to the tone of some Gallic hagiography, Napoleon was only human. As the Emperor aged, his performance was hindered by illness and infirmity as well as by dynastic ambition. His judgement became erratic and his openness to advice, always limited, was reduced yet further. The performance of any one-man system must decline when the person who is its centre of gravity himself declines.

Political and strategic failure

The strategic historian reviews the military detail of Napoleon's remarkable career and asks the trademark question of the strategist: 'So what?' What was it all about? The warfare of 1792 to 1794 was about the survival of the new republic and its radical ideology. But once the First Coalition disintegrated in 1794, with Prussia's defection, and collapsed utterly in 1797 when Austria signed the Treaty of Campo Formio (17 October), it is unarguable that France was waging war simply for gain. Viewed overall, one is obliged to argue that French, and especially Napoleon's, strategic performance was a colossal failure. Despite the Emperor's undoubted military gifts, and his remarkable ability to win almost all of his battles, he did not succeed in removing permanently from the struggle any of his principal enemies. Austria was defeated repeatedly in the 1790s, catastrophically in the Ulm and Austerlitz campaign of 1805, and yet it returned to the combat in good enough condition to win a major battle against Napoleon at Aspern (21–22 May 1809), before being defeated at Wagram (5–6 July 1809). Austria returned to the combat as a major player in the coalitions that brought Napoleon down in the warfare of 1813 and 1814, while its army was preparing to campaign in 1815 when its activity was pre-empted by the verdict of battle at Waterloo. Similarly, Prussia seemingly was smashed at Jena–Auerstädt on 14 October 1806, and subsequently was coerced into a French alliance and into cooperating in Napoleon's ill-judged Russian adventure in 1812. And yet Berlin changed sides in the wake of the French debacle, fought hard against Napoleon in 1813 and 1814, and played a crucial role in the Emperor's final defeat at Waterloo. Russia was beaten at Friedland on 14 June 1807, but proved to be distinctly unbowed, let alone accepting of a fate that required it to be a submissive servant of Napoleon's statecraft. In short, Napoleon's exemplary record of military success was not translated into lasting political advantage.

Napoleon's failure was primarily political. No matter how many battles he won, how many treaties he dictated to beaten foes, they always returned to fight him again. The problem was that Napoleon did not really function strategically at all. Time after time, at least until 1812, he held the dominant hand in European politics, a hand won by the sword. Yet he never succeeded in using – indeed, he never tried to use – his military success as the platform for a lasting peace. He seemed to have no notion that in order to secure an enduring and advantageous peace, France needed the active and willing cooperation of former enemies. Napoleon's proclivity to wage war appeared to be quite out of rational, certainly reasonable, control. There was an acute, obvious and ultimately fatal absence of restraint in his statecraft.

What was his strategy? To employ ever larger armies to win battles, which should lead to dictated peace terms. But the defeated enemy of today is certain to recover, in time, and return to the contest bent on revenge. In other words, Napoleonic warfare, whatever its technical excellence for the period, was an exercise in strategic futility. Clausewitz insisted that war had to be an instrument of policy. So what was Napoleon's policy? Even with his genius at the military helm, France, and its on-again, off-again allies, was not strong enough to establish and hold a continent-wide empire against all comers. Eventually, Napoleon's contemporaries realized that serious diplomatic business could not be done with the Emperor. He declined to accept real limitations upon his behaviour. There did not appear to be any finite limit to his ambition. In a sense, Napoleon was akin to a mad dog. He was beyond reason, and beyond discipline, so he needed to be put down. As late as 1814 the Emperor was offered a general settlement that was modestly to the French advantage; yet, despite his unhappy contemporary plight, Napoleon refused. He simply did not know when to stop. By 1814–15 the whole of Europe finally had come to appreciate that the Emperor could not be trusted to keep any promise or abide by any treaty.

Strategic theory holds that war should be waged only for reasons of policy and in pursuit of an advantageous peace. In addition, it advises that a lasting peace settlement requires its genuine acceptance by those who have just been defeated militarily (absence of such acceptance was an important factor undermining the European order after 1919). Reviewed overall, the strategic history of the Napoleonic Wars shows unmistakably that the Emperor did not wage war in search of that advantageous peace. Instead, he waged war, and then more war, in pursuit of personal glory, family advancement (Napoleon was a good Corsican-Italian), loot and simply for its own sake. Sadly for him, his many victories, no matter how brilliantly obtained, were irrelevant: they would always be succeeded by the need to fight yet more battles. No matter how competently he waged war, eventually time, fortune, friction and a bevy of vengeful foes would call him to a terminal account. And they did, between 1812 and 1815.

The strategic historian must conclude that the wars of the French Revolution and Napoleon were conducted, after 1794 on the French part, for reasons that defied strategic logic. Regardless of the quantity and quality of French military means, which were genuinely formidable for a long period, they could never suffice to meet the unbounded policy ambitions of their political master. This was a crime against the logic of both policy and strategy.

Conclusion

This chapter has reviewed and analysed the transformation of war that was enabled by the new patriotism triggered by the ideals and the chauvinism of the French Revolution, a transformation subsequently exploited and perfected by Napoleon. Particular emphasis has been laid upon the critical role of the changing political and social contexts, while the many continuities in military affairs from the eighteenth century through the two decades of upheaval which concluded at Waterloo in 1815 have also been noted. Although one may choose to criticize Napoleon for his inability to employ force to secure a lasting peace, one must give him due credit for his undoubted operational genius and extraordinary leadership skills. To describe Napoleon is virtually to define charisma.

Above all else, though, this analysis placed the Emperor in the spotlight of Clausewitzian theory and found him wanting. The Napoleonic Wars stand in sharp contrast to the situation that was to obtain in World War II, wherein the Allies would not negotiate with a German government led by Adolf Hitler, if indeed they would negotiate with any German government at all. Not until 1814 was regime change in Paris an allied demand. The Emperor passed up many opportunities to negotiate a general settlement that would be to the French advantage. Yet he also declined to accept any lasting diplomatic limitation upon his ambition. The distinctive perspective of this book, which is to say strategic history, focuses attention upon the consequences, or lack thereof, of military action. One might venture to dissent from Clausewitz with the belief that if Napoleon was the god of war, he seems to have lost the plot early in his career and confused war with warfare. Napoleon was so overfond of warfare that he forgot, if he ever knew, that warfare serves war, which must serve attainable policy goals. But for policy, war and warfare all to be singing from the same hymn sheet, there has to be a well-wrought and adaptable strategy. Analyses which make claims for the Emperor's alleged strategic genius should be laughed out of court.

Key points

1. War and warfare were transformed between 1792 and 1815.
2. Revolutions have a dynamic all their own. They begin with high ideals, but conclude with (military) dictatorship, as in France in 1799, when Napoleon staged a coup and made himself First Consul.
3. Napoleon was not a great military innovator. His skill lay in the superior use that he made of the French Army, a truly national force that he reorganized and made his own as the Grande Armée.
4. Napoleon virtually defines what is meant by the concept of the charismatic leader.
5. France educated its enemies in what constituted 'best practice' in modern warfare. In long wars, military competence tends to equalize.
6. Napoleon's lethal failures were strategic and political. Because he could accept no limit to his power, he was unable to establish a European order tolerable for other states. His military victories were strategically meaningless and politically irrelevant, because they simply led him on to new adventures.

Questions

1. **What were the main characteristics of eighteenth-century warfare?**
2. **What was the Napoleonic way of war? Identify its systemic strengths and weaknesses.**
3. **What is meant by charismatic leadership? Answer with reference to Napoleon.**
4. **Why, ultimately, did Napoleon fail?**

Further reading

D. Chandler *The Campaigns of Napoleon* (London: Weidenfeld and Nicolson, 1967).

O. Connelly *The Wars of the French Revolution and Napoleon, 1792–1815* (London: Routledge, 2006).

C. J. Esdaile *The Wars of Napoleon* (London: Longman, 1995).

D. Gates *The Napoleonic Wars, 1803–1815* (London: Arnold, 1997).

P. Griffith *The Art of War of Revolutionary France, 1789–1802* (London: Greenhill Books, 1998).

R. Muir *Tactics and the Experience of Battle in the Age of Napoleon* (New Haven, CT: Yale University Press, 1998).

G. E. Rothenberg *The Art of Warfare in the Age of Napoleon* (Bloomington, IN: Indiana University Press, 1980).

—— *Napoleon's Great Adversary: Archduke Charles and the Austrian Army, 1792–1814* (New York: Sarpendon, 1995).

S. Wilkinson *The French Army before Napoleon* (Aldershot: Gregg Revivals, 1991).

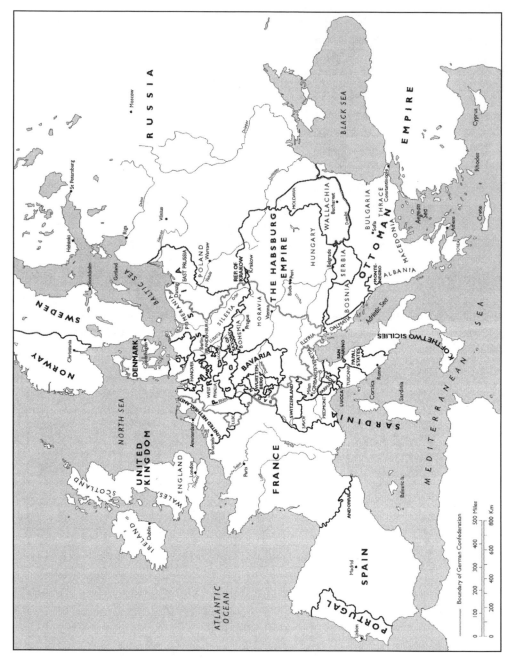

Map 4.1 Europe in 1815

4　The nineteenth century, I

A strategic view

Reader's guide: Overview of strategic history, 1815–1914. The wars of the period. The Industrial Revolution and military revolutions. The strategic consequences of the Industrial Revolution.

Introduction: the reach of strategic history

The twentieth century was dominated by wars, general and local, regular and irregular, to register an incontestable claim. It is less well appreciated that the international relations of the nineteenth century similarly were shaped and reshaped decisively by wars. Moreover, that reshaping critically contributed to the outbreak and character of what the British victory medal proclaimed to be the Great War for Civilization, or World War I. The Concert of Europe, so called, contrived in 1814–15 with its initial flurry of congresses, was a response to the wars of the French Revolution and Empire, their consequences and implications. In mid-century the succession of wars between great powers from 1854 to 1871 entirely restructured the balance of power in Europe. Those conflicts yielded a political context of enduring rivalries that enabled and eventually triggered the catastrophe of 1914. To extend the argument geopolitically, the outcome of the American Civil War of 1861–5 created the modern United States, and ensured that that country would be a giant among nations. This is not to claim inevitability to the events just cited. The point, simply, is that the strategic history of the nineteenth century, though less dramatic and obvious in its consequences than the like history of the twentieth, was just as influential over the course of events.

The master narrative of the nineteenth century has to be the Industrial Revolution, but for this book an even bigger story reposes in the strategic consequences of that protracted process. In company with historian Paul Schroeder, one might be tempted to argue that the biggest story of the century was what he discerns to have been a benign transformation of international politics away from the habits and practices of the previous century, most especially the readiness with which states resorted to war (Schroeder, 1994). Schroeder and his legion of predecessors have been seduced by the fallacy of benign transformation. They note, accurately enough, some encouraging change in the assumptions and practices of international relations. Also, they identify what they see as evidence of progress away from humankind's seemingly eternal war-prone condition. But what those optimists have done is ignore the main plot in international relations in favour of a sub-plot. Time after time in the past two centuries, progressive folk have found the very idea of major war, which is to say war between or among the great powers, to be incredible and obsolescent or even obsolete. This was so in the early 1850s, the late 1860s, the 1920s, the 1990s and the 2000s.

A violent century

The nineteenth was a very violent century. It just does not seem so to Eurocentric people who compare and contrast the ninety-nine years that separated Waterloo from Sarajevo with the periods that immediately preceded and followed them. It is not controversial to note that this was a long period that registered profound political, social, technological, economic and cultural change. And one must not forget that even though some changes, especially those of a material kind, occurred near-simultaneously in many countries, there were national differences in the ways that, and in the pace at which, modernity was welcomed. Unlike those theorists of international relations who disdain to take account of the domestic diversity of states, this text on strategic history is ever mindful of the rule that polities and their societies express themselves, indeed reveal their characteristics, in the way they prepare for and wage war, *inter alia*.

It is commonplace today to comment upon such phenomena as globalization and a supposedly frenetic rate of technological change. However, the nineteenth century suffered, or at least had to cope with, processes of globalization and rapid innovation which, if anything, were even more dramatic and potentially more significant than their successors of today. Then, as now, the real challenge was not to know what was happening, but rather to understand its significance. In strategic context, absent great power warfare for long periods, the overall meaning of technical innovations has to be eminently contestable. Forward-looking soldiers from the 1840s right until 1914 were confronted with desperately difficult questions. What would future major war be like? What did new weapons mean for the balance among warfare's trinity of fire, shock and movement? What should history, even recent experience of war, be allowed to teach? When technology changes rapidly from decade to decade, or even more rapidly than that, just how useful can historical experience be? Can one look to Napoleon, Jomini and Clausewitz for guidance in a strategic context that they neither knew nor anticipated?

It is convenient, but inevitably over-tidy, to divide a long period into phases. Risking the charge of undue simplification, this text finds it strategically meaningful to divide the nineteenth century into four phases. Each corresponds to a distinctive strategic context. If nothing else, such phasing should be effective in combating any temptation to offer unduly airy strategic generalizations about the nineteenth century.

1. *Phase One: 1815–54:* These thirty-nine years saw the decline, fall but continuing residual half-life of the so-called Concert of Europe that emerged from the Vienna Settlement of 1814.
2. *Phase Two: 1854–71:* Nearly two decades of intermittent warfare between isolated pairs of great powers, except for the Crimea, in which Russia was opposed by France and Britain. The overall consequence of the warfare of this phase was the

forcible creation of both a united Italy and, of infinitely greater significance, a united Germany. In addition, the victory of the North in the American Civil War of 1861–5 had strategic implications for the twentieth century and beyond of a significance that it would be hard to exaggerate.

3. *Phase Three: 1871–1890:* The new Imperial Germany comprised a potentially lethal threat to the ideas and practices of international order associated with Concert Europe. It was only the Machiavellian cunning and skill of Chancellor Otto von Bismarck which more or less obscured that deadly fact for a while, but only for a while.

4. *Phase Four: 1890–1914:* The post-Bismarckian German Empire of Kaiser Wilhelm II was led by men (one can hardly claim statesmen) who had neither the ability nor the intention to function as cooperative team players in a variant of Concert diplomacy. The international relations of the twenty-four years of Phase Four were characterized by the creation and extension of fixed rival alliance systems and by the conduct of competitions in both land and naval armaments.

One must focus on the strategic history of Europe in this period, because by and large European politics were world politics. But it is necessary to remember that there was continuous colonial warfare in Asia and Africa, as the European empires sought to plant their flags on every tract of extra-European land as yet unclaimed by rival imperialists. Although there were colonial disputes aplenty, sometimes of a seriousness that could threaten to trigger hostilities – especially between Britain and France in Africa, and Britain and Russia in Central Asia – colonial conflicts did not have a decisive effect upon the course of European strategic history.

The Americas too registered a strategically lively century. The former Spanish colonies asserted and sustained their independence by force of arms, following which they expended much blood and treasure in fighting among themselves in assertion of contested territorial claims. To the north, the United States redefined itself by strategic action from 1861 to 1865, in the bloodiest war in the country's history. The United States, North and South, suffered 620,000 fatalities in its Civil War, approximately 200,000 of which were from battlefield causes. In proportion to its total population, American losses from 1861 to 1865 were higher than those suffered by Britain from 1914 to 1918. The Civil War was not a minor strategic event. Much lower on the casualty scale, but in contrast near-continuous from the 1810s to the early 1890s, the United States was actively strategically engaged in hostilities with a wide range of tribes of Native Americans on its internal frontier. Such 'small warfare' was a running story throughout the century, at least until the concluding tragedy at Wounded Knee on 29 December 1890, when 150 Sioux adherents to the Ghost Dance Cult were shot by US soldiers.

Before one contrasts a nineteenth century that saw no general war with a twentieth that recorded two such, and might have gone for gold with an even more remarkable third, one should take note of a Chinese contribution to strategic history. It so happens that the bloodiest war of the nineteenth century was a most uncivil civil war waged in China between 1850 and 1864. The civil war of those years had as its political centrepiece opposition to the rebellion against the Manchu Dynasty in favour of a Han dynastic revival. This revival was inspired by an exciting ideology which attempted to fuse Confucianism with Christianity. The extensive warfare that ensued produced fatalities estimated (and one must emphasize estimated) to have totalled no fewer than 20 million. By any standard of awfulness, the Taiping Rebellion was a protracted strategic happening that would blacken the record of any century.

As was claimed in the introduction to this chapter, those in search of a grand narrative for the nineteenth century are virtually obliged to settle upon the Industrial Revolution as the multifunctional engine of their story arc. That near-compulsory choice is not contested here, but the Industrial Revolution is considered primarily with a view to unwrapping its strategic consequences and implications.

Implications of the Industrial Revolution: the strategic tale

The strategic history of 1800 to the present is the history of the conflicts, and peace-making efforts, of an ever more industrial, technological and at root scientific civilization. When Clausewitz was writing and rewriting *On War* in the 1820s, he felt under no compulsion to discuss the implications of technology and industry for his theory. Had he been writing twenty, perhaps only ten, years later, he could hardly have avoided the subject. What happened in the second quarter of the nineteenth century was the acceleration, maybe the true beginning, of what has been called the routinization of invention. From the 1830s and 1840s until today, material progress in the form of technological invention and industrial processes resting upon scientific discovery has been continuous. The rate of advance has varied, and some societies have lagged behind, but as early as the 1850s, strategic history was impacted noticeably by the challenge of coping with a novel technological context. It is fair to claim that in sharp contrast to the wars of the French Revolution and Empire, every war between great powers in the later nineteenth century and after posed new problems and opportunities that were, in good part at least, technological. The Industrial Revolution was not carried through in order to benefit strategists, but its progress was expedited at times by the needs of strategists, just as its products, by no means always welcomed wholeheartedly by soldiers, presented challenges that only experience, which is to say trial and error, could resolve.

While it is sensible to identify an Industrial Revolution in the nineteenth century, it is no less valid to think of that revolution as a process of diverse cumulative discovery and manufacture which continues to this day. It is useful to appreciate that there have been three such revolutions. The first was the introduction of steam power, following James Watt's invention of a practicable steam engine in 1764, which was a revolution fuelled by coal and capable of producing steel. The second revolution occurred slightly more than a century later with the invention of the internal combustion engine in 1885–6 by Gottlieb Daimler, the use of oil as a source of power, together with the taming and exploitation of electricity. The third revolution, dating from the 1930s, yielded nuclear energy, plastics and electronics. In the words of military historian John Terraine, 'A process of emergence, dominance, decline and fall is apparent. There are no fixed dates; elements of all three Revolutions operate today' (Terraine, 1996: 3). This chapter asks the same question that statesmen and strategists have been obliged to ask since the 1840s: what do these technological changes mean for the character and structure of international relations and for the conduct of war? The wars of the 1850s, 1860s and 1870s posed novel dilemmas. That condition of some bewilderment was not to improve in the twentieth century.

In order better to appreciate the scope, depth and significance of the Industrial Revolution of the nineteenth century, it is helpful to understand it in the context of the whole of modern strategic history. Some historians and social scientists have postulated a grand theory of military revolution (MR) (Murray and Knox, 2001: ch. 1). They argue that since the seventeenth century there have been just six truly profound revolutions either in warfare itself directly or in the most critical contexts for warfare. These revolutions, so the story goes, have been unavoidable and inescapable, and can be likened to irresistible seismic events. Statesmen, soldiers and indeed everyone else simply has had to make the best of the novel conditions wrought by the great changes. Box 4.1 summarizes the mighty six.

Box 4.1 **Modern military revolutions**

1. *The invention and the rise of the modern state in the seventeenth century.* This triggered, accompanied or was a consequence of the first of the modern MRs. Historians disagree over the issue of whether the emergence of the state as we know it is the product mainly of military necessity, or whether a monopoly of effective military power is more the consequence than the cause of the rise of the state.

2. *The French Revolution*, which, with some inspiration from the ideals and the practices of the American Revolution only a decade earlier, invented the modern concept of the nation state. The American and French revolutions postulated the radical notion that people were citizens, not subjects, and that they had an obligation, a duty as the price of their rights, to defend their nation.

3. *The Industrial Revolution* is still under way. The material character of this revolution has shifted several times since the age of steam and coal and steel, but it initiated a process of scientific, technological and industrial manufacturing, advance that has never halted or even noticeably slowed. Indeed, it has been unstoppable. In common with the other MRs, the thesis holds that the military revolution sparked and sustained by industrialization was unavoidable. All that soldiers and statesmen could do was adapt as best they could to the conditions it imposed.

4. *The Military Revolution of World War I.* Modern warfare, in the fullest sense of the term, was invented under fire and as a matter of the direst military necessity, from 1916 to 1918. This military revolution was mandated by the strategic context created by the previous, but still authoritative, MRs. In World War I the belligerents were centralized and fairly efficient states, which ruled over societies of variably patriotic citizen-subjects, with the products of unevenly mature industrial infrastructures.

5. *The Nuclear Revolution of the 1940s and 1950s.* Once the nuclear discovery was made, and especially once it had been demonstrated in weapons that worked, states had no choice other than to make the best of it. This revolution, in common with the others, could not be repealed. It could only be accepted

and, if possible, tamed and exploited for national and international security. The 'bomb' was here to stay. It could not be disinvented.

6.   *The Information Revolution of the 1980s to the present.* Again, this revolution is more of a process than an event or episode. Also, it had a host of scientific and technical antecedents. The 1980s are chosen for convenience and strategic plausibility, as well as because they marked some dramatic changes. This latest promoter of military revolution has in common with all the rest the defining feature that it is unavoidable.

One may need to add a seventh entry to this list of MRs.

7.   *The Cultural Revolution under way in the Islamic world.* This revolution in the strategic implications of faith exploits industrial and information technology, and may find employment for the products of the nuclear revolution, but it is occurring independent of technology. The dominant character of contemporary warfare is highly irregular, and therefore asymmetrical.

The Industrial Revolution, therefore, was one in a short series of mighty upheavals that shaped and reshaped modern strategic history. It could not be evaded or ignored, any more than could any of its five historical siblings. Each of these great revolutionary developments had the potential, indeed were certain, to remake the character of war. Time after time, however, responsible officials, both civil and military, had to recognize the fact of incipient revolution; then understand its implications; and finally come up with practical solutions to the political, strategic and military problems and opportunities created by the radical changes.

The Industrial Revolution which began in Britain in the late eighteenth century spread inevitably, though at varying speeds, to countries on the continent of Europe and to North America. It changed almost everything about war and warfare, except for the nature of those phenomena and possibly the 'principles' that Jomini discovered and expounded in the 1830s (Jomini, 1992). Strictly speaking, the authority of Clausewitz's theory of war is immune to the charge of an obsolescence born of cumulatively massive alterations in technological, political or socio-cultural contexts. Wisely, he crafted his general theory of war so that it would not need amendment in order to accommodate technical, or any other, developments. But one must point out that all works of strategic theory, even the greatest, are the product, and have to reflect the worldview, of a particularly encultured person located historically at a specific time and place. It is a tribute to the extraordinary quality of Clausewitz's theory that his book, inspired above all else by the experience of the wars of the French Revolution and Napoleon, has retained an undiminished relevance throughout the two centuries that are the concern of this text. One must add, however, that many of his readers, or more often skimmers and quotation-extractors from bowdlerized versions of the work, found the Clausewitz that they favoured in his sometimes apparently contradictory text.

If one fast-forwards to 1914–18, it is abundantly plain that that Great War had a character, and indeed strictly was enabled, only by the consequences of the French and Industrial revolutions. This is not to suggest that World War I was caused in some deterministic way by the burgeoning nationalism that flourished in the nineteenth and early twentieth centuries. And neither should one assert that the war was the almost natural consequence of the material transformation of many European and North American societies effected by the Industrial Revolution. Instead, the claim is simply that the general war that erupted in 1914 took the form that it did because of the political, social and material conditions that were products of the rise of national sentiment and the process of industrialization.

The Industrial Revolution affected all aspects of strategic history. Indeed, in its contemporary guise as the Information Revolution, keyed to the exploitation of the computer, technological change continues to impact, though certainly not direct, the course of strategic history in the twenty-first century. Many historians have accepted as a master strategic narrative the thesis that there was a distinct era of increasingly total – for a contested concept (Chickering, 1999) – warfare enabled initially by the revolution in national sentiment unleashed from Paris, and later by the artefacts and attitudes of an industrial age. That era is variably dated from the 1790s, the Crimea (1854–6), the American Civil War (1861–5), the Austro-Prussian War (1866) or the Franco-Prussian War (1870–1). Generally it is held to have terminated in 1945, when the appearance of the atomic bomb seemed to carry the promise of functioning as a technological trump to the military products of industrial mass production. Alternatively, a case can be made for allowing industrial-age mass warfare a lingering half-life through the Cold War decades to a final hurrah in the First Gulf War of 1991. That conflict was waged with masses of armour, fleets of ships and aircraft, mountains of ammunition and other supplies and, generally, in a style not radically different from 1945.

In tandem with, and really as a beneficiary of, radical changes in agricultural practices – in a few countries, at least – industrialization led to increasing urbanization. There was a flight of people to towns and cities, away from the countryside. Nevertheless, this was a slow process and it was distinctly uneven from country to country. Throughout the nineteenth century, Europe continued to comprise a collection of largely peasant societies. Urbanization was a matter of great concern to politicians and soldiers. With good reason, peasants were believed to be healthier than townsfolk, and hence to make more robust soldiers. Also, even more important, peasants were ill-educated, if formally educated at all, politically conservative and therefore a reliable source of military manpower for the support of traditional regimes. Population growth was rapid – if, again, uneven – among states. When one considers the mass conscript armies fielded in 1914–18, supplied and fed by the products of industrialization and a more scientific agriculture, it is important to be aware of the dynamic demographic context of the preceding century. The total population of Europe was 187 million in 1800, 266 million in 1850, 401 million in 1900 and 468 million in 1913. By 1914 the new united Germany comprised 67 million people, a total which dwarfed the human pool of the French at a severely lagging 39 million. In this period, numbers mattered profoundly. Mass armies had to be extracted from the mainstream of the public, from society broadly, not only from its marginal groups. Should warfare be protracted, size of population could, indeed must, be the vital factor determining the depth of the belligerents' manpower reserves. Moreover, should attrition play a determinative role in deciding war's outcome between competent enemies, relative numbers would be potentially the deciding difference.

The revolution in the use of coal to produce the steam which enabled the mass production of iron and then steel delivered, pre-eminently, the railway and the steamship. Both had enormous strategic implications. Troops could be moved rapidly for the first time. Moreover, they could be moved in large numbers, and then sustained logistically. The first railway was built in Britain in 1825, connecting Stockton and Darlington; Liverpool and Manchester were connected in 1830. The first major railway in France had been completed in 1828. In terms of demonstrated military utility, Prussia dispatched soldiers by train to suppress revolution in 1848. The Anglo-French expeditionary force in the Crimea constructed a light railway to connect the harbour at Balaclava with the troops inland, and the French moved an entire army by train to northern Italy in 1859 in just two weeks when they mobilized and deployed to fight the Austrians. The classic study of the strategic influence of the rise of 'rail power', written by Edwin A. Pratt in 1916, had this to say about the extraordinary meaning of the railway for the American Civil War: 'Such were the conditions under which the War of Secession in the United States was fought that without the help of railways it could hardly have been fought at all' (Pratt, 1916: 11). What Pratt refers to are the facts that the American theatres of war approximated in geographical scale the size of much of Europe. That was a far cry in time and space from Prussia's much-praised employment of its railways in its wars with Austria in 1866 and France in 1870–1. In fact, Pratt's comment on railways as a vital enabling agent for the conduct of the American Civil War could also have been made for World War I, and indeed for World War II. They were both 'railway wars', among their other qualities.

The Industrial Revolution, and the revolution in a more scientific agriculture that accompanied it in some countries, created the wealth that enabled military preparation and war to be financed. In addition, it allowed for the standardized mass production by machine tools of the equipment and weapons with interchangeable parts in quantities that large armies must have. The Victorians were proud to the point of boastfulness of the material progress they achieved through science, technology and engineering. They first showcased their technical triumphs in the Great Exhibition in London in 1851. But, inevitably, such progress also advanced the material culture of war.

In addition to the railway, which was the signature development of industrialization, the invention in 1812 of a safe and reliable means of preserving food by the process of heat sterilization and canning had profound implications for military logistics. More campaigns in history have been undone by hunger and its consequences than by the combat skills of cunning and determined foes. Grand narratives of strategic history are apt to neglect to mention that the nineteenth century registered the beginning of scientific medicine. Nevertheless, it was not until the next century that disease was tamed as a potential strategic show-stopper. Certainly it was a huge impediment to the designs of military planners and the hopes of politicians.

As well as the railway and the preservation of food, another of the principal structural achievements of the Industrial Revolution was its success in exploiting electrical impulses for communications. Samuel Morse patented the electric telegraph in 1837, and the first operational system was functioning by 1844. Morse went on to invent his eponymous code, which after 1850 greatly simplified and speeded transmission. Communication by cable was a revolution. For example, the French Army in the Crimea was linked by cable with Paris. One must add that this was a distinctly mixed blessing, since governments henceforth could exercise very near real-time control over distant armies. The electric telegraph enabled commanders to issue orders promptly over great distances, always provided they were connected by cable and that the enemy, or nature, had not imposed too much friction. Obviously, though, armies on the move would be difficult, if not impossible, to reach by telegraph.

In several respects the electric telegraph meant new challenges for civil–military relations. Governments now could intrude into operational military matters, a subject that military professionals regarded, and continue to regard, as properly and uniquely their field of expertise. Also, for the first time in history, the telegraph meant that war news could be transmitted to publics at home and abroad. The new profession of war correspondent appeared in the Crimea. The transmission of news 'from the front' to the increasingly literate and somewhat enfranchised home public produced the novel peril of public opinion for politicians over their foreign and strategic policies. The wiring of the world by the 'Victorian internet', as the electric telegraph has been called, was the vital technical enabler of the political involvement of the general public with the behaviour of its country's armed forces (Standage, 1998). In modern times, public opinion had hardly ever played a significant role in policy-making for war and peace. In the 1850s that condition changed for ever. In the uncomfortably direct democracies of ancient Greece, of course, public opinion was a decision-maker with lethal, prompt powers.

Conclusion

The Industrial Revolution allowed states to equip, train, move, command and sustain logistically in combat armies of a size unprecedented in history. There were potent strategic reasons why the decisive theatre in World War I was the Western Front in Belgium and northern France. However, there was also an eminently practical reason. In 1914–18, Belgium and northern France comprised the only area on earth where intensive mass warfare was logistically feasible. In a vital enabling sense, the Great War was a great railway war. This is not to deny that Europe had conducted a cycle of great wars from the end of the fifteenth century to the beginning of the nineteenth. But the totality of the great wars of the twentieth century was feasible only because of the marriage of mass manufacture and surplus food to a rise in national sentiment almost everywhere. M. S. Anderson has conveniently summarized the implications of the revolutions of industrialization, national feeling and even the transnational culture of attitudes towards war in a single, high-voltage sentence: 'In every great European state, therefore, armed forces in 1914 were larger, more national, more eager for conflict, and endowed with enormously more destructive power than in the year of Waterloo' (Anderson, 2003: 346).

This history moves on to look more closely at the impact of these revolutions upon the armed forces, especially the armies, that Clausewitz insisted had to be instruments of policy. The focus initially will be on technical advance, with its uncertain strategic, operational and tactical implications. Above all else, though, strategic and military history must be related to their all-important and sometimes highly dynamic political context.

Key points

1. The period 1815–1914 was not a century of peace; rather, it was only a century that did not register a general European war.
2. The Industrial Revolution introduced a routinization of the process of invention. Strategists were challenged to understand the implications of the new technologies that appeared at a near-frenetic pace.
3. The Industrial Revolution was one of the six (or seven) great military revolutions in modern strategic history.
4. The signature innovations of the Industrial Revolution were the railway and the steamship. Both posed novel risks and opportunities for strategists.
5. The invention of the electric telegraph revolutionized civilian and military communication.
6. The character of World War I was directly attributable to the consequences of the French and Industrial revolutions. Those revolutions were the vital enablers of 'total' war.

Questions

1. What was the strategic significance of the railways, food canning and the electric telegraph?
2. How persuasive do you find the theory of military revolutions? Answer with reference to the French and Industrial revolutions.
3. What intellectual and practical problems did the rapid pace of technological advance pose for strategists in the nineteenth century?
4. Why was there no general European war between 1815 and 1914?

Further reading

M. S. Anderson *The Ascendancy of Europe, 1815–1914*, 3rd edn (Harlow: Pearson Education, 2003).

C. J. Bartlett *Peace, War and the European Powers, 1814–1914* (London: Macmillan, 1991).

G. Best *War and Society in Revolutionary Europe, 1770–1870* (London: Fontana, 1982).

T. C. W. Blanning (ed.) *The Nineteenth Century: Europe, 1789–1914* (Oxford: Oxford University Press, 2000).

F. R. Bridge and R. Bullen *The Great Powers and the European States System, 1814–1914*, 2nd edn (Harlow: Pearson Education, 2005).

D. Gates *Warfare in the Nineteenth Century* (Basingstoke: Palgrave, 2001).

H. A. Kissinger *A World Restored: Europe after Napoleon: The Politics of Conservatism in a Revolutionary Age* (New York: Grosset and Dunlop, 1964).

A. D. Lambert *The Crimean War: British Grand Strategy against Russia, 1853–56* (Manchester: Manchester University Press, 1990).

P. W. Schroeder *The Transformation of European Politics, 1763–1848* (Oxford: Clarendon Press, 1994).

D. Showalter *The Wars of German Unification* (London: Arnold, 2004).

G. Wawro *Warfare and Society in Europe, 1792–1914* (London: Routledge, 2000).

5 The nineteenth century, II

Technology, warfare and international order

Reader's guide: The transformation of warfare in the nineteenth century. The improvements in armament and their implications. The changing political and strategic contexts.

Introduction: Waterloo to the Marne

Today, defence experts argue about the implications of new information technology for warfare. In the mid-nineteenth century their predecessors debated the meaning of the railway, the electric telegraph and, above all else, the new firepower available to infantry. The need to make strategic, operational and tactical sense of new technology, to find workable doctrine to govern its use, became a permanent challenge once the Industrial Revolution had gathered pace in the second quarter of the century.

Strategists in the 1840s and 1850s, for example, had to understand the promise and the potential pitfalls of the railway. Yes, it provides relatively speedy transport for men, animals, equipment and food, but only if the lines connect places useful to war-making. Will not total dependence on the railway restrict operational choice; indeed, make it predictable to an enemy? And might not the lines be sabotaged? Furthermore, what happens at the end of the line? For tactical, and possibly even operational, military movement, armies will still have to advance or retreat as the Romans did, on foot and hooves. In addition, the loading and unloading of mountains of equipment, munitions and food for men and animals is a large – or by 1914–18 a monumental – logistical task. A further consideration, one that was to become the engine pushing all the European great powers into the creation of a more or less capable general staff, was that a state whose military mobilization plans were utterly dependent upon rail transport required mastery of, and contingent control over, railway timetabling. Unless military establishments were expert in the planning and management of rail traffic, the result would be chaos in a time of crisis, probably followed promptly by defeat in a single campaign for a continental power. The experience of war in 1866 and 1870 appeared to demonstrate that decisive victory could be achieved by the outcome of an initial offensive alone. And that victorious offensive could be launched only if military professionals utilized railways efficiently.

The wars of the nineteenth century provided ample evidence of the strategic impact of an accelerating and diffuse process of industrialization. Also, they flashed a red light to those attentive to the significance of the national sentiment which had first made its presence felt as a driving element in America in the 1770s, and then in France, Prussia and Russia a generation later. The period 1815–1914 concluded with a protracted conflict between multi-million-man armies locked into indecisive combat for four and a quarter years. There were no decisive battles in World War I, as Michael Howard reminds us, perhaps with some overstatement (Howard, 2004: 53). That generally plausible claim was the consequence of the state of technology, military and civilian, and the sheer scale of the armies committed to the fight. The Great War was the temporary, if highly dynamic, conclusion to the trends and processes discussed in this and the previous chapter, but it would be a grave error to assume that the march from Waterloo to the Marne was entirely linear. Clausewitz pondered the question of whether the wars of the French Revolution and Napoleon presaged the wars of the future:

> Since Bonaparte, then, war, first among the French and subsequently among their enemies, again became the concern of the people as a whole, took on an entirely different character, or rather closely approached its true character, its absolute perfection. There seemed no end to the resources mobilized; all limits disappeared in the vigor and enthusiasm shown by governments and their subjects. Various factors powerfully increased that vigor: the vastness of available resources, the ample field of opportunity, and the depth of feeling generally aroused. The sole aim of war was to overthrow the opponent . . . War, untrammelled by any conventional restraints, had broken loose in all its elemental fury. This was due to the people's new share in these great affairs of state; and their participation, in turn, resulted partly from the impact that the Revolution had on the internal conditions of every state and partly from the danger that France posed to everyone . . . Will this always be the case in the future? From now on will every war in Europe be waged with the full resources of the state, and therefore have to be fought only over major issues that affect the people? Or shall we again see a gradual separation taking place between government and people?

The Prussian concluded his speculation by observing that 'once barriers – which in a sense consist only in man's ignorance of what is possible – are torn down, they are not so easily set up again. At least when major interests are at stake, mutual hostility will express itself in the same manner as it has in our own day' (Clausewitz, 1976: 592–3).

Clausewitz is quoted at such length because he penetrates to the heart of primary concerns. What was the character of European and American warfare in the nineteenth century? Were the theorist's fears borne out by events? Note that Clausewitz was speculating strictly with reference to the political context of warfare, not at all to its material conditions. For a fearful speculative glance at war's material future, nearly contemporary with Clausewitz's political warning, one needs to turn to the pages of Jomini. His most influential work, published in 1838, only seven years after Clausewitz's death, contained these somewhat prophetic thoughts:

The armament of armies is still susceptible of great improvements; the state which shall take the lead in making them will secure great advantages. There is little left to be desired in artillery, but the offensive and defensive arms of infantry and cavalry deserve the attention of a provident government.

The new inventions of the last twenty years [1818–38] seem to threaten a great revolution in army organization, armament, and tactics. Strategy alone will remain unaltered, with its principles the same as under the Scipios and Caesars, Frederick and Napoleon, since they are independent of the nature of the arms and organization of the troops.

The means of destruction are approaching perfection with frightful rapidity. The Congreve rockets, the effect and direction of which it is said the Austrians can now regulate – the shrapnel howitzers, which throw a stream of canister as far as the range of a bullet – the Perkins steam-guns, which vomit forth as many balls as a battalion – will multiply the chances of destruction, as though the hecatombs of Eylau, Borodino, Leipzic, and Waterloo were not sufficient to decimate the European races.

(Jomini, 1992: 48)

Jomini demonstrated the typical fallibility of specific predictions, but it is difficult to fault his general judgement, which is notably complementary to that of Clausewitz.

What occurred was a deadly synergism between material advance and popular involvement in the policy of the state understood as the national cause. The Great War for Civilization illustrated all too vividly from 1914 to 1918 that in the later decades of the nineteenth century and the early years of the twentieth, the political and social legacy of the American and French revolutions, married to the products of the Industrial Revolution, produced an approximation to total war. Although total war is a controversial concept, it does have a useful definition: a war waged with all the assets of the belligerents' societies. But the road to the Marne in 1914 was by no means a straight one, and those who were on it could not know their destination in advance.

Weapons and warfare

After 1815 the governments of the great powers of continental Europe were determined to restore those barriers of which Clausewitz was to write, designed and operated to prevent warfare becoming a dangerously popular activity. Strategic history cannot focus strictly upon the external political context of states; in addition, it must take full account of the domestic dimension. Naturally, there was intensive official effort to understand the strategic meaning of the technological developments that cascaded upon military establishments as opportunities and possibilities. But, in parallel, there was a steady concern to maintain social control and make military provision of a kind that would not undermine the traditional social and political order. One reason among several why wars between great powers in the nineteenth century were rare, conducted with limited means, and restrained in purpose was that the period 1792 to 1815 served as an awful warning. Extensive and intensive warfare promoted popular passions and, almost inevitably, led to social and political revolution. The Franco-Prussian War of 1870–1, though restricted in its purpose for both sides, demonstrated yet again that war on a large scale must engage public feeling, and could promote social chaos and even revolution. When one examines the armies of nineteenth-century Europe, armies struggling to manage the rush of technical innovation that the routinized process of innovation thrust at them for decision, one is considering institutional pillars of the political and social order as well as instruments of foreign policy. That claim, by the way, is as valid for many countries in the twenty-first century as it was in the nineteenth.

Historian Brian Holden Reid claims, 'what is undeniable is that warfare between 1815 and 1875 was transformed in scale, impact and destructiveness' (Reid, 2002: 24). One can extend this and argue that warfare between 1875 and 1914 similarly was transformed, though in that latter period there was relatively little actual experience of warfare involving the European great powers to test the claims of rival theories. If one discounts the near-continuous practice of colonial warfare in those years, only Britain and Russia waged war against a modern enemy, though in the British case the Boers were a notably irregular modern foe, albeit a well-armed, highly motivated and tactically skilful one. Chapter 7 explains how the character and conduct of warfare assuredly was transformed between 1914 and 1918. Unsurprisingly, in each of those periods – 1815–75, 1875–1914 and 1914–18 – the dominant consequence of technological innovation and industrialization was a dramatic increase in firepower. For a long while it was the firepower of the infantry which had the most significance, but from the 1890s the firepower of artillery began to catch up, and eventually surpass, the tactical potency of infantry weapons. However, at least as important as the dramatic increases in weapons' lethality were two vivid demonstrations of the potency of popular passion for the expansion of warfare.

The first example was provided by the evolution of the American Civil War from what began as a limited struggle – on the Southern side to persuade the Union to allow the secessionist states a divorce by mutual consent, and on the Northern to coerce the South into returning. By 1864 not only had both belligerents mobilized their publics and their industries, in the Confederate case creating new industries, but Union armies broke with long tradition and deliberately waged war directly upon the enemy's society. President Lincoln's Preliminary Emancipation Proclamation of 22 September 1862 was a policy initiative which struck at the heart of the Southern social order. In 1864, General Ulysses S. Grant ordered his trusted cavalry commander General Philip S. Sheridan to lay waste the Shenandoah Valley, a breadbasket of the Confederacy. Sheridan was ordered to '[t]ake all provisions, forage and stock wanted for the use of your command. Such as cannot be consumed, destroy' (Reid, 2002: 165). But the most famous, or notorious, example of the waging of war upon enemy society was General William T. Sherman's 'march to the sea' – from Atlanta to Savannah – through Georgia, and then north through the Carolinas, from November 1864 to April 1865. Sherman deliberately wrought all the material damage of which his army of increasingly ideologically motivated Western veterans was capable. Most emphatically, these cases of purposeful frightfulness were contrary to the traditional lore of war.

There was a second example which can be seen as a sign of the times, and was viewed as such by many soldiers of the period, including Field Marshal Moltke: the popular resistance to the Prussian invasion and occupation of France. To their surprise and anger, the Prussians and their German allies discovered that although they had won the war against the regular French Army by trapping the main bodies of incompetently handled enemy forces at Metz and Sedan, French society did not accept that verdict of defeat as nationally decisive. What followed was in reality a second war, one wherein the Prussians were obliged to crush enthusiastic but amateurish armies raised by patriotic Republican politicians who appealed to the spirit of the legend of 1793: '*la patrie en danger*'. Waging war against French civilians, both in uniform and not, the invaders were none too discriminating in the violence they dispensed.

There is a great deal more to warfare than firepower, just as technology is only one of war's vital contexts. Moreover, ideas for the effective use of weapons are at least as important as are the weapons themselves. And, always, the state of mind of the soldier behind the gun is of greater significance than is the gun itself. Nevertheless, weapons matter, and from the 1840s to the 1910s they were changing at a rate, and with possible implications, that challenged military comprehension and therefore military doctrine. The primary story concerns the radical, albeit evolutionary, advances in infantry fire-power. Those advances created what contemporaries referred to as 'the tactical crisis', a condition that persisted, and was never truly resolved, from the 1850s until the final year of World War I. Technical improvements in the lethality of infantry small arms, to be joined towards the close of the century by the novelty of the machine-gun and the recoilless field gun, suggested that infantry could no longer take the offensive, at least not in frontal attacks. And if soldiers could not advance in the face of modern firepower, how could wars be won?

How far did the firepower of armies progress from the 1840s to 1914? The story is simply told, though, as always in this text, it is the strategic and ultimately the political consequences that really matter. Box 5.1 provides a brief summary of more than sixty years of development in infantry small arms.

Box 5.1 The revolution in infantry firepower, 1840–1914

- *Percussion caps* replaced flintlocks on muskets, thereby negating the fatal effects of damp weather, as well as the all but proverbial 'flash in the pan' (1830s).
- *Breech-loading* was introduced, which improved the rate of fire some seven-fold over the smooth-bore muzzle-loader, though gas leakage from the breech remained a problem. Breech-loading allowed soldiers to reload lying down, which had major implications for tactics (1840s).
- The *conoidal bullet*, the 'minié ball', was invented in the 1830s, met wide-spread acceptance in the 1840s, and became the standard weapon of the infantry in modern armies, except for the Prussian, in the 1850s and 1860s. The minié rifle, or certainly the minié ball in a British Enfield rifle (1851), was a muzzle-loader that could fire two or three shots a minute. The technical principle was that the propellant caused the hollow base of the conoidal 'ball' to expand and grip the rifling grooves, thereby eliminating the negative effects of windage on both range and accuracy. The minié rifle, though still requiring soldiers to reload standing up, was sighted up to 800 yards. It could be lethal at 1,000 yards, though it was a reliable killer at only half that range. The minié

was a step-level jump in infantry lethality for the British, French and Union and Confederate armies.

- The *near perfection of breech-loading rifles*, as achieved by the French with their class-leading Chassepot (late 1860s). The Chassepot had longer range (sighted up to 1,600 yards), was more accurate and therefore more lethal than the 1840s technology with which Prussia's army was still equipped in 1870, the Dreyse needle gun, the world's first successful breech-loader.
- The introduction of repeating, and then *magazine-fed, rifles* (1860s–80s). The Prussian Dreyse needle gun, the minié rifle and the Chassepot were all single-shot weapons. Magazine loading greatly speeded the rate of fire.
- The invention of *smokeless powder* in 1884 to replace the black gunpowder, whose cartridges needed to be bitten off to be released for business, even in the minié system. Metal (brass) cartridges containing poudre blanc (1884), ballistite (1888) and cordite (1889) allowed for a smaller calibre (one-third to a half reduction), which enabled the introduction of clip-feed magazine loading. That development all but ended the previous blight of the powder fouling of barrels, and increased range and muzzle velocity. The new 'white powder' propellants on average were three times as powerful as the traditional black powder they replaced.

The modernization of the soldier's premier weapon between the 1840s and 1914, as outlined in Box 5.1, was an evolutionary triumph for science, technology, engineering, industry and military adaptability. However, it was bad news for the would-be warriors of all countries who would be using and facing these radically new products of the Industrial and Scientific revolutions in battle. Also, it was far from clear, even to the finest of contemporary military minds, what the transformation of infantry firepower meant for logistics, organization, doctrine, tactics, operations, strategy and even high policy (not that the final item generally was considered a proper military concern).

It is necessary now to devote some time to the weapons that were to dominate the battlefields of 1914–18: the machine-gun and artillery. Ironically, perhaps, despite the emphasis here that is required by the history of military advances in the nineteenth century, the Great War at the close of this period did not showcase the benefits conferred by the perfection of the infantry rifle. Instead, World War I was to be an artillery war above all else, while the machine-gun proved to be king of the killing ground of no man's land that separated the entrenched, and eventually somewhat pill-boxed, rival armies. In fact, during the middle years of the war the rifle was seriously demoted in significance and employment. It was found to be an inappropriate weapon for trench-to-trench combat and was largely displaced by grenade-throwers, mortars, an imaginative array of blunt and spiked clubs and an ever-more ubiquitous supply of automatic and semi-automatic guns.

The first truly practical machine-gun was invented in 1884 by the American Hiram Maxim. Relying on its own recoil energy, a single water-cooled barrel could fire up to 600 rounds a minute. It was prone to jam, among other technical difficulties, and it used belt-fed ammunition at a rate that frightened logistical minds. However, it could only improve, and it constituted another huge step-level jump in the lethality of weapons available to the infantry for both offence and defence. Armies differed in their choices among weapon system brands, their rate of introduction into the inventory, and their exact placement of this formidable device in the force structure. But few could deny that the machine-gun made a difference to the conduct of warfare.

The artillery story of the nineteenth century is too extensive to be developed here. Its full consequences are discussed in Chapter 7. Guns changed in their material composition from brass and iron to steel, and from being smooth-bored to rifled (1860s). Muzzle-loading gave way to breech-loading (1860s) and firing mainly solid shot gave way to firing high-explosive shells, which required the development of precise time fuses along with the older system of shrapnel (which dated from 1804 in the British Army). Thanks to a more scientific approach to gunnery, indirect fire was introduced in the Boer War by both sides, while its practice was advanced by the Russians, uncharacteristically the technical leaders in this field, in their war with Japan (1904–5). Also, technologists solved the problem of needing to re-lay a gun after every shot, with the consequent loss of time, accuracy and repeated exposure of the crew. The answer lay in the invention of a recoilless mechanism enabled by the rearward release of firing gases (1890s).

Barbed wire was a civilian technical development adjunct to, but lethally synergistic with, modern weaponry. The wire that closed the formerly open range of the American prairie was invented in 1874 and was first used in the Boer War (1899–1902). It proved deadly in its contribution to stalemate and the necessary resort to a strategy of attrition in 1914–18.

For these innovations to be directed intelligently, perhaps just effectively, if not necessarily efficiently, every state player that aspired to perform well at modern warfare was obliged to acquire a general staff of military professionals genuinely expert in the mysteries of logistics, especially of coordinated movement by railway. The railway sections of general staffs dealt with mobilization, the binding task between movement for war, which was believed to hold the key to swift victory, and war planning. The Prussians had led the way, but as always happens the leader is followed and loses much of his initial advantage, as this case illustrated.

By the closing decades of the century, aristocratic and other conservative anxieties about the political risks of creating a nation in arms by universal conscription were overridden by the more pressing demands of perceived military necessity, especially in France. The French experience in 1870–1, together with its large demographic shortfall compared with the new Germany, provided conclusive reasons why the army should be increased dramatically in size. Nevertheless, each continental great power continued to size and shape its army with at least one eye on the political perils of the undesirably democratic domestic consequences that would flow from large-scale expansion.

It may seem odd that thus far nothing has been said in this chapter of a naval, or more broadly maritime, character. The omission may appear especially unjustifiable given that the years 1890 to 1914 saw the appearance of influential books by the most accomplished strategic theorists in American and British history. Respectively, in 1890 Admiral Alfred Thayer Mahan, the American, preached the doctrine of superiority at sea via a dominant and concentrated battle fleet as the only certain route to national greatness (Mahan, 1965). The Briton, Julian Corbett, was a civilian lawyer, a gifted historian and an inspired Clausewitzian naval theorist. He wrote subtly and in terms that did not meet with wholehearted official enthusiasm in the Royal Navy (RN), pointing out the limits of the cult of battle that he believed had secured an unhealthy grip on the public and official imagination (Corbett, 1988). His nuanced appreciation of the risks that a stronger navy should and should not be willing to run in seeking battle was integral to his brilliant, if somewhat dated, view of the roles of the RN in war. His understanding of the value of a largely maritime and amphibious way of war rested heavily on historical evidence from a pre-industrial context. But what was of lasting value was his insistence upon the primacy of war on land, and therefore upon maritime, rather than narrowly naval, strategy. The title of the first chapter of his classic study of the Seven Years War (1756–63) conveyed the basic message: 'The function of the fleet in war' (Corbett, 1973). That subject merited a measure of strategic thought that it received only rarely.

Of course, navies and maritime trade were strategically important in the nineteenth century, but for the principal purposes of this text, developments in land warfare have commanded priority treatment. The significant topic of radical changes in marine architecture and naval design between Trafalgar and Jutland is well covered in a library of specialist studies. This narrative adheres closely, if austerely, to the focus that defines this whole endeavour: strategic history. So what follows is a summary of the strategic history of sea power in the nineteenth century.

The century concluded where it had begun, with Britain's Royal Navy pre-eminent at sea. It was not unchallenged in 1914, at that time by Germany, and it had been menaced occasionally by France in the preceding century. The appearance in 1848 of a French screw-propelled steam warship, the *Napoleon*, rang alarm bells in Britain over an alleged invasion danger. The French construction of an armoured frigate, the *Gloire*, in 1858, propelled similarly to the *Napoleon*, provoked an immediate British technical reply: the all-iron *Warrior*. Until the early 1900s, when the baton of rivalry was passed to Imperial Germany, France was Britain's only naval rival, albeit one that the latter had little difficulty out-competing time and again. There were at least four major reasons why Britain was the leading – one cannot quite say hegemonic – great power in the nineteenth century, periodically co-equal with continentalist Russia, depending on the issues of the day. Those reasons included its dominant commercial and naval sea power; its wealth and pre-eminent, though relatively declining, general economic strength, a strength that depended critically on the country's sea power; and an overseas empire of increasingly awesome proportions that was founded, sustained and exploited by sea power. Finally, to cite a less obvious reason, though one whose strategic implications should not be mocked, Victorian Britain was a much respected and widely envied civilization; it enjoyed the benefits of what today is known as 'soft power' (Nye, 2002: 8–12).

With respect to the wars of the period, with its ability to reach relatively rapidly and reliably into the Black Sea, the Baltic and even the North Pacific, in 1854–6 the RN enabled the temporary Anglo-French alliance to defeat Russia. Earlier, it had played an important role in helping the Greeks achieve their final independence from Turkey in 1831. That behaviour was pursued in somewhat uneasy occasional collaboration with Russia. With good reason, the Russians were suspected of being far more interested in securing control of the Turkish Straits than they were in aiding their Greek co-religionists. In the American Civil War, the Union Navy played a crucial role in exercising what eventually became a reasonably effective maritime blockade of the extensive coastline and the major and most minor ports of the Confederacy. However, given that Southern blockade runners succeeded in importing 600,000 rifles, plus fancy fashionable goods worth a fortune in a society starved of the finer things of life, obviously there were holes in the blockade. Sea power played no role worth mentioning in the wars of German unification. They were too brief for a maritime dimension to register any influence, while the military action was wholly continental. In the Balkan wars which studded the decades from the 1870s to the 1910s, sea power was sometimes a minor factor, for the more rapid transport of Russian troops, for example. But, as a general rule, the struggle to inherit as much as possible of the barely living corpse of Turkey-in-Europe was a story of strategic land power, not sea power. In sharp contrast, although the Boer War of 1899–1902 was waged entirely on land, for the British Empire it was enabled in the most fundamental sense, which is to say logistically, strictly by Britain's unchallenged control of sea communications to southern Africa. Such control was a strategic sine qua non for London. Finally, sea power showed its teeth decisively both in the Sino-Japanese War of 1894–5 and in the Russo-Japanese war of 1904–5. As an insular power, Japan depended wholly upon maritime strength to exert itself abroad, and particularly on land on the Asian continent. In both wars, despite suffering from some of the ill-fortune and errors that happen in all conflicts, the Imperial Japanese Navy covered itself with glory. Those triumphs led to its infection with the virus of the 'victory disease', a malady that would prove fatal in a later and much greater conflict.

From this brief survey of the strategic significance of sea power in the nineteenth century, one notes that although nearly everything changed in naval technologies of all kinds – propulsion, construction, armament, protective armour and, rather less than was desirable, in ship-to-ship communications – there was little actual warfare at sea, although Japan eviscerated Russia's benighted Baltic Fleet in 1904. That fleet had toiled with painful slowness from one French coaling pit stop to another, all the way from Kronstadt in the Baltic to the Sea of Japan to meet its Trafalgar in the Tsushima Strait off Korea. It was simply outclassed in all departments, except courage, by the Japanese Navy. Tsushima was a decisive sea battle. Had Japan lost, it could not have sustained its aggressive land campaign in the face of a Russian navy commanding sea communications between Korea and the Home Islands. Nevertheless, Tsushima was an exceptional event indeed in this long period. War at sea between great powers with navies of approximate symmetry, if different strengths, was not a notable feature, indeed hardly a feature at all, in the strategic history of the century. But the RN was of paramount strategic importance as the backstop to and symbol of Britain's status as the leading – certainly a leading – great power.

Politics and strategic history

When analysing the veritable torrent of technological, socio-cultural and domestic political changes of the period 1815–1914, it is all too easy to lose sight of the international political context. A striking advantage of a focus upon strategic history is that it compels attention to the major plot lines in international politics. Especially with reference to military developments, as already cited, the view of the strategist and strategic historian demands an answer to the enduring question: what is it all about? Shortly an attempt must be made to answer that question, the one that leads us to the central plot of the strategic history of the period. But first it is necessary to return briefly to where these two chapters on the nineteenth century began: politics. The dynamic international and domestic political contexts of the nineteenth century are vitally important because they, and they alone, provide strategic meaning to the largely military discussion provided here. The political end of the metaphorical bridge that strategy provides to connect policy with military effort needs to be revisited.

There were two long periods of peace among the great powers, interrupted by a twenty-year burst of brief wars (Russia against France and Britain, 1854–6; France against Austria, 1859; Prussia against Austria, 1866; and France against Prussia, 1870–1). By the Treaty of Chaumont of 9 March 1814, Britain, Austria, Prussia and Russia formed the Quadruple Alliance and committed themselves to the goal of securing Napoleon's final fall, in other words to regime change in Paris. In addition, and probably of greater significance, they committed themselves, albeit vaguely, to pursue the practice of consultation over prospective diplomatic initiatives and particularly military actions. Their purposes were to restore and sustain domestic and international order, and especially to prevent the recurrence of another period of general European war. They were not so concerned to prevent war *per se*, because they believed that it was an occasional necessity if order were to be restored. But the aims and therefore the character of warfare should be modest and defensive. Thus began the so-called Congress System, launched with rather different agendas by the eccentric apostle of Christian royal legitimacy Tsar Alexander I, the over-cunning Austrian Machiavelli Prince Klement von Metternich and the deeply conservative British Foreign Minister Viscount Robert Castlereagh, 2nd Marquis of Londonderry.

The Congress System was driven initially by fear of Napoleon, then by a residual fear of France, just as a parallel residual fear of Germany animated French policy in the 1920s and 1930s, and again in the late 1940s and early 1950s. Also, as just noted, the Congress powers were moved by fear of domestic and international disorder and its revolutionary implications, as had been demonstrated so recently by events. After seven years, though, the Congress System effectively died when Castlereagh, a key player who by then was suffering from advanced paranoia, cut his own throat. Strategic historians must never forget that the tempo of historical change, be it rapid or slow, is driven by individuals. Commitment to 'the repose of Europe', to quote Castlereagh, was not a popular political principle in British domestic politics. And his successor, George Canning, was not inclined to attempt to sustain it.

Just two months after Castlereagh took his own life, France was allowed back into the charmed circle of recognized and somewhat respected legitimate great powers at the Congress of Verona, a conclave which met to discuss the controversial topic of Spain. It is an error to write off the system of regular great power congresses as a general failure, even though that system appeared to breathe its last in Verona. The system persisted in the more adaptable and resilient form of the so-called Concert of Europe, certainly until mid-century, and in some occasionally significant residual practices even until 1914. The Concert has been described persuasively as a great power club with norms (Clark, 1989: 115). It was all about great power rights and duties, and its most vital norm was the master precept that no unilateral military action should be taken by a great power which could affect the European balance without a prior effort being exerted to concert understanding and secure at least tacit consent or tolerance. Each great power was obliged to be sensitive to the legitimate defensive concerns of the others.

The Vienna Settlement of 1814–15, and its evolution from Congress diplomacy to occasionally effective concerted behaviour, endured for several reasons. It was moderate in its terms and not drafted to demote France from the club of great powers, only to remove the possibility of its returning to trouble Europe as an aggressive superpower. France itself did not harbour strongly revisionist intentions. It had a new royal government that was regarded as legitimate by the other great powers. Moreover, for the next thirty-plus years France was more troubled by threats of a return of domestic revolution than it was moved to stage a replay of its erstwhile military rampage. A French overseas military adventure in Algeria was launched in 1830, nominally to suppress the Barbary pirates. But really it was all about refocusing disturbing domestic dreams of Napoleonic-style glory into a harmless channel. Also, one should not forget that there was a general desire among the great powers to maintain the status quo in most countries. Britain and Russia were respectively the maritime and continental superstates of the era. Prussia was the weakest club member of the Concert, while Austria was slipping because of its growing ethnic, cultural and consequentially political tensions. So, any great power motivation to change the status quo unilaterally foundered on the fear of revolution and frank recognition that it would lack the strength to impose its will.

Great power relations worked by different norms in the middle two decades of the century. In France, Napoleon III needed victories in war in order to legitimize his glittering, but somewhat counterfeit, empire. This was the fundamental reason behind the Crimean War, the war with Austria in 1859, a Mexican escapade in the 1860s and even the fatal war with Prussia in 1870. Prussia, with a much improved military machine by 1866, needed war in order to impose its hegemony upon the whole of Germany. That purpose required the forcible political expulsion of Austria, the erstwhile leading German state. To consolidate Prussia's grip upon a still disunited Germany, war with France provided the perfect fuel for an all-German patriotism keyed to Prussian leadership. Needless to say, these violent episodes of disturbance by France and Prussia were distinctly unconcerted in the great power club. In the Prussian cases, at least, they were wholly unilateral in action, and were motivated by the no less unilateral intention of gain at the expense of another great power member of the Concert club.

The Industrial Revolution was offering professional soldiers ever more lethal weapons in potentially ever larger quantities, as well as the wonders of long-term food preservation in tin cans, railways, electric telegraphic, then telephonic, then radio communications, and eventually the internal combustion engine. But the underlying international political stability of Europe was transformed very much for the worse by German unification. The new German Empire was forged by the sword in two semi-dazzling campaigns controlled by Helmuth von Moltke (the Elder). Moltke's contemporary international reputation was challenged only distantly by that of General Robert E. Lee, despite the latter's ultimate failure. The German wars all but exploded the character of great power international relations as they had generally, though far from universally, been practised since the Vienna Settlement. If the Concert System was not dead after 1871, assuredly it was on life support in intensive care. Prussia had demonstrated by its military deeds how much it cared for concerting its behaviour, for not upsetting the established order by disadvantaging other great powers, as well as for most of the other norms of the club. But while it was in the safe hands of Chancellor Otto von Bismarck, Germany after 1871 was not a revolutionary or rogue power. It was content to defend the new status quo that it had won with blood and iron.

The challenge to German security, and the prospects for great power peace in Europe over the longer term, depended critically on Berlin's ability to keep France isolated. Bismarck succeeded by adroit diplomacy, despite Austro-Russian rivalries in the Balkans and the complication of Vienna's multitude of Orthodox Christian Slav subjects. But once the 'pilot' was dropped, as a famous British cartoon showing Bismarck's dismissal by the new Kaiser, Wilhelm II, on 18 March 1890 was captioned, it was all change, and greatly for the worse for 'the repose of Europe'. Berlin decided not to renew the secret 'Reinsurance Treaty' it had signed with St Petersburg in 1887 in order to offset Russian disappointment with the League of the Three Emperors, the (German, Russian, Austrian) Dreikaiserbund of 1881. It would be a mistake to condemn out of hand Germany's abandonment of the secret treaty. The secret itself, which amounted to a general German promise to appease Russia, could be revealed at any time by the Russians, potentially to the acute embarrassment of Germany, especially in Vienna, London and Rome. In addition to the Dreikaiserbund, Bismarck had expanded his Dual Alliance (with Austria) of 7 October 1879 with a Triple Alliance which also included Italy. His dexterous and cunning diplomacy was waiting for a fall, and it came soon after his enforced retirement in 1890. It took the long-dreaded, probably inevitable, form of an agreement between France and Russia, initially in 1891 with a diplomatic understanding and three years later with a formal treaty of alliance. So, after twenty years of fancy footwork, Germany's, and therefore Europe's, strategic nightmare became a definite possibility. The continent was organized henceforth into two generally antagonistic and increasingly heavily armed camps. Only Britain among the great powers remained formally uncommitted, indeed isolated, with its freedom of diplomatic and hence strategic action as yet uncompromised. That condition was to alter somewhat, however, as a consequence of the officially unofficial 'military conversations' that soldiers at the War Office held with their French opposite numbers, beginning in 1906.

As an overall judgement, it is plain to see that the Great War was copiously and redundantly enabled. So many and potent were the diverse factors influencing events that the historian, even the strategic historian, is tempted to regard 1914–18 as an accident – or, more plausibly, as an intended event – that was bound to occur. In this view a large-scale war was a certainty. All that remained in doubt was the timing of its outbreak, the affiliations of Britain and Italy (the latter was not a happy camper within the Triple Alliance) and, last but not least, its character, duration, outcome and consequences.

Strategic historians must take a broad, inclusive view of the civilian and military transformations wrought by the long-term effects of the French and Industrial revolutions. They take due note of a Europe-wide culture that accepted warfare as a natural and even healthy activity for a dynamic society and rising state. Widespread militarism was a potent source of cultural norms. In addition, strategic history records the ever-greater rise of a new Imperial Germany intensely jealous of British global pre-eminence. That jealousy pertained especially to Britain's imperial holdings, possessions protected and interconnected by the apparently magnificent, certainly enormous, Royal Navy. London's continuing grip on world finance was another source of German jealousy, despite the relative slippage of Britain from its former primacy in science, technology and industry. The first to industrialize was bound to be the first to fade. To complete this tale of woe, by the 1900s some senior German soldiers, including the new Chief of the General Staff (from 1906 to 1914), Helmuth von Moltke (the Younger), were so convinced that Germany would be unable to win a future war against the Franco-Russian Alliance that they pressed for preventive war soon, or preferably 'now'. The rival alliance systems, and the interlocking logic of competitive mobilizations, meant that any crisis between the blocs must have the potential to engulf the whole of Europe.

Conclusion

What had the nineteenth century produced, ultimately, in strategic terms? What was its meaning strategically? The final answer was delivered in 1914–18. But here, at the end of a two-chapter discussion, one must be content to identify the grander of the enablers of the greatest of great wars in modern times to date. The nineteenth century provided the people to man mass armies; the population, science, technology and industry to equip, feed and pay for those mass armies; and a general surge both in national pride and loyalty, and in an acceptance of militaristic values. There was no effective, enduring transformation in the norms and practices of statecraft. This is not to deny that the Concert System retained some modest merit, but the fact was that the century concluded with Europe, if not poised for general war, undoubtedly structured around two rival armed, and arming, camps. And nothing has been said here about the effect of the unpredictable personality of the Kaiser upon the course of events. None of these elements made war inevitable, but they did make a general war probable, should a great power conflict occur.

As early as 14 May 1890, Field Marshal Helmuth von Moltke spoke all too presciently to the Reichstag in these terms:

> Should a war break out now, its duration and end cannot be foreseen. The largest powers of Europe armed as never before would take the field. None could be so completely defeated in one or two campaigns that it would declare itself vanquished and that it would have to accept the hard peace conditions imposed upon it. None would promise not to rise up again, even if only after years to renew the struggle. Such a war could easily become a seven years' or a thirty years' war. Woe to him who applies the torch to Europe, who is the first to throw the match into the powder cask.
>
> (Hughes, 1993: 29)

The European stage was set for an acceleration in the pace of strategic history. All that was needed was for someone to apply the torch.

Key points

1. There was a deadly synergism between material advance and popular association with state foreign policy.
2. The character of land and sea warfare was transformed several times in the nineteenth century.

continued

3. For most of the century, the principal technical advances in armaments benefited infantry weapons. But by 1900 the artillery had more than caught up and it was to prove dominant in 1914–18.
4. From the 1840s until 1918, soldiers in all countries tried to resolve the 'tactical crisis' produced by the lethality of modern firepower. No fully satisfactory answers were discovered.
5. The Congress System established in 1814–15 died an early death in the 1820s. However, its legacy in a Concert System endured weakly, albeit still usefully, at least into the late 1870s.
6. A fatal and fateful development in the 1890s was the permanent division of great power Europe into two rival armed camps.

Questions

1. What was the 'tactical crisis'? Why did it confound all attempts at solution?
2. How and why did concerns for domestic political stability constrain the military policies of the great powers?
3. How useful was Concert diplomacy in keeping international order?
4. Could Germany have kept France and Russia apart, thereby saving itself from facing the nightmare prospect of war on two fronts?

Further reading

E. Belfield *The Boer War* (London: Leo Cooper, 1993).

M. F. Boemke, R. Chickering and S. Förster (eds) *Anticipating Total War: The German and American Experiences, 1871–1914* (Cambridge: Cambridge University Press, 1999).

S. Förster and J. Nagler (eds) *On the Road to Total War: The American Civil War and the German Wars of Unification, 1861–1871* (Cambridge: Cambridge University Press, 1997).

M. Howard *The Franco-Prussian War: The German Invasion of France, 1870–1871* (London: Methuen, 1981).

P. Howes *The Catalytic Wars: A Study of the Development of Warfare, 1860–1870* (London: Minerva Press, 1998).

B. H. Reid *The Civil War and the Wars of the Nineteenth Century* (London: Cassell, 2002).

L. Sondhaus *Naval Warfare, 1815–1914* (London: Routledge, 2001).

G. Wawro *The Austro-Prussian War: Austria's War with Prussia and Italy in 1866* (Cambridge: Cambridge University Press, 1996).

—— *The Franco-Prussian War: The German Conquest of France in 1870–1871* (Cambridge: Cambridge University Press, 2003).

6   World War I, I
Controversies

Reader's guide: Controversies about World War I. The scale of the conflict. Casualties.

Introduction: the making of the twentieth century

With black humour one could argue that the Great War of 1914–18 was the kind of conflict that gives war a bad name. War should be an instrument of policy; Clausewitz is crystal clear on that fundamental. However, for four and a quarter years warfare seemed more in command of the policies of states than commanded by them. That was not quite true, but neither was it wholly an illusion. The strategic historian takes serious note of Gary Sheffield's expansive claim that 'The First World War was the key event of the twentieth century, from which everything else flowed' (Sheffield, 2001: 221). Sheffield is persuasive, provided one does not take too literally his assertion that 'everything else flowed' from the war. One has to beware of such a vague concept as the flow of events. While there is no doubt that in many vital respects the Great War made the twentieth century, certainly politically and strategically, there is good reason to question the responsibility of the war for all that followed over the next eighty years.

It is plausible to claim that the Great War against France which concluded in 1815 had reshaped, even redefined, international politics for at least a half-century. Similarly, it is scarcely less persuasive to argue that Bismarck's wars to unite Germany under Prussian tutelage reconstructed the architecture of the balance of power. The German Chancellor decisively altered the way that international politics would have to be managed by the great powers. Now the temporal domain of the strategic historical argument needs to be extended. The war of 1914–18 was uniquely responsible for setting the stage for, and thereby enabling, the major political and strategic events of the century that followed, but even the most influential of historical episodes, which tend to be strategic in character, do not drive forward along predetermined linear paths. Two fallacies beg for attention.

First, just because 1914–18 unquestionably was the product of factors traceable to trends and events in the nineteenth century, it does not follow that those factors caused the war in a direct and unavoidable sense. Second, although one can hypothesize a rich assortment of 'what ifs', specifying alternative happenings here and there, it should not

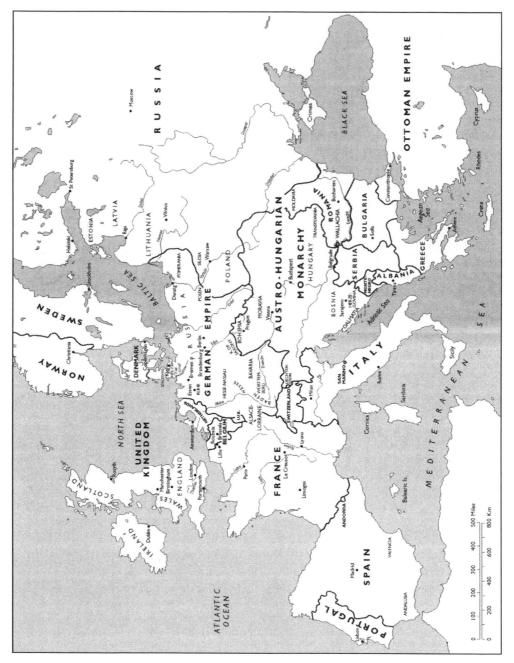

Map 6.1 Europe in 1914

be imagined that strategic history occurs randomly, ever vulnerable to course redirection by surprises, great and small. The past acts as an enabler for the particular future that did happen, not as a slave-master. Also, while one should be impressed by the potential of contingency and non-linearity, one should be similarly impressed by the argument that great strategic events are apt to have great enabling causes, or predispositions to unfold. There is some merit in the Marxist cliché 'It is no accident . . .' There are deep and compelling political and strategic reasons why the subject of this chapter and the next is 'World War I' and not 'the Third Balkan War'. Similarly, as later chapters argue, although World War II and then the Cold War were not strictly inevitable – very little is literally inevitable – there were powerful reasons why those mighty conflicts were probable.

A contested history

Historian Niall Ferguson asserts that World War I 'was nothing less than the greatest *error* of modern history' (Ferguson, 1998: 462; emphasis in original). Obviously, that proved to be the case for the defeated Central Powers, while one might claim that even the nominal victors would have been better served by the avoidance of war in 1914. However, the error thesis is profoundly arguable, with its implications of incompetent statecraft in several capitals. In 1914, indeed throughout the war, leaders made mistakes, as they always do, but as a general rule the policy-makers knew what they were doing, they understood the certain or highly probable consequences of their decisions, and they had strong and pressing reasons for the courses of action they took. This is not to deny the fact that policy-makers did not comprehend as well as they needed to the military instrument that they were using (Clausewitz, 1976: 607–8). But the generals themselves were scarcely more expert on the subject of modern warfare until the war was well advanced. Efforts to understand and explain World War I politically, strategically and militarily are bedevilled by a number of potent myths. It is necessary to expose the most misleading of these before proceeding to present the war as accurately as the evidence permits.

Whereas one can describe views of 1914–18 as 'a contested history', no such description can be applied to 1939–45. This is not to ignore the ongoing historians' debate about the origins of the war: for example, was 1939–45 strictly 'Hitler's war' (Martel, 1986; Boyce and Maiolo, 2003)? World War I holds a unique place in modern strategic historiography. It is the most misunderstood conflict of modern times. Why this should be so is a fascinating topic for enquiry, much of which needs to be undertaken by cultural and social historians, rather than by those who approach the black episode strategically. Nevertheless, today it is not particularly difficult to attain a grasp on the causes, course and consequences of the Great War in which considerable confidence can be held. New scholarship over the past twenty-five years has revealed more about the ways in which the war was waged than most of the studies conducted during the previous sixty. It is said that often it is more difficult to expel a false idea than it is to introduce a new, more correct one. Few adherents to the traditional, near-universally negative view of the performance of the major human players in the war can be persuaded that they subscribe to a legend. They resist the notion that they do not have a defensible view of the strategic history of the most important event of the twentieth century. So powerful are the negative myths that the analysis in this chapter and the next can make no progress until the primary errors are exposed. One must tackle, challenge and demolish five great myths about the Great War:

1. Allegedly, the war occurred because governments lost control of their military instrument. Once begun, the process of competitive mobilization could not be arrested. Famously, A. J. P. Taylor popularized the theory of 'war by timetable'. He argued that once the first steps towards war had been taken, Europe was driven to general war by its railway timetables (Taylor, 1969).
2. Allegedly, the war was futile. After all, the fundamental justification for the resort to war is that it should solve a vital problem when nothing else can. Since what some regard as this European civil war required a second round in 1939–45, the strategic job needed to be repeated. Plainly, the effort and costs of 1914–18 were suffered in vain.
3. Allegedly, the war was waged by all belligerents with an all but incredible military incompetence. Illustrative of this long-standing opinion is the charge that most of Britain's generals were 'butchers and bunglers' (Laffin, 1988) or, at the least, 'donkeys' leading sacrificial lions (Clark, 1961).
4. Allegedly, the military and strategic implications of modern firepower were not absorbed by military professionals. The lessons of the greater conflicts from the 1860s until the 1910s were either ignored or misassessed.
5. Allegedly, political and military leaders shared in the illusion that the next great war would be of short duration.

Even today, despite the recent appearance of a large amount of corrective scholarship, these myths live on and dominate received wisdom on the war. Each is either false or so flawed as to be seriously misleading. They will be dealt with in turn.

First, the historical record tells us unambiguously that the governments of the great powers did not lose control of their armies and navies as everybody mobilized. It is true that the Kaiser 'wobbled' once or twice, as had his predecessor in 1870, but everybody understood what their mobilization meant, as well as what its probable or even certain consequences would be. Just because countries were convulsed by the precise administrative mechanics of railway-dependent mobilization, it does not follow that the politicians had surrendered control to the generals. It would be absurd to try to explain the rush to war in late July and early August 1914 with reference to the inflexible demands of military logistics. Of course, mobilization involved rigidities – how could it not? – but the issue of most significance is not whether the war plans and their enabling steps of mobilization were sufficiently flexible and adaptable to cope with a variety of strategic demands. Rather, it concerns the political reasons why country after country chose to send its armies and navies to war.

The war was not *about* the potency of Europe's railway timetables; nor was it *about* a breakdown in civilian control of the military instrument. The war of 1914–18 was about the prevention of German domination of Europe. However, that controversial overall judgement needs to be disaggregated with reference to the decisions taken in 1914.

Austria-Hungary was spoiling for a fight with Serbia. It had been humiliated diplomatically as a bystander to the Balkan Wars of 1912–13. Its status as the greatest power in the Balkans, one able to cope well enough with its domestic ethnic troubles, was believed in Vienna to be at risk. For its part, Russia felt compelled to assert its weight in the 1914 crisis, having been shown up in 1909 over Bosnia to be an ineffective and unreliable guardian of Slav interests. Germany both wanted war with its Franco-Russian rivals (in order to prevent a further deterioration in its relative power position) and was convinced, albeit with some reluctance, that it could not permit its deeply unloved Austrian ally to be humiliated yet again, let alone defeated. If Austria were beaten by Russia, or coerced into political retreat, Germany's reputation would suffer major damage. France went to war because it had no choice. Germany had only one war plan, the so-called Schlieffen–Moltke Plan, and it mandated an all-out offensive against France as its first stage. Even had German military moves not compelled both French and Russian belligerency, the security of each required it to support the other if German power were to be checked. In fact, the mobilizations of the great powers in 1914 were more independent than interdependent, mythology to the contrary notwithstanding. Both Russia and Germany decided to mobilize despite their ignorance of the other's moves. As for Britain, it believed that it must intervene lest Germany defeat France. British security would be fatally undermined were Germany to eliminate France as a vital element in Europe's balance of power. Moreover, even should the Franco-Russian Alliance defeat Germany and Austria-Hungary, Britain's influence in European, and hence world, affairs would be critically impaired for reason of its having stood aside.

To find the common theme, it is necessary to stand back from the details of each country's mixture of motives, and from the complex narrative of cascading events. It so happens that the basic explanation of why war, a very great war, was launched in 1914 could hardly be simpler. Thucydides fingered the reason when he identified honour and its powerful associates, fear and interest, as the principal motives driving war and, indeed, all international political behaviour. Boldly stated, the great powers of Europe, without exception (although one can argue about a French exclusion), decided to fight in order to maintain, improve or prevent an anticipated decline in their relative standing in the stakes of comparative power. Rephrased, each great power believed it had compelling reasons of national security which afforded no reasonable choice other than the one it made. They knew what they were doing. Irrespective of whether they stumbled into war from a crisis slide that the diplomats were unable to discipline, given the contemporary lore of international politics they had no prudent alternative but to fight.

What of the second myth, the belief that the Great War was an appalling exercise in futility? The war proved to be neither 'the war that will end war' (Strachan, 2001: 1115), as H. G. Wells had promised in 1914, nor even, more modestly, the war that would resolve Europe's German problem. Did the nightmare of 1939–45 mean that 1914–18 had been, at best, futile; at worst responsible in its consequences for the carnage to come? This futility myth cannot be demolished by a simple argument. Fundamentally, it is incorrect because World War I did perform the duty, probably the sole duty, legitimate for war: it was uniquely effective in solving a problem. The outcome of the war decided the pressing issue of Germany's relative power and influence in Europe. For a time, at least, the military verdict of 1918 meant that Germany would not dominate continental Europe. It is true that Berlin did not issue its 'blank cheque' of support to Vienna in 1914 in the hope of sparking a general conflict that would be the perfect vehicle for Germany to drive to hegemony. But Germany did seek to enhance its standing among the powers, and it did welcome war in 1914 as a necessary means to weaken or eliminate its rivals, Russia in particular. And although the principal German strategic motive was defensive, not aggressive, the former required behaviour of the latter character. In 1914, Germany went to war out of fear, not ambition, let alone overconfidence, but an aggressive Germany still had to be stopped, no matter what its motives. The Allies achieved that end, albeit at dreadful cost, in over four years of ever more total warfare.

It cannot be denied that the devastation and costs of the war mortgaged the peace that followed. However, it would be unhistorical, and also implausible, to assert that World War II was the necessary, inevitable, consequence of World War I. The character, manner of conclusion and results of 1914–18 did contain some potentially lethal enabling factors for a return match, but whether the enabling consequences of that war would wreak fatal damage upon the European order in the 1920s and 1930s depended critically on the dynamic political context. When one searches for the fuel and the matches that produced World War II, one must look beyond the Great War, vitally important though it certainly was as a contributory factor.

The third popular myth holds that the war was waged with near-unbelievable military incompetence. As proof of this conviction, casualty figures typically are cited to pre-empt contrary argument. Of all the myths about the Great War, this is the most obviously unsound and the easiest to demolish. In the first place, the charge of exceptional military incompetence fails the test of plausibility. Is it likely, one must ask, that a whole cohort of general officers, embracing all great power belligerents, would be almost uniformly unfit for high command? If outstanding performance by military commanders of all nationalities was in short supply from 1914–18, it is rather more likely that some powerful systemic inhibitors of military genius were at work. It is not too hard to locate them. They include the technical difficulties, even impossibility, of real-time command, communications and control once battle was joined; the lack of means for tactical and operational mobility in, through and out of the battle zone; the high force-to-space ratios on the restricted geography of the Western Front, which was the only possible theatre of final decision; initially the universal lack of experience in the waging of modern warfare; and, last but not least, a military context that mandated attrition sharply limited the scope for demonstrating flair in generalship.

Naturally, military commanders varied in their abilities, and they ranged, as they do in armies at all times, from the incompetent to the exceptionally gifted. There is no good reason to believe that the distribution of military competence in the armies of 1914–18 was worse than in other periods of great and protracted conflict. Competence in generalship can be assessed only in its historical context. The relevant question, therefore, is how well or poorly did generals *and their troops* perform, given the conditions with which they had to cope and the tasks they could not avoid? The main, unavoidable, task for British and French generals was to find a way to penetrate a German defensive zone that could be 6 to 8 miles deep and which had no flanks to turn. Hopes for a dramatic break-in, breakthrough and subsequent break-out persisted in a few quarters, with Sir Douglas Haig especially, longer than they should have done. Such an unrealistic aspiration had the deadly consequence of dispersing unduly the all-important weight of artillery fire. However, by late 1917 and in 1918, military commanders on both sides had solved the problems of penetration. Everyone understood and, with variable skill, practised a combined-arms style of combat which was all but guaranteed to make limited territorial gains, even against the deep and flexible defence system that the Germans had pioneered in the construction of their Hindenburg Line in the winter of 1916–17. But what no one succeeded in achieving was a sustainable breakthrough and break-out. The Germans came closest with their mighty 'Michael' offensive of 21 March 1918, but even that tactically impressive success was brought to nought by the systemic inhibitors in the military context of the time.

On balance, military command on both sides performed competently or better, given the limitations of feasibility. The problem was that the generals had been given a task – to deliver decisive military victory – that was beyond them and their military forces except by means of protracted combat. The war was won in the only way that was possible: by a process of military attrition that came to be managed competently.

The fourth myth asserts that modern firepower was either ignored or misassessed by the armies that went to war in 1914. But the historical record shows that, far from ignoring modern firepower, European armies had been debating the tactical crisis caused by rapidly evolving firepower for more than sixty years. The crisis pertained to the need to find an answer to the question: how can soldiers advance, take the offensive, in the face of modern weaponry? The problem was first demonstrated in the Crimea, when Anglo-French minié rifles (and Enfield rifles with minié ammunition) massacred Russian infantry columns. It was illustrated repeatedly in the American Civil War, with the third day at Gettysburg serving as a prime example of the general impracticality of frontal assaults, and was revealed in 1866 when Austrian infantry melted away under the rapid fire of Prussia's breech-loading needle guns. The Franco-Prussian War told the same story of bloody repulse, when infantry or cavalry relied upon dash and spirit rather than manoeuvre and supporting fire. The arrival of the machine-gun in the 1880s, and of recoilless, quick-firing artillery in the 1890s, made the tactical crisis yet more chronic. So, the strange notion that military professionals somehow had failed to notice, or at least take due account of, the revolution in firepower that the Industrial Revolution effected is as absurd as it is totally untenable.

The difficulty did not lie in recognizing the problems but in identifying pragmatic solutions. The Schlieffen–Moltke Plan was one solution: avoid the tactical impasse by sweeping operational manoeuvre. The Germans, under Schlieffen's guidance from 1891 to 1906, developed a fondness for operational envelopment. Alternatively, one could attempt to rely on high morale on the part of the attacking infantry, and high speed in the assault as they moved across the killing zone on the offensive. The Japanese Army had shown in the war with Russia of 1905–6 that élan and a willingness to take sacrificial losses could sometimes triumph over modern weapons. By and large, though, military professionals concluded that the only practical solution had to lie in new infantry tactics favouring dispersal, the use of cover, and flexible movement by relatively small bodies of soldiers acting independently. Measures such as these, among others, were debated extensively and intensively before 1914. When war came, the unforgiving conditions of the continuous Western Front rendered the tactical crisis terminal for a while, rather than merely chronic. The armies of Europe were not collectively stupid. They were confronted with a tactical challenge to which there was no clever solution ready at hand in 1914.

Myth number five about World War I is the belief that the most senior soldiers of the great powers harboured what has come to be known as the 'short-war illusion'. There is no doubt that in 1914 many soldiers and probably most civilians did subscribe to the view that the next war between the great powers would be short, a matter of months rather than years. Such a war was expected by most people to conclude with a decisive military victory for one side. However, there is irrefutable evidence showing that the most senior soldiers in Germany, France and Britain did not expect a future great war to be 'over by Christmas' (Strachan, 2001: 1005–14). Indeed, it was precisely the Germans' fear of all but inevitable defeat in a long war against the Franco-Russian Alliance that drove them, virtually in desperation, to gamble on achieving an improbable short-war victory by means of the super-envelopment envisaged in the Schlieffen–Moltke Plan. Germany knew that it had to win a short war, because it would be impossibly outweighed in human and material resources in a long one. Should Britain fight with France and Russia, a probability with deadly negative implications for German access to vital raw materials from overseas, then the prospect of defeat in a long war would be more certain still. It may seem strange – certainly it was strategically irresponsible in the extreme – for Germany to choose to go to war at all in 1914, given its pessimism over the balance of forces. But in explanation of Germany's decision to fight, one must note that its estimate of its poor competitive position in 1914 was superior to that anticipated for later years. The German Army persuaded itself that that which was necessary, swift victory against France, would somehow, as a consequence, mysteriously prove militarily feasible. Military professionals in 1914 knew that war between great powers that could mobilize conscript armies in the millions was not at all likely to be concluded with a single battle or campaign. But the Germans felt compelled to try. Strategic history demonstrated that pre-war professional estimates of the duration of war as lasting perhaps three years, Field Marshal Lord Kitchener's best guess, were fairly accurate, if still unduly optimistic.

There is an old saying which advises that 'there is a great deal of ruin in a nation'. That claim goes far towards explaining key features of World War I. Modern, or modernizing, states blessed with a robust industrial base and a large population of tolerably patriotic citizen-subjects would not accept most military setbacks, even defeats, as being decisive. In theory, there could be a military catastrophe of such proportions that recovery would be impossible. This was especially a possibility for France, given the restricted geography of warfare in Western Europe. But, barring victory by some super-manoeuvre, such as that planned by Schlieffen, it was obvious that the great powers had the depth of means to sustain loss and damage, if not indefinitely, then certainly through several campaigns. It is worth mentioning, however, that the professional soldiers of 1914 appreciated very well that 'the soul of an army', to quote British general Sir Ian Hamilton, was its spirit, its morale (Hamilton, 1921). Men and material may be abundant, once mobilized, but how resilient would the urbanized masses in uniform prove to be to the stresses of modern combat? Also, no less important, would the increasingly urbanized societies of 1914 remain politically stable in a long war? Modern Europe was substantially literate, its working class was imbued with socialist ideas, and its patriotism might not withstand the hardships, tragedies and disappointments of a long war.

Conclusion

If the Great War is notorious for anything, it is for its casualties. This is not a myth. The casualty toll was awesome. However, the strategic history of the whole of the first half of the twentieth century demonstrates that the casualty lists for 1914–18 were the inevitable consequence of the contexts of the war. There was nothing extraordinary about

Table 6.1 Casualties in World War I

	Dead	*Wounded*	*Total casualties*
Allies	5,421,000	7,025,487	17,292,863
Central Powers	4,029,000	8,379,418	15,486,963
Total	9,450,000	15,404,905	32,779,826*

Note: * Includes prisoners of war

the casualties of 1914–18, regarded in strategic historical context, because the war of 1939–45 produced an even larger casualty count. When industrialized great powers waged war *in pursuit of decisive military victory*, the dreadful human costs recorded twice in half a century must be the result. Table 6.1 tells the story starkly.

To emphasize the greatness of this Great War, note that the Allies – all of the Allies, that is – mobilized a grand total of 42,188,810 men, while the comparable total for the Central Powers was 22,850,000. The strategic history of the two world wars shows the iron authority of a rule which determined how large or modest the relative human cost of industrial-age mass warfare would be to a particular country. In both wars, unsurprisingly, casualties were suffered in direct proportion to the duration and intensity of exposure to lethal risk. In the Great War the British Empire suffered approximately 908,371 battle deaths, contrasted with 397,762 (for Britain alone) in World War II. The difference is easily explained. Between 1914 and 1918 the British Expeditionary Force (BEF) waged continuous land warfare against the main body of the enemy's forces in the principal theatre of war. From 1939 to 1945 the BEF met the main body of the German Army for only three disastrous weeks, in May 1940. The more fighting a country's armed forces were obliged to do, the greater their casualties. This is as obvious as it is strategically significant. In both world wars, someone had to wage a lot of warfare if Germany were to be beaten, which meant someone had to suffer enormous casualties. In 1914–18, Britain, for the first and only time in its history, bore close to a full human burden of continental warfare against the most potent killing machine of the era, the Imperial German Army.

Key points

1. World War I was the most significant event of the twentieth century.
2. Every great power had strong reasons for fighting.
3. Germany went to war for defensive reasons, out of fear, not because of overconfidence or in order to advance an agenda of aggression (though victory must have yielded Berlin continental hegemony).
4. The character, especially the duration, of the war mortgaged the subsequent peace, but World War II was not the inevitable eventual consequence of World War I.

continued

5. Military commanders were all but fatally hampered in their generalship by the absence of reliable real-time communications with their troops, and by the absence of means for rapid and flexible tactical and operational mobility.
6. Casualties in the war were by no means extraordinary, when they are viewed in strategic historical perspective. When great industrialized powers wage total war for four and a quarter years, the casualty figures are going to be high. The 9.45 million military dead in 1914–18 compares favourably with the 16.8 million figure for World War II.

Questions

1. **Do you agree that World War I continues to be seriously misunderstood?**
2. **Why did the great powers go to war in 1914?**
3. **Did Germany wage what it regarded as a defensive, preventive war?**
4. **Was the casualty count far higher than it could have been if the generals had been more competent?**

Further reading

I. F. W. Beckett *The Great War, 1914–1918* (Harlow: Longman, 2001).

C. Falls *The Great War, 1914–1918* (New York: Perigee Books, 1959).

Richard F. Hamilton and Holger H. Herwig *Decisions for War, 1914–1917* (Cambridge: Cambridge University Press, 2004).

J. Keegan *The First World War* (London: Hutchinson, 1998).

A. Mombauer *Helmuth von Moltke and the Origins of the First World War* (Cambridge: Cambridge University Press, 2001).

D. Stevenson *The First World War and International* Politics (Oxford: Oxford University Press, 1988).

—— *Cataclysm: The First World War as Political Tragedy* (New York: Basic Books, 2004)

H. Strachan *The First World War: A New Illustrated History* (London: Pocket Books, 2006).

S. C. Tucker *The Great War, 1914–18* (London: UCL Press, 1998).

7   World War I, II
Modern warfare

Reader's guide: The course of the war. The invention of modern combined-arms warfare. The reasons for Germany's defeat.

Introduction: education by experience

A strategic history such as this tries to avoid becoming unduly enmeshed in the details of either policy or military tactics. It is the role of strategy to direct tactics and operations to advance policy goals. But strategy can find itself bereft of attractive options when tactics or policy is unable or unwilling to adapt pragmatically to unexpectedly non-permissive political and military contexts. A narrative of 1914–18 can be interpreted as a protracted and highly expensive education in the realities of modern warfare. Once the less than cunning plans of 1914 had failed, and the military skills of the two sides approached equality, though the Germans always retained a combat edge, victory could be achieved only by attrition in a flankless theatre of war. This chapter emphasizes the structure of the strategist's problem from 1914 to 1918. The politicians would not lower their policy goal from the demand for victory, while the soldiers spent more than three years solving the tactical problem of how to advance in the face of modern firepower. They could not solve their operational-level problem of translating tactical successes into much wider advantage, because they lacked the mobility, including mobile fire-support, to do so. It followed that the strategist found little scope to exercise his trade. The combination of extravagant political objectives and tactical stalemate produced the greatest war in history to date.

This chapter opens with a chronological review of the course of the war, and proceeds to explain how contemporary soldiers strove, with mixed success, to meet the challenges they faced.

The course of the war

1914: the war plans fail

In 1914 the Germans attempted to wage two wars in swift succession: first, to defeat the French; then, to turn on the more slowly mobilizing Russians. The Schlieffen–Moltke

Plan for the grand envelopment of the French armies was executed. It failed because of its logistical frailty and the weariness of the marching troops; because of the lack of real-time communications between the armies of the right wing and Moltke's headquarters in Luxembourg, and therefore because of the absence of command grip from the centre; because the French and British threatened to outflank and envelop exposed and isolated armies; because French lateral railways enabled a rapid shift of weight from the right to the left of the theatre; and because it was executed with too few troops.

Schlieffen's original grand design was nothing if not daring. Of Germany's seventy-eight divisions, he allocated only ten to hold the Russians in East Prussia, with the remaining sixty-eight to invade France. Fully fifty-nine of those sixty-eight were assigned to the armies of the right wing, the enveloping arm, leaving only nine to face the French on the left. Between 1906 and 1914 Moltke changed the ratio of forces between the left and the right wings, adding eight of nine new divisions to the left and only one to the right. On 25 August 1914 he compounded the damage to the basic concept of a huge disparity between the left and right wings when he acted ill-advisedly in response to panicky reports from East Prussia. He withdrew three army corps from the right wing and dispatched them to the Eastern Front. As a result, those divisions were in transit while major battles with far-reaching consequences were waged in both the East and the West.

These modifications to Schlieffen's plan certainly lessened its prospects of success. But, given the dire logistical straits in which the armies of the right wing found themselves as they approached Paris, it is not obvious that larger forces could have been sustained on the right anyway. In recent years a radical revisionist argument that there never was a Schlieffen Plan intended to defeat France in six weeks gained some credence for a while (Zuber, 2002). However, scholarly battle has since been fully joined, and the traditional understanding of a German bid to knock France out of the war in a single campaign has regained its authority (Mombauer, 2005).

The Germans were halted on the Marne, deep in France, and were compelled to retreat, albeit in good order, to the River Aisne, where they remained for the next four years. Alas, the Germans had neglected to develop a 'Plan B', as insurance against the possibility of failure of the Schlieffen gamble. For the remainder of 1914, September–December, the severely battered armies in the West extended their fronts competitively all the way to the sea. The British Expeditionary Force (BEF) was moved to the vicinity of Ypres in Belgium, where it fought itself almost to oblivion in a protracted struggle in October and November. With a great deal of French assistance, it prevented a German breakthrough which might have outflanked the still rudimentary Allied line. In the East, the Russians behaved as an exceedingly loyal ally. They attacked prematurely in East Prussia in order to relieve pressure on the French in the West, only to meet with twin disasters at Tannenberg and the Masurian Lakes at the hands of what was to become the much respected command team of Erich Ludendorff and Paul von Hindenburg. That celebrated pair received the glory, but the true architect of the German triumph of cunning manoeuvre, effective deception and exploitation of Russian incompetence was one Lieutenant Colonel Max Hoffmann.

1915: victory remains elusive

In 1915 the new German Chief of Staff, Erich von Falkenhayn, a dedicated 'Westerner', was overruled, and the victors of 1914 at Tannenberg and the Masurian Lakes, Hindenburg and Ludendorff, were allowed to make the main German effort in the East. This proved extraordinarily successful, if ultimately indecisive, as victories and defeats in the vastness of the geography in the East tended to be. The Austrians were rescued from some early disasters and German and German/Austrian assaults from north and south cleared Russian armies from nearly all of Russian Poland. The great German victory of 2 May–27 June, known to history as the Gorlice–Tarnow Breakthrough, offered a revealing commentary on the respective qualities of the German and Russian armies. But by the end of 1915 a successful conclusion to the war was still nowhere in sight. The French continued to weaken themselves severely by launching repeated abortive offensives in Artois and Champagne, while the British staged their first notable, but also abortive, attack at Loos (25–28 September).

Anglo-French disappointments on the Western Front in 1915 were fully matched by an embarrassing failure against Turkey. A British-led effort to achieve an amphibious outflanking of the Central Powers' continental fortress by seizing the Dardanelles and menacing Constantinople fell just short of constituting a military disaster. The Dardanelles venture met first with naval failure and then with a bloody stalemate on land on the Gallipoli peninsula. It was a half-baked strategic conception of Winston Churchill, then the First Lord of the Admiralty, executed with extraordinary incompetence.

1916: attrition

Having been defeated on the Marne in the West in 1914, and having failed to secure a decisive advantage in the East in 1915, despite major victories in Poland, in 1916 Germany returned to the West as the locus for its principal effort. In so doing, it pre-empted the Allies' belated plans to coordinate offensives against the Central Powers on all fronts. Falkenhayn was permitted to attack the French fortress city of Verdun. His purpose, which was not as well understood by his army as it needed to be, was not to take the city. Rather, he intended to entice the French into expending troops at a rate that they could not afford in a desperate campaign to hold the fortress, which he knew had iconic significance for Paris. The Germans had amassed an awesome weight of artillery and intended – at least, Falkenhayn intended – that Verdun and its environs should become the graveyard of the French Army. He calculated, over-optimistically, that at Verdun he could kill five Frenchmen for every two Germans. Such was the logic of victory by attrition. The 'battle' lasted from 21 February until 18 December, with the French suffering 542,000 casualties to the German 434,000. Falkenhayn had hoped that French morale would crack under the cumulative weight of French casualties and, as a consequence, that Paris would seek terms. Should that occur, Britain would find itself in an impossible position, so the Germans reasoned. Falkenhayn regarded Britain as Germany's principal enemy, one which could best, perhaps only, be defeated strategically by breaking its 'continental sword', which is to say the French Army.

Just as Allied plans for offensives were pre-empted by Germany's initiative at Verdun, so the increasingly bloody and self-defeating effort there was interdicted and weakened by the need to contain the first major British offensive of the war. From 24 June (including the seven days of artillery preparation) to 13 November, the new British Army, greatly swollen in size by the millions of volunteers of 1914–15 (between August 1914 and September 1915, 2,257,521 men volunteered), attacked repeatedly on the unpromising and strategically marginal open terrain of the Somme. Douglas Haig, the new British Commander in Chief of the BEF, failed to achieve his intended breakthrough, but, as with the French at Verdun, he did succeed in inflicting terrible and, in quality of experienced regular soldiers, irreplaceable losses on the Germans. Overall casualties on the Somme comprised 420,000 for the BEF, 195,000 for the French, and an unsustainable 650,000 for the Germans. In the context of the 434,000 losses at Verdun, it was plain for the Germans to see that they had allowed themselves to be sucked into a war of attrition which they could not possibly win, given the greatly superior numbers available to the enemy coalition.

1917: political upheaval, but growing military competence

A new German High Command, the Hindenburg–Ludendorff team, prepared for 1917 by constructing a new defence zone, the so-called Hindenburg Line, in the winter of 1916–17, in order to shorten their front and economize on manpower. As for victory, the baton was passed to the German Navy, but not to its High Seas Fleet, which was cowering in port, still traumatized by an accidental near brush with disaster at Jutland on 31 May 1916. For the third time in the war, permission was granted to wage an unrestricted submarine campaign. Beginning in February 1917, the Navy predicted that if it could sink in excess of 600,000 tons of Allied shipping each month for five months, Britain would be compelled to sue for peace. The strategic logic was reasonable, but like many plausible theories it foundered in practice. On 10 May the Royal Navy was ordered by the British government to institute a convoy system, and that wrote *finis* to the prospect of Germany winning the war by maritime blockade. Not only did the submarine campaign fail, but it had the well-anticipated effect of triggering a US declaration of war on 6 April. Much as in 1914, when execution of the Schlieffen–Moltke Plan was a reckless gamble on a short-war victory in fear of an unwinnable long war, so the U-boat campaign was a no less reckless bet on short-term victory, with the consequences of American belligerency wholly discounted.

In 1917 the Germans were on the defensive on land in the West, pending the delivery of victory by blockade at sea. But the Allies' Russian front collapsed, despite energetic efforts by the Kerensky government to fight on, and eventually there was a near cessation of hostilities by the Russian Army after the Bolshevik Revolution of 7 November. As a consequence, Germany's geopolitical context was transformed. A glittering strategic opportunity beckoned for 1918. Apart from the notable addition of the United States as a most welcome co-belligerent, 1917 was a terrible year for the Allies. Russia suffered two revolutions and left the field. France staged a spectacular, but alas unduly well-heralded, great offensive on the Aisne and in Champagne (the Nivelle Offensive – named after its boastful, smooth-talking author, General Robert Nivelle), with 1,200,000 men and 7,000 guns, from 16 to 20 April. The French lost 120,000 men in only five days, and the operation was abandoned. The result of this failure, truly a forlorn hope, was that forty-six of the 112 divisions in the French Army staged mutinies great and small between 29 April and 20 May. They mutinied not against the war, but against futile offensives conducted without apparent care for soldiers' lives. In addition, the soldiers protested about their poor terms of service (pay, rations, leave). For the remainder of the year, the French Army would hold its ground to defend the country, but it would not take the offensive. The Americans were coming, but they were not coming with large numbers of well-trained and well-equipped combat-ready troops in 1917.

That only left the BEF, now grown to some sixty divisions, still in the field as a formidable offensive fighting force. At the third Battle of Ypres, 31 July–10 November, Haig's BEF took the strain for the whole Alliance, and continued to batter the Germans in what became, in effect, a continuation of the protracted attritional battles of 1916. Haig continued to delude himself with dreams of a dramatic breakthrough, but such a happy result was no more feasible in 1917 than it had been the year before. There was a brief false dawn between 20 November and 3 December, when new artillery tactics, keyed to predicted, un-preregistered firing, enabled a surprise assault by 200 tanks to take a 5-mile bite into the Hindenburg Line along a 6-mile front. However, the attack was insufficiently supported, the Germans promptly counter-attacked effectively, and the Cambrai miracle faded instantly. It had, however, revived some long-absent hopes for success with a better way in combined-arms warfare.

In taking the strain for the vanished Russians, the inactive French and the absent Americans, the BEF weakened noticeably in 1917. At the third Battle of Ypres, for the leading case, the BEF sustained 240,000 casualties. One strategic consequence of the British disappointments of 1917 was that Haig's failure to achieve notable progress strengthened the hand of his adversary at home, Prime Minister David Lloyd George. The latter was able to withhold reinforcements from joining the BEF, convinced that Haig would only waste their lives. The result was that the BEF entered 1918 seriously under strength, both because of its losses in 1917 and because the soldiers of which it was in desperate need were detained in Britain.

1918: the Allies were the 'last men standing'

The grand finale to the Great War in 1918 was high drama. The Germans had to find an answer to their familiar strategic problem: how to win against the material odds. This time, however, thanks to the demise of the Russian Army as an effective com-batant, Hindenburg and Ludendorff were granted a brief window of opportunity to achieve and exploit numerical superiority on the Western Front. Forty-eight divisions were transferred from the Eastern to the Western Front, as well as eight from Italy. Of Germany's total of 243 divisions on 21 March 1918, 191 were in the West. The Allied total was 175 (Zabecki, 2006: 89–90). By transferring divisions from the East and Italy, Germany gambled on winning the war by a great offensive. Actually, it was to be a series of five offensives (Somme, 21 March–4 April; Lys, Flanders, 9–29 April; Aisne, 27 May–4 June; Noyon–Mondidier, 8–12 June; and Champagne–Marne, 15–17 June). Despite heroic sacrifice by the forty-seven newly formed 'attack divisions', especially their stormtroop formations, the Germans failed in their bid for victory before the Americans were in place and combat-ready in overwhelming numbers. They did, though, break through the British defences and caused some panic and heavy losses. Moreover, it seemed for a while as if the Germans might succeed in unhinging the Allied front by separating the BEF and the French Army. But 1918 was not to be a year of military or strategic miracles for Germany.

Familiar problems compromised the German gamble. Their offensives were login tically impractical – recall 1914! – and consequently the best of the German infantry, though frequently tactically successful, took disabling casualties. The Germans rapidly outran their artillery support and could not provide adequate substitutes from the air or from weapons integral to their combined-arms combat teams. With respect to the higher direction of this final, monumental effort, Ludendorff proved himself a true disciple of Moltke the Elder, who had claimed that 'strategy is a system of expedients' (Hughes, 1993: 47). There was no consistency of operational purpose for strategic effect. The Germans launched offensive after offensive against different sectors of the Allied line in obedience to no coherent strategic conception.

With the Germans exhausted, demoralized and greatly reduced in numbers by their extraordinary casualties, from July until November 1918 the Allies counter-attacked continuously all along the Western Front. Between 21 March and 25 June, German casualties totalled 1 million, suffered mainly by their better formations. Not only was the numerical and material balance moving ever more rapidly in the Allied favour, but their forces, the British and French at least, had more or less mastered a new style of combined-arms warfare. (This is discussed in the next section.) Although it is a cliché to repeat the mantra that there were no decisive battles in World War I, Amiens on 8 August was termed the 'Black Day of the German Army' by no less an authority than the highly strung generalissimo himself, Erich Ludendorff. The Allied forces were exhausted, particularly so the BEF because it was bearing the heaviest burden of the fighting, but they continued their attritional and unstoppable advance, step by step, from 8 August until 11 November. On 29 September the BEF broke into and through the Hindenburg Line (which generally consisted of six lines of defence) at the St Quentin Canal, and it was plain for all to see that the end of effective German resistance was approaching. Nevertheless, despite unsustainable casualties, some mass surrenders, a hopeless military situation and rock-bottom morale, much of the German Army retreated slowly in fair, if not reliably good, order, and continued to inflict high losses on their careful pursuers.

The fact that the German Army had been beaten but not routed in the field was registered in the signing of an Armistice on 11 November 1918. That army on the Western Front was, and always had been, the centre of gravity of the war-making of the Central Powers. It was defeated by the cumulative strategic effect of four and a quarter years of attritional combat. The Germans had always believed that they were certain to lose a protracted war against a coalition blessed with superiority in numbers of soldiers and economic resources. That belief was vindicated in 1918.

Modern warfare

World War I offers a near-perfect illustration of the wisdom in Clausewitz's trinitarian theory of war. As was explained in Chapter 2, the Prussian advised that war is composed of 'primordial violence, hatred and enmity; of the play of chance and probability within which the creative spirit is free to roam; [and] of its element of subordination, as an instrument of policy, which makes it subject to reason alone' (Clausewitz, 1976: 89). In 1914–15 none of the great powers believed they could stand aside. Policy drove strategy in all countries. Then it was up to strategy to deliver the kind of military outcome that would satisfy the demands of policy. And for that to occur, the military machines needed to secure victory, because nothing less was asked, or expected, of them. But could the armies and navies of 1914 deliver what was required by policy? What if policy demanded a military victory that was beyond the fighting power of the army of the day? Strategy is about the use of force and the threat of force for the ends of policy. But policy should change if the force available is incapable of securing a favourable outcome. From 1914 to 1918, policies did not change: military victory was still demanded. Rather than throttle back on their political goals, instead the belligerents sought to improve the combat effectiveness of their armies and navies. They strove to improve their military instrument so that it would be capable of generating the military victory which was the precondition for the necessary strategic effect.

World War I was a protracted learning experience about the mysteries of modern warfare and how those mysteries could be penetrated and overcome. Totally inexperienced armies using new weapons, or familiar weapons in new ways, had to learn how to fight under modern conditions. And they had to learn while under fire, when they were taking high casualties. It is important to note the essential symmetry between the armies of 1914. The differences were those of detail, not of structure, doctrine or equipment. Everyone had copied, adopted and adapted what they admired and found useful in the Prussian–German model, especially with respect to the creation of a general staff worthy of the name. Also, everyone was similarly armed with magazine rifles, more or fewer machine-guns, quick-firing field artillery, a rapidly mobilizable mass conscript army (Britain excepted, until 1916), and a doctrine that emphasized offensive action. In 1914, Germany did not have a lead in military technology, doctrine or indeed anything else, except, arguably, in its traditional strength in military training. However, because Moltke was obliged to use many reservists in the first line in order to achieve the numbers necessary for the grand envelopment of the French, it was inevitable that many formations were not exactly on the cutting edge of tactical excellence. (The West Army of 1.6 million men comprised twenty-three active and as many as eleven reserve corps.) Historian Antulio Echevarria has explained that while it is true that the Germans had an intelligent and appropriate tactical doctrine for coping reasonably well with modern firepower, the problem was that too few units followed it in practice (Echevarria, 2000: 217–18).

On the Western Front for the first three months in 1914, and for the final three months in 1918, the war was one of movement, albeit not usually rapid movement. On the Eastern Front, because force to space ratios were low, the war generally was one where movement, even extensive and ambitious manoeuvre, was possible. (This fact translated as a major difference between the wartime experiences of the German, French and British armies.) But for nearly four years in the West, the decisive theatre, the Great War was a gigantic siege operation. No army was properly equipped to conduct siege warfare in a flankless theatre of operations. Since such conditions had not been expected, it would have been truly remarkable had anyone been suitably prepared. However, the Germans were fortunate in their possession of a great many of their excellent 105mm field howitzers. Siege warfare called for plunging fire rather than the flat trajectory of the quick-firing field artillery. Also, it demanded guns of large calibre and high-explosive shells in numbers unanticipated in pre-war calculations.

The military problem of the war on the Western Front, the only theatre for decision, was not directly strategic, nor even operational. Instead, the long-insuperable military problem was tactical. Armies had to learn how to penetrate a continuous, fortified front. Soldiers had to be able, first, to break into a defended zone that might be 6 miles deep and contain three (or even six) lines of fortification, protected by vast aprons of barbed wire; then they had to break through the lines in that zone; and finally they had to break out of the defended zone and exploit tactical success for operational effect and ultimately for strategic advantage. In 1918, both sides came close to achieving all three steps. The Germans broke in, broke through and broke out in March and April, but their losses were too high and their logistics collapsed. As if those near-lethal developments were not sufficient to doom the great gamble, the operational direction of the offensives on the Somme and in Flanders was so poor that the incomplete success which was achieved merely ensured that the attackers created a salient that left them vulnerable to deadly counter-strokes. In truth, though badly shaken and not always in good order, the Allied forces that were beaten in the early stages of the German offensives generally were by no means routed. A similar judgement applies even to the defeat of the German Army that unfolded remorselessly from July until November 1918. There was ample evidence of disintegration: unusually high numbers of prisoners were taken by the Allies; German guns were captured on a large scale for the first time in the war; overall, the German Army was becoming ever less able to resist the repeated hammer blows it received during what is known as the 'Hundred Days Campaign' that concluded the war. However, while the Germans had no option but to yield ground, usually they yielded it only slowly and continued to inflict losses on Allied forces as heavy as those suffered in any period of the war. The Germans remained formidable and deadly right up to the Armistice.

When scholars claim that the belligerents mastered modern land warfare in 1914–18, and that they carried through a revolution in military affairs in order to achieve and exploit that mastery, it is well to remember that even the best military practice of 1917–18 was distinctly limited in its operational and strategic reach. What follows is a short discussion of the most important features of warfare in those years. It includes the innovations that were feasible and succeeded as well as those that were necessary but impractical at the time.

The military key which unlocked the Western Front was scientific gunnery. World War I was the Great Artillery War. Precise artillery fire, without precursor firing for target registration – which would forfeit surprise – stunned or destroyed the defenders, and, as important, silenced the enemy's artillery with accurate counter-battery fire.

The artillery revolution, first revealed by the Germans at Riga in September 1917, and by the British at Cambrai in November that year, could all but ensure tactical victory. At least it could deliver victory when it was employed as the most vital enabling agent for a combined-arms approach to warfare. Artillery, infantry, tanks (in the Allied case) and aircraft all had to play mutually supporting roles. By late 1917 and in 1918, 1914-style warfare was as obsolete as was the infantry square. There was no question of sequential combat, with artillery, infantry and cavalry each performing its role in its turn, effectively in isolation from one another.

Tanks were important by late 1917, but not by comparison with the artillery. Aside from their undoubted psychological effect, the principal utility of the early tanks was in crushing paths for the infantry through fields of barbed wire. This was not a minor task:

offensives would fail if the infantry could not penetrate the enemy's wire. In the absence of tanks, the wire would have to be cut by the artillery, and failures in that task were legion from 1915 to 1917.

Both sides had to learn how to use aircraft, and they needed to build planes that were militarily effective. From Verdun in early 1916 onwards, every major offensive was accompanied by combat on a large scale in the air. In 1917 and 1918 the belligerents had achieved generally effective integration of air power with their ground assets in the combined-arms concept mentioned above. In 1918 the Germans, for example, formed dedicated ground-attack squadrons that supported their infantry by flying at almost zero altitude to strafe the enemy. In this war, as in 1939–45, the close ground-support mission was extraordinarily dangerous to perform, as well as being subject to friction from the weather and from the smoke and dust of battle conditions. By the final year of the war, both sides were employing aircraft in all the ways that were to become familiar in World War II. The only exception was with regard to the massed paratroop drop, but even that was planned by the Allies, had the war continued into 1919.

Whereas the story of military innovation in the nineteenth century pre-eminently pertained to the infantry and its weapons, the like story of 1914–18, as emphasized here, related pre-eminently to the artillery. However, both sides had to learn new infantry tactics, for defence and attack, in order to survive on a battlefield dominated by guns. Also, the infantry had to acquire the skills and the equipment needed to exploit the novel opportunities granted by unprecedentedly precise gunnery. While it is probably true to claim that the Germans pioneered and exploited most fully the concept of infantry infiltration tactics (so-called 'Hutier tactics', named after General Oskar von Hutier, who used them first at Riga on 1 September 1917), in point of fact the French and the British were working from the same tactical page at more or less the same time. The Germans were not by any means alone in effecting a revolution in tactical doctrine for the infantry. Recall the familiar, dreadful image of dressed ranks of overburdened Tommies plodding doggedly towards the German lines until they were mown down by machine-gun fire. That is not a myth, but it bears little relation to battlefield tactical reality in 1917 or 1918 (or even in 1916, after 1 June). Both sides developed their assault infantry into all-arms combat teams, equipped with light machine-guns, grenade-throwers and flame-throwers, as well as some rifles. The infantry sought cover, and moved stealthily or rapidly. It advanced dispersed, and depended critically upon the closest of cooperation with the artillery. Such standard practice of 1918 was a light-year removed from ground warfare in 1914.

It is worth repeating two limiting features of warfare in 1914–18 from which much else flowed. First, uniquely in history, commanders and their troops lacked reliable, prompt tactical communications. Radio did not exist below the level of corps head-quarters. The field telephone could not accompany soldiers in the attack, at least not reliably. It was always liable to be blown away, or otherwise cut, in this artillery-dominated war. Second, the troops lacked tactical mobility. They could advance or retreat only at walking or crawling speed. These limitations meant that generals could not know in real time how their troops were progressing. Also, there was no way in which a successful break into or break through the enemy's defences could be exploited rapidly. Tactical victories could be no more than that, because the enemy nearly always was able to outpace exhausted attackers with the rapid insertion of counter-attack formations previously held back, out of hostile artillery range. In addition, the operational-level movement of troops by the lateral rail lines behind the front guaranteed that any menacing breach would soon be sealed by fresh forces.

Overall, by 1918 everyone had learnt how to wage modern warfare, albeit in styles which best suited individual national contexts. Combined-arms warfare was understood and practised. At least, it was practised when the means were available and the troops and their leaders were properly trained, which was by no means always the case. The military experience of 1918, with its succession of five mighty German offensives, followed by the drumroll of Allied counter-offensives which continued into November, demonstrated beyond any room for doubt that there was only one way to win the war. Daring operational manoeuvre, heroic and skilful infantry tactics and in general even an excellence in the conduct of combined-arms warfare depending critically on the artillery, tanks and air power could not offer a short cut to victory. The war could be won only by attrition. The belligerents were too powerful and too competent to be defeated by anything other than exhaustion.

Nothing has been said thus far about the introduction of poison gas into warfare. This secret weapon, first revealed at Ypres by the Germans in April 1915, initially was effective in panicking unprepared troops. But soldiers soon learnt how to minimize the damage from gas attacks, and specialized protective equipment was issued. Gas, which became progressively more deadly from 1915 to 1918, came to be employed on a large scale by both sides. Although it was not as lethal as conventional high explosives, when gas was delivered precisely by the artillery it was an especially fearsome weapon because of the horrific character of the injuries it caused (e.g., lung damage, blindness, blistering). But its effect on warfare was simply to add to the horror and reinforce the difficulties of tactical combat. It was not a wonder weapon that could unlock the enemy's defences on the Western Front.

Maritime matters have also been conspicuous by their absence from this analysis. In military terms this neglect has been commanded by a historical record that showed little naval action that had direct significance for the course and outcome of the war. To repeat, the war was decided, and could only be decided, on land on the Western Front. However, if one approaches the question of the maritime contribution to the history of the war strategically, as one must, it is plain to see just how significant British maritime command was for the outcome. The Royal Navy checkmated and distantly blockaded Germany's short-range High Seas Fleet, while in 1917–18 it defeated the U-boat menace by its implementation of a convoy system. Bear in mind that sea power exerts its influence strategically and slowly upon the land, the geography of decision. By commanding the seas around Europe, the Royal Navy enabled the Allies to win a long war of attrition, always assuming that the Allied armies were militarily effective. World War I was a war of competing resources. Maritime command meant that the Allies could draw upon the assets of the whole world reachable by sea. Germany suffered in two fundamental ways. On the one hand, it was deprived of access to the raw materials from overseas which it needed desperately. To cite but four vital items, Germany was cut off from supplies essential to the making of gunpowder, potentially a fatal bottleneck in a war economy: 'cotton from the United States; camphor from Japan; pyrites from Spain; and saltpetre from Chile' (Strachan, 2001: 1025). On the other hand, enjoying unrestricted maritime access, the Allies could not exhaust the material basis for their war-making, at least not unless foreigners ceased to regard them as tolerable credit risks. Finally, the Allied maritime economic blockade of the Central Powers played an important, if incalculable, role in weakening morale on the home front and generally helping to induce war-weariness. There has long been a school of thought in Britain which holds to the view that it was the Royal Navy and its blockade which ranks first among the causes of the Allied victory (Liddell Hart, 1970a: 464). The German High Seas Fleet won a tactical victory at Jutland on 31 May 1916, in the only main fleet action of the war, but it was bested strategically. The Germans effectively blockaded themselves for the remainder of the war, too fearful of the Royal Navy to risk venturing forth again in large numbers.

Conclusion

The strategic history of World War I is dominated by a political context that was of overwhelming significance. Governments required more of their armed forces than those forces could deliver, virtually no matter how competently they were handled in combat. It is commonplace to observe that the leading problem in the land warfare of 1914–18 was tactical, rather than operational or strategic. The troops could not penetrate the sophisticated continuous field fortifications of a flankless enemy. But to focus near-exclusively upon the tactical crisis and its several partial solutions is to miss the forest while being fascinated by the trees. The real problem was not tactical at all; rather, it was political. The armies struggled bloodily to resolve, or at least alleviate, the tactical impasse, because they were the instruments of policies which insisted upon decisive military victory. Such a victory was obtained, albeit barely, but only after four and a quarter years of attritional combat. If there is blame to assign, its proper targets should not be the generals and their staffs who had to learn how to wage modern warfare, still less the mass of conscripted victims of the military learning curve. Rather, blame must be heaped at the door of the people who demanded more from the use of force than such use was capable of delivering at reasonable cost.

Why did the Central Powers lose? Given that the major belligerents achieved an approximate equality of military effectiveness, as happens in all protracted conflicts, and given the impracticality of bold operational strokes, the better-resourced side was bound to win in the end. That end was a long time coming, as was predictable, given the strength of Germany and the skill and determination of its soldiers, but provided no essential member of the Allied coalition succumbed to terminal war-weariness at home, the defeat of Germany had to be only a matter of time. It is true that Russia was just such an essential coalition member, but it was replaced by the United States, albeit with a perilous military time lag.

The Allies held the strategic trump cards. Germany proved in 1914–18, as it did again in 1939–45, that it was superior in the conduct of warfare: in the first half of the twentieth century the Germans were unsurpassed at fighting. But there is much more to war than fighting. Germany did not function in a purposefully strategic manner. It had no strategy-making machinery to advise the Kaiser, and Wilhelm II was not gifted as a strategic thinker. However, to be fair, Germany's military leaders had long recognized their fundamental strategic problem: the relative shortage of means. The Schlieffen–Moltke Plan was nothing if not daring. It was a reckless attempt to finesse by operational dexterity and sheer military tempo both the tactical crisis caused by modern firepower and the strategic dilemma of having too few means to achieve the political ends demanded.

This discussion may have given the impression that Germany could not have won World War 1. That impression is intended, but it needs to be modified by the Clausewitzian thought that 'war is the realm of chance'. Nothing is certain about the course and outcome of a war, even when the dice seem to be loaded, as in this case, clearly in favour of one side. Germany lacked the means and, it transpired, the skill to force a decisive military victory in the years when it took major offensive action, 1914 and 1918. But military errors by the Allies or a failure of political nerve in the face of domestic war-weariness could have delivered conclusive success to Berlin.

To repeat, the dominant problem of 1914–18 was political, not military. The policymakers of both sides, and the societies for which they spoke, demanded a military outcome that the armies either could not deliver, or could deliver only at exorbitant cost. Military victory was certain to be pyrrhic. Now the narrative must move on to examine the political and strategic consequences of this protracted attritional catastrophe.

Key points

1. It took both sides three years to understand how to wage modern warfare. It took them at least another six months before they were able to put their new doctrine of combined-arms warfare into effective practice.
2. When the Schlieffen–Moltke Plan failed in August–September 1914, the Germans were caught without the insurance of a 'Plan B'. They did not know how to win the war.
3. The Germans had to take the offensive in 1918, before the US Army arrived in overwhelming numbers. To remain on the defensive would mean to accept defeat. They failed in good part because Ludendorff was no strategist.
4. The dominant weapon of the war was artillery. It was the key to solving 'the tactical crisis', and it caused 70 per cent of the casualties.
5. The fundamental problem in the conduct of the war was that governments demanded of their armies what those armies could not deliver.
6. The only way in which the war could be won by the Allies was by attrition.

Questions

1. Why did the Schlieffen–Moltke Plan fail in 1914?
2. How did land warfare in 1918 differ from its practice in 1914?
3. How might Germany have won the war?
4. Was there any practicable alternative to a strategy of attrition?

Further reading

J. B. A. Bailey *The First World War and the Birth of the Modern Style of Warfare*, The Occasional [monograph], No. 22 (Camberley: Strategic and Combat Studies Institute, Staff College, 1996).

R. A. Doughty *Pyrrhic Victory: French Strategy and Operations in the Great War* (Cambridge, MA: Harvard University Press, 2005).

P. Griffith *Battle Tactics of the Western Front: The British Army's Art of Attack, 1916–18* (New Haven, CT: Yale University Press, 1994).

P. G. Halpern *A Naval History of World War I* (London: UCL Press, 1994).

H. H. Herwig *The First World War: Germany and Austria-Hungary, 1914–1918* (London: Arnold, 1997).

M. S. Neiberg *Fighting the Great War: A Global History* (Cambridge, MA: Harvard University Press, 2005).

G. Sheffield *Forgotten Victory: The First World War: Myths and Realities* (London: Headline, 2001).

N. Stone *The Eastern Front, 1914–1917* (London: Hodder and Stoughton, 1975).

D. T. Zabecki *The German 1918 Offensives: A Case Study in the Operational Level of War* (London: Routledge, 2006).

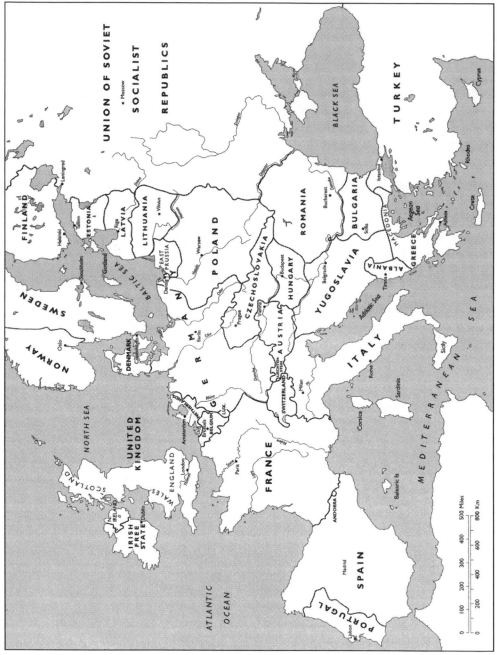

Map 8.1 Europe between the wars

8 The twenty-year armistice, 1919–39

Reader's guide: The Versailles Settlement and its consequences. The radical change in political context between the 1920s and the 1930s. The strategic implications of that difference.

Introduction: contrasting decades

The author of the pessimistic prediction in the title to this chapter was Marshal Ferdinand Foch, Commander-in-Chief of all the Allied armies on the Western Front from 3 April 1918 until 11 November (Bell, 1997: 16). His contemporary judgement on the Versailles Settlement was to prove all too accurate. But did this twenty-year armistice have to be such? Strategic history does not follow a preordained linear path, and those who write about it have to beware lest they reason backwards from a great event, such as World War II, to identify the causes that allegedly made it 'inevitable'. A great second round was always a possibility, given the terms and conditions that concluded hostilities and sought to stabilize the post-war world. But what had been only a distant possibility, and a rather implausible one at that, in the 1920s became a rock-hard certainty in the 1930s, specifically after 30 January 1933. However, one must recognize the powerful influence of contingency, including the role of such an extra-political and extra-strategic event as the Great Depression. In addition, personalities can matter critically: people do make history. By far the most potent force for war in the 1930s was, of course, the character, ideology and policy pursued by Germany's Chancellor, Adolf Hitler.

There is an obvious and undeniable unity to the years 1914 to 1945. Understandably, many historians, following popular opinion in the period itself, are satisfied with the concept of a second 'Thirty Years War'. Certainly it is true that Germany was principally responsible for both wars, and solely for 1939–45. In non-German perspective, both events were about the curbing, and eventually the annihilation (in 1945, not 1918), of German power and influence. Nevertheless, despite the many continuities between 1914–18 and 1939–45, it would be a serious error to see the two wars simply as succeeding rounds in the same conflict. Similarly, even though this book explains why a second world war eventually was inevitable, it would be a mistake to write off the 1920s and 1930s as a rather inconsequential time-out between catastrophic bloodlettings. World

War II was a different conflict from World War I, and the 1930s differed markedly, indeed decisively, from the 1920s. While one might conclude that the strategic history of 1914–19 rendered a second war of some kind all but inevitable some day, the World War II that actually happened was the product of policy choices in several capitals as well as of shifts in the contexts for international politics.

Historical empathy for the human agents of strategic history is hampered by the curse of hindsight. As a consequence, it is difficult to assess fairly the statecraft and strategic policies of the 1920s and 1930s. Almost inevitably, historians judge policies not on their contemporary merits, but with reference to their consequences. Naturally, since a world war concluded these two decades, behaviour in those years on behalf of peace with security is found to have been fatally wanting.

To understand the interwar decades and their strategic consequences, it is essential to grasp both the vastness of the shadow cast by the war so recently terminated and the major differences between the 1920s and the 1930s.

Versailles and the legacy of the Great War

Peace settlements do not make, or remake, strategic history. Instead, they reflect their political and strategic contexts. Versailles 1919 has acquired a largely undeserved reputation allegedly as a leading contributor to the eventual onset of World War II. The facts of the matter do not support such a negative view.

It is true to claim that the Versailles Settlement was thoroughly unsound, but the fault reposed in its contexts, not in the heavily constrained policy choices of the leading peacemakers. Those individuals were Georges Clemenceau for France, David Lloyd George for Britain, Woodrow Wilson for the United States and Vittorio Orlando for Italy. Versailles was a faithful reflection of the appalling political and strategic contexts created by the war. Germany was not invited, while the new and desperately insecure Bolshevik Republic was the victim of ill-judged military intervention by the principal Allied states. In addition, the new Russia was suffering from several ongoing civil wars, and was conducting extensive warfare with the newly restored state of Poland. Major combat began in January 1919 and persisted until Polish victory was conceded in the Treaty of Riga on 18 March 1921.

The Versailles Settlement broke just about every defining rule of sound statecraft for peacemaking, but it is difficult to see how the principals could have drafted a substantially different document. After over four years of increasingly total war, the victors – the nominal victors, that is – were in no mood to be magnanimous. The United States was alone among the winners in not harbouring acquisitive or vengeful motives. (President Wilson spoke of 'a peace without victory' in a speech to the US Congress on 22 January 1917.) Admittedly, those potent words were uttered prior to both American belligerency and American shock at the predatory terms of the peace imposed by a victorious Germany on the Bolsheviks at Brest-Litovsk on 3 March 1918. The settlement was an all-too-faithful expression of reality. Germany and its allies had been defeated, but not destroyed. Berlin had sued for peace, but it did not sign an instrument of unconditional surrender. The Allies could have continued the war, invaded Germany in 1919 and wrought great physical destruction upon the main instigator of the catastrophe. But, for good and ill, they chose to be satisfied with an armistice and the dictation of terms of peace.

Germany was stripped of Alsace–Lorraine; French domestic opinion would brook no plebiscite there. It also lost three small enclaves on its border with Belgium (Eupen, Malmédy and Moresnet); the ethnically Danish slice of Schleswig, conquered in 1864; most of West Prussia, and the largely German port of Danzig; the port of Memel, also ethnically German; and most of Upper Silesia. Perhaps 6 million ethnic Germans were lost to the Reich. Overall, Germany was deprived of 13 per cent of its pre-war population, 26 per cent of its coal and 15 per cent of its iron ore. Wilson's guiding principle of self-determination of peoples was not, of course, applied in an unimpeachably even-handed manner among all nationalities. The French claimed the rich coalmining district of the Saar, which was wholly German, but they were thwarted by Wilson. Instead, they were allowed to exploit the Saar coal mines and industries for fifteen years, under the authority of the newly created League of Nations. Following that period a plebiscite would be held to determine whether the Saarlanders wished to return to German sovereignty. To no one's surprise, in 1935 they voted to join the new Nazi Germany.

Germany was disarmed to the point where it could not resume the war, which was the initial concern. Indeed, it would be incapable of defending itself even against invasion by Poland, restored as a sovereign state by Versailles. The German Army was restricted to 100,000 men, to include only 4,000 officers (reduced from 34,000), and the Great General Staff was to be abolished. The army was to consist strictly of long-service regulars: officers were to serve for twenty-five years, NCOs for twelve. Germany was denied tanks, heavy artillery, military aviation, submarines and all save a token surface fleet. In addition, it was denied the right to construct frontier fortifications. The Rhineland, including a fifty-kilometre-wide strip on the eastern bank, was to be demilitarised in perpetuity.

Perhaps most damaging of all for the future peace of Europe was the so-called 'war guilt' clause of the Versailles Treaty, Article 231. Wilson prevented the French from imposing an indemnity on Germany because indemnity is the penalty paid by the loser simply for losing. But it was open season to claim reparations for the cost of the non-military damage wrought by the armed forces of the Central Powers. The famous, or infamous, Article 231 added financial injury to what nearly all Germans regarded as insult. It read as follows:

> The Allied and Associated Governments [a total of twenty-nine states] affirm and Germany accepts the responsibility of Germany and her allies for causing all the loss and damage to which the Allied and Associated Governments and their nationals have been subjected as a consequence of the war imposed upon them by the aggression of Germany and her allies.
>
> (Goldstein, 2002: 111)

The issue of reparations was to be a running sore in international relations throughout the 1920s, linked as it was to the issue of war guilt, the moral basis for the financial claims. The Reparations Commission of the Allies produced a grand total claim of 132,000 million gold marks in May 1921, most of which was to be deferred, probably indefinitely, pending a marked improvement in Germany's ability to pay. In 1924 the 'Dawes Plan', devised by US Director of the Bureau of the Budget, Charles G. Dawes, sought to stabilize the German currency after hyperinflation had rendered it worthless, and reschedule reparations payments more realistically. Finally, in 1929, the reparations problem was tackled yet again, this time by a committee chaired by American banker Owen D. Young. The 'Young Plan' envisaged German payment of reparations that would not conclude until 1988.

Not only did the reparations controversy poison international relations in what otherwise was generally a period of cooperative statecraft, but it was linked in Europe, and in London in particular, to the pace, and even the fact, of the Allied repayment of war loans from the United States. Britain had borrowed $4,661 million and France $3,991 million from the Americans. And after the war the Americans were insistent upon strict repayment. European debtors sought to tie their repayment of debts to the United States to their receipt of reparations payments from Germany. Unsurprisingly, the United States rejected this nexus out of hand.

Germany lost all of its colonies to the Allies, though the transfer was effected under the authority of mandates from the new League of Nations. Compared with the war guilt clause, the loss of territory and ethnic Germans in Europe, and disarmament, though, the loss of overseas colonies was a matter of little consequence for Germany. Given that Germany was able to evade making much more than token payments towards the shifting totals of reparations demands, and that the territorial and population losses were more insulting than crippling, the settlement cannot be judged, objectively, to have been especially harsh. There was an important area of exception to that judgement, however. Despite its many successful and systematic evasions of treaty obligations, there is no doubt that Germany was decisively disarmed. Its Versailles-sanctioned 100,000-man Army was incapable of defending the country, let alone of taking offensive action against a neighbour, while France maintained a notable military presence in the Rhineland until 1930. That French military occupation, two corps strong, was tied to German performance on reparations; so the French wished to maintain their military presence for as long as possible.

Thus far, nothing has been said about the League of Nations, the covenant of which was incorporated into the Versailles Treaty and all of the other peace treaties concluded with the defeated former Central Powers (Austria, Bulgaria, Hungary and Turkey). The League, which admitted Germany in 1925, was the brainchild of many optimists, pre-eminently British and American, though its founding is associated popularly with President Wilson. The last of his 'fourteen points' of 8 January 1918 insisted that 'A general association of nations must be formed under specific covenants for the purpose of affording mutual guarantees of political independence and territorial integrity to great and small states alike.' It cannot be denied that there was a great deal of conference diplomacy in the 1920s, some of it facilitated by the existence of the League. However, the League did not, and could not, transform the conduct of international relations. Alas, its fundamental premise was unsound. That premise was that the whole community of nations, and certainly the great powers permanently on the League's Council, would act together to deter, and if need be resist, aggression. This is the theory of international order by collective security. The fallacy in the theory is that states will take costly steps to resist aggression even when their own vital interests are not at stake.

The Versailles Settlement was the inevitable product of the war. Unwisely, it offered maximum offence to Germany while inflicting only minimal long-term damage upon it. One of the rules of international relations holds that no post-war political order can be stable if it is judged unacceptably unjust by a disadvantaged great power. Making an enduring peace is more of a challenge than making war. But the subsequent peace is, after all, what the preceding war was all about. If a somewhat punitive peace settlement is dictated without negotiation to a defeated great power, its authors require a robust plan which will deny that great power the ability to seek eventual violent, or other coercive, redress of its grievances. Spencer C. Tucker penetrates to the heart of the problem with Versailles and the international relations of the next twenty years when he writes: 'the peace rested not so much on French strength as on German weakness' (Tucker, 1998: 227). Over those twenty years, that Franco-German strategic imbalance eventually would be reversed.

Germany's army had been beaten in the field, but its territory had been barely touched physically by the war. In fact, many Germans had difficulty believing that the war had really been lost. In truth, Versailles trod an indecisive course between a punitive and a moderate settlement. It was as punitive as France could impose, and as conciliatory as the United States and Britain could achieve in the face of French anger and anxiety. The details of the case signified a great deal less than did national perceptions of what had been perpetrated. The whole peace settlement comprised treaties with Germany (Versailles, 28 June 1919), Austria (Saint-Germain, 10 September 1919), Bulgaria (Neuilly, 27 November 1919), Hungary (Trianon, 4 June 1920) and Turkey (Sèvres, 10 August 1920). The last of these needed to be revised comprehensively by the Treaty of Lausanne of 24 July 1923, following a period of intense warfare between Greece and Turkey and a massive enforced exchange of populations across the Aegean. It is probably most sensible to regard the establishment of the peace settlement as being completed, save with respect to reparations and disarmament, by the Locarno Treaty of 16 October 1925. This signified the general acceptance of Weimar Germany back into the family of respectable powers. By its terms, Germany, France and Belgium guaranteed 'the maintenance of the territorial *status quo* resulting from the frontiers between Germany and Belgium and between Germany and France, and the inviolability of the said frontiers as fixed by or in pursuance of the Treaty of Paris signed at Versailles on June 28, 1919' (Article 1; quoted in Goldstein, 2002: 120).

The peace settlement to World War I could not help but be a legacy of that long struggle to the future. Its terms and the ways in which they worked, or failed to work, depended wholly upon the dynamic political context and its associated strategic context. The crucial changes in those contexts are examined in the next section. The settlement satisfied no one. It humiliated and punished the Germans. In the view of the French it made no reliable provisions for their future security. In the eyes of the British it was unduly harsh on Germany, especially in its economic dimension. And it made unacceptable demands upon the Americans. They would not sign up for a League whose Covenant was keyed to the principle of collective security, a principle that would require the United States to take action abroad, not always at its own discretion. It left Italy convinced that it had been short-changed in rewards for its wartime sacrifices. Rome had received promises of extensive territorial acquisition at the expense of Austria, Hungary, Turkey and even Germany. That was how London and Paris had bribed the country into belligerency in 1915. And, last but not least, Japan, a successfully opportunistic ally in the war, was thoroughly aggrieved by the failure of its allies and co-belligerents, especially the United States, to support its predatory demands upon China. However, this list of discontents was of no great significance in the 1920s. During that decade the political and strategic contexts placed strict practical limits upon the potential of discontented states to make trouble. The question of the 1920s, had anyone been minded to look to the future in this way, was whether the discontented parties could, or would, come to accept the post-war environment. As an aid to such acceptance, could they adjust the settlement to a meaningful degree before the course of strategic history staged some surprises and tested the stability of the existing order?

Box 8.1 Principal features of the Versailles Settlement

- *War guilt:* Germany and its allies accepted sole responsibility for the damage and costs of the war caused by their aggression.
- *Territorial loss:* Germany suffered modest losses of territory, population (13 per cent) and resources.
- *Reparations:* Germany agreed to make financial reparation to the victors for the non-military damage that its war-making had effected. The amount to be paid and the time schedule for payment were not part of the settlement.
- *Disarmament:* Germany was effectively disarmed, even though it cheated systematically on its obligations. Also, the victors committed themselves to disarmament, at least in principle.
- *New states:* In accordance with the principle of national self-determination, the geopolitics of Eastern Europe were transformed from a condition of domination by three rival empires – the Austrian, Russian and Ottoman – into one characterized by an array of squabbling small states. Most importantly, Poland reappeared on the map for the first time since 1795, and the new multi-ethnic state of Czechoslovakia was created.
- *The League of Nations:* The League was founded to keep the peace. It was to do so through application of the principle of collective security. The whole collectivity of nations was supposed to combine to resist an aggressor.
- *The Locarno Treaty of 1925:* This final element in the post-war settlement registered the mutual acceptance of the Franco-German and Belgian–German frontiers, and guaranteed the integrity of those frontiers. Britain and Italy were the treaty's 'guarantors'. Locarno marked Germany's re-entry into the community of nations. The treaty guaranteed frontiers only in Western Europe, not in the East.

It would be difficult to exaggerate the impact of World War I upon the course of twentieth-century history, so the more significant of the war's consequences need to be cited.

Both international relations and the domestic functioning of societies were all but turned upside down. What became a total war, requiring belligerents to mobilize all of their assets of all kinds, had revolutionary, certainly far-reaching, implications for relations between classes, capital and labour, between sexes, between government and industry, and between governments and the governed.

Four empires were removed from the map: the Imperial German, the Austro-Hungarian, the Russian and the Ottoman. In place of being dominated by the shifting relations among Germany, Austria-Hungary and Russia, East–Central Europe suddenly was populated by an array of new, weak states. These states, especially Poland and Czechoslovakia, separated Germany from Russia. But they could not possibly serve a serious barrier function once Germany or Russia, or both, recovered from their low condition of the 1920s.

The war shifted global financial leadership from Britain to the United States.

Because of its devastation, intensity and duration, the war reintroduced ideology into international relations. The Bolshevik coup of October 1917 introduced a regime whose formal *raison d'être*, beliefs and behaviour were at least as fundamentally menacing to world order as had been the ideology and actions of the first French Republic in the 1790s. In addition, the entry of the United States into the war, also in 1917, introduced a popularly inspiring, but naïvely idealistic, liberal ideology into the statecraft of peacemaking. Some elements of that ideology were widely shared in Britain.

The way the war was concluded, with an armistice and the subsequent settlement, left the defeated states, and even some of the victors (e.g., Italy and Japan), vengeful and determined upon revision. The victors did not seek to destroy Germany's potential to return one day to the ranks of the great powers. The peacemakers of 1919 neglected the most fundamental rule of sound peacemaking: specifically, if a post-war order is to endure and provide only for stable and orderly changes, it is essential that the defeated parties should accept their defeat. They have to be granted a vital stake in the new international order and, after a probationary period, gradually be reabsorbed into the general and full working of international relations. The war should not be conducted militarily, or concluded diplomatically, in such a way that defeated states are left with a permanent sense of acute grievance.

The process of peacemaking revealed with crystal clarity the deep divisions among the leaders of the victorious coalition. They agreed on almost nothing of great importance. The Alliance, plus its American co-belligerent, that had won the war dissolved almost as rapidly as did the armies of its offshore members, Britain and the United States. At root, the problem was that the war had not concluded with the destruction of Germany. With good reason, France was obsessively worried about a future threat from Germany, but Britain and the United States were all but indifferent to that distinctively French concern, a concern that seemed absurd to Britons and Americans at the time.

The events of 1914–18 had a near-traumatic impact upon popular attitudes to warfare, particularly in the Western democracies. It would be hard to overstate the war's socio-cultural reach. At least 65 million men in total had been mobilized, more than 9 million had died, and the grand total of casualties was of the order of 32 million (killed, wounded and POWs). World War I left a legacy of profound aversion to war among the peoples who might one day be challenged to protect the international order that succeeded it.

Although not a direct consequence of the war, it is essential not to forget the great pandemic of Spanish influenza which struck globally in 1918–19. This ghastly episode was far more deadly than was the warfare of the period. It is generally estimated that it killed at least 50 million people world-wide, with some suggesting the figure was nearer to 100 million. And, as John M. Barry notes, the world's population in 1918 was only 1.8 billion, 28 per cent of what it is today (Barry, 2005: 452).

The war did not give birth directly to Nazi Germany and its malevolent leader, but Adolf Hitler and his party were the results of the domestic conditions produced by it. In permissive political, economic and socio-cultural contexts, the Nazis and other extremists who were a legacy of the war and the subsequent economic crises would have a unique opportunity to make history.

Finally, World War I bequeathed as a legacy to future strategic history an incomplete revolution in military affairs. This was keyed to the ways in which the internal combustion engine could be employed, and its foci were tanks and aircraft. Even today, it is still not sufficiently appreciated that 'The Great War of 1914–18 arguably had a greater impact on military change than any modern conflict before or since' (Showalter, 2000: 220).

The changing political context: strategic implications

It is commonplace and necessary to highlight the historical importance of particular events and individuals. In keeping with that tradition, due respect must be paid to the vital importance of the Great Depression and, of course, to Adolf Hitler. However, as a strategic history, this book must explain the structure of the strategic context that rendered particular events and personalities so potentially lethal in their capacity to foment international disorder. History's makers and shakers need the opportunity to act; they require their strategic moment. But the potential in that opportunity is governed by the strategic context.

The strategic context of the 1920s was fundamentally different from that of the 1930s. In the earlier decade, statesmen and publics may have been seduced by 'the illusion of peace' (Marks, 2003). Plainly, the international order at that time was not seaworthy in heavy weather, though one might question whether any order can be. The war had demolished the old balance of power system. The pre-war and wartime alliances were defunct. Peace and stability in the post-war era were hoped by optimists to be guaranteed by the working of the collective security principle under the aegis of the novel League of Nations. In practice, though, every international order requires, though does not always enjoy, the service of an effective policing agent or guardian. The peace settlement was a faithful expression of the strategic context at the time of its creation. The dissatisfied states, the would-be revisionists, temporarily were strategically impotent, a fact which left the anxiety-racked French with a seemingly simple task. Despite British hostility, France was able to play the role of heavy-handed hegemonic ordering power in Europe in the 1920s. And since Germany was effectively disarmed, a relatively benign international political context prevailed.

The Weimar Republic, more sincerely than its Nazi successor, was committed unswervingly to the repeal, or avoidance, of as much of the Versailles Settlement as it could negotiate or ignore. The dominant European statesman of the 1920s was Germany's Foreign Minister from 1923 until his death in 1929, Gustav Streseman. With much British connivance, Streseman succeeded in undermining and chipping away at much of the constraining edifice and legacy of Versailles. He played to perfection the role of responsible statesman of a respectable country that deserved to be treated as a normal, senior member of the community of (great) powers. The decade saw a cascade of conferences, large and small, formal and informal, typically conducted in one or other of the more agreeable watering holes on Lake Geneva or one of the Italian lakes. A notable high point of the decade was the signing of the Locarno Pact in 1925, which seemed to bury for ever the prospect of war between France and Germany. The popular ecstasy with which it was greeted, especially in Britain, was not seriously reduced by what should have been regarded as the disturbing point that Streseman declined to match frontier guarantees in the West with any like agreement for the East. In other words, Weimar Germany did not consider its eastern frontiers to be finished business.

Three years after Locarno, statesmen delighted the credulous among their publics with the drafting and signing of the International Treaty for the Renunciation of War as an Instrument of National Policy, to be known to contemporaries and posterity alike as the Kellogg–Briand Pact. Frank Kellogg was America's Secretary of State, while Aristide Briand was the President of France. No fewer than fifty-one countries were pleased to sign up and declare thereby that they were against war. It is both easy and appropriate to be scornful of this vacuous document, but Sally Marks notes the historical novelty, and possibly even the significance, of the pact. She writes that it 'constituted the first formal renunciation ever of war as an instrument of national policy and the first step toward the slowly spreading view that war is immoral' (Marks, 2003: 109). The strategic historian, not to mention the cunning German Foreign Minister of the day, may regard the pact with an amused cynicism, but millions of people who constituted the force of public opinion were all too willing to take it at face value. Only ten years on from the catastrophe of 1914–18, it is difficult to be other than sympathetic to their pitiful naïvety. After all, in Britain alone, 37,780 war memorials were erected in the 1920s in a historically unique memorialization of national grief.

The 1920s were a time of hope and, on balance, a time when considerable progress seemed to be made towards repairing the damage wrought by the war to international order. Germany was slowly accepted as a responsible international player and, as a reward for its cooperative behaviour, many of the burdens of Versailles were eased or lifted. However, one humiliating burden against which Streseman struggled in vain until his premature death was the continued French military occupation of the Rhineland. That insult to Germany, so comforting to France in its strategic meaning, was finally removed in 1930.

The basic reason why the 1920s were a period of progress in international comity, real or illusory, was that the balance of power was loaded unchallengeably in favour of the new status quo established, or recorded, by Versailles. The treaty reflected the strategic context of 1919. As long as those who were motivated strongly to revise the peace settlement were unable to act upon their dissatisfaction, it would endure, at least in its essentials. Alone among the victors of 1914–18, France appreciated that it had not really won the war strategically. The Allied victory of 1918, with its consequent settlement, translated into a potentially disastrous strategic context for France. Before 1914 the country had secured a powerful ally in Russia that posed Germany both the nightmarish dilemma of a war on two fronts and the prospect of defeat because of the seriously adverse imbalance in resources between the rival alliances. In the war itself, France had acquired Britain as an ally of the first rank and, in 1915, Italy as an ally of the second. When Russia left the war in 1917, the United States took its place. The French need for allies had been amply met. However, France was acutely aware that in the vital matter of allies it had needed the assistance of them all in order to beat Germany.

The strategic context of the 1920s could hardly have been more different from the perspective of French security. No longer was there a great power ally in the East, threatening Germany with a two-front war. Instead, France could only seek some solace in treaties of alliance with the array of weak new, or controversially expanded, states that had been created from the collapse or reduction of the Austro-Hungarian, Russian and German empires. Despite the nominal commitment to collective security that was the keystone in the arch of the League of Nations, France hastened to assemble an allied team of minor players located to the east and south of Germany, signing treaties of alliance with Poland (19 February 1921), Czechoslovakia (25 January 1924), Romania (10 June 1926) and Yugoslavia (11 November 1927) (the latter three known collectively as the 'Little Entente'). The French strategic problem was that it shared Western Europe with a Germany that was potentially unmatchably powerful. This did not matter in the 1920s, because Germany, though energetically revisionist, was in no position to take action to restore its position by threat or force. France recognized, however, that that satisfactory condition could only be temporary. None of France's former great power allies were willing or able to play an active role in supporting the European order which they had helped establish at Versailles. Russia was a pariah state, distrusted and self-absorbed, though willing to collaborate secretly with Weimar Germany on innovative military projects for mutual advantage. The United States had rejected the League of Nations because of the theoretical obligation to take action for collective security which membership entailed. As a result, America definitely was not available as a likely ally of France against a Germany that was recovering. Last, but not least, Britain was more worried about French hegemony in Europe than it was sympathetic to French security anxieties, so it, too, was not available as an ally, even an unreliable one. That political condition was to endure until early 1939.

France had need either of allies or of a benign transformation in the character and foreign policy of its German neighbour. For nearly twenty years it could acquire only state minnows as allies, while after January 1933, of course, there was indeed a transformation of Germany, but it was far from benign. The basis of French anxiety was demographic. It had a population of 40 million, which was declining, while Germany's population was 75 million and rising. Furthermore, given French interests in the Mediterranean, a potentially hostile Fascist Italy had a population of 40 million. Beyond the promise of menacing demography, Germany's industrial base was second to none in Europe and had been damaged neither in the war nor very seriously by the Versailles Settlement. So, in the 1920s, the bottom line to French appreciation of its strategic context was that effectively it stood alone as the guardian of the new European order. That position of great strategic responsibility would be undemanding only while Germany could be kept in a condition of strategic impotence. Revisionist Weimar was strategically impotent and was obliged to pursue a responsible diplomatic course, but that course was designed to unravel Versailles, strand by strand.

This text has emphasized the importance of context. The 1920s showed real and apparent progress in international cooperation. Conference diplomacy bloomed as never before. The 1920s out-conferenced the post-1815 Congress System. It is possible that had the economic, political and strategic contexts of that decade continued into the 1930s with no abrupt, non-linear shifts, Germany might have completed the process of reabsorption into the ranks of responsible, respectable and essential great powers. But history was not going to permit that. Genuine or illusory, the progress achieved in the 1920s towards international reconciliation and cooperation was brutally halted by an appalling change in the economic context. That change altered the political context, which – inevitably – shifted the strategic context. The French nightmare became a reality. In the 1930s, France was alone as the policeman for the status quo of a European order that was challenged by a potentially, and predictably, unmatchably powerful revisionist Germany.

The structure of the strategic history of the 1920s and 1930s could hardly be simpler. With France as the only senior player on the erstwhile victors' team available to police the peace settlement, it looked to a strategic future wherein the principal loser of 1918 would be the strongest power on the Continent. France could try to persuade or bribe Britain to join in the policing role, it could seek allies among the small states of East–Central Europe, and it could try to conciliate – appease – Germany on matters that were less than vital to French security. Fundamentally, though, France could not escape a strategic context wherein eventually it must be on the wrong side of an imbalance of power vis-à-vis a revisionist Germany.

There is little profit pursuing some intriguing 'what ifs' of history. The fact is that the 1930s were strategically radically different from the 1920s. One might try to argue that another world war would have occurred anyway, at some time, virtually regardless of the course of events in the 1920s and 1930s, and that view merits serious consideration. It is anchored by the proposition that there was a redundancy of possible causal factors for war, but it is unduly deterministic. What separated the two decades was the Great Depression, with its political, economic and eventually strategic consequences. The collapse of the New York stock market on 29 October 1929 was a panic that both reflected and signalled a traumatic loss of business confidence. It had knock-on effects that damaged most countries' economies, though some more than others, and some more immediately than others. The two countries hit the hardest were the United States itself and Germany. Adolf Hitler and the Nazi Party were the products of the Great War, though in the 1920s not very significant ones. Hitler's assumption of the chancellorship of Germany on 30 January 1933 is attributable almost wholly to the social, economic and political effects of Germany's economic meltdown and the associated political disarray. Germany had 6 million unemployed in 1932. That was the most potent fact contributing to a 1930s drastically different from the 1920s. Hitler and the Nazis came to power on the back of economic chaos and popular economic anxiety. He promised to restore stability, confidence, jobs and in general a condition of, and status for, Germany in which Germans could take pride.

'The Hitler factor' is considered in detail in Chapter 11. The strategic history of the 1930s is the tale of a German regime determined to effect a revolutionary transformation in the map of Europe. Needless to say, perhaps, few people in the 1930s, at least until 1939, realized that in Hitler and his Third Reich they were not dealing with a normal, if unusually bold, statesman who was seeking only to improve his country's geostrategic position and remove the evidence of the humiliation of defeat in 1918–19.

Hitler's political and strategic achievements in the 1930s were impressive indeed. In only six years, 1933 to 1939, Germany changed from being strategically among the weaker states of Europe to being the strongest. In fact, by 1939 Germany was already the dominant state. The Versailles Settlement was dead and essentially buried, except as a source of some useful pretexts for aggression. Until 1939, all of Germany's forward strategic moves were ethically and politically defensible in terms of the former Allies' grand principle of the national self-determination of peoples. Germany reoccupied and remilitarized the Rhineland (7 March 1936), a move illegal under the Locarno Treaty of 1925; effected union with Austria, the Anschluss, on 12 March 1938, which was expressly forbidden by Versailles; and it absorbed the largely German-populated Sudetenland of Czechoslovakia after the Munich Conference of 29 September 1938. Where and when Hitler crossed his Rubicon was in the occupation of the substantial, and emphatically non-German, remnant of Czechoslovakia on 14–15 March 1939, in flagrant breach of the Munich Agreement. For the first time, Germany lacked even the pretence of a respectable ethnic rationale for its action. From March 1939 it was obvious to all except the wilfully strategically blind that Hitler's Germany was embarked upon a path of expansion that had no obvious limit.

Systematically, even carefully – though many of his generals did not agree – Hitler moved step by step to alter Germany's strategic context as the necessary enabler for realization of his political ambitions. On 14 October 1933 he withdrew from the overlong awaited and futile World Disarmament Conference, and from its parent, the League of Nations. In 1935 he flouted Versailles' injunction against Germany having any military aviation by announcing the existence of the Luftwaffe. Also in 1935, Germany put the final nail in the coffin of the disarmament provisions of Versailles when it reintroduced conscription. By far the most fateful step taken by the new regime, however, was the reoccupation and remilitarization of the Rhineland the following year. The action was dramatic, and caused panic attacks among senior German soldiers, but Hitler was correct in his belief that France would not move to resist the illegal action. The initial German military advance into the Rhineland was almost trivial in scale: just twelve infantry battalions and eight groups of artillery entered the demilitarized zone, and most of those remained on the east bank of the Rhine. Still, France, politically and militarily the only possible opponent of the reoccupation, was entirely incapable of mounting resistance.

Many historians and other commentators have argued that 7 March 1936 was the last opportunity to prevent World War II (e.g. Aron, 2002: 94). It is claimed that had France ejected German troops forcibly from the legally demilitarized zone, Hitler would have suffered such a loss of domestic prestige that he and his Nazi regime could well have been swept away by a military coup. One cannot know whether such speculation is well founded. However, what is known is that the Rhineland move, succeeding as it did the open steps towards headlong rearmament, was the first of what became a series of political triumphs for Hitler's statecraft. His self-confidence and popularity grew with each further proof of the soundness of his judgement. It is not entirely obvious that military defeat and the subsequent political humiliation over the Rhineland in 1936 would have resulted in regime change in Berlin, but it is fairly certain that after the Rhineland the only way to avert a great war would have been by a change of German government. Of course, what is obvious today, and was almost equally obvious to many observers across Europe by 1939, was not at all self-evident until that year. What is unarguable about Germany's unopposed military occupation of the Rhineland is that it caused a gigantic loss in French prestige. The Russians, who had signed a treaty of alliance with France in 1935, drew the appropriate conclusion from French inaction: the policeman of the European order was not up to the job. French alliance value suffered a catastrophic drop, while Hitler realized that Paris lacked the will to resist his designs. This was taken as definitive evidence in support of his conviction of French decline.

As strategic history, the 1930s registered an exceptionally unavoidable journey towards war, or at least so it appears with the benefit of hindsight. Nazi Germany could not be appeased or, ultimately, deterred. By 1939, France and Britain, belatedly and more than a little reluctantly playing the roles of policemen for European order, had only two policy options: to acquiesce in an open-ended process of German aggression or to fight. There was no third way. Much earlier in the decade, probably no later than March 1936, a great war might have been avoided if a method could have been found to bring down the Nazi regime. Unfortunately, by the time it became obvious that Germany had to be stopped, and that the only ways to do that were by deterrence if possible and by war if deterrence failed, the Third Reich had constructed a fragile, but formidable, military machine. Sad to say, Berlin's material gains through the Anschluss with Austria and in Czechoslovakia in 1938–9 strengthened the Reich's economic and military positions considerably. So long as Germany was ruled by Adolf Hitler, a great European war literally was inevitable.

As for those abroad who might have aborted the Nazi adventure in its early stages, none was in a condition to act, either alone or in concert. France, the declining European hegemon, was content with its 1918-style military doctrine of 'the methodical battle'. It believed that a future war would be waged and won in much the same way as had the previous one. Victory would be achieved by the long-term application of superior resources; through meticulous planning for attritional combat dependent upon artillery firepower provided by a nation fully mobilized for total war, in the context of another British, and hopefully American, alliance. The French Army, nominally the most powerful in Europe in the interwar years, was completely unsuited to serve as an instrument of anything short of general war. Because of domestic politics, as of 1930 conscripts served only a year with the colours, and no part of the metropolitan army was ready for war. French foreign policy required a military agent capable of taking offensive action to support allies in Eastern Europe and, if need be, to enforce the demilitarized status of the Rhineland. The French Army was not such an agent. Jeffrey Record argues as follows:

> The foundation of French appeasement was military incapacity to act against Germany. This incapacity was inexcusable, given that France was, unlike Britain, directly menaced overland by Germany, suffered fewer illusions about Nazi ambitions in Europe, required allies in Eastern Europe, possessed the largest army in Europe (upon mobilization), and was far less stressed than Britain by threatened imperial defense obligations.
>
> (Record, 2005: 19)

France's defensive military doctrine was mandated by the highly ideologized domestic politics which prohibited a professional army, by the long shadow of Verdun, and, as the 1930s progressed, by policy in London. It knew that it could defeat a rearmed Germany only with Britain as an ally, as it had before, albeit in that case with an expanding scale of help from the United States. French hands were tied since Britain was determined to go the extra mile for peace in its well-intentioned endeavours to appease Hitler, at least until the winter of 1938–9. This is not to suggest that prior to 1939 French public opinion was any more ready for war with Germany than was British. In the 1930s, therefore, the French Army placed its confidence in its impressive system of frontier fortification, the so-called Maginot Line (which did not cover the Franco-Belgian border), and in its ability, *with allies*, to mobilize for the conduct of a long total war of resources. But Britain did not have an army worthy of the name by European standards, and until early 1939 had not the slightest intention of staging a second major intervention in a land war on the Continent. Thus, it is not difficult to see how it was that in the 1930s Hitler's aggressive moves can be likened to applying pressure upon a door that was already ajar.

Conclusion

The more closely one examines the 1920s and 1930s, the more unavoidable World War II appears to have been in the latter years, and the less likely in the former. It is intellectually unfashionable as well as strictly unsound to claim that an event was inevitable. Nevertheless, once Hitler became Chancellor of Germany on 30 January 1933, and while he held that office, another great war *was* unavoidable. This admittedly deterministic claim rests with confidence on the evidence of Hitler's well-known character and purpose. It is not entirely correct historically to claim that he could not be deterred. He was deterred from potentially rash foreign policy behaviour in the early and mid-1930s by his understanding of Germany's contemporary military weakness. Moreover, even as late as 1938 he was deterred twice over Czechoslovakia by threats from Britain and France. However, some limited success with deterrence could have only a temporary tactical impact upon Hitler's plans for expansion and continental domination.

There was a night-and-day difference between the 1920s and 1930s. Whereas another great war was almost certainly unavoidable in the latter decade, such a conflict is almost unimaginable from the perspective of the former one. That is not to say that in the 1920s people were seduced by the illusion of an enduring peace. Illusion was rife, as usually is the case, but it was no illusion in those years to believe that the prospect of a second round of great power armed struggle was remote. Of course, there were many continuing irritants in relations between Germany and the erstwhile victorious Allies. But Jeffrey Record advances a powerful argument when he claims that 'it is hard to see how Europe gets to World War II without Hitler' (Record, 2005: 43–4). As Record argues, while any German government in the 1930s would have sought energetically to have the remaining humiliating and constraining terms of the Versailles Settlement removed, Hitler was surely unique both in desiring, indeed needing, war and in his absence of any sense of the practical limitations that should restrain German ambition and behaviour.

For the 1930s to be so different politically and strategically from the 1920s, intervention was required by a dramatic cause of historical non-linearity. In this case it was the Great Depression, with its malign consequences for domestic politics in Germany. The sharp strategic contrast between the two interwar decades serves as an eloquent warning to those who are addicted to the comforting, but ever-misleading, phrase 'the foreseeable future'. Only rarely is future strategic history foreseeable. The 1930s were not strategically foreseeable by reasonable people in the 1920s. But, alas, World War II was unavoidable in the 1930s. The latter point is made with all the advantages of hindsight. We know that the 1930s, unlike the 1920s, turned out to be the path to war. At the time, of course, at least until the late winter of 1938–9, statesmen other than

Hitler believed that they were preventing another great war, and could point to some recent successes in that area, one must add.

Key points

1. Another great war was only a distant possibility in the 1920s. In the 1930s, it was a certainty.
2. The two world wars were very distinctive in their origins and in the motivation of the belligerents. Therefore, the theory that the 1914–45 period constituted a second Thirty Years War is seriously flawed.
3. The Versailles Settlement reflected the political context of 1919. A completely different character of settlement was not politically feasible.
4. Great power conflict was largely absent from the 1920s, because the would-be revisionist states (Germany, Italy and Japan) were on the disadvantaged end of an imbalance of power.
5. The true character and most probable purpose of Hitler's foreign policy was not fully revealed until March 1939, with the seizure of the remainder of Czechoslovakia.
6. Without the Great Depression there would have been no Nazi regime, and hence no World War II with the total character of that which occurred from 1939 to 1945. Also, there would have been no Holocaust.

Questions

1. **What are the strengths and weaknesses of the thesis that 1914–45 comprised a second Thirty Years War?**
2. **Was the Versailles Settlement unjust to Germany?**
3. **Explain the basis for French security anxiety in the interwar years.**
4. **Was another great war inevitable in the 1930s?**

Further reading

P. M. H. Bell *The Origins of the Second World War in Europe*, 2nd edn (London: Longman, 1997).

M. F. Boemke, G. D. Feldman and E. Glaser (eds) *The Treaty of Versailles: A Reassessment after 75 years* (Cambridge: Cambridge University Press, 1998).

R. Boyce and J. A. Maiolo (eds) *The Origins of World War Two: The Debate Continues* (Basingstoke: Palgrave Macmillan, 2003).

R. Chickering and S. Förster (eds) *The Shadows of Total War: Europe, East Asia, and the United States, 1919–1939* (Cambridge: Cambridge University Press, 2003).

P. Finney (ed.) *The Origins of the Second World War* (London: Arnold, 1997).

M. Kitchen *Europe between the Wars: A Political History* (Harlow: Pearson Education, 2000).

M. Lamb and N. Tarling *From Versailles to Pearl Harbor: The Origins of the Second World War in Europe and Asia* (Basingstoke: Palgrave, 2001).

S. Marks *The Illusion of Peace: International Relations in Europe, 1918–1933*, 2nd edn (Basingstoke: Palgrave Macmillan, 2003).

J. Record *Appeasement Reconsidered: Investigating the Mythology of the 1930s* (Carlisle, PA: Strategic Studies Institute, US Army War College, 2005).

Z. Steiner *The Lights that Failed: European International History, 1919–1933* (Oxford: Oxford University Press, 2005).

9   The mechanization of war

Reader's guide: The mechanization revolution in military affairs. The technical development of armies, air forces and navies. The problems of coping with rapid technological change.

Introduction: revolution in military affairs (RMA)

The principal weapon for war-making in 1914–18 was the artillery. Although World War I compelled the invention of modern combined-arms warfare, it was really the great artillery war. Infantry and tanks could not advance once they had outrun their artillery support, except at the cost of suffering prohibitive losses. By way of sharp contrast, the principal war-making machines in 1939–45 were armoured fighting vehicles and aircraft. Between 1918 and 1940 there had been a mechanization of warfare that most scholars now regard as a revolution in military affairs (RMA). By that we mean a radical change in the character and conduct of war. However, RMA is a contested concept. Some historians discern evolution rather than revolution, and they emphasize the complexity of war and strategy, which can significantly limit the tactical and operational impact of new technologies (Black, 2004: 225). Moreover, the leading challenge to military establishments between the wars – beyond the nightmare of unaffordability, that is – was to decide what doctrinal sense to make of the novel military– technical possibilities.

The previous chapter gave pride of place to the changing political context from the 1920s to the 1930s. However, while broad political subjects were forging and altering the strategic context, the military dimension to that context was the subject of intense controversy in all modern states. Everyone needed to make strategic, operational, tactical, logistical and fiscal sense of the options for mechanization that appeared to be on offer. No one could afford to be left behind. But each power had different political, and hence military-strategic, needs. Furthermore, each had distinctive strategic and military cultures, distinctive recent experiences of war, and distinctive limitations in the critical realm of affordability.

The technologies for the mechanization of war on land and in the air effectively were common to all interested states. Two main sets of questions assailed the military establishments of the period. First, what would work, how well would it work, by when would it work, and what would it cost? That set was of lesser importance. Countries could build whatever they chose, given the fairly well-understood technical constraints (e.g., attainable engine power) of the time. Second, and far more significant, were the questions that bore on the fundamental matter of what *should* be built. It was not simply a question of discovering what new machines for land and air combat could offer; rather, it was a matter of deciding upon the tasks in need of performance by the machines. For new military technologies to effect a radical change in the character and conduct of warfare, first there has to be a doctrine suitable for their employment. Furthermore, that doctrine should match the tasks laid by foreign policy upon the military establishment.

Land warfare

RMAs are not always entirely self-evident in their strategic implications. Rarely has that point been as pertinent as it was to the problems and opportunities presented by mechanization in the 1920s and 1930s. Consider the following crucial issues. Would tanks be the dominant weapon in future ground warfare? Would they be effective only in the context of combined arms, rather than in isolation as tank forces? If tanks were to be dominant, or at least critically important, how much of the rest of the army needed to be mechanized or motorized? What does mechanization imply for the relevance of recent historical experience? Is mechanization and motorization affordable? How should tanks be employed? What ought to be their roles? Given the high cost of procuring mechanized forces and the dynamism of technical innovation, when should one settle upon particular designs and order mass production? How many different types of tank will one need? If a country's foreign and strategic policy is essentially defensive, what are the best technical and doctrinal answers to a mechanized style of threat from abroad? One can easily assemble a like listing for military aircraft. The point is that during this twenty-year period, governments and their military establishments were required to make decisions about military mechanization in the face of profound uncertainty. Moreover, as suggested by the different terms employed, mechanization posed complex challenges, not least to slim defence budgets in a period of severe economic constraint. The three key concepts were armoured warfare, meaning tanks; mechanization, meaning all-terrain tracked (or half-tracked) vehicles, including tanks; and motorization, meaning wheeled vehicles. One might invest expensively in the mobility provided by motorization, but be militarily embarrassed if one's truck-borne troops ran into an enemy's armoured fighting vehicles.

Strategic history was to provide the necessary education on the benefits and hazards of armoured warfare, for example, but as always the context was crucial. There was no single correct doctrine for armoured warfare, but even if there had been, most countries would not be in a position to exploit that knowledge fully, given their local needs and constraints.

France and Britain had been the great exponents of the mechanization of war in 1917–18. Germany decided not to acquire a tank force, a decision that post-war critical analysis recognized to have been a mistake. In the 1920s and into the early 1930s, Britain retained both a technical and a theoretical lead in the development of tanks. There was lively debate led by such controversialists as Brigadier General J. F. C. Fuller and, in good part following his lead for a while, Captain Basil Liddell Hart. British experiments in 1927 with a fully mechanized combat brigade were monitored assiduously by interested foreigners. Unfortunately, the brigade, encouragingly renamed the Experi-mental Armoured Force, was precipitately disbanded in 1928. Despite being on the cutting edge of this possible RMA in the 1920s, the British Army did not sustain its lead in the 1930s. The main reasons were basically mundane: mechanization was expensive; the Army had no high-priority mission that called for a powerful tank force; and it was last in line among the three services for budgetary largesse. Furthermore, with European continental warfare as the Army's fourth, and lowest, priority, it was difficult to make a case for an urgent need to develop mechanized fighting units. Also, controversy persisted between the advocates of two radically different visions of armoured warfare; indeed, of land warfare as a whole. On the one hand, there was the view that tanks should be massed in all-tank, or at least very tank-heavy, formations. On the other hand, the vision of armour as a component, albeit the leading component, of a combined-arms combat team attracted many followers. The latter view undoubtedly was the sounder of the two, and eventually generally was to be accepted by all belligerents, though often more in principle than in practice.

With some difficulty, the French Army fitted mechanization into its existing military doctrine of *la bataille conduite*, or the methodical battle. It agreed with the Germans, and indeed with most of British opinion, that tanks were vulnerable to anti-tank weapons unless they were protected by infantry. Mechanization was not permitted to effect revolutionary change in French doctrine. Given that the French were perfectly content with their defensive doctrine, that they had no intention of attempting bold offensives and that their industrial base was incapable of producing large numbers of tanks rapidly, this conservative approach was understandable.

The German Army, under both Weimar and the Nazis, also did not alter its military doctrine noticeably in order to accommodate mechanization. It had no need to. The ideas expressed in action in 1918, reinforced by the views of Chief of Staff Hans von Seeckt (1920–6) and the conclusions of the rigorous studies conducted by fifty-seven com-mittees in the immediate aftermath of the Great War, were well suited to an army with a large mechanized element. Contrary to legend, the Nazis did not invent a new way of war called *Blitzkrieg*. That attention-getting concept was the invention of a journalist, though the Germans would come to believe that their victories from 1939 until the late autumn of 1941 were attributable to their unique mastery of the secrets of modern warfare. German military doctrine evolved in detail from World War I to World War II, but it did not deviate from a fundamental commitment to a manoeuvrist style. The arrival of tanks and half-tracked infantry carriers simply enabled the elite mechanized elements of the German forces to manoeuvre much more rapidly than previously. What the Germans accomplished against the French and British armies in May and June 1940 did not differ significantly from their intentions and style in 1918. The latter battles witnessed infiltration tactics effected by some genuinely mobile units. The successes of *Blitzkrieg* were highly contextual. In common with the French, albeit following experiments with tank-heavy formations, the Germans decided that their new panzer divisions – the first three of which were activated in 1935 – had to contain all arms, not only tanks. The experience of war was to prove the wisdom of that judgement.

For a while, at least, the Red Army, assisted technically and doctrinally by Germany's illicit experiments in Russia under Weimar, had the boldest doctrine for the offensive exploitation of the mechanization RMA. Soviet theorists developed the idea of 'deep battle'. They envisaged tank-heavy striking forces moving far and fast into the enemy's rear. Alas, Stalin's purge of the officer corps in 1937–9 put a stop to radical ideas for the exploitation of mechanized forces: at least 30,000 out of a total officer corps of 75,000 were executed or imprisoned. When the Germans invaded on 22 June 1941, much of the Red Army was caught out of position geographically and it had far from recovered from the damage to its effectiveness wrought by Stalin in his wholesale military purge.

Air power

Unlike the tank, the half-track and the truck, aircraft possessed a genuinely revolutionary potential. At least, that is what some theorists maintained. The Great War effected an acceleration of technical and tactical advance in the air, such that by 1918 the shape of wars to come seemed to have been revealed. The air power RMA took different forms in different countries. National choices among air power alternatives reflected differences in resources, in geostrategic context and in strength of existing army and navy doctrines of warfare. Following a brief dalliance with the strategic bomber, Nazi Germany decided that it lacked the industrial strength, the technology and really the strategic need to build a long-range bomber force. As a result, the new Luftwaffe constructed an outstanding force of short- and medium-range bombers, as well as dive bombers. However, British and French observers somehow failed to notice the blatant deficiencies of the German bomber force, and especially its unsuitability as an instrument of coercion in the strategic bombing role. In the 1930s, and particularly at the time of Munich in September 1938, both the British and the French governments were intimidated by the latent menace of German air attacks on London and Paris. An important reason why Britain at last elected to say 'no' to Hitler in 1939 was that it believed it had constructed an effective answer to the threat of the 'knockout blow' from the air. Air rearmament favouring fighter aircraft together with the technological marvel of radar, all bound together in the world's first air-defence *system*, promised credibly to neutralize, or at least severely blunt, the potential strategic effect of the German bomber force.

Only two countries in the interwar decades subscribed to the theory, then the doctrine, of strategic air power: Britain and the United States. Germany, France and Russia all took an understandably continental view of air power. They intended that their air forces should assist their armies in what today is known as 'joint' warfare. Just how important aircraft would be as a factor in war on land and at sea remained to be demonstrated convincingly. However, the theorists of strategic air power did not offer a concept of joint warfare, which means land–air or sea–air cooperation. Instead, they maintained that air power alone could win future wars, and that most of the resources expended on armies and navies would be wasted.

The best known, certainly the most coherent, of the theorists of strategic air power was an Italian general, Giulio Douhet. His theory insisted that the first duty of an air force was to win command of the air – the title of his 1921 book (Douhet, 1972) – an accomplishment to be secured by destroying an enemy's air force on the ground. Once the enemy could not threaten from the air, one would be at strategic liberty to assault its civilian population with poison gas, incendiaries and high explosives dropped from planes. As a result of this coercive bombardment, or perhaps just the threat of it, the enemy's public would demand that the government surrender, or at least seek terms for an armistice. Douhet, though, was theorizing prior to the appearance of radar. He assumed that air defence was futile, that 'the bomber will always get through', to quote Stanley Baldwin, Britain's Conservative leader, on 10 November 1932 (Bialer, 1980: 14). Radar changed the military–technical context fundamentally. With its invention and improvement in the 1930s, the theory and practice of strategic bombing were critically challenged. Furthermore, the 1930s saw the appearance of new generations of specialized fighter aircraft whose combat performance was significantly superior to that of bombers. The Americans believed that the heavy bomber could be self-protecting, provided it was abundantly armed with machine-guns and was flown in tight formation. The air war over Germany in 1943 was to prove that they were wrong. It was the experience of World War II that prohibitive losses would be suffered in a strategic air campaign unless air superiority were achieved first. The enemy's air defences had to be defeated before the strategic bomber force could demonstrate its potential.

The statecraft of the 1930s was conducted in the context of air rearmament by each of the great powers, as well as deep uncertainty over the true peril from the air. It is a well-attested fact, however, that fear of strategic bombing played a significant, possibly even a determining, role in British, and hence French, policy over Czechoslovakia in September 1938. Because Britain gave credence to the theory of strategic air power, of victory by the bombing of civilians in cities, it assumed that Germany shared that same belief. However, Germany did not, and, as the events of 1940 were to reveal, it lacked aircraft capable of posing a credible threat of strategic bombing.

In the 1930s, despite dubious evidence from Abyssinia and Spain, modern air power, both offensive and defensive, essentially was an untried, but greatly feared, instrument. 'The shadow of the bomber' hung over international relations. Radar seemed to have tilted the playing field in favour of the defence, but only future strategic history would tell whether that really was the case.

Sea power

It is paradoxical that unjustified fear of the bomber had a powerful strategic effect upon the course of events in the mid- and late 1930s, while the strategically more deadly submarine was not a political factor at all. Admiral Dönitz's U-boat campaign was to be hampered critically by a shortage of long-range boats, as well as by the periodic transparency of its radio-transmitted coded operational messages. Nevertheless, the U-boat made a more substantial strategic contribution to the German war effort in the West than did Göring's Luftwaffe. Submarines were held in such low strategic regard in Britain in the 1930s that in its 1935 Naval Agreement with Germany the latter was permitted to construct a U-boat force up to the level of parity with the Royal Navy's. This agreement, negotiated by Britain without consulting Paris, licensed German naval construction forbidden by Versailles – no submarines for Germany – and rested upon a quite unjustified British complacency over the menace of submarines in future war. The Royal Navy believed that it had the magical elixir that deprived submarines of most of their menace. Sonar (sound navigation and ranging; or, as the British called it, ASDIC – the Anti-Submarine Detection Investigating Committee) had been invented in both Britain and France in 1918, but too late to be employed in the war. Tests and sea trials in the 1920s and 1930s appeared to demonstrate that it had defanged the submarine. So, until war came in 1939 and the operational limitations of sonar were revealed, there was an international consensus among naval experts that the maritime powers had little to fear from the submarine in future warfare.

The air threat to sea power, both naval and commercial, was taken more seriously. But in Britain, still the leading sea power, an influential school of thought believed that ships could defend themselves against air attack. The Fleet Air Arm was relatively neglected by the Navy, as it had also been while under the jurisdiction of the RAF, a control that concluded as late as 1937. Certainly, the Navy had no intention of transferring its capital ship affection from the big guns of battleships and battle-cruisers to aircraft carriers. The latter were held to be fatally vulnerable to attack by enemy surface vessels and land-based aircraft.

The influence on strategic history of Britain's evolving naval context in the 1930s was considerable. If resistance were to be offered to German aggression, Britain was the key strategic player in the second half of the decade because France would not move on its own. Paris knew that it could succeed in a new war with Germany only if Britain was a reliable ally. The maritime dimension to Britain's foreign policy in the 1930s was of fundamental importance yet became ever less permissive of British discretion in policy and strategy. Britain's standing and capabilities as a great power rested in good part upon its sea power. But in the 1930s that sea power was menaced by the reality of an impressive-looking Italian fleet in the Mediterranean, by an aggressive Japan that formally exited the Washington–London naval arms limitation regime in 1936, and by a new German Kriegsmarine which, though still modest in scale, was high in quality, certain to grow larger and, moreover, based perilously close to British home waters. Britain's theory of victory in a future war with Germany, a theory shared with the French, depended utterly upon Allied command of the seas. The Anglo-French intention in 1939 was to draw Germany into a long attritional war wherein the balance of resources would prove decisive, as it had in 1914–18. The theory made strategic sense in its own terms only if the Allies controlled the sea lines of communication essential to their mobilized war effort. British statecraft in the 1930s thus was exercised in a strategic context perceived at the time to contain twin lethal dangers. On the one hand, Britain faced catastrophe from the air. On the other, the diplomatic linking of Germany, Italy and eventually (1940) Japan posed a potentially fatal maritime threat to the integrity of British, and hence Allied, strategy altogether.

Disarmament for land and air forces proved thoroughly non-negotiable at the League's Disarmament Conference in 1932–4. But naval disarmament had registered some major achievements much earlier, principally at a conference held in Washington in 1921–2, and at a long-delayed follow-up conference in London in 1930. The Washington and London treaties imposed a ten-year building 'holiday' on the construction of capital ships (battleships and battle-cruisers), subsequently extended for another five years; a 5:5:3 ratio between Britain, the United States and Japan in capital ship and aircraft-carrier displacement, extended in 1930 to include cruisers, destroyers and submarines; a 35,000-ton limit on capital ship displacement and a 16-inch calibre limit on main armament; and a prohibition on the further fortification of naval bases in the Pacific, with Singapore excluded on British insistence. These were the major provisions, but the full strategic context for the discussion of naval disarmament was complicated by the distinctive geostrategic situations of each country, as well as by the regional interests of such second-tier naval powers as France and Italy. Although the Washington treaty system may have helped head off an impending Anglo-American naval competition, even though that was improbable on financial grounds, it was not particularly sensible for the world's two great maritime democracies to devote extensive effort to their mutual naval disarmament. As an influence upon strategic history, the Washington–London naval disarmament regime of the 1920s and 1930s has been controversial from the time it was signed in 1922 until the present day. Appraised overall, it conceded naval superiority to Japan in East Asian waters. As always is the case with disarmament and arms control, the treaties were negotiable in a politically permissive context, which is to say in 1921–2, and just barely in 1930. But they collapsed when the political context grew threatening.

The relative significance of sea power depends critically upon the strategic importance of leading sea powers. Maritime anxiety had a debilitating effect upon British statecraft in the 1930s, as if 'air panic' were not enough, while American foreign and strategic policy worried more about Japanese misbehaviour than it did German. By geopolitical and geostrategic decree, the military context for American and Japanese hostility had to be maritime. If, one day, Japan's forward moves in East Asia, especially in China, were to be arrested and reversed, the only plausible agent of strategic discipline would have to be the US Navy.

Conclusion

One can claim that there was a mechanization RMA in the interwar decades. That RMA carried the promise of a radical change in both land and air warfare. In addition, though this was not perceived so clearly at the time, the air power version of the RMA contained deadly threats both to surface vessels of all kinds and to the primacy of the battleship and the 'gun line' in main battle fleets.

The strategic history of the 1930s was not especially revealing of military trends. In Spain, Germany's Condor Legion achieved international notoriety with its destruction of Guernica, in particular, but its contribution to the Nationalist victory was modest. Observing the war in Spain, many experts were also convinced that modern anti-tank guns could duel successfully with tanks. Mussolini's air force, which performed poorly in Spain, had been rather more impressive as an aid to the ground forces that invaded Abyssinia in 1936. But what could be learnt from that episode?

Given the high financial cost of mechanization, and the deep uncertainties about what should be bought, for what purpose and when, it is appropriate to have some sympathy for the defence and military planners of the period. They could not know when war would come. With the exception of the Soviet Union after the military purge, every great power made its investment decisions on air power and mechanized ground forces for reasons that made sense locally. Strategic and military culture, the distinctive strategic context for each state and, as always, resource constraints collectively ensured that one size in doctrine and procurement would not fit all demands. So, the mechanization RMA, on land and in the air, was effected differently from country to country.

With only two major exceptions, there was no universally correct doctrine for land warfare with armoured fighting vehicles, or for the most effective use of air power. The two exceptions were, first, the necessity for a combined-arms approach to combat and, second, the universal truth that air power could not be applied effectively until air superiority had been gained. However, these two fundamental principles were by no means self-evident truths to military experts in the 1930s.

The military and strategic meaning of the mechanization RMA would only be revealed by historical experience. The next four chapters are about mechanized warfare waged on the grandest of scales for the most total of political objectives.

Key points

1.   There was a mechanization RMA between the two world wars.
2.   The technologies of mechanization were common to all major states, but their strategic contexts, cultures and therefore investment decisions differed.
3.   There were uncertainties about the roles of tanks that only the experience of war could resolve. Some theorists believed that tanks should be employed all but independently, *en masse*. Others believed that tanks should be a component in a combined-arms team.
4.   When technology is changing fast, doctrine is controversial, money is scarce and the date of a future war is unknowable, it is inherently difficult to make prudent investment choices.
5.   The air power menace to the civilian population, London in particular, frightened British politicians in the 1930s and encouraged the policy of appeasement.
6.   All navies were imprudently confident that in sonar they had a good enough answer to the challenge of the submarine.

Questions

1.   **What were the principal uncertainties that military planners needed to resolve in their decisions on mechanization in the interwar years?**
2.   **What were the main competing ideas on the proper use of tanks?**
3.   **How did technological developments from 1918 to 1940 affect the military promise in different forms of air power?**
4.   **How did strategic and military culture, as well as considerations of geostrategy, influence different countries' choices in mechanization?**

Further reading

U. Bialer *The Shadow of the Bomber: The Fear of Air Attack and British Politics, 1932–1939* (London: Royal Historical Society, 1980).

J. S. Corum *The Roots of Blitzkrieg: Hans von Seeckt and German Military Reform* (Lawrence, KS: University Press of Kansas, 1992).

G. Douhet *The Command of the Air* (New York: Arno Press, 1972).

A. Gat *Fascist and Liberal Visions of War: Fuller, Liddell Hart, Douhet, and Other Modernists* (Oxford: Clarendon Press, 1998).

E. Goldstein and J. Maurer (eds) *The Washington Conference 1921–22: Naval Rivalry, East Asian Stability and the Road to Pearl Harbor* (London: Frank Cass, 1994).

J. P. Harris *Men, Ideas, and Tanks: British Military Thought and Armoured Forces, 1903–1939* (Manchester: Manchester University Press, 1995).

R. W. Harrison *The Russian Way of War: Operational Art, 1904–1940* (Lawrence, KS: University Press of Kansas, 2001).

R. G. Kaufman *Arms Control during the Pre-nuclear Era: The United States and Naval Limitation between the Two World Wars* (New York: Columbia University Press, 1990).

E. Kiesling *Arming against Hitler: France and the Limits of Military Planning* (Lawrence, KS: University Press of Kansas, 1996).

M. Knox and W. Murray (eds) *The Dynamics of Military Revolution, 1300–2050* (Cambridge: Cambridge University Press, 2001).

T. G. Mahnken *Uncovering Ways of War: US Intelligence and Foreign Military Innovation, 1918–1941* (Ithaca, NY: Cornell University Press, 2002).

W. Murray and A. R. Millett (eds) *Military Innovation in the Interwar Period* (Cambridge: Cambridge University Press, 1996).

H. R. Winton and D. R. Mets (eds) *The Challenge of Change: Military Institutions and New Realities, 1918–1941* (Lincoln, NE: University of Nebraska Press, 2000).

10 World War II in Europe, I

The structure and course of total war

Reader's guide: Casualties. The wars that comprised World War II. A strategic narrative of the war. The Holocaust.

Introduction: total war

The actuality or the threat of war was by far the most important influence on international relations in the twentieth century. Its outcomes reshaped societies and enforced regime changes, added and deleted states to and from the geopolitical map, and accelerated the long process of global decolonization. Warfare, its memories, legends and consequences of all kinds, virtually defined the European experience in the century. Two total wars dominated the first fifty years, while the threat of a potentially total nuclear war overhung, even dominated, all but ten of the second.

World War II brought casualty figures to new heights. If one includes the Sino-Japanese War that opened in earnest in 1937, the total death toll in the war was of the order of 53.5 million. That figure is of course suspect in detail, but it is reliable as to order of magnitude. Whereas in 1914–18 some 65 million men were mobilized for military duty, in 1939–45 the comparable figure was 105 million, a fraction of which were women. Also, unusually in modern times, the civilian death toll exceeded the military, and by a wide margin (perhaps 36.5 million to 17 million) (see Table 10.1) There were three principal reasons why this was so. First, the growing maturity of air power guaranteed that civilians would be targets, both inadvertently as collateral damage and intentionally as required by the new doctrine of seeking victory, or at least to coerce, by strategic air power. Second, everywhere, even eventually in Germany following the defeat at Stalingrad in the winter of 1942–3, the war was explained and conducted as a 'people's war': everybody was at war. Since economic blockade and aerial bombing placed civilians on the front line, the vital legal distinction between combatants and non-combatants was eroded almost into oblivion. However, the third reason for the appalling civilian death toll resides in the realm of the ideological dimension to national culture. Nazi Germany set out to wage a war of annihilation against its Slav neighbours to the east and against the whole Jewish population of Europe. Naturally, that intention could be pursued only in stages, as opportunities permitted. In 1939, most of Europe's Jews

Table 10.1 Casualties in World War II

	Total forces mobilized (million)	Military dead	Military wounded	Civilian dead
United States	14.9	292,100	571,822	Negligible
United Kingdom	6.2	397,762	475,000	65,000
France	6.0	210,671	400,000	108,000
Soviet Union	25.0	9,500,000	16,000,000	17,500,000
China	6–10	500,000	1,700,000	1,000,000
Germany	12.5	2,850,000	7,250,000	500,000
Italy	4.5	77,500	120,000	40–100,000
Japan	7.4	1,506,000	500,000	300,000
All Others	20.0	1,500,000	No estimate	14–17,000,000
Total	105.0	16,834,033	No estimate	36,573,000

Principal source: Dupuy and Dupuy, 1993: 1309, with some estimates adjusted in light of more recent evidence

were not yet under German control, but that situation had changed dramatically by early 1942. The Holocaust was a crime waiting to be committed, when circumstance allowed. It could be translated from German culture to German policy only as a consequence of military success.

The Holocaust is justly infamous, but mass murder of the innocent was also a commonplace practice by the Japanese Army in China. To return to the German war in the East, the law of war was a dead letter, and officially so. German soldiers were assured of immunity from prosecution for war crimes for any death, injury or damage they inflicted upon enemy civilians. This release from normal restraints contrasted sharply with the Wehrmacht's ferocious combat discipline. Because of the total – which is to say cultural and social – character of the Russo-German War of 1941–5, there was no sure safety in surrender or in subsequent POW status. On the one hand, prisoners frequently were not taken at all; while on the other, the POW survival rate was not impressive. The German Army and the Waffen SS did not usually kill their Russian prisoners directly; they simply neglected to feed or house them adequately, if at all. Of the 3 million Russian POWs taken in 1941–2, 2 million were allowed to starve to death or die of exposure. Overall, only 2.4 million of the Russian POWs held by the Germans in the war survived out of a grand total of 5.7 million. Germany's domestic labour shortage in industry and agriculture became increasingly chronic after 1941–2, and, belatedly, it was recognized that the POW catch was a convenient, free and expendable source of labour, though one that was always a cause of security and racial– cultural anxiety. Much as Spartans feared revolt by their helot slaves, so Germans were uneasy at the prospect, then the reality, of the Reich being inundated by millions of 'racially inferior' slave labourers.

In an obvious sense, World War II was a round two: it was Germany's War of Revenge; unfinished national business. But it was much more than that, too: 1939–45 was not just a continuation of 1914–18, following the twenty-one-year time-out of an armistice. First, it was much more of a total war. This was the result of its being ideological to a degree not approached in 1914–18. Also, totality became more possible as the instruments and practices of central state control improved. When the whole of society is regarded as a resource for the war effort, it follows logically that civilians and their property become legitimate targets for assault, both direct and indirect. And that, of course, is before one even considers the distinctively German policy of genocide. In 1914–18 the armies in the West were essentially stationary, a condition which permitted minimal interface with enemy civilians. It is true that there was much mobility in the warfare in the East, but those campaigns, though conducted with great brutality fed by racial prejudice on the German side, were not intended to have genocidal effect. The mechanization of warfare by 1939, and its subsequent immense geographical expansion, had the inevitable consequence of granting the major combatants direct access to enemy civilians on a scale radically greater than in 1914–18. Performance followed opportunity, as the British practice of indiscriminate 'area' (i.e., civilian urban area) bombing and Germany's genocidal endeavours in the East demonstrated to malign perfection. (One must hasten to add that the Royal Air Force's 'area' bombing was a forced choice: British bombers at night were technically incapable of precision targeting, at least until late in the war.)

It is standard practice and convenient to refer to World War II in the singular. But 1939–45 witnessed several wars, each influencing the others to a greater or lesser degree. Thematic or geographically focused analysis is attractive, but it has the limitation of obscuring the historical reality that strategic behaviour in all the wars within the war occurred simultaneously. If one is to grasp the problems of the time as they had to be approached at that time, one should not lose touch with the binding thread of historical narrative. The plan of attack on World War II adopted here is to open with a broadly chronological treatment of the course of the war in Europe, keyed to explanation of the structure of the conflict. The discussion here sets the scene for an analytical examination in Chapter 11 of what the war was about, how it was fought and why Germany lost. Chapters 12 and 13 are then devoted to the conflict in the Pacific and East Asia, and to the connections between what were, in reality, two separate struggles.

The structure of the war

Hitler's Third Reich was a state made for war. It was to be the historic vehicle that its charismatic founder intended to employ to deliver world dominion to the Germanic race. The exact timing of the succession of wars that he envisaged was uncertain, but the purpose was not. In October 1936, Germany launched a Four-Year Plan of economic mobilization, the mission of which was explained unambiguously by its highly incompetent director, Hermann Göring. In his words, the task of the plan was 'preparing the German economy for total war' (Bessel, 2004: 48). Hitler concluded his Memorandum on the plan with these demands: 'I. The German Army must be operational within four years. II. The German Army must be prepared for war within four years' (Bessel, 2004: 49). Should any doubt remain as to Hitler's intentions, in a now notorious gathering of the leaders of each of the armed services of the Reich on 5 November 1937, he explained explicitly that Germany would have to go to war by 1943–5 in order to solve its deficiency in 'living space' (Snyder, 1981: 263–73). Germany needed to be economically self-sufficient, which is to say blockade-proof. Hitler recognized that he was running a race between Germany's readiness to wage war in order to implement his dreams of Aryan domination and the response time of his intended victims.

World War II was nothing if not complex, with combat on three continents and on land, at sea and in the air. However, the conflict did have an almost elegant simplicity in its essential course and structure. The conflicts in Europe and Asia were separate wars, though they influenced each other critically, even decisively, at times. For the leading example of the latter, Japan's desperately ill-judged gamble in attacking the US Navy at Pearl Harbor on 7 December 1941 triggered Hitler's gratuitous declaration of war on the United States four days later. It is true that he had promised Tokyo that he would take that step should Japan go to war with the United States, but since when were political promises sacred to the Führer? It is a revealing fact that the wars in Europe and Asia can be treated as distinct, albeit connected, phenomena. The two contests were gigantic siege operations. The war against Germany was continental, the one against Japan maritime, and both were increasingly prosecuted in the air.

Germany's territorial imperium expanded for three years; there was a period of equilibrium; and then it contracted for two years. If the interwar years divide neatly into two distinctive periods, so does the war in Europe. From September 1939 until July 1943, Germany held the initiative and the Third Reich expanded to the point where nearly all of continental Europe, from the Pyrenees to the Volga, was either conquered or dominated. The advance was halted in November 1942; and after July 1943 the Germans were forced back. Thereafter, the military narrative of Germany's war was one of irregular, but inexorable, retreat. It would be an exaggeration to claim that Stalingrad and Kursk were the decisive battles of the war, the battles which decided the ultimate outcome, but there can be no doubt that they serve as two of the clearest markers in all of military history of a definitive shift of strategic fortune and momentum. Following, first, the encirclement of the German Sixth Army on the Volga between 19 and 23 November 1942 and its formal surrender on 31 January 1943, and, second, the defeat of the great armoured offensive at Kursk between 5 and 16 July 1943, German soldiers were going nowhere other than home, if they were fortunate.

There can be no doubt that Hitler passed what one might call 'the Clausewitz test' with flying colours in 1939. As *On War* insists, 'The first, the supreme, the most far-reaching act of judgement that the statesman and commander have to make is to establish by that test [of a war as an instrument of policy] the kind of war on which they are embarking, neither mistaking it for, nor trying to turn it into, something that is alien to its nature' (Clausewitz, 1976: 89). When Hitler invaded Poland on 1 September 1939, he knew that he was embarking upon his long-visualized and intended bid for world conquest. Although he would act opportunistically, improvise when necessary, and react to surprising events, his course was set and his goal was fixed. He would have only one chance in his lifetime to realize his dream of a racially pure Germanic empire. It was a case of victory or destruction. Should Germany fail, its bloodied and vengeful victims would neither be merciful in victory nor leave Germany in any condition to make a second attempt. There would be no repeat of the peace settlement of 1919.

Historians have debated whether Hitler planned a series of short wars, with victory in each strengthening the Reich for the next encounter, or whether he anticipated a single, great, protracted conflict. Naturally, he preferred the former, but strategic history dealt him the latter. Ever alert to the lessons of 1914–18, for a while he met with success in avoiding the enervating problems of war on more than one front at a time. He was surprised, but not alarmed, by the decision of Britain and France to declare war over

Poland, a country that they were in no position to assist militarily. In confident and accurate expectation of Anglo-French impotence, Stalin had cut a deal with Hitler on 23 August 1939 which made the Soviet Union an active participant in, and beneficiary of, Germany's conquest of Poland. From 1939 to 1941, Moscow chose collaboration rather than what would most probably have been a lonely and hopeless path of resistance.

Hitler was a statesman in a hurry. He had to stay ahead of the health problems, real and imagined, that threatened his own mortality as well as the willingness and ability of others to mobilize to oppose him. As a consequence, he knew that his ideal course of fighting wars one at a time against isolated enemies might be impossible. And so it proved. Britain and France did not fight directly for Poland, but neither did they seek to make peace. However, with his new Soviet alliance providing tolerable security for Germany in the East, after Poland Hitler enjoyed a strategic luxury denied his predecessors in 1914. He could fight a one-front war in the West and, by destroying France and possibly neutralizing Britain as a consequence, he would thereby set up the Soviet Union for the isolated assault that was the most necessary step on his march to continental, and later world, empire. But what happened in 1940–1 was that Germany's inability to conclude its war with maritime Britain obliged it to open the next phase of conquest, against the Soviet Union, in the strategic context of a greatly undesired multi-front war. Germany certainly did not intend to begin a general world war on 1 September 1939, and indeed it did not do so, but the consequences of the short, victorious war against Poland were ultimately to prove fatal for Hitler's dreams of empire. Strategic history is not linear; its course is unpredictable.

The strategic history of the war in Europe is one of paradox. In its three years of typically successful aggression, until October 1942, Germany sowed the seeds, set the stage, for its own eventual demise. This is not to claim that Germany could not still have won after October 1942, but it is to suggest strongly that it had overreached with its available and mobilizable assets. Hitler's Reich behaved like a reckless gambler, determined to play either to win all or to lose all. An important concept in Clausewitz's writing is the idea of 'the culminating point of victory' (Clausewitz, 1976: 566–73). Somewhere on the road to Stalingrad, German arms passed that point. The deeper they penetrated into Russia, the weaker they became. This is known as the loss of strength gradient (Boulding, 1962: 245–7): military power diminishes with distance. Unfortunately for German soldiers, their military system was characteristically casual about logistics, while Hitler's aim of conquest could accept no recognition of practical material limits. Germany's war in the East was one from which it could not withdraw, politically, ideologically or militarily, even had Stalin offered it the opportunity to do so.

The Russo-German War was the real World War II in Europe. Everything else that occurred was secondary to that main event. The principal axis of Germany's march of conquest was eastwards. That march was not an opportunistic lunge during a brief window of strategic opportunity; rather, it was the central purpose of the entire Nazi enterprise. To understand the structure and dynamics of World War II, one has to grasp the fact that for Hitler the realization of his vision of a great racial state mandated the destruction of the Soviet Union. It can be difficult for British and American commentators to accept the full implications of this historical reality. Although blood was spilt in abundance all around Europe, and despite Germany's sometimes reluctant dispersion of effort, especially to the Mediterranean theatre, the focus was always in the East. As one historian reminds us, 'More than 80 per cent of all combat during World War II took place on the Eastern Front. The Germans suffered in excess of 90 per cent of their total war losses on the Eastern Front . . . ; 10 million dead, wounded, missing or captured' (Roberts, 2002: 9). This is not to suggest that other military campaigns did not matter, but they mattered primarily for their impact upon the course of the struggle in the East. The strategic logic is inescapable. Germany had to be defeated utterly, since a compromise peace with Hitler was neither possible nor desirable, and that defeat could be imposed on the necessary scale only in the East. The centre of gravity of the Third Reich, apart from the Führer himself, was the main body of the army. From 1941 until the end of the war that was always on the Eastern Front. This fact parallels the situation in World War I. In order to defeat Germany from 1914 to 1918, there was no alternative to beating its principal concentration of fighting power, which in that war was always on the Western Front.

The text now proceeds chronologically, an approach the merits of which are easily lost if one analyses thematically or geographically. It is important to attempt to understand the flow of events and their consequences as they occurred at the time.

The course of the war

1939: first moves

The war should have begun in 1938. That had been Hitler's intention, and as late as 1945 he was convinced that all would have been well for his grand design for conquest had he not been outmanoeuvred by British Prime Minister Neville Chamberlain at Munich. As a result, the war had to be postponed to 1939, with the excuse shifted from Czechoslovakia to Poland. The delay and change of country target allowed all parties a further year to rearm, but, more pertinently, it produced a critical political mobilization in Britain and France. Germany's seizure of the ethnically non-German remainder of Czechoslovakia in March set the stage for a decision for war by the Western powers next time. And next time was expected to be Poland, especially over the issue of the Polish 'corridor' to the sea and the ethnically largely German port of Danzig granted to Warsaw by Versailles. With the security of its pact with the Soviet Union in its pocket after 23 August, Germany duly destroyed the Polish state and its armed forces in a five-week campaign, from 1 September until 6 October, when Polish resistance ceased. There was war at sea, as Hitler's small U-boat arm made its modest presence felt, and also some action in the air. Britain's Royal Air Force (RAF) discovered that its medium-bomber force was nowhere near functioning as a great deterrent and, indeed, could attack Germany in daylight only at the cost of suicidal losses. Moreover, RAF bombers lacked the numbers, the range, the navigation aids and the ordnance to do Germany much damage.

Hitler toyed seriously with the notion of swinging the fifty-four divisions (and the Luftwaffe) with which he had subdued Poland in September westwards for a late autumn campaign against France and Britain. He was, however, dissuaded from such a move by military advisers who anticipated that France would be a much tougher opponent than Poland, requiring more time to subdue. It was judged to be too late in the year to attack. In addition, the German military discovered much about their forces' performance in Poland which a process of ruthless self-criticism indicated was in urgent need of improvement. Poland in 1939 had been the first combat outing for the new-model Wehrmacht.

But if the somewhat ragged German military triumph demonstrated the need to improve combat effectiveness, especially against a foe more formidable than the Poles, the Soviet Red Army seemed determined to show just how poorly a great power could perform strategically. On 30 November 1939, Soviet forces invaded Finland, but to the embarrassment of Moscow those forces were humiliated and repulsed. In fact, diminutive Finland managed to resist Soviet aggression all through the winter of 1939–40, only surrendering on 12 March 1940. What was strategically significant about Stalin's war on Finland was not its eventual outcome, which was certain to favour Moscow, but rather the negative conclusion that all interested observers drew about the competence of the Red Army.

1940: Germany's 'happy time'

The year 1940 registered the indecisive end of the first phase of what plainly had the potential to become a long war. Hitler occupied Denmark and Norway in April, and launched his great offensive in the West on 10 May with 123 divisions (10 panzer). What the Kaiser's army could not accomplish in over four years from 1914 to 1918, Hitler's new Wehrmacht achieved in six weeks. France and Germany signed an armistice on 22 June. Demonstrating a modern, highly mobile version of their long-standing combined-arms doctrine, the Germans outflanked the Maginot Line and cut in behind the Anglo-French mobile forces which had advanced conveniently, if incautiously, into Belgium, as their standard plan required. The stunning German operational success was hardly the product of military genius, let alone of some miraculous new formula for victory known as *Blitzkrieg*. Rather, it was primarily the result of enemy operational mistakes and vastly superior German training. The deadly surprise thrust through the Ardennes was not the brainchild of Erich von Manstein or Adolf Hitler, though both claimed the credit. Instead, the principal author of the bold move was none other than Germany's Army Chief of Staff, the compliant Franz Halder. Both Manstein and Hitler had a more limited vision of the scope for operational victory in this instance than did Halder.

Some 226,000 men of the British Expeditionary Force (BEF) and 112,000 French and Belgian soldiers were able to escape from the only port open to them, Dunkirk, in what was close to a strategic miracle effected between 26 May and 4 June. The panzers could have closed the port of Dunkirk to the retreating Allied forces, but they were restrained by the famous 'halt' order until 28 May. Typically, Hitler is blamed for the order, but the truth is that it was issued by the Commander-in-Chief, West, Field Marshal Gerd von Rundstedt, and was only endorsed by the Führer. There is little doubt that it saved the BEF. The British Army lost all of its heavy equipment, but it saved itself to fight again. Almost as much to the point, the British escape prevented a military catastrophe of a character that Winston Churchill most probably could not have survived as Prime Minister. That is not a trivial point. Had the British Army gone into the POW bag, Germany could well have found itself in the strategically attractive position of being able to dictate the terms of a favourable armistice to London. Not all of Churchill's cabinet colleagues were convinced that Britain should continue the struggle, given the obvious absence of any plausible theory of victory in the summer of 1940.

The strategic history of the remainder of 1940 is the story of a Western Front that Hitler could not close down, despite his Continental triumphs. He waited through the summer for British signals of willingness to cut a deal, but such signals did not appear. The strategic challenge now was either to apply sufficient coercive pressure to change British minds in favour of an accommodation or to launch an invasion and settle the matter definitively. Visible invasion preparations were made, and Göring's Luftwaffe began its campaign to defeat the RAF. But the Luftwaffe followed up its failure to blockade and destroy the BEF at Dunkirk, as Göring had promised Hitler, with an inability to beat RAF Fighter Command and its integrated, radar-vectored air-defence system in August and September. Thanks to German operational errors, too little concentration of effort, insufficient maintenance of purpose, the technical limitations of Luftwaffe aircraft, unfriendly British geography, and an RAF Fighter Command that was both well commanded and larger than German intelligence had estimated, Germany lost the attritional struggle that came to be known as the Battle of Britain. With good reason, Hitler was profoundly uneasy at the prospect of hazarding his reputation and his thus far all-victorious land force on a decidedly risky amphibious venture. As a consequence, he was not at all displeased to be able to hold the launching of the invasion hostage to the defeat of the RAF. Since that did not occur, and it was growing too late in the year for a cross-Channel invasion, the final settlement of accounts with Britain was deferred to some time in the future, well into 1941 at least. Except, of course, that the Führer had other, much greater, plans for 1941.

One needs to look across the Atlantic for the principal, albeit longer-term, strategic consequence of Germany's failure to conclude its war in the West in 1940. America was in no way ready to enter the war in Europe in 1940. But by remaining a belligerent, albeit undeniably a strategically ineffective one, Britain ensured that if and when the United States did join the war, it would be able to project its power over, and eventually into, continental Europe. Without Britain, the US armed forces would have been unable to reach Hitler's continental fortress. War is waged with logistics; they are the arbiter of strategic opportunity. British territory was literally essential if Americans were to be able to apply their mobilizable power. In 1940, Britain's main strategic contribution to the course and outcome of the war as a whole simply took the form of remaining lightly active within it. Britain itself could not create and challenge Germany with a Western Front, but it could, and did, enable such a front to be forged in due course. It is worth mentioning that one result of Italy rushing to the aid of the victor on 10 June 1940 was that it presented the British Army with an enemy it could beat, and it enabled British forces at least to be active in the Mediterranean, far from Germany's military centre of gravity.

1941: the real war

The great war within the war of 1939–45 was launched by Germany on 22 June 1941. The Wehrmacht plunged into the Soviet Union with 3.6 million men in 145 divisions, comprising 102 infantry, 19 panzer, 14 motorized, 1 cavalry and 9 for line of communications security. Allies (Romania, Hungary and Finland) provided a further 37 divisions amounting to 705,000 men. In June 1941 the German Army had a total order of battle of

205 divisions, but 60 were not available for the war in the East: 38 were deployed in France, 12 in Norway, 1 in Denmark, 7 in the Balkans and 1 in North Africa.

This was to be the war of decision for Germany. It is true that Hitler chose to wage war on two fronts (actually three, given the Mediterranean complications wished on him by Mussolini), but the unfinished strategic business with Britain should not matter for long, given the near-universal expectation of swift victory in the East. Planning for the attack on Russia began in July 1940, well before the outcome of the Battle of Britain was known. When Russia was defeated, it was reasoned, Britain's strategic position as an active belligerent would be hopeless. Traditionally, Britain required a 'Continental sword' to complement its maritime power. In 1940, Britain's French sword had snapped, while in mid-1941 Hitler, and nearly everybody else, expected its *de facto* Soviet sword to snap also. At that time the United States was not a strategic factor of much signifi-cance, and Germany's conquest of Russia would pose an Anglo-American alliance a strategic challenge beyond their joint ability to meet.

Some claim that the German Army and Air Force were delayed from launching Operation Barbarossa, the invasion of Russia, for perhaps a month in May 1941 by the need to rescue Italy from an unfolding strategic disaster in Greece, as well as in North Africa: 15 May had been the date chosen for the invasion. Hitler did not much care strategically about the Mediterranean, but he did care about the reputation for military competence of his Italian ally, and he felt at least some sense of personal obligation to his fellow dictator. Content to stave off disaster in the desert for Italy, as well as humili-ation in the Balkans, where Hitler had at least one truly vital interest, the oil field at Ploesti in Romania, the Führer was obliged to settle for containment of his open-ended British problem. Britain would be coerced by bombing and by the maritime blockade enforced by Dönitz's U-boats. However, the main event, the one to which all other strands of the conflict would be subordinate, was the conquest of Russia.

For all its excellence as a fighting machine, the German Army was traditionally weak in the fields of intelligence and logistics. Superior training, class-leading doctrine, high morale, and tactical and operational skills were what really counted in German military estimation. Staff training emphasized the overriding importance of the operational concept. Intelligence on the enemy was somewhat discounted, because apart from its often inherent uncertainty, a German Army with the initiative would deny the foe the opportunity to recover from initial defeats and regroup in order to implement its own plans. As for logistical problems, while they could slow or even halt offensive action for a while, as in 1914, 1918 and even 1940, it was an item of faith that improvised solutions somehow would always be found. Logistical calculation tended to fade into a vague realm of hope, even among the supposedly highly professional German General Staff. However, a swift glance at a map of Eastern Europe reveals that from the perspective of an invader from the west, Russia is shaped like an ever-widening funnel. The deeper an invader plunges into Russia, the wider becomes the battle space. An invading army of 145 German divisions is a mighty concentration of power, but if that army takes heavy losses and is committed to combat from Leningrad on the Baltic to the foothills of the Caucasus, it readily becomes apparent that it is likely to be far too small for its operational tasks.

The strategic story of 1941 is keyed to a deadly lack of German operational focus. The Soviet Union was to be defeated in a single campaign, but how and where should that be achieved? And how long might it take? The German Army advanced on three diverging axes: Army Group North swept through the former Baltic States, towards Leningrad; Army Group Centre moved towards Moscow, via Minsk and, in due course, Smolensk; Army Group South speared into the Ukraine. But which thrust had priority? Did any of them? It is relevant to note that German military intelligence – almost an oxymoron – estimated on 22 June 1941 a total Red Army strength of approximately 240 divisions and division equivalents in all theatres. That figure was at least fifty divisions too low (Boog *et al.*, 1998), with current research suggesting a Soviet order of battle of 303 divisions (Tucker, 2004: 84). By the time that the German forces in Stalingrad surrendered, on 31 January 1943, the Red Army had an order of battle of an incredible 581 divisions, a figure which grew to 603 by 1 December that year. However, it must be emphasized that all divisions were more or less below their authorized strength, and that Soviet divisions were smaller than German. But German intelligence had absolutely no detailed information on the location or production capability of the most vital elements of Soviet defence industry. Of course, if one is supremely confident of achieving complete military victory in a ten- to fourteen-week summer campaign, the potential size and equipment holdings of the Red Army are not matters for concern.

The strategic story of 1941 in the East was one of apparent triumph, but concluding with near catastrophe. The Wehrmacht was successful everywhere, at least up to a point. The Red Army was caught in mid-reorganization and incomplete redeployment forward. Stalin, its political master, had refused to believe the abundant intelligence about the impending German attack. The Red Air Force was all but destroyed on the ground on day one as an effective fighting force. Nevertheless, despite securing Russian POWs by the million, and advancing hundreds of miles on each axis, the summer passed without German registration of decisive victory.

The German theory of strategic victory was identical to Napoleon's in 1812. Both Napoleon and Hitler foresaw defeat of Russia by means of great envelopments of Russia's armies close to the frontier, with the Russian Army expected to collapse as a consequence. The theory was as unsound in 1941 as it had been in 1812. Leningrad was not taken. The drive on Moscow was slowed and then stopped, to allow for an opportunistic swing south by the panzers of Army Group Centre to assist Army Group South around Kiev. In the late summer the Germans could have taken Moscow with relative ease, had they concentrated upon it as the overriding operational goal. As it was, the large commitments in the north and the south, the wear and tear on mechanized and motorized forces imposed by the unprecedented distances that had to be travelled, the heavy casualties suffered in the fighting and the ever-critical fuel situation translated into an eventual bid for Moscow that was conducted by a Wehrmacht that was too weary, too battered, too small and was attacking too late in the year. The Germans had already lost 400,000 men by the end of August, a figure that grew to the insupportable level of 743,000 by the end of November. That number needs to be considered in the context of the Eastern Army's total average strength of 3.5 million.

Hitler was always nervous of the road to Moscow. He was acutely aware of Napoleon's dilemma once the Emperor had occupied the city. Was Moscow that important? The German military high command was firmly convinced that, notwithstanding the Führer's enthusiasm for the industrial and historical significance of Leningrad, and the resources of the Ukraine and the Caucasus, the only way to defeat the Soviet Union rapidly was by taking Moscow. After all, it was the national capital, it had priceless political symbolic value, it was the hub of Russian rail communications, and it was an industrial centre with an importance second to none. Eventually, therefore, the Germans did launch a concentrated drive on the city. Codenamed Operation Typhoon, it opened on 1 October 1941. Unfortunately for the Wehrmacht, though gravely wounded in June, July and August, by the autumn the Red Army had begun to recover its poise. The Russians mobilized fresh armies to replace those destroyed in the summer and they were ultimately able to redeploy most of their Siberian divisions from the Far Eastern provinces, where they had been watching, and deterring attack by, Japan's Kwantung Army. The Russians had also been given the time to construct serious lines of fortification to protect their capital, and the Russian winter was beginning in earnest. On the night of 4 December the temperature on the approaches to Moscow fell to –25°F.

The net result of these competing strategic efforts was that somewhere between Smolensk and Moscow the German attack, indeed the German way of manoeuvre warfare, ran out of steam as well as ideas. Advance units of Army Group Centre were literally in Moscow's suburbs, on the tram route, when on 5 December they were hit by the first major Soviet counter-offensive of the war. The result was a massive German defeat, nearly a disastrous rout. The Battle for Moscow in November, December and January 1941–2 was nothing short of a titanic struggle. As many as 7 million soldiers from both sides participated. In this battle alone, Soviet fatalities numbered some 926,000, a figure close to the British Empire total for 1914–18. This was war on a scale unmatched, indeed unmatchable, in any other theatre. The German Army survived, though barely. It retreated some way, while at Hitler's insistence it held its ground where it could. The Führer took over operational command of the Army, so contemptuous was he of the competence, lack of determination and deficient spirit of his generals.

The one-year, one-campaign bid for total victory in the East had failed dismally. And it had failed at a cost in experienced manpower as well as machines that could not be made good. The German Army of Operation Barbarossa was always walking wounded after the protracted Battle for Moscow. Among its problems, erroneous strategy and the Russian climate merit special notice. As noted already, German strategy intended to win the war by so damaging the Red Army in great battles of encirclement close to the frontier that the Russians would collapse as a coherent fighting force. The Red Army did suffer great damage, but it did not collapse. With respect to the Russian climate, a recent study claims that 'The weather did not defeat the Germans: their failure to plan for it did' (Megargee, 2006: 103).

1942: the tipping point

The year 1942 had been heralded by both good and bad news for Germany. The bad news has just been outlined: Russia was still in the field, fighting. But Germany had acquired a maritime ally of the first rank. Hitler was delighted by the Japanese attack on the Americans in Hawaii and the Philippines. Indeed, so delighted was he that he chose to declare war on the United States on 11 December. He calculated that the Japanese would keep America occupied strategically for a long time to come, while Japan would prove to be both the naval ally Germany needed and a potentially lethal continental threat to the Soviet Union in Asia. Sad to say for Germany, President Roosevelt adhered to a policy principle he had already agreed with the British of defeating Germany first. However, one must record the fact that in practice in 1942 American military resources of all kinds, as they were mobilized, headed in at least as great quantities for the Pacific theatre as they did towards Europe. The reasons for this were straightforward. In the Pacific, strategic opportunity knocked and there was a combat job of immediate significance to be done in order to slow, arrest and reverse Japan's forward surge. In Europe, by contrast, there was no near-term military task for American forces to perform.

In broad strategic terms, 1942 was the high-water mark for the Axis, as well as the year which provided unmistakeable evidence that Berlin and Tokyo had far exceeded Clausewitz's 'culminating point of victory'. In Russia, Stalin foolishly insisted on continuing the Great Winter Offensive, even to, and beyond, the point of the exhaustion of current Red Army reserves. In due course, the Germans counter-attacked a much weakened Red Army and then were at liberty to plan and execute their grand campaign design for the year. Chastened by the near catastrophe in the Battle for Moscow, Hitler elected to pursue a less direct approach. Codenamed Operation Blau, the principal German thrust in 1942 would be to the south, specifically to secure the oil fields at Grozny and eventually at Baku on the Caspian Sea. This caught the Russians by surprise: they had expected a renewal of the attack on Moscow. It would not be the last time they were wrong-footed by Hitler's irregular, not to say eccentric, operational choices. So, while still besieging Leningrad and watching the road to Moscow, the Germans committed some of their most potent formations to drive east and south. The result, as history records, was the disaster at Stalingrad and a near disaster for the German forces that had penetrated as far south as the foothills of the Caucasus.

The Russians fought hard, when eventually they did stand and fight, and the distances were a logistical nightmare for the Germans. But the German defeats in Russia in late 1942 were mainly the product of their own operational incompetence. The German Army in the summer of 1942 was probably still strong enough to secure a major objective in the south, had it only been concentrated for the task. In other words, the Germans could have taken Stalingrad, which the Sixth Army first reached as early as 19 August. Similarly, they could have forced their way through the relatively modest opposition to seize and hold the critical oil fields at Maikop and Grozny. By and large, Russian forces retreated rather than contested every foot of ground in 1942. The Germans were lured to overreach themselves logistically. What the Germans could not do was seize and hold both the Caucasian oil fields and Stalingrad on the Volga *and* protect the long lines of communication to, and the flanks of, these hugely divergent objectives. They needed to choose. On 19 July, just three weeks after launching Operation Blau, Hitler decided that the forces advancing towards objectives in the Caucasus, 600 miles from their start line, should detach six divisions (three infantry, two motorized infantry and one panzer) to assist the Sixth Army in its none too potent drive on Stalingrad. Murray and Millett argue that Caucasian oil was logistically beyond German grasp (Murray and Millett, 2000: 278–83). What cannot be contested is that Hitler's belated weakening of the attack to the south condemned that venture to failure and possible disaster, while the slow-moving approach to Stalingrad still would not be strong enough to ensure success.

Hitler was not a war leader to make operational choices between desirable goals. He favoured multiple ambitious tasks that translated militarily into a reckless dispersal of effort. So, 1942 turned out to be something of an operational replay of 1941. A still mighty German Army attempted to accomplish too much, in too many divergent directions, for its strength. The strategic difference was that by late 1942 the Russian enemy had recovered its breath, learnt much about the modern trade of warfare from its earlier mistakes and from close study of German practice, and had mobilized on a scale unanticipated by the Germans. In short, the strategic context was growing ever less permissive of German strategic and operational errors.

Also in 1942, from a necessarily slow beginning, the United States was establishing what must become a major land and air presence in the European theatre; the Italo-German situation in North Africa proceeded from bad to worse; Germany at home was now under serious aerial bombardment; and its Japanese ally had lost the strategic initiative with its defeat at Midway on 4–6 June. But at the end of 1942 Germany still remained formidable. Its troops stood near the Volga, though admittedly they were encircled. The Luftwaffe, though sorely weakened by its heroic efforts to resupply the Sixth Army at Stalingrad, was still very much in business. And the Kriegsmarine, the U-boat arm in particular, had had a strategically excellent year for Germany: 1942 was its second 'happy time', with 1940 having been the first. But the tide of war was turning, and possibly might have turned already. Irrespective of whether that fact was fully recognized in Berlin, 1943 was to witness Germany's final throw of the dice in the hope of shifting the military momentum on the Eastern Front.

1943: the final throw and reversal

Strategically appraised, 1943 was a year of preparation for the reckoning that would come due in 1944. The latter year saw the collapse of Germany's strategic position on all fronts except, perhaps, the Italian. In 1943, Hitler assembled every available new Panther and Tiger tank in order to deliver crushing pincer blows to a Red Army that had suffered more than a million casualties in the Stalingrad campaign. In fact, he delayed the offensive, codenamed Citadel, by at least six weeks to allow more time for new tank deliveries. The Red Army was temporarily exhausted. With much operational dexterity, and a new armoured force, the Germans aspired to win a great victory. There was a large bulge in the Soviet line around the city of Kursk which seemed to beg to be pinched off by complementary assaults from north and south. Given Soviet spies, poor German operational security and the unmistakeable attraction of the salient, it is scarcely surprising that the Russians had detailed foreknowledge of the Kursk offensive. They prepared defences in great depth, including no fewer than six defensive belts and massed armoured reserves to meet such panzers as managed to survive the minefields, anti-tank artillery and tank-destroyer aircraft. Despite initial penetrations, the German assault failed at a lethal cost in irreplaceable armour and experienced tank crews and panzer grenadiers. Kursk was the greatest tank-to-tank battle in history. Germany could wage it only once. The Germans committed 3,155 tanks – of which they lost 3,000 – 9,960 pieces of artillery and 435,000 soldiers; the Soviets defended with 3,275 tanks, 13,013 artillery pieces and a million men, plus large reserves. Hitler saved face by using the Anglo-American landing in Sicily on 9–10 July as an expedient excuse for calling off the offensive, but it had already failed.

Although Stalingrad was a very significant defeat – twenty-two German divisions were destroyed – and a huge blow to German prestige, Kursk was the true military turning point of the war. Hitler's intention there was literally to smash the Red Army. The battle was not about the Kursk Salient or any other geographical asset; rather, it was truly the greatest trial of strength between the two armies. Had Citadel succeeded in destroying the best formations in the Red Army, 20 per cent of which was committed to the Kursk battle, Germany might have been able to erect a military 'Eastern Wall' to all but close down the Eastern Front. That would have enabled Berlin to shift forces on a large scale from Russia to the West, where they should have been more than capable of either deterring or defeating Anglo-American invasions. Kursk was Germany's last real opportunity to reverse its strategic fortunes, and the last time in the war that Hitler was able to dictate the terms of engagement.

For reasons known only to himself, Hitler, whose strategic interest in North Africa had only ever been reluctant, episodic and marginal, also elected to stage a major campaign of forlorn resistance to the Anglo-American armies in Tunisia. Since Germany and Italy did not command air or sea communications between Africa and Sicily, this was a most unwise decision. The fully predictable result was that the initially inexperienced Americans, and the British Eighth Army, managed to inflict more casualties on the Germans in Tunisia than they had suffered at Stalingrad. Strangely and foolishly, purportedly for reasons of prestige and morale, Hitler refused to permit the evacuation from Tunisia of experienced but tank-less panzer crews. The Allies took 130,000 Germans and 120,000 Italians prisoner. Tunis finally fell to the Allies on 11 May, and they followed up this triumph, despite American strategic unhappiness, by invading first Sicily on 9–10 July and then Italy proper on 9 September.

So, the strategic picture towards the close of 1943 had the following prime features. In Russia, Germany had lost the initiative and, after its irreplaceable losses of armour and men at Kursk, in addition to the losses at Stalingrad and Tunis, that initiative could not be recovered. But the German Army was still very much in the field and it remained a formidable fighting machine. Indeed, as its military context grew ever more desperate, so its resistance became even more fanatical, especially when conducted by the expanding number of Waffen SS divisions, of which thirty-six in total were raised. The war in the Mediterranean went badly, but given the geography of that theatre, the strategic consequences of defeat were distinctly tolerable, as was the defection of the erstwhile, much despised, Italian ally.

The air war over Germany was bad news for the civilians of the Reich, but the Anglo-American Combined Bomber Offensive (CBO), announced to be such at the Casablanca Conference on 30–31 January 1943, was not wreaking fatal damage on either civilian morale or Germany's defence industries. On balance, in fact, in 1943 Germany's multi-layered air defence system defeated both arms of the Allied CBO: the Americans by day and the British by night.

The picture was less agreeable for Germany at sea. Thanks to a combination of Allied code-breaking, very long-range patrol aircraft, airborne centimetric radar for detection of U-boats on the surface and much improved convoy escort tactics, the submarine offensive was defeated in May. As for Germany's Japanese ally, it was reading the strategic runes without benefit of reliable insight into Hitler's vision of world conquest. As a consequence, Tokyo urged Hitler to come to terms with the Russians while acceptable terms might still be negotiable.

Overall, then, the close of 1943 did not present a pretty strategic picture for Germany.

1944: the trap closes

In 1944 the promise of strategic disaster was duly, though not quite inevitably, realized. After the failure of the Kursk offensive in July 1943, it is hard to discern any German strategy. Hitler's residual hopes for victory rested upon the possibility of a break-up of the Grand Alliance that opposed him; the defeat of the amphibious second front that was certain to be launched in 1944; and the strategic effect of his 'vengeance' secret weapons – the V-1 cruise and the V-2 ballistic missiles. It may not be an exaggeration to say that Hitler would simply fight on to the bitter end, possibly confident until the very last stage that something would turn up to save him and his uniracial Reich. Well, nothing did turn up.

The fighting in Italy rumbled on indecisively as a modest drain on both German and Allied resources, but the three military events that shaped and paced the course of strategic history in 1944 were, first, the defeat of the Luftwaffe in the so-called 'Big Week' air offensive against German air power, launched on 20–21 March; second, the successful Allied landings in Normandy on 6 June; and, last but not least, the destruction in twelve days of the twenty-five divisions of Army Group Centre in Operation Bagration, which the Red Army initiated on 9 June. It was crisis time in both East and West for the Reich, and the Luftwaffe's fighter force had been all but eliminated in the attritional struggle against the new long-range fighter escorts to the daylight bombing campaign conducted by the US Army Air Forces (USAAF).

Bagration effectively destroyed any real coherence in Germany's Eastern Front. By the end of 1944 the Red Army stood on the Vistula, it threatened Budapest, it had reached Czechoslovakia, it had cleared the Balkans, and it had isolated as many as fifty German divisions in Baltic enclaves and East Prussia. That isolation was far from complete, however, given the naval superiority exercised in the Baltic by the Kriegsmarine. Plainly, the end was approaching for Nazi Germany. The only question was: how quickly?

On the Western Front a combination of inspired Allied deception – Operation Fortitude, the absence of unified command by the Germans, Hitler's habit of sleeping late, doctrinal and operational disagreements on the proper deployment of the panzer reserves, and complete Allied command of the air – allowed a secure beachhead to be established in Normandy in early June. However, the German defenders conducted a spirited defence, and certainly frustrated the initial Allied plan to effect a rapid breakout into the open tank-friendly country beyond the coast. Despite suffering crippling losses, the German Army also succeeded in evacuating many of its more valuable personnel from the meat grinder in Normandy. The result was that the Western Allies failed to achieve a defeat of the German Army in France of such magnitude that it would be unable to rally and regroup for the defence of its home territory. Also, as the Germans fell back towards their own soil, their logistic problems eased dramatically, while those of the Allies multiplied.

It is difficult to resist the judgement that with more Allied drive and determination, and a greater willingness to take risks and casualties, Germany should have been beaten in 1944. As it was, by December of that year the Reich itself was menaced everywhere, but its greatly reduced and decidedly ragged military assets were still battle-worthy and battle-willing, in the East and the West. From 16 December 1944 until 28 January 1945, Germany launched its final major offensive of the war, in what came to be known as the

Battle of the Bulge. Hitler assembled in secret virtually the last remaining panzer reserves available, and concentrated them in the West for what he hoped would be an operational and strategic replay of the Ardennes thrust of May 1940. In bad weather, when Allied aircraft were grounded, strong German armoured forces routed some weak and inexperienced American divisions. They aimed to seize crossings over the River Meuse, and then to race on in the direction of the vital port of Antwerp, in the process splitting the British and Canadian forces in the Netherlands from the Americans in France and Belgium. It was always a forlorn hope. The Germans were short of fuel and dependent upon bad weather to keep the Allied fighter-bombers at bay. The whole enterprise was hopelessly ambitious. More to the point, strategically viewed, the armour and motorized infantry expended in the Bulge were to be desperately needed for the defence of the capital of the Reich.

In the West, Germany could delay the end by the astute use of prepared fortifications, especially the Westwall or Siegfried Line of 1939 vintage, as well as urban, hilly and densely forested terrain that channelled and slowed a cautious enemy. In the East, by contrast, there were few useful geographical features providing natural protection for Germany. Given the peril posed by a Red Army which already was investing Warsaw, a mighty offensive in the West in late 1944 was a luxury Germany could not afford.

1945: vision denied

By 1945 the conclusion to the European tragedy engineered by Adolf Hitler was as inevitable as it was terrible. After the failure of the Ardennes offensive, and with the CBO paralysing Germany's ability either to sustain its armies in the field or to move fuel to, and products from, industry, the country was running on close to empty. But, incredibly, it was still running. Field Marshal Keitel did not sign the formal, comprehensive instrument of surrender in Berlin until 8 May. On 29 April, three days before the surrender of Berlin, Hitler had committed suicide in his bunker.

The strategic history of 1945 from January to May unfolded inexorably. Allied armies pressed in on Germany from East and West, while Allied bombers continued to do their best, or worst, to ensure that post-war Germany would resemble a wasteland. The strategic justification for massive urban bombing in a war that was already won was exceedingly weak. The problem was that the American and British heavy bomber forces had reached their peak of near perfection by late 1944. It was impossible to decline to employ them. This was a case of the triumph of the law of the instrument. The heavy bomber force existed and now was a tool capable of employment with great precision, so it would be used.

There were no strategic surprises in the European war in 1945. It was far too late for the Reich to be saved by a falling out among the Grand Allies; though, admittedly, an Anglo-American bid to be first to Berlin most likely would have led to heavy fighting with Soviet troops. The legacy of the thousand-year Reich was rubble: close to 10 million prisoners of war, the largest refugee flows in history, economic destitution and a geo-strategic transformation of Europe. Soviet arms were in Berlin, Vienna and on the Elbe, and they were there to stay.

Conclusion

Some readers may regard the strategic history told in this chapter virtually as a choreographed tragedy for Germany and a similarly predetermined course, though a mixture of tragedy and eventual triumph, for the Allies. Others may be impressed by the power of contingency and will be inclined to speculate that a decision here, a change in the weather there and so forth might have sufficed to produce a German victory. So how fragile was the Allied victory? Was it vulnerable to one or two serious strategic or operational errors, or was it massively and redundantly overdetermined? There is no way of knowing. Moreover, further research will not tell us. This is the realm of historical judgement. It is useful to remember that people today are infinitely more confident of the ultimate victory of the Grand Alliance than were the historical players at the time, at least until late 1944. For example, it seemed highly improbable that Germany would succeed in developing an atomic bomb, but the Allies could not be absolutely certain of that. From Stalin's ideological and realpolitikal perspective, there was always some risk of his Western Allies making a separate peace with Germany and joining it in a new Grand Alliance, this time against the Soviet Union.

The strategic history of 1939–45 in Europe can be summarized with a simple claim. After the United States entered the fray at Hitler's irresistible invitation on 11 December 1941, Germany was certain to lose eventually, provided the Grand Alliance did not make some terrible mistake or suffer appalling bad luck. However, one should recall Clausewitz's warning about war being 'the realm of chance', and the experience of 2,500 years warns that history can, and sometimes does, mount great surprises. Although Germany's defeat was strongly probable, at least from late 1942 onwards, it was not an absolute certainty before the autumn of 1944.

The next chapter unwraps the ways in which the war was waged, and explores the plausibility of somewhat rival explanations of Germany's defeat. But a subject of immense importance, if not strategically so, has thus far been ignored in these pages: the Holocaust. So, this chapter now concludes with a brief explanation of how the Holocaust relates to strategic history.

The Holocaust was a tragedy. A crime, certainly. But it might be claimed that it played no strategic role of significance to the course and outcome of the war. Such a view has strategic merit, but there is a lot more to strategic history than narrowly strategic concerns alone. Hitler's visceral hatred of the Jews was entirely genuine; at least, it became so after the Great War. This commitment to their persecution and physical eradication was founded on an ideology that regarded Jews as both a racial virus to be eliminated as a duty for public health and as the authors and agents of a malevolent and hostile international conspiracy. One cannot just dismiss this nonsense with ridicule, because Hitler believed it, and from 1933 to 1945 he was increasingly able to match his beliefs with deadly actions.

The Third Reich did not have well-prepared plans for the extermination of all of the Jews in Europe (and eventually the world, had the war in Europe been won). But in a speech to the Reichstag on 30 January 1939, to which he referred many times during the war, Hitler declared that in any new war the Jews of Europe would all be killed. Since he himself intended to begin that war in 1939, one is entitled to regard his prediction as a serious intention.

Persecution and murder, even mass murder, became the industrial-scale slaughter of the Holocaust as a direct consequence of Germany's military victories. Until 1941, most of Europe's Jewish population was not under German control. The invasion of the Soviet Union changed that situation. Persecution in Germany in the 1930s escalated to a campaign of mass murder in Poland in 1939, a policy that continued in the wake of the German advance in Russia in 1941. But the Holocaust proper, the change from murder squads (*Einsatzkommandos*) to murder factories, was effected in 1942. The new policy of wholesale murder, genocide, and of the industrial process to achieve it in dedicated death camps such as Auschwitz was decided at the notorious Wannsee Conference of 20 January 1942, convened by Reinhard Heydrich, Heinrich Himmler's SS deputy. Hitler himself was careful never to affix his signature to a document ordering genocide. As a result, there are scholars, as well as apologists, who argue that he did not know what was going on. That is unconvincing (Longerich, 2005). The Holocaust, as the genocidal programme was to be known to history, was always implicit in Nazi ideology, and the intention to carry it through was articulated guardedly in Hitler's speeches and explicitly in conversations with his intimates. It was opportunistic in that Germany could implement genocide only when it controlled most of the Jewish population of Europe. The war provided both the political and the ethical cover for the programme, as well as the historic opportunity. The death camps with gas chambers were invented to solve the 'problem' of how to kill people in numbers that overwhelmed the physical and moral–psychological capacities of the SS murder squads. But the policy of genocide itself was anything but improvised. In the 1930s, Hitler might have been amenable to a policy of mass Jewish emigration, but by 1939 such an option was neither logistically nor politically feasible. The Holocaust always lurked as a strong probability in Hitler's firm commitment to the seizure of land in the East to provide a racially pure Aryan state.

From a narrowly strategic perspective, as has been said, the Holocaust may be viewed as a costly irrelevance. It tied up invaluable manpower and railway assets, and above all it blackened further the already dark reputation of the regime. Indeed, so heinous was the policy of industrial-scale killing that the Allies initially were sceptical of the reports of genocide that they received. Recall that the Holocaust proper was perpetuated from 1942 to 1945, albeit in succession to a growing record of mass murder in the earlier years. The murder of Jews and others contributed nothing at all strategically positive for the German war effort. That said, it must not be forgotten that Hitler's was an ideological war. His Germany was not fighting to improve its competitive place in the hierarchy of nations. Rather, he was fighting to conquer first Europe and then the whole world. Cleansing Europe of its Jewish inhabitants was not simply a bonus generated by military success: it was at the heart of what gave military success its purpose and meaning. Hitler may have loved war, but he had a definite and sincerely held political and cultural vision. The Holocaust was a cultural necessity for Nazi Germany. It cannot be understood in strategic terms, save as a vital part of the Nazi vision that could be enabled only as consequence of strategic success. It is worth noting that in addition to the 6 million Jews who were murdered, at least a further 6 million people died in concentration camps and in the network of Germany's slave labour camps and industrial facilities. Also, as was noted earlier, at least 3.3 million Russian POWs died.

Key points

1. The war was a total struggle between societies.
2. The Russo-German War was the core of World War II. Its course decided the outcome of the war as a whole.
3. By remaining a belligerent into 1941, Britain ensured that American military power, once mobilized, could be projected into continental Europe.
4. The armed forces of Germany and its allies were not large enough to conquer the Soviet Union, a problem accentuated by the German lack of operational focus.
5. Stalingrad was a devastating blow to German pride and prestige, and did some damage to German military strength. But the defeat at Kursk in July 1943 was strategically more significant.
6. The Holocaust was strategically irrelevant to the course of the war. However, it was central to the values of the Nazi state.

Questions

1. Was there a decisive battle in World War II?
2. What were the strategic consequences of Germany's failure to take Britain out of the war in 1940?
3. Why did the Soviet Union survive the German invasion?
4. Why did Nazi Germany perpetrate the Holocaust?

Further reading

J. Black *World War Two: A Military History* (London: Routledge, 2003).

P. Calvocoressi, Guy Wint and John Pritchard *The Penguin History of the Second World War* (London: Penguin, 1999).

I. C. B. Dear and M. R. D. Foot (eds) *The Oxford Companion to the Second World War* (Oxford: Oxford University Press, 1995).

D. M. Glantz and J. House *When Titans Clashed: How the Red Army Stopped Hitler* (Lawrence, KS: University Press of Kansas, 1995).

D. J. Goldhagen *Hitler's Willing Executioners: Ordinary Germans and the Holocaust* (London: Abacus, 1997).

J. Keegan *The Second World War* (London: Hutchinson, 1989).

B. H. Liddell Hart *History of the Second World War* (New York: G. P. Putnam's Sons, 1970).

E. Maudsley *Thunder in the East: The Nazi–Soviet War, 1941–1945* (London: Hodder Arnold, 2005).

W. Murray and A. R. Millett *A War to be Won: Fighting the Second World War* (Cambridge, MA: Harvard University Press, 2000).

S. C. Tucker *The Second World War* (Basingstoke: Palgrave Macmillan, 2004).

G. L. Weinberg *A World at Arms: A Global History of World War II* (Cambridge: Cambridge University Press, 1994).

11 World War II in Europe, II
Understanding the war

> *Reader's guide*: Hitler's purpose and role in the war. How the war was waged. Reasons for Germany's defeat. The war and themes in strategic history.

Introduction: what was the war about?

When delving into the rich contextuality and contingency of events, there is a risk that somewhere amid the detail and the complexities, the essential historical plot is obscured or even lost. The origins, causes, enabling conditions and triggering occurrences that generated World War II attract a host of expert scholars, and rightly so. But at the end of the day, as the cliché has it, the necessary and sufficient explanation for the outbreak and general course of the war could hardly be more straightforward. After 30 January 1933, Germany was led – one can hardly say governed, since Hitler did very little governing – by a man who needed to wage war in order to realize his vision of a racially pure Greater Germany occupying territory suitably expansive for a burgeoning populace of Aryan settlers. That land was in the East; currently it was held by Slavs, and it would have to be seized by force. In order to take this land and construct a strategically secure Germanic continental fortress, Hitler needed to abolish the European balance of power and replace it with German hegemony. Exactly how and when this visionary purpose could be achieved were as uncertain in detail as its pursuit was to be unswervingly steady. Hitler intended to achieve world domination via the successful conduct of a series of wars, and he expected that process to be completed by 1950. Alone among the great powers of the 1930s, Germany had a leader who knew what he wanted and what he would, and would not, accept. He could be flexible, rationally prudent at times, and even deterred when opportunities faded temporarily. However, he could not be deflected from pursuit of his vision of a Europe dominated, actually owned, by a new, imperial Nazi German Reich.

As so often is the case at the highest level of international politics, culture, the source of political vision, drove policy. That is the core explanation of World War II. Historical contingency would decide how effectively Germany would be opposed.

Hitler's war

The war was not about Germany seeking to reverse the few remaining terms of the Versailles Settlement. Between them, Gustav Streseman in the 1920s and Hitler himself in the 1930s had rendered Versailles a thoroughly dead letter. This is not to forget that the symbolically politically important and geographically inconvenient Polish corridor to the Baltic port of Danzig remained outstanding as an issue in August 1939. It is well-nigh certain that Danzig and the corridor could have been reacquired by Germany without the necessity of embarking upon a reign of conquest. But Hitler was not interested in the terms of Versailles, save as a banner to wave to excite Germans, and as a reminder to guilt-ridden Britons and Frenchmen that injustice had been done.

Hitler's overriding war aim, for the purpose was intensely personal, never deviated from the policy implications of the deeply cultural vision that he had outlined with great clarity in Chapter 14 of Volume II of *Mein Kampf*, written in Landsberg Prison in 1924. One cannot improve on his own deathless prose. The words quoted in Box 11.1 state unambiguously that Germany must expand its national territory by seizing land in the East, particularly from Russia.

Box 11.1 Hitler's vision and war aims as revealed in *Mein Kampf*

[T]he aim which is to be pursued in our political conduct must be twofold: namely (1) the acquisition of territory as the objective of our foreign policy and (2) the establishment of a new and uniform foundation as the objective of our political activities at home, in accordance with our doctrine of nationhood . . .

To demand that the 1914 frontiers should be restored is a glaring political absurdity that is fraught with such consequences as to make the claim itself appear criminal. The confines of the *Reich* as they existed in 1914 were thoroughly illogical; because they were not really complete, in the sense of including all the members of the German nation. Nor were they reasonable, in view of the geographical exigencies of military defence. They were not the consequence of a political plan which had been well considered and carried out. But they were temporary frontiers established in virtue of a political struggle that had not been brought to a finish . . .

The fact that a nation has acquired an enormous territorial area is no reason why it should hold that territory perpetually. At most, the possession of such territory is a proof of the strength of the conqueror and the weakness of those who submit to him. And in this strength alone lives the right of possession . . .

[W]hen we speak of new territory in Europe to-day we must principally think of Russia and the border states subject to her . . .

The future goal of our foreign policy ought not to involve an orientation to the East or the West, but it ought to be an Eastern policy which will have in view the acquisition of such territory as is necessary for our German people

(Hitler, 2003: 606, 607, 610, 612, 622)

There it was, the grand vision (almost design) laid out clearly in 1924. There is no reason to doubt either the sincerity of Hitler's manifesto or the steadiness of his purpose through all the vicissitudes of political life in the 1920s, the bold diplomacy of the 1930s and then the shifting fortunes of an ever more total war from 1939 to 1945. The world had been warned. However, *Mein Kampf* and Hitler's public rhetoric could not be taken seriously by responsible statesmen. His vision of a great racially based Germanic continental empire was an example of thinking wildly 'out of the box'. It was so extraordinary that sophisticated practitioners of normal statecraft may be excused for declining to take Hitler's words at face value. And at first he did not need to be taken seriously, because he and his party were only marginal players in German politics. When he did seize his opportunity to assume the chancellorship, most observers were convinced, not unreasonably, that he would be tamed both by the responsibilities of office and by the many sober and experienced advisers to whom he would be politically beholden. Germany was bereft neither of a prudent political class nor of a body of cautious soldiers.

The problem was that Adolf Hitler was that (fortunately) true rarity: a conviction politician with a vision that could not be accommodated within the existing international order. In addition, by securing control of potentially the most powerful state in Europe, a process fully complete only in 1938, he commanded the means to attempt to translate vision into action. The all but demonic truth about Nazi Germany was so improbable to mid-century Europeans that for many years they could not accept it within their mental universe. Even well into the war itself, and in the face of accumulating evidence, the existence and purpose of dedicated death camps, as contrasted with the long-familiar concentration camps, was seriously doubted.

Hitler may be likened to a gangster in a hurry. He had to secure world domination for his racial state before his health and energy failed: he was fifty years old in 1939. He calculated that his Third Reich had a rearmament lead that would prove to be a rapidly wasting asset after 1943. To offset the real, if potential, danger in the last point, he believed that each of his succession of ever-greater wars of conquest would improve Germany's strategic competitive position for the next one. They were to be stepping stones to nothing short of world conquest and domination.

World War II was not an accident, a mistake or a blunder, though its timing, character, course and outcome certainly could be so judged by many. In retrospect, it is unarguable that Hitler's Germany had to be destroyed. It is equally unarguable that the essential, possibly the sufficient as well the necessary, step was to change the regime and destroy its charismatic leader, his legend and the quasi-religion of Nazism. But that which was plain for nearly all to see in the summer of 1939 had not been at all obvious to normal, decent (if mediocre) politicians in previous years. They and their ilk lacked training in how to cope with one of the greatest threats in all of strategic history. They tried to conduct diplomatic business according to the usual rules with a man who recognized no rules and no limits to his ambition. Hitler was neither clinically insane nor irrational, but he was wholly unreasonable in terms of the standard discourse of international relations. Britain and France chose to go to war over Poland on 3 September 1939 because they were eventually convinced that Hitler's words, his promises, were worthless. There could be no final compromise and settlement with a Germany led by that man. London and Paris did not fight for ideological goals, though there was increasing recognition of a dark dimension to the Third Reich that certainly put moral and emotional fuel behind the belated decision to resist it. Nevertheless, in the 1930s, how the German government behaved at home was accepted in Britain and France as being strictly Germany's concern. The war began when it did, with the teams that it did, because the policy of appeasement had failed. The German seizure of Bohemia and Moravia in March 1939 demonstrated that British and French vital interests were now at severe risk. Germany was seen as galloping towards a position of European dominance, and that had to be stopped while it was still possible to do so.

To fast-forward, there was never any realistic prospect of World War II concluding with a compromise peace settlement. The character of British leadership after 10 May 1940 – which is to say Winston Churchill, of course – would not entertain the notion. As much to the point, after 22 June 1941, Hitler and Stalin were to be locked into a struggle literally for survival. Moreover, the enormous dimensions of Germany's war crimes and crimes against humanity came to preclude such a deal. In addition, and of most practical importance, unconditional military victory was the only condition for peace upon which Russia, the United States and Britain could possibly agree. If anything could have fractured an already strained coalition, it would have been bitter inter-Allied negotiation over the terms to be offered to Germany for a compromise peace. The formula of unconditional surrender announced by Roosevelt at Casablanca in January 1943 was not only wise policy; it was unavoidable. Unfortunately, it had the inescapable consequence of leaving all Germans, convinced Nazis and the rest, no alternative other than to go down with the sinking ship, a fate that innocent and guilty alike would have to share.

Warfare, 1939–45

The experience of warfare from 1939 to 1945 is characterized and reviewed by means of seven broad claims.

First, World War II, as eventually with its predecessor, was a conflict waged in the style of combined arms. There was no wonder weapon. The mechanization RMA of the 1920s and 1930s simply facilitated, even enabled, the more effective prosecution of combined-arms warfare. In 1918, neither side possessed the means for the rapid exploitation of what might be only a fleeting tactical success. In 1939–45, rapid exploitation was generally possible, always assuming that the enemy was not alert to the danger and therefore had not taken counter-measures. The tank played a crucial role in World War II, but it was a role in both offence and defence that could be effective only in the context of combined arms. Tanks alone were fatally vulnerable. Even tanks in large numbers could achieve little in the absence of supporting infantry, artillery, engineers and air power.

Second, there were some dazzling manoeuvres in this war, but that is not how the war was won and lost. Armed forces as large as those of the Third Reich – 12.5 million men were mobilized – and loyal, even fanatically loyal, to Hitler could not be defeated by the operational artistry of deft manoeuvre. Such manoeuvre certainly could, and did, play a role in the German defeat, but it wrought its damage in the context of a long attritional struggle. The Soviet encirclement of the Sixth Army at Stalingrad in November 1942 and the trapping and annihilation of Army Group Centre in June 1944 were two outstanding examples of successful manoeuvre warfare. However, neither event was the decisive defeat that ensured Soviet victory. There was no single decisive defeat of the German

Army in World War II, although Kursk in July 1943 is a strong candidate. The Wehrmacht suffered heavy losses in Russia from the outset in the summer of 1941 until the end of the war, a constant drain augmented by the casualties suffered in North Africa, Italy and eventually in France, the Low Countries and the Reich itself. No single stroke of operational genius on any front could have brought down Hitler's regime, so strong was it overall. Defeat could be imposed only gradually. It is true that mechanization and motorization had restored mobility to warfare, but, contrary to the expectations of many, except in a very permissive context that RMA did not offer a short cut to victory via annihilating manoeuvre.

Third, *Blitzkrieg* was not a new way of war. Rather, it was simply the adaptation of long-standing German military doctrine to exploit mechanization and enemy errors. The Germans did not discover a new formula for victory. Instead, they demonstrated in Poland, France and initially the Soviet Union that fast-moving panzer forces, supported closely by air power, could run rings around slower-moving opponents. The Germans fell victim to the familiar malady of 'victory disease', and in 1940 began to believe that their forces and way of war were so superior that defeat was all but unthinkable. One important reason why the planning for Operation Barbarossa was so casual with regard to logistics was that the Germans were convinced that they would defeat the Russians in short order, virtually no matter how they conducted the invasion. Certainly the Germans pioneered the large-scale employment of armoured and other mechanized forces, and in Poland, France and Russia they demonstrated what those forces could achieve when they were handled with dash and imagination. Alas for them, though, they did not grasp the extent to which a so-called *Blitzkrieg* style of warfare was intensely contextual in its effectiveness. Mechanized forces do not fare well when campaigning over great distances with only the most tenuous of logistic support. Also, if the enemy has an abundance of mobilizable manpower and a continent of space, even dramatic encirclements will not deliver truly decisive military success. Furthermore, at the tactical level, *Blitzkrieg* warfare met its match as first Russian, then British and American, soldiers applied effective attritional answers to the challenges that it posed. After the Kursk offensive of July 1943 the German Army really showed its operational and tactical mettle when, in a context of growing adversity, it had to manage a fighting retreat all the way back to Germany. That was manoeuvre warfare in reverse; defensive manoeuvre when the enemy generally had both the initiative and a massive superiority of military assets.

Fourth, World War II tested everybody's theory of air power. The theories of the advocates of the strategic bombing of civilians, of economic 'key nodes' and of the 'industrial web', of close ground support including dive bombing, and of air power as an instrument to deliver light infantry from the sky behind enemy lines were all tested extensively in practice. The strategic impact of air power of all kinds on the course and outcome of the war is fairly clear. The experience of war showed beyond room for argument that in the early 1940s victory on the ground or at sea was unlikely, perhaps impossible, unless the enemy's air power had been defeated first. This does not mean that air power won the war, but it does mean that air power was more than just another player on the combined-arms team. It became a critical, arguably the decisive, source of Allied advantage. The failure of the Luftwaffe in early 1944 to defend the Reich at home, and its subsequent, consequential inability to protect and assist the German Army in the West, amounted to a war-losing development, although one of a number, it should be added. Air power came of age between 1939 and 1945. Inevitably, it disappointed those who harboured exaggerated expectations of its potential to deliver victory unaided by land and sea forces. But, equally, its potency embarrassed those who had believed that ground forces and fleets could manoeuvre and fight even under unfriendly skies. They could not; or at least they could not for long, and certainly not effectively.

Fifth, even though the purpose and heart of this war were always in the East, geostrategically the conflict was a repeat of the experience of 1914–18, in that it was a strategic triumph for the side that was a maritime coalition. Sea power was the great enabler of the victory of the Grand Alliance. It bound the Allies together, maintained and exploited the essential – maritime – lines of communication, and it was superior sea power that allowed the Grand Alliance to draw upon the resources of the entire world. '[A]ll the seas of the world are one,' as J. H. Parry (1981: xi) has observed. Hitler's landlocked imperium was impressive in scale in 1942 and 1943, but it could not compete successfully with an enemy coalition that used the world's sea lanes at will, contested though they were; which enjoyed the power of the strategic initiative granted by maritime superiority; and which used its sea power to help sustain its essential continental member. Air power was more visible than sea power, and to many people certainly appeared more modern and more directly relevant to the task of bringing war to the enemy, but the most vital logistical infrastructure of the war effort of the Grand Alliance was maritime, not aerial.

Sixth, as World War II repeated the experience of World War I with respect to the enabling essentiality of sea power, so also it demonstrated yet again the strategic benefits that can accrue from mastery of the black arts of signals intelligence. Unknown beyond a small, closed circle of officials and military beneficiaries until the early 1970s, the Allies, Britain in particular, secured and by and large maintained a decisive advantage in the intelligence competition of the war. Of the greatest strategic importance was Britain's success – with Polish assistance – in breaking the German codes that were transmitted on their supposedly unbreakable Enigma encoding machines. The vital intelligence so gathered was codenamed Ultra. British success over Enigma was not steady or, for a while, complete, but it was sufficient to make a strategic difference. In fact, Ultra intelligence could be so useful that there was always a problem in protecting the source. The Allies had to be supremely careful not to take military action that the Germans would be certain to interpret as being based on a breach of Enigma security. As with air power and sea power, both of which benefited greatly from its aid, intelligence from code-breaking was a great enabler of the victory over Germany. In neither world war did Germany shine in the intelligence field. This was a costly weakness.

Seventh and finally, the warfare of 1939 to 1945 showed for the second time in the century that the German Army was the most formidable killing machine in the world. Indeed, it was among the most efficient such in all strategic history. German military methods and fighting power have attracted a great deal of professional admiration among Anglo-American historians and defence analysts. With at least 9.5 million military dead, Russian analysts have been in no need of reminders of German combat prowess. It is a fact that in both world wars the Germans were unsurpassed at fighting. Whether on the offence or the defence, whether they were winning or losing, German soldiers regularly exacted an unequal exchange ratio, or toll, of casualties upon their enemies. One can isolate particular factors at particular times that probably made some difference to German morale and fighting power. For example, it is plausible to argue that throughout

World War II, and especially in the war on the Eastern Front, Nazi ideology contributed positively to morale and fighting spirit. For another example, one may claim that as the end neared in 1944 and 1945 in the East, German soldiers fought with the determination of desperation for hearth and home. They knew that they had no real choice, in the historical context of a surging enemy who would exact revenge for the crimes committed by Germans in Russia. Nevertheless, the German military system, especially its rigorous training and its flexible and adaptive approach to command in battle, manifestly produced a superior combat performance to that achieved by any other belligerent. However, as this was so, one must ask: why did Germany lose?

Why did Germany lose?

There is more to war than warfare. Hitler's Reich proved superb at the latter but grossly incompetent at the former. Germany suffered from a strategy deficit. Neither world war was waged with strategic competence. Means and ends were never calculated, at least not beyond the mid-1930s. Hitler's experience of succeeding against the odds with a poor hand of assets persuaded him that some mystical force was with him and that his destiny, intuition or luck would not fail him. The completeness of the German catastrophe of 1945 can blind one to the probable fact that the outcome of the war was by no means preordained. Germany did not lose the war because it was misgoverned by an immoral leader whose beliefs and purposes were an affront to civilized values. Many such men have prospered through the centuries (although, admittedly, Hitler was an extreme example of a malignant actor, one rendered truly threatening to all of humanity by his command of a great power).

Explanations for Germany's defeat have been well aired over the past sixty years. Most contain some merit, but the more popular among them are seriously flawed. There are three species of explanation, with each concentrating on one aspect of Nazi Germany: the country's resources deficit; the nature of the Nazi regime and the character of its leader; and its strategic and military errors.

First, it is easy to argue that Germany was simply out-resourced. It waged total war against the world's mightiest economies, and strategic history delivered its inevitable verdict. In a long, bloody war of attrition, the larger belligerent wins. This view is not to be dismissed, but there are two principal problems with it. First, it undervalues the extent of the German Empire of 1942–3. In those years the Third Reich was a true superpower. Indeed, one could argue that in 1942 the war was Germany's to lose. Second, resources have to be mobilized and translated into fighting power. By chalking up rapid military victories, Germany might well have ambushed adverse resources and their implications for long-term defeat. If Germany could have beaten Russia in 1941 or 1942, it would not have much mattered what Russian, British or American tank and aircraft production rates would have been, had those countries still been in the fight in 1944 or 1945.

The second approach to the explanation of defeat is somewhat, though not entirely, moral. It holds that Nazi ideology was a fatal weakness. Since it was ideology that drove Hitler's war-making, and his vision that was in command of policy, there was nothing that Germany could do to correct its ideological flaws, short of regime change. Plainly, an ideology that mandated the violent pursuit of a territorially vastly expanded uniracial Germanic superstate must have little appeal abroad. In principle, and perhaps in some practice, German grand strategy was hindered by the unswerving commitment to achievement of world dominance for a racially pure German state. Such a vision (one hesitates to say aim) must trigger ever-greater opposition. It should be noted that in both world wars, despite the radical differences in German regimes, Germany signally failed to assemble an impressive, let alone war-winning, coalition. Nazi ideology, though the essential motor for the strategic enterprise of world war, certainly was diplomatically unhelpful.

Some historians and a host of popular commentators favour an approach to the explanation of defeat that emphasizes Nazi Germany's moral deficit as a weakness that derived from the attitudes encouraged by the quasi-religion of Nazism (Overy, 1995: ch. 9). One knows what they mean, and there is some merit in this view. Germany's misbehaviour was so abominable that it convinced the country's enemies that they had no practical or ethical choice other than to wage the war to a military conclusion. Germany's crimes were so extreme and extensive that it must either win the war or go down to complete destruction. It is true that German crimes in the East – crimes that were sanctioned, even encouraged, by the racist ideology – had dire strategic consequences. Crimes against the civilian populace and POWs denied Germany local allies among the occupied population that almost certainly would have sufficed to enable victory over the Soviet Union. But those crimes should not be regarded as German *mistakes*; rather, they were the inevitable product of the character of the Nazi regime and its army. Germany's Nazified armed forces behaved as their nature commanded.

The leading problem with the moral deficit explanation is that it is too moralistic and insufficiently strategic. Causes that one deems morally atrocious do not usually fail for reason of divine, or natural, justice. Had Hitler and his generals directed their war more competently, the Third Reich's moral failings would not have registered in the strategic history of the period. One must acknowledge that it is all too easy to succumb to an undue subjectivity in moral judgement. Without for one moment softening one's disgust at German crimes, it is necessary to recognize that for millions of Germans in the early 1940s, Nazism propelled them with a moral imperative to conquer and to do so without pity for civilian victims.

The third approach to explaining Germany's defeat points to the incompetence with which the war was directed, politically, strategically and operationally. The implicit assumption here is that Germany might have won had its magnificent armed forces been led more intelligently. In other words, what Germany lacked was a strategy worthy of the name. It certainly had a political vision, the creation of a world-dominant racially pure super-state. It also had a clear policy: to wage a succession of wars to achieve that great goal. And it developed a fighting machine second to none in its tactical skills. But somehow, between tactics and policy, in the regions of grand strategy, military strategy and operations, the Germans' grip was uncertain. There is not much to be gained in playing the 'what if' game that publishers have found to be so profitable in recent years. However, Germany may, and one must emphasize 'may', have had a narrow window for victory in 1941. This thesis requires one to credit two propositions. First, it can be argued that Moscow could have been taken in the late summer or early autumn of 1941, had it been assigned overriding priority as an invasion objective. Second, the argument requires one to agree that the fall of Moscow would have set in train the definitive unravelling of the Soviet Union. There is no way of knowing for sure whether either of these would have happened, but they were both at least possible, perhaps probable. By 1942 it was almost certainly too late for Germany. The window of opportunity had already closed, even as the Sixth Army slowly moved up to the Volga at Stalingrad. By that time, the Wehrmacht had suffered too many losses in the Battle of Moscow, and the Red Army was recovering rapidly from the disasters, and successes, of 1941 and early 1942, and learning how best to fight the invader.

Germany could not win a long war of attrition against the fully mobilized economies of the Soviet Union, the United States and Britain. It could win only either if the Grand Alliance made a fatal operational mistake or two or if it could devise or exploit an operational opportunity to achieve a rapid, decisive victory. Britain and then the United States were operationally effectively unreachable until they committed themselves on the Continent with D-Day in June 1944. So that left the Soviet Union, always Germany's most important, as well as most accessible, enemy. To win the war, Hitler had to destroy the Soviet Union while that outcome was still a practicable goal, assuming that it ever was, albeit briefly.

Because of Germany's failure to concentrate its limited, though still massive, combat power upon potentially strategically decisive objectives   Moscow in 1941; the oilfields of the Caucasus in 1942 – it forfeited its short-lived chance of victory in the war. But it is just possible that had Germany won the smashing trial of strength it intended at Kursk as late as July 1943, the operational victory could have had far-reaching strategic consequences. If the Red Army had been badly beaten, though still in the field, the Western Allies could not have launched their invasion of France. One can speculate that a timely concentration of military effort, in the form of the panzer reserve divisions, against the initially tenuous Allied beachhead in Normandy might have defeated the invasion. Such a success should have had the strategic consequence, at the very least, of buying time for Germany. With the Western Front secure for a while, Hitler would have been able to shift resources to the East, possibly enforce a stalemate there, and secure an armistice. Alternatively, the Red Army might have been strong enough in mid-1944 to defeat Germany in the absence of the Allied diversion of German forces in the West.

This third approach to Germany's defeat favours the systemically contingent view that Hitler made a series of great mistakes. There is a danger of tautology. Unless one subscribes to the extreme and implausible belief that Germany could not have won, irrespective of how its statecraft and war-making were conducted, one is in danger of simply stating an obvious and logically necessary truth: specifically, an improbably error-free performance by Hitler as warlord would, or should, have delivered victory for the Thousand Year Reich-to-be. On close examination, however, it becomes apparent that most, if not all, of Hitler's alleged mistakes were in fact nothing of the kind. At least, they were not errors from his perspective. It makes little sense to measure Hitler's strategic prowess, or lack thereof, against some absolute standard of strategic excellence. Hitler, and hence the German conduct of war, was moved by a cultural dynamic, an ideology, not by a cool strategic calculation indifferent to political ideas and values.

It is commonplace to believe that the Grand Alliance won World War II on Hitler's mistakes. In one sense there is some truth in this: strategic and operational errors in 1941, and possibly in 1942 and 1943, *might* have cost Germany the war. However, there is a major problem with the usual lists of 'Hitler's mistakes' (Lewin, 1984; Macksey, 1987, 1994): the alleged mistakes all flowed naturally from Hitler's ideology and, hence, from the imperial and cultural purposes of his regime. If Hitler and his Germany were to have avoided these great mistakes, they would need to have been other than who and what they were in historical reality.

What follows is a typical list of Hitler's alleged mistakes. To repeat, it obscures the content of Nazi ideology and the degree to which it shaped assumptions and subsequent behaviour. It is alleged that it was a grave mistake by Hitler:

- *To seize the non-German remainder of Czechoslovakia in March 1939.* This belatedly mobilized Anglo-French opinion and policy for war 'next time'. But Hitler was determined on war in 1939. Consolidation of Germany's position in Central Europe and the acquisition of Czech military assets were necessary as preparation for the war to come.

- *To invade Poland.* After all, this action triggered Anglo-French belligerency. But the destruction of Poland was the essential first step on the march to the East. War with France, and possibly Britain, was always viewed as a necessity.

- *To invade Norway in April 1940.* Although it was an effective joint operation by the three armed services, it was a strategic disaster because Germany lost too much of its already unduly small navy in the exercise. Later that year, the ships lost or damaged off Norway might have made the difference to the feasibility of a cross-Channel invasion. But in April 1940 Hitler could not foresee the need to prepare for an invasion of Britain. However, he did appreciate the long-term value of bases in Norway. The successful Norwegian venture was not a mistake. It was a pre-emptive move to forestall an Anglo-French landing.

- *Not to invade Britain.* If such an invasion had been likely to succeed, then indeed it was a great mistake. On balance, though, the decision not to invade, keyed for public consumption to the plausible excuse of the continued existence and combat readiness of the RAF, was not a mistake. It is highly improbable that the German invasion armada could have survived what undoubtedly would have been assault by droves of the Royal Navy's smaller warships, assault pressed home with suicidal determination. Of particular note was the fact that the Royal Navy had as many as eighty destroyers in home waters. Even had the Luftwaffe performed better than it did against RAF Fighter Command, it is a certainty that the Royal Navy would have delivered Hitler his first crushing defeat.

- *To help Mussolini in North Africa and in Greece in the spring of 1941.* It was a nuisance to divert from preparation for Barbarossa to invade Yugoslavia and Greece. But it was necessary to eject the British from Greece, because of the threat that their air power would have posed to Germany's vital oil supply from Ploesti in Romania. Also, it was prudent to consolidate Germany's southern flank before invading Russia. Although the armoured and air assets lent to the Italians in North Africa were only modest in scale, there is no denying that they would have been of greater strategic value to Germany in Russia than in North Africa. Hitler sent Erwin Rommel with the Afrika Korps, later titled Panzer Armee Afrika, which eventually was to comprise two panzer and two under-strength infantry divisions. Also, he dispatched the Luftwaffe's Air Corps X from Norway to Sicily (with 500 planes). At the end of 1941 the Germans were obliged to divert Luftflotte 2 from Russia in order to rescue Rommel from impending logistical disaster.

- *To invade Russia*. Many people make the mistake of arguing that because Germany failed in Russia, the attack must have been an error. But the invasion of the Soviet Union was not a German mistake; rather, it was the essential step towards seizing the territory needed for establishment of the German racial empire. War with Russia was ideologically and strategically necessary. There is a sense in which the offensive against Russia was what Nazi Germany was all about. It could not fulfil its destiny unless it attacked Russia. And 1941 was a prudent choice for the timing of the invasion: the Red Army appeared still to be a rabble; there was no menace of note from Britain in the West; and the German people had to be prevented from settling into a post-war frame of mind, satisfied with the victory over France in June 1940. Nazi Germany was an ideologically driven state built for war. Russia was both next in line geostrategically and the current tenant of the land that the Reich must seize if it were to realize its destiny as visualized by the Führer.
- *To declare war on the United States*. This was a gratuitous act by Hitler on 11 December 1941. But it is worth noting that war with the United States was accepted by Hitler as an inevitability. His was an act of solidarity with his Japanese ally, in keeping with a promise he had made, committed in a mood of some euphoria occasioned by Pearl Harbor. Hitler overvalued the strategic worth of Japan as a first-class maritime ally. Also, he undervalued the ability of the United States to wage what would amount to two separate wars half a world apart. In retrospect, Hitler's needless declaration of war was a grave error in statecraft. However, if one is faithful to the historical context, one has to recognize that in early December 1941, despite the bad news from the Moscow front, Hitler anticipated winning the war in Russia in 1942. Had Germany won its continental war in that year, American belligerency most probably would have been a strategic irrelevance.

To recap, three broad explanations of Germany's defeat have been suggested here, each of which has some merit: (1) a resources shortfall – Germany attempted to wage too much war with too few assets; (2) the hideous nature of the regime, and the personality and beliefs of its all-powerful leader; (3) errors in statecraft, military strategy and operational direction. One can argue the case for the inevitability of German defeat based on any one of these explanations, let alone a compilation of all three. Because of the extravagance of its goals and the extremity of its aggressive and criminal behaviour, it is probable that the Third Reich was doomed to go down in the flames of total defeat. However, it is well to remember that no country conducts foreign policy faultlessly or military campaigns immaculately. In other words, to claim credibly, even self-evidently, that Hitler made mistakes in his direction of the war is not to offer a penetrating insight. Germany's problem in the early 1940s was that the nature of its regime and the character of its leader afforded it, and its enemies, no way out from a total struggle for victory and survival or death. Hitler's Germany could not, and would not be permitted by others to, arrest or reverse its course, except by the military pressure of its enemies.

Conclusion

Chapter 1 introduced six themes which run throughout the strategic history in this text. Generally, the themes have not been highlighted explicitly, but rather have been allowed a silent role of influence over the narrative and argument. However, so rich – indeed extreme – was the strategic history of World War II that it is useful to employ the themes directly at this juncture.

The first theme is the relationship between continuity and discontinuity. The years 1939–45 demonstrated both in abundance, as well as much misunderstanding of both. On the one hand, despite widespread mechanization and motorization, the continuities in 'best practice' in warfare, emphasizing combined arms, far outweighed the discontinuities. Modern warfare was invented and developed between 1916 and 1918, not 1939 and 1941. On the other hand, at the political level, World War II registered a massive discontinuity with World War I. Nazi Germany was not simply out to reverse the verdict of 1918. While there were some continuities of territorial ambition, as one would expect, Hitler's vision of a uni-racial superstate that would establish global dominance by war was a sharp discontinuity even from the outer boundary of German ambitions, let alone intentions, in 1914–18.

The second theme pointed to the close and essential connection between politics and war. Again, World War II reveals the key significance of this nexus. The war was solely about a violent bid to realize Hitler's political vision, and that vision was the heart and soul of the quasi-religion of Nazi ideology. Often it can appear to be the case that the proper relationship between war and politics is reversed in practice: politics seems to serve war, rather than vice versa. It is true that war has a 'grammar' all its own, as Clausewitz claims (Clausewitz, 1976: 605), and even that its course will be shifted by military contingency. But a strictly military history of World War II would lack integrity; it could make no sense. The entire black episode was driven by politics. For an unusually clear example of this theme in action, once Stalin was convinced that Russia could not lose the war, he directed his country's military effort more towards the shaping of post-war Europe than to defeating the Wehrmacht as rapidly as possible. Stalin, at least, was not confused about the superiority of the political over the military, always provided the military context is permissive.

The third theme is the strangely ill-understood relationship between war and warfare. Germany was supreme at warfare, but hopelessly incompetent at war. Merely to cite 1918 and 1945 points to conclusive proof of this claim. On the evidence of World War II, Germany had a clear state ideology which inspired policy. Also, it had an excellent military machine that was highly skilled tactically and, generally, operationally. But between the elevated heights of ideology and policy, on the one hand, and expert military behaviour, on the other, there is the difficult realm of strategy, especially grand strategy. Time after time in Russia, German military prowess and increasingly scarce assets were committed to operational tasks that could not yield strategic benefits proportionate to their costs of attainment. At the level of grand strategy, in both world wars Germany's soldiers were handicapped severely by their politicians' inability to assemble politically an array of allies that looked like a potentially winning team.

Theme four is civil–military relations. In World War II, Hitler was unique among the warlords in not allowing a true dialogue between civilian policy-makers and soldiers. Stalin and Churchill could be ruthless and unreasonable, but both were open to persuasion and would change their minds when confronted with powerful arguments or incontrovertible evidence. Not so Hitler. In both world wars, German war-making was handicapped fatally by the absence of genuine debate between civilian leaders and the military.

The importance of the fifth theme, the connection between war and society, was demonstrated in all respects by World War II. This was a total war, a people's war. It was a war of total mobilization. Civilians were combatants, both literally as the targets for bombs, and functionally as the providers of the material sinews of war. Moreover, in all belligerent countries, even Nazi Germany, public opinion – which is to say morale – was courted, manipulated where possible, and sometimes measured fearfully. Between 1939 and 1945, societies, not merely states, made war.

Finally, the sixth theme is the thread that links war and peace and peace and war. World War II was born not so much out of the result of 1918 and the peace settlement of 1919, but rather out of the purpose and character of the Nazi regime that came to power on 30 January 1933. The strategic context that Hitler was able to exploit in the 1930s was a direct consequence of World War I, which had destroyed the old balance of power, and also of the way in which that war was terminated.

Moving forward in time, the international stage for the Soviet–American Cold War largely was set by the ways in which the members of the temporary anti-German Grand Alliance chose to conduct their military operations. But first one must address the other war of 1941–5: the conflict in the Pacific and Asia against Japan. It is remarkable how separate were the two conflicts. Of course the wars were connected, but it is also true to say that the United States was alone among the belligerents in its commitment to the waging of warfare on the largest of scales in Europe and Asia simultaneously.

Key points

1. Nazi Germany had to wage war if it were to fulfil its ideologically mandated purpose.
2. Despite extensive, though still very incomplete, mechanization, 1939–45 was another great war of attrition.
3. Air power did not win the war, but the war could not have been won without superiority in the air.
4. Allied maritime dominance was a crucial enabler of victory in global war.
5. For the second time in the twentieth century, Germany was as proficient at warfare as it was incompetent in the conduct of war.
6. The verdict remains open on whether Germany could have won the war in 1941, 1942 or even 1943.

Questions

1. Is it an exaggeration to claim that World War II was 'Hitler's war'?
2. What difficulties did the Wehrmacht face in its invasion of Russia?
3. How important was Allied air power in the defeat of Germany?
4. Could Germany have won the war in 1941, 1942 or 1943?

Further reading

C. Barnett *Engage the Enemy More Closely: The Royal Navy in the Second World War* (New York: W. W. Norton, 1991).

R. Bessel *Nazism and War* (London: Weidenfeld and Nicolson, 2004).

R. Evans *The Third Reich in Power* (London: Allen Lane, 2005).

J. Keegan *The Battle for History: Re-fighting World War Two* (London: Hutchinson, 1995).

I. Kershaw *Hitler, 1936–45: Nemesis* (London: Allen Lane, 2000).

R. Lewin *Ultra Goes to War* (New York: McGraw Hill, 1978).

—— *Hitler's Mistakes* (London: Leo Cooper, 1984).

A. R. Millett and W. Murray (eds) *Military Effectiveness*, Vol. III: *The Second World War* (Boston: Allen and Unwin, 1988).

R. J. Overy *The Air War, 1939–1945* (New York: Stein and Day, 1981).

—— *Why the Allies Won* (London: Jonathan Cape, 1995).

A. Tooze *The Wages of Destruction: The Making and Breaking of the Nazi Economy* (London: Allen Lane, 2006).

G. L. Weinberg *Germany, Hitler, and World War II* (Cambridge: Cambridge University Press, 1995).

H. P. Willmott *The Great Crusade: A New Complete History of the Second World War* (New York: Free Press, 1989).

12 World War II in Asia–Pacific, I

Japan and the politics of empire

Reader's guide: The connections between the two wars. The growth of the Japanese Empire. US–Japanese relations and the approach to war.

Introduction: global war

In its origins, stakes and purposes, the war in Asia–Pacific was all but entirely unrelated to the war in Europe. Nevertheless, it is still accurate, if strangely so, to regard the war against Japan as an integral part of World War II. The principal connection between the two wars, half a world apart, was that it was only the ongoing war in Europe that emboldened Japan to seek a grand military solution to its strategic problems. Had there been no active conflict in Europe, Japanese prospects for success would have been so poor that war almost certainly would have been rejected as the policy choice. Even as it was, in 1941 Japanese leaders were far from united in a determination to fight. Context is vital. In 1940–1, as Japan's material strategic condition worsened as a result of American-led economic sanctions, so the radical changes in the global strategic context effected by Germany's victories appeared to offer a unique opportunity for Japan to exploit.

It is useful to draw attention to an obvious political difference between the war in Europe and that in Asia–Pacific. By 1939, perhaps after 1936, or even as early as 1933, it is plausible to argue that war in Europe was unavoidable. Germany, which is to say Adolf Hitler, wanted war. He might briefly be deterred tactically, but not strategically or politically. By way of contrast, Imperial Japan did not want war with the United States, though war with the British and the Dutch was unavoidable, given Tokyo's need for the raw material resources of South East Asia. It should have been possible to persuade Japan not to embark on a course of war. But for a potential combatant to agree to be deterred when the stakes are very high, it must be deprived of even an unreasonable hope of military success. Also, it should be offered a politically tolerable alternative to war. In 1941, alas, those crucial conditions did not apply, as the world learnt on 7 December, when the Imperial Japanese Navy attacked Pearl Harbor.

Considered as one global conflagration, World War II comprised two geostrategically immense siege operations. The contrasting geographies of the Axis empires in Europe

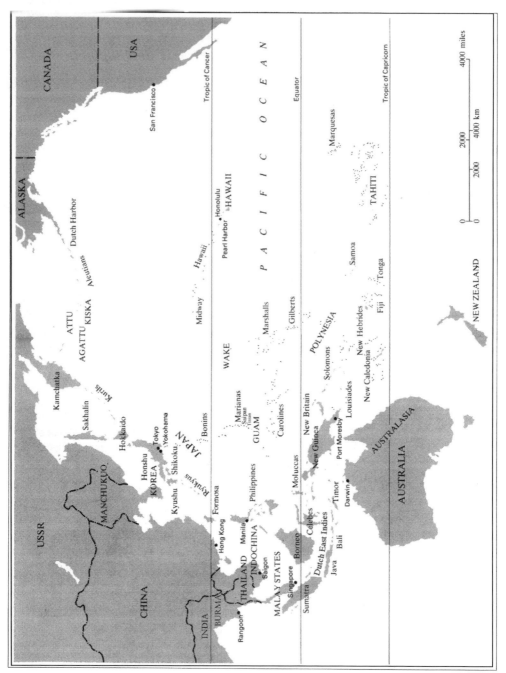

Map 12.1 The Pacific in 1939

and Asia–Pacific determined that the former ultimately would have to be brought down by continental warfare. The latter, by contrast, might succumb primarily either to continental pressure exercised in and from China or to maritime and maritime–air assault; or, indeed, it might fall to both. In practice, the Chinese continental road to the Japanese Home Islands proved impracticable, for a mixture of geographical, political, logistical and military reasons. Although the wars in Europe and Asia–Pacific were intimately linked politically, strategically and certainly logistically (at least they were for one belligerent – the United States), it is an easy matter to exaggerate the connections. These were two distinct wars. To say that is to risk overstatement, but it is one that registers a vital truth. The Grand Alliance did not wage a global war against the Axis powers, if only because those powers did not themselves wage a global war.

It is true that the war in Europe was global in that the British Empire was truly global, and it mobilized its global assets to fight, just as it had in World War I. Also, on 22 June 1941, Germany attacked a country, the Soviet Union, that was both a European and an Asian power, though the latter status rested logistically on the thin ribbon of steel of the single-track trans-Siberian railway. *True* globality to conflict from 1941 to 1945 was therefore conferred uniquely by the United States. Washington alone played major roles in both wars, and it was alone in having the strategic discretion to choose to swing its mobilized resources more in favour of one contest than the other. All the other belligerents lacked such freedom of strategic choice.

It is possible that the Asia–Pacific war might have had a determinative effect upon the war in Europe. There could have been a genuinely global war. But, fortunately, that did not occur because Berlin and Tokyo did not conduct their statecraft, or wage their wars, with an enlightened view to helping themselves by helping each other. They did not develop, or even seriously consider developing, a coordinated strategy in pursuit of mutually agreed policy goals.

Two points serve to illustrate the potential of the Tripartite Pact of 27 September 1940, the formal basis for the German–Japanese Alliance (Italy was the third member). First, the Soviet Union was able to save Moscow in December 1941 by transferring more than half of its Siberian divisions from the Far East, where they had been guarding against attack by Japan's Kwantung Army. It is at least possible that had Japan attacked the Soviet Union in the East, the Germans might have secured a decisive victory at Moscow. (Earlier in the year, the option of joining the Germans in the attack on Russia had found some articulate supporters in Tokyo.) Second, unlike Nazi Germany, Imperial Japan conducted serious debates over policy and strategy. It was reasonably obvious to the leaders in Tokyo that Japan could win its war only if Germany won, too. If Germany were to lose, it would only be a matter of time before the Allies massed their forces to conclude strategic business in Asia–Pacific. In practice, it is little short of amazing to realize just how minimal was the content of the Axis partnership because, in theory, the German–Japanese Axis had formidable strategic potential.

The Japanese bid for empire

From the time of the Meiji Restoration in 1868 until nemesis in August 1945, a modernizing Imperial Japan strove to become the dominant power in East Asia. Primarily, this drive entailed a bid for continental imperium, an effort focused overwhelmingly on

China. By the time of the crisis in relations with the United States in 1941, Japan had long detached Korea, *de facto* Manchuria and *de jure* Taiwan from China. The decline and fall of imperial rule in China with the end of the Manchu Dynasty (1911), and the subsequent protracted turmoil which consumed the new Republic of China, offered to a predatory Japan an irresistible temptation to expand. Henry Kissinger has explained the phenomenon in general terms. He wrote about 'the realities of global power, one of the lessons of which is that vacuums always get filled and that the principal issue is not whether but by whom' (Kissinger, 1994: 548). Japan was ready and ruthlessly willing to provide Kissinger's 'whom'. As China ceased to function as a centralized state that was able to protect its interests effectively against rapacious colonial powers, so Japan stepped in, time and again, to take what it could.

Japanese expansion at China's expense began in earnest as early as 1879, with the annexation of the Ryuku Islands. In the 1880s, Japan intervened militarily in Korea, a country nominally under Chinese sovereignty, and war was only narrowly avoided by the Convention of Tientsin (18 April 1885). The pace of Japanese strategic history accelerated from the 1890s onwards. In 1894–5, Tokyo announced to the world that it had arrived as a major regional power in East Asia by decisively defeating the largely moribund, but still functioning, China of the Manchus. Japan was rewarded diplomatically for its strategic arrival as a state of some significance when, in 1902, it was offered, and accepted, alliance with Britain. This was diplomatic promotion indeed. In British calculation, the Japanese alliance provided valuable insurance against Russian troublemaking in Central Asia, especially in Afghanistan on the most obvious invasion route to India.

But Japan's debut on the world stage, as opposed merely to the regional platform, was declared and then strategically demonstrated in 1904–5 in a way that stunned most foreign observers. In 1904, Japan moved to assert its interests in Korea and forcefully to expel its Russian competitor. Japan was victorious on land and sea, and the Russians were humiliated, although it is true that the latter had to fight at a great logistical disadvantage. As noted already, their army in Korea and Manchuria was connected to European Russia by means of a solitary single-track railway line, 5,500 miles in length, with the added complication of a 100-mile gap at Lake Baikal. Also, when Russia decided to reinforce its naval power in Korean waters, particularly in support of the besieged naval base of Port Arthur, it was obliged to dispatch its Baltic Fleet from Kronstadt, all the way around Europe, Africa and Asia. Given Britain's alliance with Japan and France's alliance with Russia, the unfortunate Russian fleet staggered from one French coaling station to another at a painfully slow pace. Alas, when it arrived off Korea it was met and all but annihilated by a more modern and better-handled Japanese opponent in the Strait of Tsushima.

On land, the fighting was bitter and in many tactical respects it anticipated the conditions of 1914–18. However, the Japanese Army appeared to demonstrate that it had found a workable solution to the tactical crisis discussed in earlier chapters. Soldiers could advance in the face of modern firepower, provided they were willing to accept very high casualties. The keys to such acceptance, of course, were discipline and, above all else, morale or fighting spirit. Russia, struggling to survive revolution at home in 1905, was in no condition to impose a long war on the Japanese. The latter's consequent victory carried the implication that they had arrived as a great power. The military standard for membership in the ranks of the great powers was the ability 'to put up a serious fight in an all-out conventional war against the most powerful state in the world' (Mearsheimer, 2001: 5). Japan had met that standard. The event was all the more surprising, not to say shocking, given the racist assumptions of European statesmen at the time. Japan's victory demonstrated Asian strategic superiority over a great European power.

Japan fought with the Allies in World War I, and the war provided a glorious and unique opportunity to siphon up all of Germany's extensive island possessions in the Pacific north of the equator, as well as its valuable concession on the Chinese coast. The principal gain from Germany was the port of Kaiochow, with the fortress of Tsingtao, on the Shantung peninsula. Not one to let the political opportunity for notable advantage pass unexploited, in 1915 Japan served its notorious 'Twenty-one Demands' on the Republic of China. In effect, the demands amounted to a Japanese claim for unique extra-territorial rights. The Chinese Nationalist leader Chiang Kai-shek judged them to be 'the grand culmination of all the unequal treaties' (quoted in Lamb and Tarling, 2001: 16). But China had no practicable option other than to agree to most of the demands, since its potential supporters had their minds and strategic endeavours focused on the contemporary trauma in Europe. Nevertheless, it is important to note that the demands were a direct challenge to American policy on China. Since the turn of the century, Washington had sought to insist that China must be able to present an 'open door' to the whole world. It should not be permitted to fall under the sway of one or two great powers exclusively. Subsequently, at Versailles in 1919, the United States succeeded in thwarting at least the most outrageous of the Japanese demands. And in the package of treaties that comprised the 'Washington system' of naval disarmament of 1922, the Nine-Power Treaty guaranteed that China would be approached diplomatically and strategically on a multilateral basis by the great power signatories. This, needless to say, was a major political defeat for Japan, and was to be the source of much anti-American sentiment in Tokyo in the 1920s and 1930s. Japan believed that it had been denied its just deserts as a loyal ally in the Great War.

Against the background of political instability in Tokyo – with the Army collectively as well as smaller groups of military officers intervening frequently and sometimes murderously in public affairs: for example, Prime Minister Hamaguchi was assassinated in November 1930 – Japan's drive for continental empire changed its character in the 1930s. Beginning on 18 September 1931 with the so-called Mukden Incident, Japan's effectively autonomous Kwantung Army effectively took control of policy and strategy towards China. Ignoring a barrage of international protests, though greatly irritated by China's ability to rally diplomatic support through the League of Nations, the Japanese Army proceeded to turn Manchuria into a Japanese dependency. This dramatic step, which was extended and consolidated in succeeding years, was the first blatant Japanese challenge to the Washington system for stability in East Asia. Tokyo was widely denounced for flouting the Nine-Power Treaty of 1922 on relations with China as well as the Pact of Paris of 1928 which had obliged its contracting parties, including Japan, to forswear the use of force in the conduct of their foreign relations.

Manchuria in 1931 was followed by half a decade of Sino-Japanese tension and minor military clashes, which culminated fatefully in an unplanned skirmish at the Marco Polo Bridge in Beijing on 7 July 1937. The incident entailed Chinese troops firing at Japanese troops and the latter retaliating. Certainly on the Japanese side, the incident was not pre-arranged. Although Japan bore heavy responsibility for the inflammatory political context of Sino-Japanese relations, the evidence shows that the exchange of fire occurred strictly by local initiative, and on the Chinese side at that. But once the touch-paper was lit and political passions were aroused in China and Japan, the strategic fire could not be doused. The Japanese Army seized the opportunity created by the incident and commenced what was to be an eight-year war to subdue the Republic of China by force of arms. It was this change in policy, above all else, that set Tokyo on a collision course with Washington.

Japan had long embraced an imperial dream which, though limited, was certainly extensive. It sought to establish a great empire in East Asia, primarily on the continent at the expense of Chinese independence. For this empire to be defensible and prosperous, it had to be robustly self-sufficient in raw materials. Alas, the necessary natural resources lay at some distance from the Japanese Home Islands and were currently owned by other powers, chiefly European colonialists. In particular, Japan stood in acute need of oil, tin and rubber, itself possessing adequate stocks only of coal and iron ore. The Japanese Empire would be hopelessly vulnerable to blockade unless it expanded its territorial holdings into South East Asia.

Japan's strategic context in the 1930s was not enviable. Wherever it looked for support, it came up empty. Tokyo had no allies, and once it left the League of Nations in 1932 over that body's expressed unhappiness at Japanese aggression against China in Manchuria, there seemed to be menaces on all geostrategic fronts. In summary, in the mid- to late 1930s, Japan's quest for self-sufficient empire was opposed militarily in China by the Nationalist leader, Chiang Kai-shek; threatened by large Soviet armed forces deployed in Outer Mongolia and in the Soviet Far Eastern provinces; blocked by the European empires of Britain and the Netherlands from South and South East Asia; and menaced by the US Navy, which, though normally based near San Diego on the American West Coast, as an intended deterrent was moved far forward to Pearl Harbor on Oahu in the Hawaiian Islands in January 1940. The Philippines were an American colony and military dependency, and were situated with great geostrategic inconvenience for Japan between the Home Islands and the South Seas Resources Area in South East Asia. Geostrategically, then, America was in the way. Indeed, unless Japan was blessed with an unusually permissive window of strategic opportunity, and was cunning as well as lucky, there was a distinct possibility that it might find itself alone at war with a wholly unmatchable coalition of enemies. Adding yet more fuel to the strategic flames, by the late 1930s Japanese–American political and cultural relations already had recorded a legacy of forty-plus years of mutual antagonism.

Japan and the United States: the drift to war

The American acquisition of the Philippines from Spain, booty from a short, victorious war in 1898, all but guaranteed a long-term, tension-fraught relationship with Japan. As the new owner of the Philippines, the United States became by definition an Asian power. Moreover, as a simple consequence of strategic geography, the United States had acquired instantly a defence obligation in the far Western Pacific. From the turn of the century until 1941 there was only one plausible threat to America's new Asian empire, Imperial Japan. The latter demonstrated a highly aggressive policy and strategy regionally – towards China in 1894–5 and Russia in 1904–5 – and was committed to building a first-class navy. One did not require a crystal ball in order to anticipate trouble in the future for Japanese–American relations.

For more than thirty years the US Navy planned how it would defend the Philippines. Basically, its operational task would be to fight its way across the Pacific, seizing island bases as it went, leading to a heroic showdown with the Imperial Japanese Navy either in Philippine waters or close to Japan itself. Japan constructed a world-class navy that even in the context of the Washington Naval Arms Limitation Treaty with its 5:5:3 tonnage ratio (USA:Britain: Japan) would be superior in fighting power to that of the United States in Asian waters. It would be difficult to exaggerate the magnitude of the American naval task. To be blunt, the United States could not defend the Philippines. No matter how competently American and Filipino forces performed, they could not possibly hold out until the cavalry arrived from over the eastern horizon. Physical geography decreed that the centre of America's power was too remote from the scene of the needful action in Asian waters. In the absence of an existing well-fortified American or usable Allied base structure in East Asia, swift American military moves to counter Japanese aggression were simply a logistical impossibility. Japanese naval and military superiority over the United States and Britain in Asia was guaranteed by the deadly item in the Washington system which forbade the construction of new fortifications west of Hawaii and north of Singapore.

In addition to the unpromising strategic dimension to Japanese–American relations, one must not neglect the power of reciprocal cultural antipathy and the political antagonism that it stirred. Popular American distaste for Japan and the Japanese had two principal sources. First, there was elemental racism: many Americans despised Asians simply on racial grounds, though it is only fair to note that such racism was fully reciprocated by the Japanese. American disdain for the Japanese as Asians found expression in both legal and extra-legal discrimination against Japanese immigrants, especially in California. Furthermore, for all its high-flown rhetoric, the administration of Woodrow Wilson (he of the Fourteen Points and other declarations of universal virtues) steadfastly declined to endorse the principle of racial equality. This may have been a necessary contemporary evil, given America's domestic racial context, as well as the severe complication of the multiracial colonial empires of the European victors of 1918, but to reasonable Japanese in the 1920s it was unambiguous evidence of both a lack of respect and, indeed, hypocrisy.

The second major source of socio-cultural tension between Japan and the United States concerned the future of China. To the Japanese, China was the site of the origins of their culture, a vast domain with which they had a long, troubled special relationship mandated by history and geography. Also, China was viewed as the necessary continental anchor to the empire that they judged it essential to build if they were to win promotion to the premier league of great powers. The Japanese were genuinely puzzled by America's strange obsession with China. After all, the United States had no obvious strategic stake there and no extraordinary economic ties with Chinese society. One had to strain the imagination in order to understand just why so many Americans appeared to care deeply about China's fate. The Japanese never quite grasped the cultural fact that American society, notwithstanding its brutally racist mistreatment of Chinese immigrant labour, felt a powerful sentimental and paternalistic tie to China. Far from being respectful of

China as an ancient and highly sophisticated civilization, many Americans viewed it as a potential Asian America. They saw China as backward and corrupt, and therefore vulnerable to exploitation by profit-seeking foreigners, although not Americans, of course. The leading sources of this desire to improve China and save the Chinese were the thousands of American Christian missionaries who toiled selflessly to bring the Gospels and American values to what they found to be a medieval society. Of course, eventually there came to be strategic reasons to oppose Japanese misbehaviour in China, but behind the strategic rationales was always a profound American belief that Washington had a unique moral responsibility to protect China from unscrupulous predators. And by far the most unscrupulous predator in Asia in the 1930s and early 1940s was Imperial Japan.

If the events of 1940 in Europe created a strategic moment for those who wished to give history a helping push, so those same events had a like consequence in East Asia. The German victories over France, the Netherlands and soon, perhaps, even Britain and its empire seemed to transform Japan's strategic context. Opportunity appeared to beckon.

The German victory and consequent European ascendancy in 1940 altered Japan's strategic situation radically, probably for the better. But Tokyo never forgot that it was fundamentally isolated politically in its ambitions in East Asia, and that unless it were careful it might find itself facing a coalition of such combined strength that it would stand no realistic prospect of strategic success. Although Germany had defeated France and the Netherlands, and was obliging Britain to focus its strategic effort upon Europe – though Churchill did boldly reinforce the British garrison in Egypt – Japan's strategic situation was still heavily risk-prone in 1940. Notwithstanding the Tripartite Alliance of 27 September with Germany and Italy, Russia and Germany were still allies, Britain remained undefeated and the United States, though formally neutral, had assumed the role of coalition leader for those states that were seeking to arrest and reverse the continuing Japanese effort to achieve dominion over China. One did not need to be an overly paranoid Japanese leader to worry about the possibility of having to wage war against an enemy coalition comprising the United States, China, the Soviet Union, Britain and the Dutch East Indies. Tokyo harboured few illusions about the probable fidelity of Berlin, should the Germans need to choose between the Soviet Union and their new ally in Asia.

Domestic politics in Japan and the international diplomacy bearing on the issue of war in 1940–1 were complex indeed. The Japanese were not of one mind about their policy options; nor were they united in interpreting the meaning of the dynamic strategic context in Europe after 22 June 1941, the date of the German invasion of Russia. Amid the fine detail of policy conferences, proposals and counter-proposals, it is all too easy to lose sight of the central thread of the plot of strategic history. In particular, it is possible to be persuaded that since neither Japan nor the United States wanted war, a compromise settlement somehow might have been arranged. Perhaps a concession here, a compromise there, and the Asia–Pacific War might have been averted. That is not wholly fanciful, but on balance the evidence does not support it. It is well to remember that although Japan harboured antagonistic feelings towards the United States, feelings that had been greatly fuelled by the successful US efforts at Versailles in 1919 and then in Washington in 1921–2 to confine and limit Japanese power in China, war with the United

States was understood to be, at best, futile. Japan could not defeat the United States, and US possessions in the Western Pacific were anyway of no inherent material interest. In Japanese perspective the value of the Philippines was political and geostrategic: they were important to Japan because of their location and American ownership.

The central plot to this strategic historical narrative was, on the one hand, Japan's determination to construct a great East Asian empire, bulked up by a totally subordinated China, and, on the other hand, America's mounting determination to prevent this from happening. The diplomatic story of 1940–1 is one of repeated, ever-escalating American efforts to deter Japanese forward moves, and of the Japanese search for some political formula for its relations with China which Washington would find tolerable. But it could not be done. Both parties were sincere. Neither wanted to go to war with the other. American pressure was applied in two policy steps, both keyed to Japanese behaviour towards French Indo-China. Following the French surrender on 22 June 1940, and given Britain's understandable preoccupation with home defence, Japan sought to exploit the situation by closing the two overland routes by which Western aid was reaching China: the road from northern Indo-China and the specially constructed 'Burma Road'. The French and the British acquiesced and Japanese military intervention became large scale with an actual invasion of the north of Indo-China on 23 September 1940. The United States, however, was not ready to appease Japan just because Germany was triumphant in Europe. In July 1940, Washington imposed a selective embargo on aviation gasoline, on some lubricants and on scrap iron and steel. This was more of a warning than a severe punishment, but it was an unmistakable shot across the bows for Japan.

The strategic history of 1941, of the drift to war in the Pacific, can appear almost to have been scripted. Nothing in history is truly inevitable: possible contingency always may lurk in the unknown future to ambush those who believe that they can foresee how events will unfold. Nevertheless, by 1941 it is difficult to see how the Pacific War could have been prevented. At issue was the future of the Japanese Empire, particularly its expanding imperium over the coastal third of China. If Tokyo would not change its policy fundamentally towards China, a policy that it had pursued, in fits and starts, for half a century, then there could be no political accommodation with the United States. By 1941, indeed by 1940, Washington was the leader and essential mover of an anti-Japanese coalition, one that was known informally as the ABCD powers (America, Britain, China, Dutch East Indies).

By 1941 the United States was determined to reverse Japan's continuing efforts to subjugate China, not merely to prevent further Japanese aggression. Japanese offers to settle for what they had seized already did not meet with a friendly response in Washington. Given that the United States was by no means ready for war in the Pacific, or anywhere else, in 1941, and was committed to the defeat of Germany as the first priority should the country become a formal belligerent, its strategic options were distinctly limited. However, those options were to prove potent, and provocatively so. The drift to war in 1941 was the result of reciprocal strategic misjudgements by Tokyo and Washington.

In an effort to reduce the number of its potential enemies, at least for a while, Japan signed a five-year neutrality pact with the Soviet Union on 13 April 1941. The German invasion on 22 June caused a brief period of euphoria in Tokyo. The apparent defeat of the Red Army in the first month enabled Japanese leaders to persuade themselves that the United States now would be so acutely worried about developments in Europe that it would have no appetite for a firm policy in Asia–Pacific. As a result, Japan seized the strategic moment and in July 1941 moved its forces into the south of Indo-China. This aggressive forward move, one long anticipated by friend and foe alike, set in train the events that produced the Pearl Harbor attack of 7 December. Far from bowing to the inevitable, and acquiescing with a poor grace to this latest Japanese outrage, the United States took the second of its major strategic decisions: it froze all Japanese funds and assets in the United States and, in effect, imposed a total embargo on oil and other strategic materials. Economic sanctions have a notably mixed record of success and failure in strategic history, but this time the American economic sanctions were probably too effective. They created a policy crisis for Japan. No oil was received from the United States or the Dutch East Indies after 5 August 1941, and the Imperial Japanese Navy had reserves that would last only two years, at most.

Conclusion

Japan had a clear choice. On the one hand, it could agree to be coerced and bow to American pressure. This would mean meeting at least the minimum slate of American demands, the centrepiece of which was the abandonment of the war in China. On the other, it could reject the US insistence that it forswear its long-standing China policy, indeed its policy of imperial expansion altogether, and instead fight to secure the raw material resources that it needed to sustain and expand the imperium. Japanese opinion was divided, but not over the most essential of matters. The commitment to continental empire in China was uncontroversial, while the strategic implications of the total oil embargo were stark and undeniable. The only issue for debate was whether it was worth pursuing a diplomatic solution. It is clear enough in retrospect, as it was to many at the time, that while Japan insisted upon a forward policy in China, a compromise solution was not available. Since the Japanese vision of a Greater East Asian Co-prosperity Sphere – Japanese regional hegemony – required the domination of China, there simply was no diplomatic solution.

Given their ambitions and assumptions, Japanese leaders were in an unenviable position in late 1941. They could not abandon the war in China. They could not endure the oil embargo, because it must have the consequence that the armed forces, especially the Imperial Navy, would grow progressively weaker, to the point where they would be unable to move and fight. Furthermore, Japan was well aware that the United States was in mid-course of a programme of headlong rearmament. As a military adversary, it would be far more formidable in 1943 and after than it had been in 1941 and would be in 1942. Predictably – dare one say inevitably? – diplomacy failed to produce an acceptable compromise. Japan decided to strike and to attempt to fight its way out of its strategic dilemma. But where to strike? What would be the objectives? How would the new acquisitions be defended? And, given the inherent strength of the United States, how could Japan avoid eventual defeat?

Key points

1. World War II in Europe appeared to provide Japan with the permissive strategic context it needed in order to solve its economic and strategic problems.
2. The decline of China, and the chaos there that succeeded the 1911 Revolution, created the opportunity for Japan to seek a great continental empire.
3. US–Japanese antagonism pre-dated Pearl Harbor by nearly forty years. It was fed by racial and cultural disdain, but above all else it centred upon Japanese policy towards China.
4. In 1941, Japan's decision not to join Germany in the war against the Soviet Union was probably a strategic error.
5. US-led efforts to deter Japan from further aggression in 1940–1 had the reverse effect from the one intended. Economic sanctions drove Japan to war.
6. Japan and the United States did not wish to fight each other, but their policies towards China were comprehensively irreconcilable. Compromise was impossible.

Questions

1. What were Japan's foreign policy objectives?
2. How did the events of 1939–41 in Europe influence Japanese policy and strategy?
3. Explain the significance of China as the principal cause of US–Japanese antagonism.
4. Why did Japan decide to fight in 1941?

Further reading

M. A. Barnhart *Japan Prepares for Total War: The Search for Economic Security, 1919–1941* (Ithaca, NY: Cornell University Press, 1987).

J. W. Dower *War without Mercy: Race and Power in the Pacific War* (New York: Pantheon Books, 1986).

H. Feis *The Road to Pearl Harbor: The Coming of the War between the United States and Japan* (Princeton, NJ: Princeton University Press, 1971).

A. Iriye *The Origins of the Second World War in Asia and the Pacific* (London: Longman, 1987).

R. H. Spector *Eagle against the Sun: The American War with Japan* (New York: Free Press, 1985).

J. Toland *The Rising Sun: The Decline and Fall of the Japanese Empire, 1936–1945* (New York: Random House, 1970).

J. G. Utley *Going to War with Japan, 1937–1941* (Knoxville, TN: University of Tennessee Press, 1985).

H. P. Willmott *The Second World War in the Far East* (London: Cassell, 1999).

13 World War II in Asia–Pacific, II
Strategy and warfare

Reader's guide: Japan's decision to fight. Japanese strategy. US strategy. The character of the war, and of warfare, in Asia–Pacific.

Introduction: over the cliff

There was much diplomatic activity in the second half of 1941 between Japan and its opponents, primarily the United States. In addition, the internal Japanese debate was certainly active virtually all the way to Pearl Harbor. But really the die was cast in a key policy document of 6 September 1941, 'Guidelines for implementing national policies', which was formally adopted by national leaders in the presence of the Emperor. In the judgement of one Japanese historian, 'That document may be regarded as a virtual declaration of war by Japan. It clearly implied that war would come unless a peaceful settlement could be worked out with the United States' (Iriye, 1987: 160). The 'guide-lines' document said that the Americans, British and Dutch would have to halt their aid to China, eschew establishing military facilities in Thailand, the Dutch East Indies (modern Indonesia), China itself or the Far Eastern provinces of the Soviet Union, and restore normal cooperative trading relations with Japan. In return, Japan would promise to refrain from further military expansion in Asia, and would withdraw its forces from Indo-China 'upon the establishment of a just peace in Asia'. In other words, Japan insisted upon holding on to its ill-gotten gains and was offering only a promise of good behaviour in the future. General Tojo Hideki took over as Prime Minister on 17 October, in place of the rather more flexible, not to say weak and inadequate, Konoye Funimaro. As a result, the prospects for a last-minute shift in Japanese policy towards an offer that might just be on the outer edge of negotiability moved from exceedingly low to zero. Japan would not abandon its China policy, and the United States would not acquiesce in that policy.

Japanese strategy

Unlike the quasi-religious vision that inspired Adolf Hitler's decidedly open-ended policy goals for expansion, Japan had a fairly precise notion both of what it wanted to achieve and of how it could accomplish it. In July–August 1941, despite the temptation to jump on the German military bandwagon, Tokyo decided firmly not to abandon its recent neutrality pact with Moscow. This seemed to be a prudent case of 'heads we win and tails we also win'. Should Germany defeat the Soviet Union, then Japan would face no threat from the north, which would be a highly satisfactory situation. Should the Soviet Union resist successfully (an unlikely possibility, but one that could not be ruled out), then again Japan would not be troubled by a Soviet threat, because the USSR would be far too preoccupied with Germany to be at all interested in fighting Japan for many years to come. Furthermore, should the Soviet Union defeat Germany, it would be prudent for Japan not to have lined up as an active belligerent in that conflict.

Japan adopted a necessarily limited strategy for limited objectives. As just noted, it assumed that it would not have to fight Russia. Conveniently, Germany had reshaped Japan's strategic context by both removing the Soviet menace, for a while at least, and occupying British and American strategic attention in Europe, even though the United States was yet to enter the war. Japan's strategic grand design in late 1941 was to seize by force what it termed the Southern Resources Area of South East Asia, primarily the Dutch East Indies and Malaya. Then Japan would construct a defensible perimeter to protect the greatly expanded geographical scope of the new Japanese Empire. From 31 January 1941, Tokyo began referring officially to its imperium, actual and intended, as the 'Greater East Asian Co-prosperity Sphere'. (Strategic history is well populated with such self-serving euphemisms for exploitative political designs.) Japanese naval and military planners were confident that they could make the necessary gains in a campaign of only five months' duration. In this, if in little else, they proved correct.

For this huge smash-and-grab operation to the south to be strategically feasible, the Japanese Navy reasoned that it must disable or otherwise neutralize the only armed force in the Pacific that, in theory at least, might offer effective opposition. That threat, of course, was the US Navy, forward-based on Oahu at Pearl Harbor, as well as the long-range, land-based air power of the US Army Air Corps' B-17s, based in the Philippines. With those assets neutralized, nothing could hinder the brief but highly ambitious march of conquest. The Philippines were a vital military objective for Japan both because of General Douglas MacArthur's B-17s and, more fundamentally, because geostrategically the islands sat astride Japan's crucial sea lines of communication to the Southern Resources Area of South East Asia. In short, there was never any prospect of Japan restricting its attacks to Dutch and British territories alone and leaving American assets untouched. Not only was the United States the leader of the anti-Japanese ABCD coalition, but its brief imperial moment at the end of the nineteenth century had bequeathed it political responsibilities which happened to lie directly in the path of Japanese expansion.

The Japanese plan for the security of its expanded empire comprised the following essential elements: establish an extensive maritime defence perimeter in the Central and South Pacific; provide strong garrisons, including land-based air power, for selected islands on and behind that perimeter, for defence in depth; and support those otherwise isolated garrisons with the Imperial Navy. From such advanced, fortified bases as Rabaul in New Britain and Truk in the Caroline Islands, the fleet, operating from a central position, would enjoy the Napoleonic advantage of interior lines of communication. So much for the necessarily maritime menace from the east. What about the south and the west?

As a matter of a strategic geography, the Japanese Empire in the early 1940s was, in theory, at risk from four directions. The menace from the east posed by the US Navy in the Central Pacific would be eliminated by direct military action. The threat from the north, which is to say the Soviet Union, had been dispelled temporarily by a combination of prudent Japanese diplomacy and German war-making. From the south, it was just possible that an enemy coalition might be able to base itself in Australia and New Zealand, and then slowly crawl up the extensive island chains of Papua New Guinea and the erstwhile Dutch East Indies, on the way to Singapore, Malaya and points north. From the west, the Japanese were obliged to take seriously the danger that a militarily revived China could serve as a launch pad for a land, sea and air threat to the Home Islands themselves.

Japan's answers to these unpleasant possibilities were to seek to foreclose at least on the threats from the south and the west. By controlling all of Indo-China, persuading Thailand to be cooperative, ejecting British imperial forces from much of Burma, and waging warfare ever more ferociously in China, the Japanese sought to close down the China option as a base and threat vector for their enemies. Despite President Roosevelt's ambition to the contrary, such unforgiving realities of geography as sheer distance, terrain and weather were to render China a hopeless candidate for the direction from which Japan would be brought to book. As for potential peril from the south, in practice Japan needed to prevent Australia and New Zealand serving as advanced bases for American military power. To that end, it was essential to sever America's maritime lines of communication across the South Pacific and, to be doubly sure, to conquer Australia and New Zealand. But Japan suffered its first notable strategic setback when its geographically final move before reaching Australia itself was frustrated by the US Navy in the Battle of the Coral Sea (7–8 May 1942). The outcome of the battle was indecisive, but strategically it was an American victory, because a Japanese troop convoy heading for Port Moresby in New Guinea was obliged to abandon its intended invasion.

It may be helpful at this point to note that of the four geostrategic threat vectors – from Hawaii and the Central Pacific; from Australia and the south; from China in the west; and from the Soviet Union in the north – that from the Central Pacific was by far the most menacing. The Soviet Union was not in this war until 8 August 1945. China was never sufficiently secure as a base for ambitious Allied operations, and it was logistically impracticable save at disproportionate cost. And the advance up the Dutch East Indies towards Singapore and the Philippines promised to be a protracted venture, one that would not yield high strategic returns for a long time.

But what was the Japanese theory of victory? It is true that the Japanese and the Americans lacked mutual cultural empathy, a fact which had political, strategic and tactical consequences. However, ethnocentric and deeply prejudiced though each side certainly was, neither Washington nor Tokyo was deaf to strategic analysis, notwithstanding the wishful thinking that coloured some of that analysis. The Japanese knew that alone they could not protect their new empire by force of arms over the long term. Their strategic challenge was to present the Americans with a strategic context in Asia–Pacific that they would choose to accept, no matter how reluctantly. The Japanese theory of victory, therefore, amounted to the hope – one hesitates to say calculation – that the United States would judge the cost of defeating Japan to be too heavy, too disproportionate to the worth of the US interests at stake. If Germany were to beat the

Soviet Union – which remained a distinct possibility until quite late in 1942, and feasible even in 1943 – and as a consequence dominate Europe, it was reasoned in Tokyo to be improbable that Washington would be willing to conduct a total war in the Pacific.

This Japanese theory of victory was as weak as it sounds in the brief outline above. It might have had some small merit in the event of a German victory, but that, of course, was out of Tokyo's hands to control. And, if anything, Tokyo had hurt its own strategic prospects by declining to join in the assault on the Soviet Union.

Four erroneous Japanese assumptions foredoomed the Japanese bid for expanded empire. First, the surprise attack on Pearl Harbor was a cultural mistake of the first order. Regardless of its substantial tactical success, it so incensed the American public that no US government could accept any outcome short of virtually total, unconditional Japanese surrender. (The only condition that the United States did accept, at the last minute, was preservation of the symbolic role of the Emperor.) It is almost a law of strategy that one must not wage war in such a way as to foreclose upon the kind of political outcome that is desired. Since Japan sought to wage a limited war for limited, albeit territorially extravagant, gains, it was not wise strategy to open proceedings with tactical actions which would drive the materially superior enemy to seek total revenge.

Second, Germany did not defeat the Soviet Union. This had not quite been an assumption behind Japanese policy, at least not for long beyond June–July 1941, but it was a far more vital necessity for the security of the Japanese Empire than Tokyo appeared to recognize.

Third, Japan was well advised by military and industrial professionals who believed that they understood the depth of America's war-making potential. But few, if any, of them appreciated that the United States would prove strong enough to mobilize on a scale adequate to wage a two-ocean war, *simultaneously*.

Fourth and finally, the Japanese strategy for imperial defence was fundamentally flawed because it could be only as robust as the military balance that supported it. The strength of the fortifications and garrisons on geographically isolated atolls and islands did not really matter strategically; their protection had to be systemic, or it was nothing. Japan's Pacific island barriers comprised a network held together, and indeed to be defended directly, by the maritime–air strength of the Imperial Navy employed in conjunction with local, land-based air power. If the Imperial Japanese Navy was too weak to contest an American advance, then the island garrisons were simply *de facto* POW camps. The United States could pick and choose which islands it would assault and which it would ignore. Many of the necessary amphibious assaults would prove hugely expensive in casualties, but Japanese defeat, island by island, was as inevitable as the bravery shown by the defenders was strategically irrelevant and culturally faithful.

As Japanese military leaders had predicted, the strategic initiative was theirs for five months. But two critical naval–air battles in May and June 1942 effectively marked the end of the short period wherein Japan controlled the character and geostrategic direction of the war. As noted already, at the Coral Sea on 7–8 May the US Navy ambushed the Japanese invasion fleet bound for Port Moresby. Aside from the significant tactical fact that the Coral Sea was the first sea battle wherein the combatants' ships were always out of sight of each other, the indecisive tactical outcome was sufficient to thwart the Japanese invasion plan. Port Moresby was the last stop before Port Darwin in Australia's sparsely populated Northern Territory.

A month later, and again with heartfelt thanks to superior code-breaking, the US Navy succeeded in ambushing the carriers which were leading the main body of the Imperial Japanese fleet off the island of Midway, an extension of the Hawaiian chain. Thanks to good luck, extreme bravery and prudent military practice, American naval aviators sank four Japanese fleet carriers on 4–5 June. Admiral Isoroku Yamamoto, Japan's naval commander-in-chief, had decided that the partial success at Pearl Harbor – no American carriers were in port – needed to be augmented by the imposition of a truly crushing blow against the US Navy at sea. Alas for him, the crushing blow was suffered by Japan. The four carriers could and would be replaced eventually, but what could not be replaced was the experienced elite of naval aviators, of whom Japan was to discover it possessed far too few.

In the summer of 1942, with the Japanese failures at the Coral Sea and Midway, and with the United States at least a year away from reaping the benefit of its rearmament surge, the belligerents were in a condition of rough strategic balance. The Japanese had lost the initiative, while the United States had yet to seize it and decide what to do with it, and where. The strategic history of late 1942 to 1945 was driven principally by American behaviour and Japanese responses. As a consequence, the focus now shifts from Japanese to American strategy in order to explain the further course and character of the war in Asia–Pacific.

American strategy

The United States did not really have a dominant strategy for the defeat of Japan. Rather, it had several, each promoted by a separate armed service. Everyone agreed on the geostrategic destination of American military power: Tokyo. But a clear choice of route there was never made. One of the many benefits of a growing, and eventually great, military superiority is that agonizing decisions between alternative courses of actions can be evaded; one simply pursues each of the principal options. Americans did not, perhaps could not, have a clear idea as to exactly how Japan would be brought to surrender. The USAAF intended eventually to bomb Japan back into the Stone Age with its brand-new B-29 Superfortresses (whose first combat mission was on 5 June 1944). The US Navy expected to strangle Japan into impotence with a blockade enforced by its surface, sub-surface and air assets, having first defeated the Imperial Japanese Navy in battle, while the US Army anticipated launching, and planned to launch, a massive invasion of Japan's Home Islands. This view and approach reflected the respected dictum expressed by Rear Admiral J. C. Wylie: 'The ultimate determinant in war is the man on the scene with the gun' (Wylie, 1989: 72). However, given the fanatical quality of Japanese resistance, ubiquitously, there were no illusions as to just how bloody a business an invasion would prove to be.

The previous section advanced the story to the summer of 1942, when Japan lost the strategic initiative; or, more precisely, when Japanese strategic options were significantly reduced. This point was reached because of Germany's continuing failure to knock the Soviet Union out of the war and, more directly, because of the Imperial Navy's defeat at Midway in June. By way of an express overview, for the next two years, from June 1942 until June 1944, the two great navies of Japan and the United States were careful to avoid each other, at least with respect to fleet-to-fleet combat. Both needed a major victory, but both were reluctant to take needless risks. These were two formidable navies. It is worth remembering that despite the combat at the Coral Sea and Midway, the two battle fleets had yet to meet. The age of carrier air power had arrived, or at least was arriving, but many admirals, especially in Japan, still expected a great naval battle to be concluded by the gun power of the battle line. With Germany in deep trouble in the Soviet Union – as it demonstrated by its own formidable negative example just what Clausewitz had meant by 'the culminating point of victory', and why one should not exceed it – Japan could identify only one theory of victory. The Imperial Japanese Navy, the guardian of the new empire, had to inflict defeat in battle upon the US Navy. If the latter could be beaten, all might yet be well. The theory had some merit, but the American enemy was sufficiently high in quality and was expanding so rapidly in quantity by 1943 that the Imperial Navy's hopes of inflicting a Tsushima (the battle on 27 May 1905 where Vice-Admiral Heihachiro Togo annihilated Russia's Baltic Fleet) on the Americans could be fulfilled only if the latter committed fatal operational errors.

The pull of the Pacific

Long prior to Pearl Harbor, the United States had agreed with Britain on the strategic principle of 'Germany First'. As the most dangerous enemy, Germany had to be defeated first. Once that was achieved, strategically, the subsequent fall of Japan could be only a matter of time. If the principle were reversed, the defeat of Japan would mean little for the prospects of defeating Germany. But strategic history is fond of abusing sound intentions and robust plans with inconvenient and unexpected contingencies. Surprises happen. And the flow of events led Americans to want to fight the Japanese, not the Germans. Primarily this was the result of Japan's 'day of infamy' with the Pearl Harbor attack on 7 December 1941. But it was a sentiment notably amplified by subsequent knowledge of Japanese brutality towards, and murder of, American POWs in the Philippines. The iconic event in the public consciousness was the so-called 'Bataan death march', when the American and Filipino survivors of the defence of the Bataan peninsula were force-marched deep inland. Under appalling conditions, 600 out of 12,000 Americans died during the trek, as did up to 7,000 of 60,000 Filipinos.

Throughout the war, from December 1941, US policy was subject to the pull of the Pacific. That pull was exerted by the military and strategic logic of events in that part of the world, and, of scarcely less importance, by the force of American public opinion. The Pacific pull was useful as a source of pressure on America's British ally. Roosevelt could threaten to put America's contribution to the European war on hold, while a near-maximum effort was exerted in the Pacific against Japan. This was not what the President favoured, but the pressure on him to devote ever more resources to the war against Japan was real enough, and the British knew it. The Pacific War did have a major strategic consequence for the conduct of the Anglo-American war in Europe, though not as major as it might have been. When it came to inter-Allied strategic argument, the British were a formidable adversary: they waged war by committee and their staffwork was in a class of its own. But the pull of the Pacific could not help but have the strategic consequence of putting the United States under pressure to win quickly in Europe, and the American Joint Chiefs of Staff were always in favour of adopting the most direct path to Berlin. This was helpful as a partial corrective to Britain's preference for what some commentators have disdainfully termed a strategy of 'indecisive encirclement'. However, the American liking for a rapid, direct approach to Hitler's Fortress Europe was also a formula all but guaranteed to produce military disaster. America's inclination towards haste in Europe needed to be disciplined by a realistic appreciation of the continuing strengths of the Wehrmacht. Fortunately, in 1942 and 1943 the United States was the junior partner in the Anglo-American Alliance. Therefore, it was in no position to insist that the invasion of France must be undertaken immediately. Any such venture would have had to be carried out largely by British and Canadian troops, not American.

Needless to say, the American public mood in 1941–2, and the country's strategic preferences, were very far removed from Japan's pre-war expectations. Such is the price of cultural ignorance and a lack of imagination. The Pearl Harbor attack was an assault on American honour, as well as on its battle fleet. And when honour has been besmirched, the offended party is not likely to be interested in the conduct of a strictly limited conflict. It is worth noting that the racially homogeneous Japanese, in common with their German nominal ally, had scant respect for Americans as members of a polyglot society. In contrast, German and Japanese soldiers regarded themselves as racially privileged warriors in a sacred cause. It was not a large leap of prejudice for them to see their American opponents as inherently inferior soldiers because of their racially varied ancestry.

The paths taken by what passed for US strategy in the war against Japan illustrate a number of enduring themes in strategic history. To be specific: history has a dynamic all its own that defies close management and control. Also, contingency and surprise may compel a radical change of course. Furthermore, opportunity can beckon as the strategic context changes. Finally, military events will have a momentum all their own. It is all very well to agree to defeat Germany first, but if Americans are heavily committed operationally and tactically in the Pacific, there must be a military logic to their behaviour and to its consequences which high policy will be almost impotent to frustrate for the sake of a general principle.

Despite the Germany First policy (from which Roosevelt never deviated), the course of events in the Pacific drew the United States more deeply, and sooner, into the war against Japan than had been expected. This was the result of public anger over Pearl Harbor and, even more, because of American surprise at the success and speed of the Japanese wave of conquest. It was recognized that unless the Japanese rampage were slowed and stopped, it could pose an unduly formidable strategic challenge to meet in years to come. There was thus an urgent need to limit the damage. Where would the Japanese halt?

The American counter-attack

The balance of military power in the Central Pacific, at least, was altered radically (though it was certainly not reversed) by the surprising American victory at Midway in June 1942. In fact, the US Navy probably inflicted even more damage upon the Japanese than it appreciated at the time by wiping out the core of Japan's elite naval aviators. For historical perspective, it should be noted that although there were dozens of minor engagements between the two navies from 1942 to 1945, there were really only three grand clashes. One can speculate as to why that was the case, but the most plausible explanation is that the stakes were too high for a fleet-to-fleet encounter to be risked for anything other than the most pressing of reasons, and only in the most favourable circumstances. This was an example of a long-standing truth about war at sea.

The margin between victory and defeat can be narrow in a naval battle, where the major combatant units will number only in the tens, or even less. Because battle is always a risky undertaking, fleet preservation typically takes strategic precedence over the chance for glory and advantage. It is true that the Imperial Japanese Navy had a doctrine that emphasized battle, but it is undeniable that it husbanded the main body of its fleet in home waters throughout the war. It sought battle on a large scale with its American counterpart only three times: in June 1942 at Midway; in June 1944 at Saipan (or the Philippine Sea); and in October 1944 at Leyte Gulf in the Philippines.

With the Japanese and US navies reluctant to expose themselves, especially their precious carriers, to the hazards of major battle for the better part of two years after Midway, the Americans took their first initiative to arrest and reverse the Japanese advance. On 7 August 1942 the First Marine Division landed on Guadalcanal and Tulagi in the southern Solomons, while an Allied army of Australians and Americans took on the unenviable task of ejecting the Japanese from the north coast of New Guinea. The Guadalcanal campaign was of great significance. It was conducted at the high-water mark of Japan's penetration of the South Seas, and it developed into an attritional struggle of six months' duration. The Americans eventually won, though the Japanese had the better of much of the naval combat, especially at night. And attritional warfare played to America's growing strength and exposed Japan's endemic material weakness.

Strategic empathy can be hard to achieve, but the effort is worthwhile because it offers useful insight into the nature of strategy as well as the realities of strategic history. Although the United States was firmly committed to defeating Germany first, in 1942 and 1943 there was not much of great strategic significance for American forces to do in the European theatre. So, it followed that political resistance to an aggressive strategy in the Pacific was easily overcome. The Japanese Navy had been wounded at Midway and effectively went into hiding subsequently, except for its piecemeal commitment of scarce surface vessels to the Solomons and New Guinea campaigns in the autumn and winter of 1942–3.

Several roads to Tokyo

The United States faced the dilemma of too many viable choices, each favoured by a different armed service and each proposing a different main character of warfare. There were several roads to Tokyo.

First, the United States could continue the war that it was fighting already in the South-West Pacific. The plan would be to advance up the Solomons and along the coast of New Guinea into the Dutch East Indies. This largely Army venture, led by none other than the all-American hero General Douglas MacArthur, he of the Medal of Honor (granted as a morale-raiser at home in order to offset the bad news of defeat in the Philippines), would proceed northwards to the Philippines. The Navy would support this grand drive.

Second, the United States might try to defeat Japan in and from China. By assisting Generalissimo Chiang Kai-shek, Chinese and some American forces would defeat the

Japanese Army and Air Force in China. Then they would launch a bombing campaign against Japan's Home Islands from Chinese bases and stage invasions of Japanese home territory from the Chinese mainland.

Third, the US Navy could implement a variant of its thirty-year-old Plan Orange and fight its way across the Central Pacific, seizing island bases and depending heavily upon its newly developed fleet train for resupply under way at sea, defeating the Imperial Japanese Navy as and when it offered itself in battle (Miller, 1991). Geopolitics and geostrategy mandated that this drive must head for the Japanese Marianas. From there the drive could veer north-westwards directly for Japan itself, move on Taiwan or reach for the Philippines.

Which of the three options did the United States choose? In practice, it chose not to choose. The drive north from Australia towards the Dutch East Indies, and eventually the Philippines, was endorsed because it was MacArthur's. After all, he had been created a national hero by Washington for his supposedly heroic defence of Bataan and the island of Corregidor in Manila Bay. Also, this land-oriented, albeit sea- and air-dependent, thrust into the Japanese Empire appealed to the Army. The Navy's understandable preference for the ocean road to Tokyo was irresistible. Its strategic promise was high, and it was complementary to MacArthur's push. Exactly where the two thrusts would meet – at the Philippines, Taiwan or Japan itself – would have to wait upon events. And finally, the United States did attempt, seriously if unwisely, to construct an army in China that could beat the Japanese and provide a safe continental haven from which a long-range bombing campaign against the Home Islands could be conducted. But in 1944, Japanese offensives in China were so successful that Chiang's armies were obliged to retreat deep into the country and US air bases for the bombing campaign were over-run. As a result, China, the third threat vector, was belatedly taken off the American strategy board, after the wasting of a mountain of *matériel* and thousands of lives. Japan would be defeated by MacArthur from the south and Admiral Nimitz from the east. Was it strategically essential to endorse both approaches? Probably not, though it may well have confused the Japanese as to which threat was the main one. Since the Americans themselves could not answer that question, one can excuse the Japanese for being puzzled.

How was Japan defeated? In a material sense, by the US economy. The 'Two-Ocean' Navy Act of 1940 looked to achieve a 70 per cent increase in the size of the Navy, while the country mobilized in depth in all dimensions of its war-making needs. The Japanese were surprised by the scale and pace of the US mobilization, as well as by the character and speed of the US Navy's recovery from its losses at Pearl Harbor, the Coral Sea and Midway. But Tokyo had never treasured any illusions as to the ultimate military-industrial strength of the United States. It knew that it must lose a long war of attrition. It would be a profound error, however, to attribute Japan's defeat largely to the weight of America's military production. The US Navy and Marine Corps invented new ways of warfare, and learnt to execute them effectively. With inadvertent assistance from Admiral Yamamoto, the US Navy changed from being a battleship navy to being a carrier navy. The latter assumed the fleet crown of being the 'capital ship' in the drive across the Central Pacific. The thrust that from November 1943 until June 1944 took the Japanese-held Gilberts, Marshalls, Carolines and Marianas on Tokyo's 14,200-mile maritime defence perimeter was led by joint carrier task forces. This was completely new in the history of warfare.

In its geographical scope, speed, operational agility and, above all, strategic effectiveness, carrier-led warfare was revolutionary. Scarcely less novel was the demonstration under fire of the effectiveness of the US Marine Corps' new doctrine of amphibious assault. The marines' learning curve was expensive in blood, but it was steep and rapid.

The fast-forward movement of the American fleet, led by its carrier task forces, was, of course, an invitation to the Imperial Japanese Navy to come out and fight. This reality had a parallel in the war in Europe. Daylight bombing by the USAAF's Eighth Air Force had the effect of all but obliging a rapidly declining Luftwaffe air defence force to take to the skies. Aloft, by March 1944 at least, it could be shot down in droves by the Allies' new escort fighters. The Japanese impotently witnessed the demolition of their theory and practice of extended perimeter defence of their empire. They knew that they had to stop the US Navy somewhere, or eventually it would appear in Tokyo Bay. But where should decisive battle be offered? Strategic geography provided just one answer: the Marianas. These islands were the innermost elements in the entire maritime defence perimeter. From them, the US Navy could reach directly for the Japanese Home Islands, via the Bonins – including a tiny volcanic island called Iwo Jima – or westwards to the Philippines or Taiwan. Also, from air bases in the Marianas, particularly on the larger islands of Guam, Tinian and Saipan, America's land-based heavy bombers would be within range of Japan. Take the Marianas, therefore, and the new B-29s would have no need of bases in China.

Victory in the Marianas

US Army and Marine units stormed ashore on Saipan on 15 June 1944, opening a campaign that was to last until 13 July and cost 14,000 casualties. The climactic encounter at sea that both sides sought, albeit cautiously (especially on the American side, strangely), occurred on 19–20 July. As at the Coral Sea and Midway, the Battle of the Philippine Sea was entirely an aerial encounter. The only exception was provided by inept Japanese submarine forays which cost an incredible seventeen boats for no return. For good reason, American pilots called the battle off Saipan 'the Marianas Turkey Shoot'. Japanese carrier aircraft made 328 sorties and managed to lose 243 planes. The island-based First Air Fleet lost a further fifty. American losses numbered only twenty aircraft from enemy action. There was nothing mysterious about the crushing American victory. By June 1944, American carrier air power enjoyed decisive advantages in the form of new models, airborne radar and, more important still, pilots who were tactically superior to their Japanese foes. The result was a massacre that marked the effective end of Japan's once world-leading carrier air power. However, because of poor intelligence and overcautious leadership by Admiral Raymond A. Spruance, commander of the US Navy's Fifth Fleet, the Japanese carriers and other surface vessels were not engaged by American aircraft. The US Navy lost more planes and pilots in an ill-judged, heroic, yet futile effort to find and engage the Japanese carriers than it did in the battle. The Pacific at night is vast and lonely when you are running low on fuel and you cannot be sure of the exact location of your mobile home. The Imperial Japanese Navy lived to fight again, but henceforth it would have to fight bereft of an offensive, or defensive, air arm.

The Japanese had hoped to deliver a painful, if not necessarily disabling, blow to the principal American carrier force off Saipan. Instead, they had hastened their own demise.

The course of the war from June 1944 until August 1945 was characterized by skilful Japanese ground defence of the Philippines (beginning on 20 October 1944 at Leyte), then of Iwo Jima (19–26 February 1945) and finally of Okinawa (1 April–4 August 1945) In addition, there were sacrificial assaults by a surface fleet naked of air cover and by 'kamikaze' suicide sorties by novice pilots.

American forces gradually – and one must emphasize that it was a gradual process – closed in upon the Japanese homeland. On balance, American military and naval leadership was less than stellar. American soldiers, sailors, marines and airmen fought far better than they were led. The missed opportunity off Saipan has already been noted. But there were other examples. In the greatest surface battle of the war, at Leyte Gulf on 24–26 October 1944, it is difficult to be certain which side demonstrated the lesser operational skill. On land, a clear verdict is easier to reach. The Japanese out-generalled the Americans in the Philippines, a fact for which MacArthur could not forgive his talented opponent, General Tomoyuki Yamashita (the victor in Malaya and Singapore). MacArthur had his revenge upon this opponent who had tarnished his reputation for infallibility by arranging for his trial and execution as a war criminal. On Iwo Jima and especially Okinawa, the Japanese played losing hands with consummate skill and terrifying determination.

The end for Japan

But, for Tokyo, resistance was in vain. By July 1945 the country was decisively beaten in several different respects. The first B-29 raid on Japan from the Marianas, 100 strong, was launched on 24 November 1944, and from that point onwards what had once been urban Japan was systematically deconstructed by fire. At sea, Japan was totally block-aded. American submarines – once they had worked out how to make their torpedoes explode, by late 1943 – had long since reduced the Japanese merchant marine to a shadow of its former self. By July 1945 the US Navy had imposed a complete submarine, surface and air blockade of the Japanese Home Islands. The Japanese at home were therefore on their own. It did not matter which Japanese forces were still in the field, or afloat, elsewhere in Asia–Pacific, they were both too weak to intervene in the principal strategic drama and had no means of returning to provide reinforcements for a last-ditch defence of the homeland.

The war in Asia–Pacific concluded with two large bangs, on 6 and 9 August 1945. A single B-29 Superfortress, flying from Tinian, delivered an atomic bomb on Hiroshima, then another did the same to Nagasaki. By the summer of 1945 the Japanese were short of everything except fanatical and strategically irrelevant courage. A powerful faction in Tokyo wanted to fight on. Mercifully, the atomic bombs provided the tipping weight in the scales that permitted Emperor Hirohito to insist upon surrender. Japan requested a ceasefire on 15 August and surrendered formally on 2 September. Should anyone doubt the significance of culture and cultural differences in strategic history, they could do worse than reflect upon the meaning of a public campaign launched in Japan in the summer of 1945 that was intended to energize the public to be ready to resist the invader: 'The Glorious Death of One Hundred Million'. The war in Asia and the Pacific certainly had a potent cultural dimension.

The British imperial dimension

Readers may have noticed the neglect here of the long and bitter struggle in Burma. The war in Burma is a tale of great courage on both sides, of the mutual difficulty of surviving nature as well as the enemy, and of the eventual achievement of military competence by British and Indian troops, well led by General William J. Slim. The reason for the silence on Burma thus far is that, despite the see-sawing of military advantage there, and the eventual fact that the Japanese Army was handed its single largest defeat of the war, the campaign ultimately was of no strategic significance for the war as a whole. The only meaning it might have had was for the opening of the Burma Road (from Lashio in Burma to Kunming in China) for aid to China. However, it became undeniable that the path to Tokyo could not proceed through China, not even for the purpose of basing B-29s for the bombardment of the Home Islands. The Japanese Army in China was too strong, and the Chinese Army too weak and uninterested in fighting the invader. It has to follow that the Burma campaign lacked significant value for the course and outcome of the war. But it did have both symbolic and substantive value for the restoration of some of the prestige of the British Empire. In 1941–2 that prestige had suffered what ultimately would prove to be terminal damage at Japanese hands. Of course, the Americans were less than sympathetic to British strategic ideas that appeared motivated more by an interest in imperial recovery than by calculation of strategic effect upon Japan.

It is only fair to observe that the British in Asia in 1942–5, whatever one's views on their empire, did behave in a strategically responsible and rational manner. They conducted the war for the post-war order that they desired. The main event was the maritime struggle between Japan and the United States. Britain was too heavily engaged in Europe and the Middle East to commit other than a small fraction of its forces to Asia. But with the United States carrying the truly heavy load in the maritime war against Japan, Britain was at liberty to wage the Asian war that was mandated by the needs of its failing, indeed failed, empire. Britain paid token obeisance to what it judged to be the American fantasy of a powerful China, but its prime concern was to save strategically, and hence politically, what it could from the appalling wreckage of the surrender at Singapore on 15 January 1942 and the subsequent rout in Burma. As Stalin waged war in 1944–5 with his eyes firmly fixed on the post-war order, so too did the British in Asia in the same period.

Box 13.1 provides a terse summary of the more distinctive characteristics of the war and warfare in Asia–Pacific from 1941 to 1945.

Box 13.1 **Characteristics of war and warfare in Asia–Pacific, 1941–5**

- It was a war of amphibious manoeuvre in an essentially maritime theatre.
- The distances were so vast, indeed were transoceanic, that any and all considerations of strategy were moot, pending solution to the logistic challenges (the distance from Yokohama, Tokyo's port, to San Francisco is 5,530 miles).

- The Asia–Pacific War was cross-cultural and was marked by deep racial and cultural antipathies on both sides. This made for extreme brutality in the fighting, and in the treatment of prisoners and enemy civilians.
- Both Japan and the United States transformed the ways their navies fought, privileging carrier task forces, although faith in the guns of the battle line did not entirely die, especially in the Imperial Japanese Navy.
- This war demonstrated almost perfectly the flexibility of sea power.
- Inter-service rivalries and suspicions on both sides hindered and often prevented unity of command and concentration of effort. To a marked degree, the US Navy and Marine Corps, the Army and the Army Air Force waged separate wars. As for the Japanese, they never really possessed or pursued a coherent joint war plan embracing the Army and the Navy.
- The United States flouted the principle of war which requires concentration of effort. The two-vector assault upon the Japanese Empire, by MacArthur from the South West Pacific and by Nimitz from the east, was a division of effort. However, it was a division that the United States could afford.
- The bigger battalions of the United States increased in size as the war progressed, just as the Japanese had anticipated. With growing quantity matched by a high quality of combat, planning and logistical skills, the outcome of the fighting was not in doubt.
- Intelligence, especially code-breaking, played a vital role.
- Warfare in Asia–Pacific was as much, if not more, a struggle against nature as against the human enemy. US forces regularly suffered more from disease and hardship in the field than they did from enemy fire.
- Time was an American asset. This most unforgiving of strategy's dimensions was always running against the Japanese. They could not escape from a relatively long war in which they were increasingly overmatched in everything except courage.
- Despite the American affection for technology, especially heavy firepower, and notwithstanding the fact that this was a war waged by maritime manoeuvre on a monumental scale, there was a great deal of island combat that was up close and very personal. The sharp end of this war was very sharp indeed. There are few places to hide on a beach or a small island.
- Strategically assessed, the Asia–Pacific War was an American war. Only the United States had the military means, and the economy to produce those means, to deny Japan hegemony over East Asia and the Western Pacific.

Conclusion

Strategically viewed, the war in Asia–Pacific revealed a familiar weakness in statecraft on the part of Japan. In common with the belligerents in World War I, Japan was committed to a policy that was not achievable. Its strategic choices, operational dexterity and tactical skills were beside the point. They could not deliver victory against a militarily competent United States. The latter was undefeatable by Japan, as Tokyo always recognized, and would never acquiesce in Japanese establishment by force of arms its notion of a Greater East Asia Co-prosperity Sphere. In other words, Japanese high policy placed demands upon its armed forces that could not possibly be met. The surprise attack on Pearl Harbor, whatever its tactical success, was a strategic disaster. It so offended the American public that Japan was denied even the remote possibility of being allowed to wage the only kind of war it might conclude with advantage: a limited struggle for limited ends.

Just as Japanese policy set unattainable goals – or, more precisely, unsustainable ones – so its military strategy was thoroughly unsound, given the dynamic military context. Japan created a network of island fortresses in the Gilberts, Marshalls, Carolines and Marianas, intended to protect the main ocean approach from across the Pacific to Japan itself. But these defences in depth could be effective only in the context of their being supported by a strength in naval–air power that would be at least competitive with the strength of the US Navy. Alas, by late 1943 and thenceforth, the Imperial Japanese Navy, though still formidable, became less and less competitive with a US Navy that demonstrated skill in fighting at least as impressive as its sheer size.

Individuals matter. From October 1941 until July 1944, General Tojo Hideki was the dominant war leader of Imperial Japan. He was both Prime Minister and Minister of War. But unlike the Third Reich, Tojo's Japan was not a dictatorship. He had to contend with powerful interest groups in the Army and the Navy. Also, although the Emperor's role was more symbolic than substantive, it had the potential to serve as the focus for effective opposition. Events in August 1945 were to prove just how useful the Emperor could be when a government is uncertain what to do in a moment of national crisis. Even a Bismarck would have found it close to impossible to steer the Japanese ship of state safely towards its regionally hegemonic goal, and Tojo was no Bismarck. He gave every impression of presiding over a losing war, while utterly bereft of ideas as to how Japan's strategic fortunes might be improved. Japan's civilian leaders, though Prime Minister Tojo was a career soldier, failed abysmally in their duty to conduct an 'unequal dialogue' on strategy with their subordinate military leaders (Cohen, 2002). The Navy had been permitted to open proceedings on 7 December 1941 with its ill-conceived blow to American honour. As Japanese military fortunes worsened markedly through late 1943 and the first half of 1944, concluding with the defeat off Saipan in the Marianas, Tokyo simply did not know what to do. More to the point, there was no one in Tokyo in authority with the imagination, skill and ruthlessness to demand and secure a change in policy or strategy. Tojo resigned as Prime Minister following the humiliation of defeat at Saipan, but his departure did not herald any improvement in Japanese statecraft or strategy.

After defeat at Saipan in June 1944, Japan was in very much the same situation as its German nominal ally had been following the defeat at Kursk in July 1943. Both countries ceased to function by direction from purposeful strategy. When the Imperial Japanese Navy lost its real striking power, which is to say its carrier aviation, especially the experienced pilots, it could no longer claim to be fighting for any operational objectives or strategic purpose. Courage, sometimes skill, and American mistakes enabled the Japanese armed forces thereafter to exact a heavy toll upon their enemy, but to what end? In 1944–5, Japan lacked a theory of victory, even its original, thoroughly unconvincing one.

Little has been said thus far of those analytically convenient concepts, the 'decisive battle', or event, and the 'turning point'. It is an elementary matter to identify several significant military events in the Asia–Pacific War: Midway, of course; the Guadalcanal campaign, certainly; and assuredly the American victory at Saipan. But none of those encounters, the brief and the protracted, should be regarded as decisive or as turning points. An earlier chapter noted the common belief that there were no decisive battles in World War I. The same can be said for the Asia–Pacific War, albeit for a different reason. In 1914–18, victory was achieved piecemeal, by attrition. In 1941–5, although the geography of the war compelled maritime and amphibious manoeuvre on the grandest of scales, at the tip of the spears of the belligerents men died and machines were destroyed. As Napoleon did, the US Navy manoeuvred in order to fight with maximum advantage.

As has been stated many times, one is reluctant to claim that the outcome of a war is inevitable. Did not Clausewitz insist that 'war is the realm of chance'? But strategic history is not a lottery. If a country chooses to fight when its strategic context offers no realistic prospect of eventual success, as did Japan in 1941, the outcomes of particular battles are unlikely to signify much for very long. The Asia–Pacific War of 1941–5 was a conflict that Imperial Japan was *always* going to lose. It remains a cultural and strategic puzzle why so many Japanese military and political leaders endorsed the decision to go to war in 1941 while knowing that fact.

Key points

1. Japan faced a brutal choice: fight or abandon its fifty-year drive for empire and great power status.
2. Japan was obliged to strike at US air and naval forces because they posed the only credible threat to the establishment of an expanded empire in South East Asia.
3. Japan's theory of imperial defence was to fortify a network of island bases, supported by the mobile strength of the Navy.
4. Japan's theory of victory in a limited war held that a well-defended maritime perimeter would deter the United States from undertaking the difficult and expensive task of reconquest.
5. Japan never regained the strategic initiative after its defeat at Midway in June 1942.
6. This was a war that Japan could not win.

Questions

1. How plausible do you find the Japanese theory of victory?
2. Could Japan have expanded in South East Asia without attacking the United States?
3. What were the advantages and disadvantages of the American strategic options for the conduct of its war against Japan?
4. How did warfare in the Asia–Pacific theatre differ from warfare in Europe?

Further reading

H. Agawa *The Reluctant Admiral: Yamamoto and the Imperial Navy* (New York: Kodansha International/US, 1982).

C. Bayly and T. Harper *Forgotten Armies: The Fall of British Asia, 1941–1945* (London: Allen Lane, 2004).

P. S. Dull *A Battle History of the Imperial Japanese Navy (1941–1945)* (Annapolis, MD: Naval Institute Press, 1978).

D. C. Evans and M. R. Peattie *Kaigun: Strategy, Tactics, and Technology in the Imperial Japanese Navy 1887–1941* (Annapolis, MD: Naval Institute Press, 1997).

R. Lewin *The American Magic: Codes, Ciphers and the Defeat of Japan* (London: Penguin Books, 1983).

W. Murray and A. Millett *A War to be Won: Fighting the Second World War* (Cambridge, MA: Harvard University Press, 2000).

C. G. Reynolds *The Fast Carriers: The Forging of an Air Navy* (Huntington, NY: Robert E. Krieger, 1978).

A. Schom *The Eagle and the Rising Sun: The Japanese–American War, 1941–1943, Pearl Harbor through Guadalcanal* (New York: W. W. Norton, 2004).

D. van der Vat *The Pacific Campaign: World War II, the US–Japanese Naval War, 1941–1945* (New York: Simon and Schuster, 1991).

K. P. Werrell *Blankets of Fire: US Bombers over Japan during World War II* (Washington, DC: Smithsonian Institution Press, 1996).

14 The Cold War, I
Politics and ideology

Reader's guide: The legacy of World War II. The onset of the Cold War. The course of the conflict. Soviet and US performance. Soviet failures.

Introduction: from war to peace – the consequences of World War II

The Cold War has passed into history, but the nuclear bomb and the nuclear revolution are here to stay, prospectively for ever. Between them, the bomb and the political context of the Cold War nearly brought strategic history to an abrupt full stop. The human experience in its entirety might well have been concluded violently. How did this happen? And, more to the point, why? This chapter offers a fresh look at the Soviet–American Cold War of 1947– 89, while the chapter that follows pays particular attention to its historically novel nuclear dimension.

The events and non-events, but possible events, of the Cold War years comprise a contested history among scholars today (Westad, 2000; Herrman and Lebow, 2004). Almost everything about the Cold War is uncertain; at least, it is uncertain if one focuses on issues of motivation and causation. There is no solid consensus on why the Cold War began, who was most responsible for it, or why it concluded with barely a whimper with the loss of the will to power of the Soviet ruling elite in the late 1980s. Fortunately, the historical record provides some compensation for the deeper uncertainties. Even if one cannot be sure exactly why particular decisions were taken, one can secure an adequate grasp of who did what and when. Furthermore, one can proceed to ask and answer the strategist's question: so what? Deeds and their consequences are less mysterious than are motives.

One of the themes of this text is the intimate connection between war and peace, and indeed between peace and war. Peace, at least some semblance thereof, follows war. Moreover, peace of a particular character is what a war is all about. It is easy to forget this fundamental fact amid the stress, excitement and difficulties of waging war. The Cold War was a consequence of the changes in context produced by World War II. It is vital to recognize the complex authority of context. It is not quite everything, because individuals matter. But the Stalins, Kennedys and Gorbachevs must exercise their judgement, their somewhat free will, in political, socio-cultural, economic, technological,

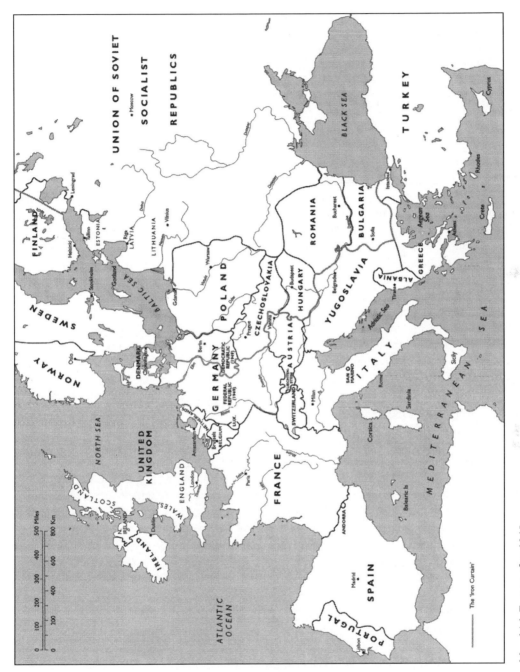

Map 14.1 Europe after 1945

military–strategic, geographical and historical contexts for which they are largely not responsible.

Nothing in history is strictly inevitable. However, history, for all its non-linearities, is by no means a random sequence of happenings. It is plausible to argue that the Soviet–American Cold War was an inevitable or, if preferred, a highly probable outcome of the war against Germany. The old European balance of power had just been destroyed utterly – not that it had been at all healthy in the 1930s, one might add. Only two states were still standing as truly great powers. Britain, France and China were treated as great powers, but that was more attributable to habit, courtesy, convenience and interests than to real strength. In the traditional logic of international politics, when two polities stand far above the rest, sooner or later they are bound to be rivals. Much of the history of the Cold War is debatable, but there are no convincing grounds for believing that the conflict was a mistake, an accident or an avoidable product of misunderstanding. This is not to argue that Moscow and Washington understood each other at all well; they did not. But in its essentials the conflict emerged, and was prosecuted, for sound enough reasons, given the ideologies and geopolitical interests of the two potential rivals. The Cold War may have been pursued overenthusiastically, even recklessly, at times by one or both parties, but each side quite accurately viewed the other as an enemy. In terms of capabilities broadly understood – which is to say grand-strategically, not narrowly militarily – the United States and the Soviet Union correctly regarded each other as their only serious enemy on the planet. Grand strategy refers to the purposeful employment of all of the assets of a state, not only to the use of the military instrument.

Why did the Cold War happen? The most convincing answer must eschew any mono-causal determinant. Instead, three structural reasons can be identified and one of human agency. The structural reasons can be summarized thus: each superpower was, globally, the sole major threat to the other; they were deadly ideological rivals; and their political differences, especially with respect to East–Central Europe, which is where the Cold War began, were non-negotiable. As for human agency, the Soviet Union was led by one of the most paranoid men in history, Joseph Stalin.

The conflict did not burst into life at a certain date, but rather emerged slowly between 1944 and 1947–8. Its emergence happened, in tactical detail, as a result of the interaction of Soviet and American behaviour. Context is not everything in strategic history, but it certainly explains, or helps explain, most things, always provided one makes due allowance for human agency and the occasional surprise. It is important to recognize fully just how significant and pervasive were the consequences of World War II. The 'peace' that came to be dominated almost immediately by the Cold War was the result of the great conflict that ended in 1945. The Cold War was not by any means made wholly in, or by, World War II, but its occurrence and much of its detail assuredly were. So, to understand the Cold War it is necessary to view it in good part, albeit not entirely (e.g., not with respect to the rival ideologies), as a consequence of World War II.

It would be difficult to exaggerate the consequences of that war for all aspects of international life in the years that followed. It may be recalled that it is a premise of this venture in strategic history that organized violence has been, and continues to be, the most potent of influences upon the course of events. Rather than simply claim as a generality the consequential sovereignty of World War II, Box 14.1 provides an itemization of the war's major consequences. This list describes the world of the Cold War.

Repeatedly, this book has emphasized the consequences of war for the peace that followed. This introduction concludes by specifying the principal consequences of the very great war, or wars, waged from 1939 to 1945. Most of the fuel for the Cold War was produced by the events of those years, and Box 14.1 offers a formidable accounting of the deeds and misdeeds of global warfare. It should be emphasized that the principal consequence of World War II was the creation of the political, economic, cultural and strategic contexts both for the Cold War that did follow and for a highly nuclear World War III which might have followed.

Box 14.1 The consequences of World War II

World War II:

1. Resolved the 'German problem', defined as the difficulty of balancing German power, but at the price of creating a 'Soviet problem'.
2. By concluding with the utter defeat of Germany and Japan, completely destroyed the balance of power in Europe and Asia.
3. Produced a physical and ideological confrontation between two very great powers with ideologies which claimed global authority.
4. Introduced truly global politics and war.
5. Shaped a new global geopolitics and geostrategy.
6. Concluded 500 years of European domination of world politics.
7. Promoted the United States to the rank of first-class superpower, a rank it alone has held until the present day.
8. Produced in its aftermath a context of such political, economic and strategic insecurity in Europe that the United States reversed its 200-year principle of avoiding entangling alliances, especially in peacetime.
9. Enmeshed the United States in European security affairs, a condition that still obtains, through NATO, in the twenty-first century.
10. Eventually produced a uniting Europe. The European Union is a child of the French, Belgian and German experiences of the war years.
11. Ended militarism in most of Europe, with the noteworthy exception of the Balkans. Any residual attractions of war that remained after 1914–18 were definitively removed by the ghastly happenings of 1939–45.
12. Conclusively delegitimized fascist ideologies, though, alas, not all fascist practices.
13. Led to the creation of the state of Israel.
14. Produced yet another attempt, the most ambitious yet, to create a multinational institution capable of policing international order with justice – the United Nations (UN). This was the third great power club, following the Congress (and Concert) System of the nineteenth century and the League of Nations of the interwar years.
15. Accelerated decolonization by delegitimizing the overseas European empires.
16. Led to the innovation of international war crimes trials.

17. Promoted the institutionalization of management tools to discipline international financial affairs, promote freer trade and encourage economic development and recovery. The institutions created under US sponsorship were the International Monetary Fund (IMF), the International Bank for Reconstruction and Development (IBRD) (popularly known as the World Bank) and the General Agreement on Tariffs and Trade (GATT).
18. Accelerated progress in both theoretical and experimental nuclear physics, to the point of their weaponization in 1945.
19. In its atomic conclusion on 6 and 9 August 1945, cast doubt upon the strategic utility of all traditional means and methods of warfare.
20. In its nuclear legacy, changed the conduct and goals of foreign policy, perhaps for ever.
21. Created the largest refugee flows in history, which had the unplanned consequence of completing most of what remained to fulfil the Wilsonian principle of 1919: the national self-determination of peoples.
22. Promoted rapid progress in medicine, especially in antibiotics.
23. Accelerated cultural awareness of the importance of human rights, a development made manifest in the drafting of the Universal Declaration of Human Rights. This was incorporated into the Charter of the UN in 1948.
24. Accelerated social change everywhere, as great wars invariably do – the only exception being the cases where authoritarian governments were able to resist the pressure for changes that might threaten their authority.

From cold peace to Cold War

The nuclear age dawned explosively almost simultaneously with the first visible stirrings of what was to become the Cold War, but that was simply a coincidence of history. The nuclear revolution neither was a cause of the Cold War nor, as a general rule, provided significant fuel for its continuance. With a few noteworthy historical exceptions, it is plausible to argue that on balance the nuclear dimension to the interstate competition probably made a positive contribution to international order and the avoidance of war. Today, the products of the nuclear revolution are still with us, while the Cold War, and one of its principals, is no more. However, for a long period the competition in nuclear weaponry between the United States and the Soviet Union was the primary focus and instrument of their interaction. Certainly, it seemed as if the nuclear arms race had taken on a life, and had a strategic meaning, all its own. If that were so, it was a violation of the Clausewitzian dictum which mandates the dominance of the political over the military. But when and why did the Cold War erupt – or, more accurately, emerge – among the members of the Grand Alliance against Germany and, eventually, Japan?

It is reasonable to date the Cold War from 1945, but there is a persuasive case for maintaining that it emerged and took shape gradually from August 1944 to June 1950. The former date is more contentious than is the latter, but the Soviet refusal to assist the Polish uprising against the Germans in Warsaw in August 1944 was a political marker of importance in Soviet–American relations. In fact, Soviet misbehaviour of several kinds in Poland was the single most potent source of fuel for the growing Western suspicion that their current, soon to be erstwhile, ally was going to pose a major problem for stability and order in post-war Europe. After all, Poland was not only a friendly state but the country that had provided the trigger for British and French belligerency in September 1939. The future of Germany was of far greater political and strategic importance than was the future of Poland, but at least the Western members of the Grand Alliance had a real vote there, a vote which rested on a physical presence as well as on prior agreements. With respect to Poland, Stalin did what he wanted, regardless of promises made to Roosevelt and Churchill at a summit meeting in Yalta in February 1945. June 1950 is the most suitable date to select for the full emergence of the Cold War, because the invasion of South Korea by the North on the 25th of that month had a near-traumatic, and certainly a galvanizing, effect upon American and some other Western opinion, policy and defence spending. The Korean invasion promoted the militarization of the Cold War as nothing to that date had done. A communist power crossed a recognized border in a campaign of conquest. That was a new development and it caused the United States and the recently established NATO to redefine their understanding of the character of threat they faced. This, though, is not to deny that America's South Korean client, Syngman Rhee, was at least as willing to invade the North as his counterpart in Pyongyang was to move south.

It is not difficult to trace the political course of mounting suspicion and outright hostility between the Soviet Union and the United States which marked the years 1944 to 1950. One needs to recognize the relatively slow-moving, but inexorable, Soviet campaign to install 'friendly' governments in those countries liberated (or conquered – the difference between the two was not always obvious) by the Red Army. The final straw which broke the camel's back of Western optimism was the Soviet staging of a coup in Prague in February 1948. The coup was completed with the murder (or assisted suicide) of Foreign Minister Jan Masaryk. In June 1946, Stalin had rejected the Baruch Plan to place all developments in nuclear energy under the authority of the United Nations. A year later, he had been equally negative towards the Marshall Plan. The United States had hoped that the plan's financial infusions would jump-start the moribund economies of devastated Europe. Seeking to demonstrate to the people in the Western zones of Berlin that they could not be protected by the Americans, the British or the French, Stalin imposed a blockade on the city on 24 June 1948. It lasted until 12 May 1949. And so it went on. Year after year, from 1944 to 1950, there was fresh evidence of ill intent on the Soviet part, evidence to which the Western powers reacted. Of course, in some cases the Soviet moves were, in their turn, reactions to what Stalin perceived, generally correctly in his terms, to be unfriendly Western acts.

But the story just outlined selectively and in only the barest of detail was not merely one of Western perception and recognition of Soviet perfidy and aggressive purpose. From the Soviet, which is to say Stalin's, perspective, the Western powers played their role, as Moscow had expected them to do, in promoting harm to Soviet interests. The Cold War emerged by a process of interaction; it was by no means entirely a product of Western reactions to Soviet initiatives. One must hasten to add that to recognize an interactive dynamic is not to assert a moral or political equivalency between East and West. The fact that both sides contributed to the escalation of political hostility should not be permitted to obscure the evidence which points overwhelmingly to Stalin's responsibility for the onset, emergence and maturing of the Cold War. The question of blame for the Cold War carries the misleading implication that had only the most guilty party behaved better, the conflict might have been avoided, or at least greatly mitigated. Such a view is easily justifiable. Indeed, a lack of appreciation of contemporary contextual realities is apt to lead the historian blessed with hindsight seriously astray. So, it is necessary to break with the common habit among Anglo-American historians of focusing unduly upon the world as it appeared to Western leaders in the mid- and late 1940s. How did the world appear to Joseph Stalin in the autumn of 1945?

His armies had done most of the fighting and most of the dying. But while the Soviet Union had suffered approximately 27 million fatalities, only 9.5 million of them had been military. Stalin and his countrymen believed they were owed revenge, recompense and guarantees of future security. As a result, the Soviet Union plundered, looted and generally added to the existing devastation in Central Europe, especially, though not exclusively, in Germany. Obviously, the Red Army's misbehaviour did nothing to commend it as a liberating force to those who might otherwise have been inclined to regard it with favour. It was now in place in Central Europe; indeed, it was as far west as the Elbe. As the armies of the United States and Britain melted away by demobilization or, in the British case, were diverted to strenuous end-of-empire duties in South Asia and the Middle East, the Russians became militarily ever more dominant in Europe. The Red Army was there by right of conquest, and increasingly it was unchallenged and unchallengeable. American forces in Europe were shrinking rapidly in the summer of 1945 because of demobilization and a wholesale switching of military focus to the Pacific, in preparation for the anticipated invasion of Japan.

The political context for Soviet power and influence in Europe looked distinctly promising. The communist parties in France and Italy, for the prime examples, were within reach of achieving national power. Indeed, throughout Europe, and even to some useful degree in Britain and the United States, the Soviet Union was understandably popular as the principal conqueror of Nazi Germany. And one should not forget that the Western Allies had praised 'Uncle Joe' Stalin for four years, presenting him to their publics as a rather cuddly, if somewhat strict, warrior against Nazi evil. They had even described the Soviet Union as a democracy 'of a kind'.

On the evidence of deeds, as well as from the archives that have been opened, it is reasonably clear that Stalin neither sought nor expected a Cold War with the West. Certainly, he did not anticipate an intense forty-five-year struggle focused upon military high technology. However, he was committed to a policy of security consolidation in Europe for the Soviet Union, including the expansion of Soviet influence where feasible. That commitment ran a high risk of triggering hostile Western responses, but Stalin was not a reckless gambler; in his style, he was far removed from his fellow dictator, Adolf Hitler. Stalin was not a gangster in a hurry but the guardian, and conveniently the sole authoritative interpreter, of a political doctrine which provided understanding, guidance and high expectations for the future. Few people in the West, in 1945 or since, seemed to appreciate that in Stalin's mind the Soviet Union was always at war with the capitalist powers. But that ideological fact did not preclude any necessary measures of expedient tactical flexibility – witness the Molotov–Ribbentrop Pact of 23 August 1939. Furthermore, communist doctrine insisted that the leading capitalist states, though the deadly enemies of the Soviet Union, would fight among themselves for a dominant share of world markets. In the immediate post-war years, Stalin sincerely expected Anglo-American relations to deteriorate to the point of active hostilities for reason of economic rivalry. With a misplaced confidence born of his ideological convictions, he believed that the Soviet Union would be the beneficiary of inter-capitalist conflicts in the post-war world. He had harboured the same illusion in 1939, when he expected to be able to sit out a lengthy and exhausting struggle between Germany and the Anglo-French alliance.

What did all this mean for East–West relations? It is obvious that serious mis-understandings hampered accurate assessments by both sides. Stalin's Soviet Union, courtesy of a fallacious theory of historical change, mistakenly anticipated war among the capitalists. Liberal America and socialist Britain did not appreciate that their former Soviet ally regarded itself as being permanently in a state of war with them. Of course, that was a state that could be, and had been, at least semi-suspended for immediate tactical reasons from 1941 until 1944, or possibly early 1945. Stalin assumed that American and British policy-makers regarded the Soviet Union much as he regarded their countries. Such is the power of ideology to mislead.

Although Stalin had no intention of launching the Cold War, he never had any intention of cooperating with the Western Allies either, except when it suited his calculation of Soviet interests – and those interests did not mesh well with Western hopes. It is true that the United States took actions and launched policy initiatives that were regarded in Moscow as threatening to Soviet interests. The most serious of these pertained to the governance of Germany and, especially, to the prospective economic recovery of Europe through the Marshall Plan that was announced in 1947 (and passed by Congress the following year). Stalin correctly identified American proposals for a UN monopoly of atomic technology as a threat to Soviet achievement of technical equivalence. Also, he was right in his reading of US and British moves to organize their zones of occupation in Germany as a threat to his plans to communize the whole of that country. Furthermore, he was surely correct in identifying the Marshall Plan as a deadly menace to Soviet political and economic intentions in East–Central Europe.

It is easy to find Soviet and Western initiatives which, by a process of interaction, fed suspicions, confirmed fears and reinforced ideological convictions. But the details of Soviet– American relations in the immediate post-war years really did not greatly matter. Mistakes were made by both sides, some conflicts probably could have been avoided, but, overall, a context of general hostility and antagonism was unavoidable. Although there was fault on both sides, the record is clear enough in revealing that Stalin, personally, was principally responsible for what came to be known as the Cold War. However, one needs to add hastily that regardless of the character of the Soviet leader, it was never likely that the two greatest powers left standing in 1945 would be able to forge a cooperative relationship for the joint ordering of a secure post-war world. When the logic of realpolitik is added to the unhelpful incompatibility of two ideologies with global pretensions – communism and democratic capitalism – the onset of the Cold War becomes anything but mysterious.

Into the political context just described intruded the military novelty of atomic weapons. Just when Soviet military power peaked in 1945, as indeed had American, the appearance of the atomic bomb threatened to alter all strategic calculations. But for four years, while the Soviet Union strove with maximum effort to recapture lost scientific and technological ground in the weaponization of nuclear physics, Western countries did not identify Moscow primarily as a military threat. The existence of the American atomic bomb was a potent source of reassurance. In fact, it served almost as a talisman that seemed to preclude the necessity for rigorous thought about military strategy. Given the unprecedentedly destructive character of atomic weapons, one must be sympathetic to those in the late 1940s who were uncertain as to what the new weapons of mass destruction portended for future warfare.

Politically, though not militarily, the Cold War was up and running in the West by 1947. President Truman had proclaimed his expansive doctrine of supporting free people everywhere in March of that year. In June, Secretary of State George Marshall was persuaded, if not bullied, by the British to turn his rhetoric into a definite plan for European economic recovery and reconstruction. Both of those momentous policy initiatives were plainly anti-Soviet in purpose, though the Marshall Plan made sense regardless of the anti-Soviet dimension to American reasoning. Meanwhile, Stalin proceeded slowly but surely to secure his new empire in East–Central Europe, with the subordination of Czechoslovakia in February 1948 comprising the final move. His greatest disappointment was the failure to render the whole of Germany open to political control by a Soviet-directed communist, or more probably a left coalition, government. It should not be forgotten that Germany held the central place in the international politics of the period. In addition to its appalling record of repeated aggression, it was the geopolitical centre of Europe as well as the most highly industrialized country in the region, which meant that it had a large working class to whom the logic of Marxism should appeal. In addition, Germany was the birthplace of the ideology that provided legitimacy for the rule of the Communist Party of the Soviet Union (CPSU) and of its General Secretary, Joseph Stalin. Last but not least, geostrategically Germany was the meeting place of Soviet and American arms.

By 1949 the Cold War was a fact, though the conflict was yet to be pursued in its military dimension with the diligence that came to characterize the years after 1950. Stalin had failed to intimidate the West or the Germans with his blockade of Berlin, but inadvertently he had greatly assisted those who were organizing what became the NATO Alliance. The bare bones of what was to become an impressive structure were created on 4 April 1949 in Washington. Then, in September of that year, the new Federal Republic of Germany was created out of the former American, British and French zones of occupation. Soviet schemes to add what was to become West Germany, as well as West Berlin, to their security barrier had failed conclusively.

The Cold War reconsidered

The plot

It would be convenient and satisfying were one able to identify a simple, one-dimensional master narrative which could explain the origins, outbreak, course and outcome of the Cold War. But one cannot. Historical perspective is still lacking for a conflict that concluded as recently as 1989 (or 25 December 1991, for the formal dissolution of the USSR). Nevertheless, the accumulating body of multinational scholarship on the Cold War does lead to a few important, if as yet tentative, conclusions (Gaddis, 2006; Gorlizki and Khlevniuk, 2004; Westad, 2000). It is useful to cite these explicitly before discussing the course of the conflict in detail. The events of 1947–89 are easier to comprehend once the plot of the Cold War is laid bare.

1. The conflict was about both ideology and geopolitics. Any explanation which effectively excludes either factor is fatally flawed.
2. It is not difficult to fault Stalin for his apparent policy turn early in 1946 towards non-cooperation with the Western Allies. But that turn was certain to happen, given that Western policies, especially towards Germany, were contrary to the Soviet definition of Soviet interests. Stalin, admittedly, was exceptionally paranoid, but it is highly improbable that any other Soviet leader of the period would have chosen to cooperate with the West in the reconstruction of Europe along lines favoured in Washington. Although Stalin died in 1953, the Cold War persisted until 1989. Had the conflict been strictly Stalin's personal project, it is likely that one or other of his successors would have managed to wind it down long before the 1980s.
3. It is clear enough from the evidence that neither side wanted war. It is also quite apparent that both genuinely believed they had good reason to fear attack. Ideologically and geopolitically, the United States and the Soviet Union truly were enemies. Their reciprocated perceptions of enmity were correct. It was but a short step from enemy identification to the anticipation of threat. By mid-1950 at the latest, both sides had added military threat to the political menace that their ideologies defined for them.
4. In common with all wars, the Cold War was a duel. It was a protracted struggle that had periods of both greater and lesser political tension. Above all else, though, it proceeded by interaction. This popular, rather obvious, point lends itself to misunderstanding. Not everything about East–West relations from 1947 to 1989 can be explained in terms of interaction. The two superpowers, with their friends and allies generally in policy attendance, though sometimes in advance or behind on policy, behaved according to their own socio-cultural natures and in ways that fitted what each understood to be its geopolitical interests. However, that behaviour was shaped by a context of overarching conflict, and it was always liable to influence from initiatives emerging from the other side.
5. Despite the fact that neither party desired war, the Cold War was extraordinarily dangerous. It is probably just as well that a non-war outcome was the product of several mutually supporting factors, because the protagonists played with the most deadly of fires for forty years. The armed forces of East and West were permanently in contact on land in Central Europe, and they frequently harassed each other at sea and in the air. Also, the great engines of nuclear destruction that both sides constructed could not be 100 per cent proofed against accident, technical malfunction, command failure, launch by miscalculation or simple bad luck. If a nuclear strike on a modest scale had evolved rapidly into a nuclear 'exchange', it would probably have been impossible to arrest the process of escalation short of utter, general devastation.

The adventurous leadership of Nikita Khrushchev

It is generally agreed that the Cold War divides fairly neatly into two periods: pre- and post the Cuban Missile Crisis of October 1962. That shocking event, the most dangerous in all of human history, scared all the participants on both sides (with the exception of Fidel Castro), not to mention the general public. It brought home to everyone, as nothing quite had to date, how necessary it was for the superpowers to exercise more self-discipline in both policy and actual military behaviour. Also, the crisis demonstrated the necessity of maintaining greater control over one's armed forces and, in the Soviet case, over the actions of a local ally. It suggested to the frightened people in Moscow and Washington that limited measures of cooperation, especially with respect to the provision of emergency means of crisis communication, as well as adoption of a generally more cautious style in foreign policy, were long overdue. On the Soviet side, Nikita Khrushchev's peers decided that the Cold War was far too perilous to be directed from Moscow by his impulsive adventurism. They had a long list of complaints about his leadership, but the brush with catastrophe in October 1962 was the final straw. However, Khrushchev did survive in power until 14 October 1964, when he was permitted to retire to write his memoirs.

From 1958 until 1961, Khrushchev, acting under severe pressure from the all too independent Walter Ulbricht, had repeatedly threatened to sign a peace treaty with East Germany and surrender control of East Berlin to his German satellite–ally. Thanks to a wartime agreement and to the final course of the war, Berlin was marooned as a Four-Power island deep inside what became the German Democratic Republic (a reluctant Soviet creation, to match the Federal Republic of Germany). It had not featured as an East–West flashpoint since Stalin abandoned his blockade of the city in May 1949, but in the 1950s, geopolitically and geostrategically, it was a crisis waiting to happen. West Berlin was NATO's most vulnerable asset. The city was literally indefensible, except by nuclear deterrence or in the context of actual nuclear use. To the relief of most thoughtful observers, Khrushchev reluctantly agreed to the building of a wall to seal off West Berlin from East Germany and East Berlin, and thereby prevent the undesirable emigration of East Germans from their dismal 'workers' state'. The Berlin Wall began to go up on 13 August 1961. Many in the West interpreted this as an aggressive Soviet move, intended to apply pressure upon West Germany, but really quite the reverse was true. The Wall was a desperate measure to plug the hole through which East Germany was losing its most educated people. Its construction was a humiliating confession of the failure of East Germany to hold its 'best and brightest', but Central Europe was considerably safer as a result of its appearance. The brutal material isolation of West Berlin at least foreclosed upon most possibilities of accidental armed conflict erupting in the city.

Although the Cold War endured for forty-four years, with only two exceptions there was no direct clash of arms between the superpowers – and even those exceptions were unacknowledged by both sides. First, there were the air battles over North Korea between US and Soviet fighter pilots from 1950 to 1953. Second, there was heavy combat from 1965 to 1973 between US aircraft and Soviet crews manning some of the air-defence missile systems that protected North Vietnam. But, by and large, the Cold War was prosecuted on both sides indirectly, through local proxies in the Third World. This was because both sides considered it unduly risky to pursue conflict in Europe. The two Asian clashes aside, direct US–Soviet competition was restricted to a furious arms race. However, to their surprise, scholars have discovered since the end of the Cold War that Khrushchev's dominant motive for introducing intermediate and medium-range ballistic missiles into Cuba in 1962 was not to boost Soviet strength in the central balance of strategic nuclear power but to render Cuba invasion-proof, and to encourage the spread of communism in Latin America (Gaddis, 2006: 75–7). Policy-makers in the Kennedy administration could not imagine that Moscow would take such a risky initiative on behalf of a distant client. Those American policy-makers did not know just how risky Soviet policy had become. While their attention was focused on the missiles that could reach the United States, they were blissfully unaware of the fact that Moscow had already deployed 162 tactical nuclear weapons on Cuba. A US invasion most probably would have been met with a local nuclear response. This reflected a failure of empathy with the Soviet worldview, or at least with the view of Nikita Khrushchev. Despite its increasingly parlous economic condition from the 1960s to the 1980s, the Soviet Union devoted substantial scarce resources to supporting unpromising clients in Asia and Africa. Sometimes the prime motive was simply to keep pace with China as a competitor, as in Vietnam, but elsewhere it was just poor judgement, as in the Horn of Africa. Moscow discovered that its role as ideological leader in a world that contained an erratic but active communist China obliged it to meet at least the minimum expectations of assistance from its allies. For example, the protracted Cuban adventure in Angola in the mid-1970s was an especially unwelcome draw on Soviet resources that Moscow had little option other than to suffer. To policy-makers in the West, Soviet intervention both in Ethiopia in 1977 (in opposition to its former client, Somalia) and in Angola in 1976 was not interpreted as it should have been – as a reluctant bowing to Cuban pressure – but rather as bold Soviet geopolitical moves. Moscow had its eyes on possible communist rule in Lisbon, not Luanda. One of the genuine revelations of recent scholarship on the Cold War is the extent to which both superpowers were manipulated by their allies (Gaddis, 2006: 134).

Détente

There were periods of lesser tension in the Cold War. Those years sparked speculation at the time and since to the effect that opportunities may have existed, but remained unexploited, to bring the Cold War to an end. It is improbable that there were any such genuine opportunities from 1947 to 1989. Although the two sides coexisted with few strategic alarms, especially after October 1962, the ideological contest was hard fought and mutually inalienable. Furthermore, the geopolitical confrontation in Europe did not allow for any disengagement by either side that would be judged safe. The first period of détente, of a lessening of tension, characterized the mid-1950s (though the French term was not in general currency until the 1970s), and was occasioned, briefly, by the new post-Stalin, somewhat collective leadership. It was in 1956 at the Twentieth Party Congress in Moscow (14–25 February) that Khrushchev both attacked the record of Stalin's leadership and announced the new policy of 'peaceful coexistence'. These bold departures had unexpectedly destabilizing consequences in Eastern Europe, especially in Hungary and Poland. The disorder in Hungary escalated uncontrollably until a thoroughgoing revolution was under way. East–West détente could not survive the subsequent Soviet suppression of the revolt in November 1956. That Soviet military response was followed by its first experiment with rocket diplomacy when it threatened Britain and France with nuclear missiles unless they evacuated their troops from Egypt, a new Soviet client. It was all bluff by Moscow, but in the context of the action in Hungary it was more than sufficient to cast a further chill over East–West relations.

Détente prospered again in the 1960s and 1970s, albeit with occasional setbacks and some difficulty, given the political and strategic context of the US war in South Vietnam and Soviet military intervention in Czechoslovakia on 20 August 1968. While the post-Khrushchev Soviet leadership team of Leonid Brezhnev and Alexei Kosygin tentatively improved relations with the United States, the American half of the détente process was busy bombing communist North Vietnam. Allowing a decent interval of fifteen months to pass after the Soviet intervention in Prague, the new Nixon administration permitted an innovative process of strategic arms limitation talks (SALT) to begin in November 1969. While Soviet relations with its former ally and supposed ideological soulmate China had deteriorated to the point of actual combat along the Ussuri River in the Far East in March 1969, its relations with the United States gradually warmed. In fact, they warmed to such a degree that Moscow even suggested joint military action against China. The United States, led by the geopolitically astute Richard Nixon and his no less skilful right-hand man, Henry Kissinger (initially as National Security Adviser, later as Secretary of State), deftly played triangular Cold War politics. They pursued détente not only with Moscow but, from 1972, with China.

The Soviet–American détente of the early 1970s registered its most signal achievement with the SALT agreements of May 1972. These comprised a five-year interim agreement constraining further growth in the number of missile 'launchers', and the ABM (Anti-Ballistic Missile) Treaty, which prohibited defence of the superpowers' homelands, though ABM deployment at a single site was allowed. However, the ink was scarcely dry on what became known as SALT I before the political context which sustained détente began to deteriorate. (SALT I was so labelled because it was intended to be succeeded within five years by a more enduring SALT II.)

The dominant narrative of the Cold War in the 1970s was a combination of the return of acute distrust on the American part and evidence of a gradual slackening of grip and loss of judgement on the Soviet. The SALT I package proved exceptionally controversial in the United States. Anti-détente opinion in Washington sought to embarrass both the US and the Soviet governments over Moscow's dreadful human rights record. That determination, focused especially upon the issue of Soviet policy towards Jewish emigration, secured a historic victory which was to have unexpectedly far-reaching results. It achieved reluctant Soviet endorsement of the human rights provisions of the accord produced by the Helsinki Conference on Security and Cooperation in Europe on 1 August 1975. The conference had been up and running – well, ambling – since September 1973.

It is ironic that the conference was greatly favoured by the Soviet Union, because Soviet policy-makers saw it, as they saw détente as a whole, as a significant endorsement of the permanence of the status quo in Europe. In practice, inadvertently the Soviet Union signed up to a standard of behaviour towards the rights of individuals to which it could be held by critical domestic monitoring groups. At the time, in 1975, cynical geopoliticians in the West assumed that the Helsinki Accords were simply empty verbiage. Meanwhile, the critics of détente were unhappy that so blatant a violator of human rights as the Soviet Union should be allowed to be a party to an agreement on standards of behaviour that it was certain to ignore. Everyone was wrong. Henry Kissinger, by then Secretary of State, was to comment that 'Rarely has a diplomatic process so illuminated the limitations of human foresight' (Kissinger, 1999: 635). The 'Final Act' (on human rights) of the Helsinki Accords sowed seeds that were to grow both at home in the Soviet Union and abroad in Eastern Europe, until they became a significant factor threatening to destabilize the imperium.

The SALT process limped on through the 1970s until eventually, by 1979, a draft treaty emerged that was both exceedingly complex and highly controversial. However, despite the historically unusual public attention that strategic arms control attracted in those years, the real story was political, not military-technical. While experts debated the fine print of a strategic arms limitation treaty, and the problems of its verification, the political climate deteriorated from bad, to worse, to impossible. The United States was not in a mood to be active in the world in the 1970s. Congress had pulled the plug on the executive's ability to assist or even supply America's clients in South East Asia. Also, it had passed a War Powers Act on 7 November 1973 which, in theory at least, greatly constrained the President's freedom of action to employ force at his own discretion as Commander-in-Chief. And America was badly wounded in two further ways as a Cold War competitor in the 1970s. First, there was the collapse of the US strategic mission in Vietnam; and, second, there was the self-destruction of presidential authority when the Nixon presidency imploded and was destroyed by the Watergate scandal. The President resigned on 10 August 1974, rather than face impeachment.

The fragile détente of the early 1970s was stressed to breaking point by political developments on both sides and by the interaction between them. The White House lacked authority in the wake of Watergate, and the United States generally was content to lick its wounds, both the self-inflicted ones and the other kind, such as those suffered in Vietnam. America's client in Saigon finally fell to a North Vietnamese military offensive on 30 April 1975. Meanwhile, the Soviet Union was producing a new generation of long-range ballistic missiles and appeared determined to achieve some variant of strategic superiority. Whether such a condition was possible, and whether it would be politically or strategically exploitable, was debatable, and was duly debated acrimoniously in Washington.

Soviet foreign policy was highly active. For the first time, the Soviet Union was assisting clients and allies in Africa, especially, as has been said, in Ethiopia and Angola. This new activism, and demonstration of long-distance logistic competence, helped sour the political context of Soviet–American relations. The new Carter administration, which succeeded Gerald Ford's caretaker government in January 1977, attempted to keep détente alive, but it proved to be mission impossible. The final straw was the extremely ill-judged Soviet intervention in Afghanistan in 1979. With exquisitely awful timing, the Soviet Union invaded Afghanistan on 25 December with 75,000 troops and murdered its own client leader, Hafizullah Amin, who was believed to be ineffective. The SALT process, which by now had produced the SALT II Treaty, was dead in the water, at least for a while. Soviet–American relations sank to their lowest point since the heyday of Khrushchev's missile diplomacy in 1958–62. In the presidential election of 1980, both candidates, President Jimmy Carter and the challenger, Ronald Reagan, in effect ran against the Soviet Union.

Contributing to the mood of international crisis in Washington was the fall of the Shah of Iran on 16 January 1979. Iran had been America's client in the Gulf, and the assumption of power on 12 February by an Islamic fundamentalist regime led by the charismatic Ayatollah Khomeini did not augur well for that to continue. The seizure of the US Embassy in Teheran on 3 November 1979, and as a consequence the taking of sixty-three (principally) American hostages, convinced many Americans that their superpower was apparently impotent while it was in the hands of Jimmy Carter.

From crisis to collapse: the 1980s

The crisis of public confidence in leadership in the United States that led to the election of Ronald Reagan in November 1980 really was as nothing compared with the protracted leadership crisis in Moscow. Between November 1982 and March 1985 the Soviet Union had no fewer than four leaders. Leonid Brezhnev, who had been visibly ailing for years, finally departed this world on 10 November 1982. He was succeeded by the head of the KGB, the gifted but ailing Yuri Andropov, who died on 9 February 1984. Next, and emphatically least, an apparatchik of no known distinction, Konstantin Chernenko, reigned (one can hardly say ruled) from the time of Andropov's demise for barely thirteen months, until on 10 March 1985 he too succumbed to the ravages of age, illness and the Soviet lifestyle. Which brings us to the fateful – and, for the Soviet Union, fatal – stewardship of an erstwhile agricultural expert, Mikhail Gorbachev.

While it was musical chairs in the Kremlin, the Cold War passed through a period of exceptional peril. Not for nothing has the period from the Soviet invasion of Afghanistan in December 1979 until the elevation of Gorbachev in March 1985 been referred to as 'the second Cold War'. But that characterization, though not wholly unwarranted, is probably misleading. There was no first or second Cold War; there was only a single conflict, albeit one with periods of lower and higher tension. The period from late 1979 until early 1985 was a case of the latter. Indeed, the political tension between the superpowers became so acute that the Soviet government persuaded itself that the hostile rhetoric from the Reagan administration signalled an intention to launch an attack. In May 1981, Soviet intelligence agencies were placed on the highest alert status, charged with identifying warning signs of an anticipated attack (Pry, 1999: ch. 2). This paranoid condition, of which the United States and NATO were blissfully, if dangerously, unaware, produced a unilateral crisis of the most severe kind in 1983. An annual US and NATO military command exercise, codenamed 'Able Archer 83' (2–11 November), was mis-interpreted by some suspicious elements in Moscow as being preparatory to an attack. The crisis passed, but it could conceivably have led to World War III. Evidence of the shortness of the fuse to military action by Moscow in 1983 had already been provided on 1 September, when Soviet air defences shot down a South Korean 747 civilian airliner (KAL007). It had been mistaken for a US reconnaissance aircraft. This event also had the potential to trigger a military confrontation.

Individuals can make a vital difference to the course of history. It is true that their options will be limited by the contexts in which they find themselves, but still they usually have choices. For two potent reasons, the Soviet Union could not possibly win the Cold War: it was economically thoroughly outclassed by the United States, and its ideology dictated a character of political, economic and social organization that did not work adequately. The ideology, the Marxist theory of historical change, that it bore was false. However, although the Soviet Union had no prospect of winning the Cold War, a fact not recognized in Moscow until the late 1960s or early 1970s, it certainly had the military means to guarantee that the United States would not win either. The world has reason to be grateful to Gorbachev for his brave willingness to face the facts of Soviet incapacity, to seek systemic remedies and to eschew desperate military measures in an attempt to hold on to the Soviet Empire and buy time for domestic reform to effect some miracle cure for his country's ills.

It is no exaggeration to say that the Cold War ended gradually between 1987 and 1989 because Mikhail Gorbachev decided to end it. A twofold explanation is required. First, Gorbachev recognized, as indeed did almost everybody else in the Soviet Union, that the Soviet system had proved an abysmal failure: it had not delivered the good life predicted by theory and promised by politicians. This undeniable comprehensive failure did not merely have implications for policy; in addition, it had the most traumatic meaning for the legitimacy of the Soviet Union itself. The state and the character of its rule rested wholly on the presumed infallibility of Marxist theory. But by the 1980s, if not earlier, it was almost impossible to argue against claims that the ideology behind the state was wrong. It had been proved false by history. The capitalist powers had not fought among themselves, as the ideology insisted they must, and those powers had outperformed the Soviet Union economically to a degree that could no longer be explained away. In order to maintain its strategic military position as a worthy superpower competitor, since the 1960s the Soviet Union had shifted scarce resources, especially talented individuals, from the civilian to the military sector of the economy. The result, predictably, was an ever more embarrassing decline in the Soviet standard of living.

Coming to power in March 1985, Gorbachev first attempted to reform the Soviet system, but a combination of his own limitations and, of greater significance, the resistance of the system to radical change foredoomed the effort. His novel watchwords of *glasnost* and *perestroika*, openness and restructuring, could not point the way to the rescue of the system. Gorbachev had been a fairly slow learner. For example, when a reactor at Chernobyl exploded on 26 April 1986, Soviet citizens heard the truth only from Western broadcasts which exposed the lies that Moscow was telling its people about the accident. Nevertheless, it is to Gorbachev's credit that eventually he recognized the impracticality of reform and decided that instead the entire basis and character of Soviet rule and life must alter. He abandoned the ideology that both legitimized the authority of the Communist Party, of which he was General Secretary, and mandated permanent hostility to the capitalist powers. The change of course in Moscow was flagged by the signing of the long-languishing treaty on intermediate-range nuclear forces on 8 December 1987. Suddenly, with Moscow determined no longer to be an enemy of the West, arms control agreements became negotiable. When the political context warms, the barriers to agreement that render substantive arms control agreements a forlorn hope simply fade away.

The Cold War did not end on some magic date, any more than it had begun on a particular day. It is convenient and plausible, however, to pick 22 December 1989 as a date of extraordinary significance. That was when the Berlin Wall came down as a result of popular pressure, both political and physical. Gorbachev had decided that the Soviet Empire in Eastern Europe was an expensive drag upon, and political embarrassment to, an impoverished Soviet Union. Contrary to much Western commentary at the time, the intervention in Czechoslovakia in August 1968 had been a sign of weakness, not strength, and was deeply embarrassing. It was not attractive for a superpower that was just attaining strategic nuclear parity with the United States to be seen to have to coerce its Czech ally into maintaining good behaviour. It was noticeable that when the Solidarity trade union movement created a revolutionary situation in Poland in 1981, the Soviet Union decided not to take control of events itself by military means. The so-called Brezhnev Doctrine, which held that once a state was communist it must remain communist – on pain of enforcement by Soviet arms – was dead and buried, if it had ever truly existed, that is.

Some interim judgements

The beginning of the Cold War was not at all surprising. The combination of antagonistic ideologies, geopolitics, the personalities of Stalin and Truman and the historical context of victory in World War II made Soviet–American rivalry as close to a certainty as anything in the history of international relations could be. But, in contrast, the conclusion to the struggle was as extraordinary as it was unexpected. The 1980s began with several years of intense verbal fencing between Moscow and Washington, with a large escalation in the level of American defence spending, and a coordinated US grand strategy to put pressure on the Soviet economy. Washington had considerable success in depressing the price of oil, draining Moscow's convertible currency, and causing trouble for Soviet clients in Asia, Africa and Central America. The decade concluded with the leader of the Soviet Union, a man scarcely known in the West in 1980, abandoning the ideology that legitimized the state. Gorbachev left Soviet client states on their own to make peace with their peoples if they could, and he abandoned the forty-plus years of enmity with the United States. Remarkably, although the Soviet economy was in a terrible condition, the state and its essential services were still functioning, and the country's military power was more formidable than it had ever been. Gorbachev ended the Cold War as a discretionary act, not out of immediate desperation. Another leader – any of Gorbachev's three immediate predecessors, for example – probably would have attempted to maintain the Soviet Union on its steady course to economic ruin. Moreover, they might well not have left the satraps in Eastern Europe to find their own salvation.

It is unusual in strategic history for great empires that have not suffered military catastrophe or domestic revolution simply to stand down from international competition. The West had been right to worry that if the Soviet Union did implode politically, for whatever mixture of reasons, the consequences could well include interstate warfare. During the Cold War it was an article of faith among Western security experts that the rule of the Soviet Communist Party, the maintenance of political control, was the highest value of the Soviet state. And that article of Western faith came to be reflected in the nuclear war plans of the United States. In the late 1970s, US nuclear strategy was reoriented towards being able to menace the Soviet political control structure as a discrete target set.

What had it been about? How could a virtual 'war' that lasted for more than forty years end so tamely? Had it all been a dreadful mistake? If the Soviet Union could collapse so precipitately, so unexpectedly and with so little violence, had it really been the formidable menace that the Western powers had assumed for so many years?

It is far too soon to make confident judgements about many aspects of the Cold War's origins, course and conclusion. But one is in a position to offer some interim opinions. Also, given that the Russian story, as well as the nuclear era, in world politics is far from over, it is necessary that one does one's best to understand what happened and why. While admitting readily their controversial nature, this chapter now offers five broad points which attempt to explain the course and outcome of the Cold War.

First, the Soviet Union and its empire imploded for reasons of internal weakness. With respect to the delivery of goods and services to its citizens, the Soviet Union was a failed state whose failure provided demonstrable proof that the official ideology was unsound. Since the infallibility of Marxist ideology was the basis for the legitimacy of the state, its failure had to call into question the system of government, and especially the right to rule of the Communist Party, supposedly the vanguard of the proletariat.

Second, it is relevant to ask whether the Soviet Union fell in the 1980s because of its own weakness or because it was pushed. The answer would seem to be that although the Soviet system was doomed to lose an economic competition with a democratic capitalist rival, American competitive moves, particularly in the military and economic fields, aggravated Soviet domestic problems. It would be an exaggeration to claim that the robust rhetoric and policies of the Reagan administration were responsible for the Soviet demise, but one should give some credit to US policy and strategy for accentuating the crisis that Gorbachev initially sought to meet with reform, and later to answer with systemic change.

Third, although the Soviet Union had competed effectively with the United States in military power throughout the Cold War years, by the 1980s the true limitations of its economy and its system of central planning were revealed by the emergence of the Information Age in the West. If any one thing condemned the Soviet Union to defeat in the Cold War, it was the computer. Moscow lacked a vibrant civilian economy to explore and exploit information technologies, while its effective, if scarcely efficient, defence industrial sector lagged behind the United States' by a generation or two in the crucial field of electronics. Militarily, and therefore strategically, this meant that by the 1980s senior Soviet soldiers were anticipating critical technical shortfalls. It seemed as if the West's lead in computer technology, when translated into military effectiveness, would enable the development of what Soviet military theorists called 'reconnaissance–strike complexes'. Soviet armour would be massacred at a distance by smart conventional sub-munitions delivered by missile or by long-range artillery shells. The menace of the Soviet armoured *Blitzkrieg* would be cancelled by Western technology.

Fourth, the United States performed well and generally responsibly during the forty years of the conflict. One can see today that the Soviet threat probably was overestimated, but there were plausible contemporary reasons for that error. The American doctrine of 'containment', with its origins in the famous 'Long Telegram' (an 8,000-word cable) sent from Moscow by American diplomat George F. Kennan on 22 February 1946, provided conceptual navigation for the struggle (Etzold and Gaddis, 1978: 50–63). On balance, with the benefit of hindsight, one may judge that Kennan exaggerated the need for the

Soviet imperium to expand, and hence he overstated the necessity to contain Soviet power and influence. But when one bears in mind the historical context of his message, his emphasis upon the need to resist Soviet political expansion becomes entirely understandable. In 1946, pre-Marshall Plan Europe was an economic ruin alive with activecommunist parties seeking power. Truman's America, and indeed Attlee's Britain, correctly identified Stalin's Soviet Union as an enemy. That enemy came to be defined heavily in military terms only after the shock of the North Korean invasion of South Korea in June 1950. In reaction to the war that followed, NATO was reshaped and developed as a notably military, as well as a political, alliance deploying forces for an integrated multinational defence. Eventually, from 1955, that defence included a controversial German contribution. American defence expenditure tripled, a fact which enabled the Strategic Air Command to procure the new all-jet B-47 and then B-52 medium- and long-range bombers. Stalin therefore had much to regret about his decision to allow Kim Il-sung to invade the South in June 1950.

For forty years the United States performed the containment function, though whether the Soviet Union required much containing is a controversial matter. American policy, even if occasionally indiscriminately overactive in its anti-communism and prone to confuse nationalist sentiment with Soviet or Chinese influence, was prosecuted at bearable economic cost at home and in a manner, militarily, that was at least safe enough, vis-à-vis nuclear dangers. This is not to ignore American mistakes, particularly in the Middle East, South East Asia and Central America, but it is to claim that as a country with no history of protracted conflict in peacetime, indeed with no prior history of intense involvement in world security politics except in time of declared war, the United States performed competently or better, if not always admirably. When one considers the historical record, it is important not to judge contemporary leaders in terms of a standard of perfection. Historical figures should be assessed only with reference to what they could know at the time.

Fifth, nuclear war was a real possibility, so much so that many officials and commentators occasionally viewed it as a probability. There is no way of knowing whether the latent menace of nuclear weapons kept the Cold War cold. On the one hand, according to the available evidence, neither side was ever motivated to launch an attack. That should mean that nuclear deterrence was never actively in play to discourage military action. On the other, had there been no nuclear dimension to East–West strategic relations, it is not unduly fanciful to speculate that the Soviet Union might have decided to solve its German problems by force of arms. So-called 'virtual histories' built on 'what ifs' can be misleading. One can invent a general war triggered by the Hungarian Revolution of 1956 in a world without nuclear weapons. But what would NATO's military posture have been in such a world? The most that can be said with absolute confidence is that the nuclear reality encouraged great caution on both sides. As often as not, the more perilous moments of the Cold War were the result of a superpower patron attempting to meet the needs or wishes of an ally to which it was, in some measure, hostage.

Conclusion

It is plausible to interpret the entire history of the Cold War with reference to a series of Soviet failures. Such an approach may seem to emphasize Soviet policy unduly, but the historical record is fairly clear in suggesting that the initiative in the conflict typically was taken by Moscow, albeit often probably for defensive reasons. So what were these major failures?

1. Stalin failed to consolidate the Soviet security zone, or barrier, in Eastern Europe without alarming the West. He triggered the beginning of an organized political and economic resistance led by the United States.
2. Stalin failed to secure the real prize in Central Europe: the whole of Germany. Instead, with his blockade of Berlin in 1948–9, he galvanized Western resistance, inadvertently stilled much Western criticism of the creation of a new Federal Republic of Germany (West Germany), and greatly facilitated American membership in and leadership of the novel NATO Alliance.
3. By permitting Kim Il-sung to invade South Korea, Stalin led, or misled, the United States to redefine the conflict in far more military terms than it had before. The Korean adventure both failed in and of itself, and triggered a threefold jump in American defence expenditure. That jump enabled the United States to fund a new generation of strategic nuclear delivery vehicles, bombers and eventually missiles, and to expand its nuclear arsenal exponentially.
4. Khrushchev's missile diplomacy in its several forms was a complete and embarrassing failure. The Soviet Union derived no benefit from its missile threats, and it appeared irresponsibly adventurous in its dangerous failure over Cuba in October 1962.
5. The Soviet forward policy in Africa and Asia in the 1970s under Brezhnev was an expensive failure that helped bankrupt the state.
6. Gorbachev's well-intentioned efforts, initially to reform the Soviet system and then to transform it rapidly into a capitalist-model economic system, failed in almost all respects. The Soviet system could not be reformed and nor could it be transformed from above by officials who did not understand how a capitalist economy functioned. The result, as history records (unambiguously for once), was Gorbachev's ouster and the demise of the Soviet Union on 25 December 1991.

Why it was so difficult for the West to make peace with the Soviet Union? Why did the Cold War endure for more than forty years? One could cite geopolitical rivalry, the key roles of individuals, and contingency, but pride of place needs to be accorded to ideology. The evidence suggests strongly that the Cold War could not end until the Soviet Union abandoned a state ideology which mandated definition of capitalist powers as enemies. When Gorbachev retired the ideology, the Cold War was over. Unfortunately for him, though, the abrupt retirement of Marxism to the dustbin of history also removed the basis for the legitimacy of the Soviet state.

The story now must turn to consider explicitly the meaning of the nuclear discovery and the implications of the subsequent strategic revolution.

Key points

1. Cold War history is hotly contested today.
2. World War II had revolutionary consequences for all the contexts of international relations.
3. The Cold War emerged slowly, by a process of interaction between rivals, from 1944 until 1947, or even 1950 (the war in Korea).
4. Because of geopolitics and ideology, the conflict was unavoidable.
5. The Soviet Union was fatally outclassed in economic strength by the United States.
6. Although it was inevitable that the Soviet Union would lose the competition, it was not inevitable that it would accept defeat peacefully.

Questions

1. **Who or what caused the Cold War?**
2. **Why did the Cold War last for forty years?**
3. **Why did the Cold War not conclude with World War III?**
4. **Did the Soviet Union expire mainly for internal reasons or was external pressure a factor?**

Further reading

R. Crockatt *The Fifty Years War: The United States and the Soviet Union in World Politics, 1941–1991* (New York: Routledge, 1995).

N. Friedman *The Fifty-Year War: Conflict and Strategy in the Cold War* (Annapolis, MD: Naval Institute Press, 2000)

A. Fursenko and T. Naftali *'One Hell of a Gamble': Khrushchev, Castro, Kennedy, and the Cuban Missile Crisis, 1958–1964* (London: John Murray, 1997).

J. L. Gaddis *Strategies of Containment: A Critical Appraisal of Postwar American National Security Policy* (New York: Oxford University Press, 1982).

—— *We Now Know: Rethinking Cold War History* (Oxford: Clarendon Press, 1997).

—— *The Cold War* (London: Allen Lane, 2006).

M. P. Leffler *A Preponderance of Power: National Security, the Truman Administration, and the Cold War* (Stanford, CA: Stanford University Press, 1992).

V. Mastry *The Cold War and Soviet Insecurity: The Stalin Years* (New York: Oxford University Press, 1996).

J. A. Nathan (ed.) *The Cuban Missile Crisis Revisited* (New York: St Martin's Press, 1992).

M. Trachtenberg *A Constructed Peace: The Making of the European Settlement, 1945–1963* (Princeton, NJ: Princeton University Press, 1999).

O. A. Westad (ed.) *Reviewing the Cold War: Approaches, Interpretations, Theory* (London: Frank Cass, 2000).

V. Zubok and C. Pleshakov *Inside the Kremlin's Cold War: From Stalin to Khrushchev* (Cambridge, MA: Harvard University Press, 1996).

15 The Cold War, II

The nuclear revolution

Reader's guide: The shock of the nuclear revolution. Nuclear weapons. The meaning of the nuclear revolution. Nuclear strategy. The nuclear arms competition.

Introduction: the strategic challenge

On reading the *New York Times'* report on the atomic bombing of Hiroshima on 6 August 1945, America's leading scholar of naval strategy, Bernard Brodie, is reported to have lamented, 'everything that I have written is obsolete' (Kaplan, 1983: 10). Today, it is difficult to recapture the shock, bafflement and sense of the vastness of the strategic challenge felt by strategists in 1945 when confronted for the first time with the demonstrated fact of the atomic bomb. Nuclear weapons can be bracketed with air power, space power and now cyber-power as comprising a clutch of wholly new means of warfare. Each has required its users to understand what it can and cannot do. It is unprecedented in strategic history for a century to produce four essentially technological revolutions in military affairs. But the nuclear revolution was distinctive, in good part for reason of the unprecedented menace that it brought to international relations. Air power, space power and cyber-power all arrived over a period of years, though the pace of air power's development was accelerated by the Great War of 1914–18. That slow arrival meant that each was subject to much speculation and debate prior to its being accorded major importance in strategic affairs. Not so the nuclear weapon.

Because of the secrecy surrounding the Manhattan Project, there was no strategic theory, military doctrine or policy ready and waiting for the new weapon. It was developed initially for the major purpose of pre-empting a possible German bomb, and later for the immediate purpose hopefully of substituting for a bloody invasion of the Japanese Home Islands. The atomic programme was not pursued for its possible coercive effect in Moscow, but that was regarded by Washington as a useful bonus. The best minds among America's strategic thinkers in the mid-1940s were suddenly (and one must emphasize the unexpectedness of Hiroshima and Nagasaki) confronted with the need to make strategic and therefore political sense of a weapon whose very existence had been unknown to them shortly before. Ironically, the historical context for meeting this challenge was America's 'strategic moment'. In 1945, the United States, with help from its allies of course, had triumphed simultaneously in two wars on opposite sides of the globe. Moreover, America was the superpower: its economic strength placed it in a class of its own. Indeed, throughout the Cold War years it is appropriate to think of the United States as the first-class superpower and the Soviet Union as the second-class one. That real distinction was to have black consequences for Soviet competitive prospects.

This chapter comments on the apparent autonomy of the nuclear arms competition of the Cold War. For several decades there was little genuine political dialogue between Moscow and Washington. The two dared not compete directly by force of arms. As a consequence, the arms race and discussion of its limitation became a, perhaps *the*, prime avenue of communication between the protagonists. From the 1960s to the 1980s, the convening of, and positions in, Soviet–American arms-control negotiations took diplomatic centre-stage. This did not mean that the weapons competition was driving the foreign policies of the superpowers, but it did reflect the contemporary reality that Washington and Moscow could not talk productively about settling their political differences. Instead, they could possibly ease political tensions and improve mutual understanding by engaging in highly technical discussions on the limitation of arms. To quote Marshall McLuhan's popular maxim of the late 1960s, 'the medium is the message'. The world found it reassuring that there was an ongoing, albeit on–off, arms-control discussion–negotiating process. Its very existence was talismanic. 'At least the superpowers are talking' was the popular judgement.

There may have been some utility for international security in Soviet–American, and other East–West arms negotiations, but agreements of strategic significance were impossible until the political context was changed beyond all recognition by the domestic revolution in the Soviet Union effected by Mikhail Gorbachev after 1985 and by Boris Yeltsin in 1991. While the Soviet Union was in business as an ideological antagonist to the world of democratic capitalism, useful progress towards better relations could not be made by means of arms control. Politics could not be evaded by technical agreements. The ABM Treaty of 1972 was not an exception to this rule. In Soviet eyes, though not in most American, that treaty denied the United States the option of pursuing its technological advantage in defensive systems. When the Soviet Empire was dissolving in the late 1980s, its extensive nuclear and conventional armaments, and the vested interests in their future, proved not to pose obstacles to what amounted to a political revolution.

It would be difficult to exaggerate the scale of the strategic challenge that the United States, its allies and the Soviet Union had to meet with the dawning of the Nuclear Age. Blessed with the wisdom of hindsight, there is some basis for confidence in beliefs concerning nuclear weapons. But in the 1940s and 1950s, policy-makers, soldiers and hostage publics were moving into and through unknown strategic terrain.

The bomb

The Cold War and nuclear weapons are connected inextricably. The strategic history of the period 1945 to 1989 seemingly was driven, assuredly was shaped, by what became a shared realization of the danger that lurked in the nuclear arsenals. This was strategic history in its most literal sense. Some commentators, scholars and policy-makers, in the West at least, came to believe that the real enemy was not the Soviet Union, but rather the awesome nuclear engines of mass destruction that both sides constructed and maintained. Although those weapons and the political context of the Cold War were vitally linked, neither depended on the other for its existence. As was explained in Chapter 14, the Cold War was the product of the clash between Soviet and American ideologies, the struggle for advantage between two very great powers, and the personality of Joseph Stalin. The competition in nuclear arms was an expression of ideological and geopolitical rivalry; it was not its cause. Over time, however, the scale of the threat posed by the nuclear arsenals did seem to many people to overshadow and even dominate the political context, while it largely ordered the strategic context of the struggle.

The story of 'the bomb' may be quickly told. The atomic bomb, in two variants (uranium and plutonium), was developed in an Anglo-American crash programme, the Manhattan Project, between early 1943 and July 1945. Thanks to its agents in place, especially Klaus Fuchs, seconded to the project from Britain, the Soviet Union knew what was going on. But Moscow was too heavily committed to its war of survival against Germany to devote desperately scarce resources to a serious nuclear weapons programme until the end of the war.

The political impetus to attempt to weaponize nuclear physics was initially strictly precautionary. In the years 1939–42, and even residually thereafter, there were some good reasons to fear that Germany might succeed in building an atomic bomb. Politically and strategically, that possibility simply could not be ignored, although it receded increasingly as the war proceeded. Had Germany built the first atomic bomb, the strategic and political consequences most likely would have been catastrophic, certainly for its enemies and possibly, ultimately, for itself, too.

Germany had been the world leader in physics, at least before the Nazis caused an international elite of German and Hungarian Jewish scientists to emigrate. Typically they moved to Britain initially, and then on to the United States, where their research was better supported. However, Germany did harbour a native son of acceptable ethnicity in the person of the world-famous mathematician and theoretical nuclear physicist Werner Heisenberg. Allied knowledge of his leadership of the German nuclear programme provided reasonable grounds for concern.

The origins of the Nuclear Age that is still with us can be traced through 100 years of progress in physics, chemistry and mathematics. Until World War II the Republic of Science was truly international, with the partial exception of those working in the Soviet Union. Discoveries and theories were shared across frontiers without political restriction. There was no military demand for the atomic bomb. The impulse to weaponize nuclear physics was entirely political, and therefore strategic. Because the British and American governments recognized the appalling probable consequences should Nazi Germany be the first to construct an atomic bomb, they were obliged to find out whether such a venture was scientifically and technically feasible. The only way to do that was to try to build a bomb themselves: hence the Manhattan Project.

Box 15.1 **The scientific and technological feasibility of atomic weapons**

The scientific trail to Hiroshima and Nagasaki is clear enough. The neutron was discovered in 1932, while in 1933 that discovery sparked realization that the neutron could be employed to trigger an explosive chain reaction. An even more significant scientific breakthrough was achieved in January 1939, when Otto Hahn and Fritz Strassmann managed to achieve nuclear fission, the splitting of uranium atoms. They demonstrated that by means of neutron bombardment the atom could be split and a self-sustaining process, a chain reaction, of atomic fission might be achieved. But theoretical physics and an isolated experiment were not remotely the same as bomb building. The crucial step towards a practicable bomb was taken when two German émigré physicists, Otto Frisch and Rudolf Peierls, working at the University of Birmingham in Britain in March 1940, calculated the critical mass of fissile material required for a self-sustaining fission chain reaction. They were amazed to discover that the necessary critical mass of the isotope of uranium (^{235}U) that had to be extracted from natural uranium (^{238}U) was only approximately 11 pounds. Prior to their findings, it was widely believed among nuclear physicists that possibly as much as 30,000 pounds of ^{235}U would be needed. Apart from the impracticality of extracting that much of the isotope from ^{238}U, any bomb that resulted would be so large and heavy that it could be delivered only by ship. In other words, it was thoroughly impractical as a weapon. The calculations of Frisch and Peierls changed all that. Their calculations impressed first the British government and then the American. In theory, at least, the atomic bomb should be technically feasible. Another fissionable element (element 94) was discovered – or rather made, since it did not occur in nature – on 28 March 1941 in the form of plutonium (^{239}Pu). The atomic bomb that devastated Hiroshima 6 August 1945 was made with a critical mass of ^{235}U, while the Nagasaki bomb used ^{239}Pu.

There were several reasons why Nazi Germany made little progress towards the development of an atomic bomb, notwithstanding the understandable anxieties of British and American leaders and their scientific advisers. First, Hitler had little or no interest in physics. In fact, he actively disliked the discipline, regarding it as a 'Jewish science'. Second, the atomic bomb, even if it should prove feasible, was believed to be strictly a long-term project, capable of producing useful results, if at all, only years after the current war had reached its conclusion. In 1942–3, Nazi Germany was not much interested in heavy investment in the next war. Third, Germany's premier scientist, Werner Heisenberg, advised Minister of Armaments Albert Speer, who duly advised the Führer, that the atomic project faced all but insuperable technical difficulties. In particular, he said, it would be almost impossible to gather or create the necessary critical mass of fissionable ^{235}U. Heisenberg did not claim that a bomb could not be built, but he did say that it could not possibly be built for many years, and only then at very great expense. After the war, Heisenberg claimed that he deliberately sabotaged Nazi bomb research by misinforming Speer about the scale of the technical difficulties; there has been a long-running debate among scholars on the question of whether he lied in that matter (Powers, 1993; Cornwell, 2004: 406–10). The balance of scholarship today favours the view that Heisenberg, for all his undoubted brilliance as a theorist, was not a gifted experimental physicist. Furthermore, despite being a mathematical genius, he was notoriously casual in his calculations. In short, it seems he misinformed his government inadvertently. He had not correctly calculated the necessary critical mass for a self-sustaining chain reaction, and he had no practical idea of how to build a bomb.

When one considers the scale and diversity of effort, and therefore the cost ($1.9 billion in 1945 dollars; which equates to $24.2 billion in 2005 dollars), of the Manhattan Project, it is evident that the Germans never even approached the level of material commitment that would have been necessary. But it is worth noting that, had Hitler been captivated by the prospect of an Aryan atomic bomb, he probably could have achieved it in the three years taken by the Manhattan Project. The claim can be made because, from 1942 to 1945, Nazi Germany did undertake a Manhattan-scale project. It was the strategically futile programme to mass-produce long-range rockets: the air-breathing V-1 and the ballistic V-2. These were mighty technological accomplishments, but, unlike atomic bombs, they carried no potential to change the course of strategic history.

The nuclear revolution

What was revolutionary about atomic fission, then hydrogen fusion, weapons? Note that the nuclear revolution occurred in two stages, with the better part of a decade between them. Stage one was the development in 1945 of the atomic bomb (A-bomb), a weapon whose energy was produced by fission. Stage two, accomplished in 1952 and 1953, was the development of the hydrogen bomb (H-bomb), whose energy was generated by the process of fusion, albeit with a fission trigger (see Box 15.2). The vital difference between the A-bomb and the H-bomb is that the explosive energy yield of the former is strictly limited by the nature of the materials, their dynamic interaction, and consequently there is a problem in keeping the weapon stable. The H-bomb is distinguished by having no theoretical limit to its energy yield. Americans were shocked by their BRAVO hydrogen (thermonuclear) bomb test of 1 March 1954, which produced 15 megatons instead of the design yield of 5. Control of the energy yield failed. In 1961, as an act of intended political intimidation, Nikita Khrushchev announced the intention to test a thermonuclear weapon of 100 megatons. In practice, the yield was restrained to 50.7 megatons. This monstrous explosion was the largest test to be carried out during the Cold War.

Box 15.2 Two kinds of nuclear weapons

Atomic weapons

- Atomic weapons derive their energy from the process of nuclear fission.
- Nuclear fission is achieved by breaking up the nuclei of uranium (^{235}U) or plutonium (^{239}Pu) through bombardment by neutrons.

- The splitting of the atomic nuclei creates a self-sustaining chain reaction that releases explosive energy.
- The nuclear weapons dropped on Hiroshima and Nagasaki had explosive yields, respectively, of 15 kilotons and 20 kilotons (15,000 and 20,000 tons of TNT equivalent, respectively).
- Atomic weapons are limited in their explosive yield by the relative inefficiency of the fission process, as compared with fusion, as well as by constraints imposed by physical size and safety considerations.

Thermonuclear weapons

- These weapons require the nuclear fusion of two lighter (than ^{235}U or ^{239}Pu) elements, usually deuterium and tritium (isotopes of hydrogen) to form helium.
- A thermonuclear weapon employs a fission explosion as a trigger to compress the deuterium and tritium together by implosion sufficiently for them to fuse.
- These weapons are generally called hydrogen bombs. There is no theoretical or practical limit to the explosive yield that can be achieved by such bombs. Typically, strategic nuclear weapons have been deployed with yields ranging from several hundred kilotons to the low megatons (a megaton is 1,000,000 tons of TNT equivalent.)

The hydrogen fusion bomb changed the strategic context radically. From atomic weapons in the tens of kilotons, the Cold War protagonists were able, after 1953–4, to field fusion weapons in the megaton range. Until the H-bomb was deployed in large numbers in the mid- to late 1950s, it was just possible to argue that a World War III would be like World War II but with the addition of precursor bilateral atomic campaigns. Those campaigns were not expected to conclude the war. But once the H-bomb was deployed, such an argument could no longer be advanced and sustained. The H-bomb was so destructive that a new set of strategic ideas and a new policy were required to fit the changed strategic context. Now it is necessary to return to a thus far unanswered question: what was revolutionary about nuclear, in particular fusion or hydrogen, weapons? Five answers command attention.

First, these novel weapons seem to fracture the link between means and ends which is the instrumental essence of strategy itself. Nuclear weapons appeared to be, indeed may be, too powerful and too destructive, if used, to serve any political ends. Whatever their utility as a threat, nuclear weapons are commonly not really seen as weapons at all, while 'nuclear strategy' is a contradiction in terms. The problem was, and is, that the weapons exist. Governments and the armed forces of nuclear-armed states have had no choice but to devise policy, strategy and doctrine for these fearsome devices.

Second, if nuclear weapons are held by both sides in a war, they should render decisive military victory impossible. Provided a fraction of both nuclear arsenals are secure against attack, nuclear retaliation could, and almost certainly would, follow any nuclear attack. Even decisive military victory in a conventional war between nuclear-weapon states should be improbable. The belligerent facing such defeat would be strongly motivated to resort to its nuclear arms rather than suffer conventional defeat.

Third, a nuclear-armed state can defeat an enemy without first defeating its armed forces, but if that enemy also was nuclear armed the net result would be bilateral defeat. This condition renders the prospect of high-intensity conflict distinctly unattractive.

Fourth, as the Cold War probably illustrated, nuclear weapons raise the threshold for the resort to force. Nuclear-armed states are, or ought to be, much more reluctant to fight each other than are non-nuclear states. One must add the caveat that this claim for the revolutionary effect of nuclear weapons rests uneasily on negative evidence, which is to say on events that did *not* happen. There is no way to be certain why possible wars did not occur. For a further caveat, the extant body of nuclear lore still derives overwhelmingly from the Cold War. It is entirely possible that the twenty-first century will witness nuclear-armed polities behaving with less restraint than did protagonists in the twentieth.

Fifth, nuclear weapons have the effect of freezing conditions of political confrontation. It is not only war that is too perilous to contemplate as a policy option. Even dangerous behaviour short of war is likely to be judged irresponsibly risky. Nuclear weapons appear to have deprived war of its prime traditional rationale. No longer can it be regarded as an instrument of policy to solve a problem that cannot be settled in any other way, at least not in conflicts between nuclear-armed rivals.

These points comprise the strategic core of the nuclear revolution. That revolution appeared to have consequences that were anti-strategic; antipathetic to the possibility of victory; potentially mutually suicidal; encouraging of super-cautious behaviour by nuclear-armed rivals; and promoting of geopolitical immobility. But the nuclear narrative of the Cold War was not quite that simple and certain.

Nuclear strategy

If nuclear weapons cannot serve political purposes as weapons in military use, they can certainly serve policy by the threat of their employment. Eventually, both superpowers recognized that large-scale nuclear use would be self-defeating, since a disarming first strike ceased to be militarily feasible by the mid- to late 1960s. Until that time, the United States might have succeeded with a surprise attack upon Soviet nuclear forces. The rival nuclear arsenals were dynamic in quantity and quality. Not until the 1960s were both the United States and the Soviet Union able to deploy long-range nuclear-armed forces in the diversity of basing modes that should render a successful surprise attack against them impossible. The now familiar strategic forces triad – comprising ICBMs (intercontinental ballistic missiles), SLBMs (submarine-launched ballistic missiles) and manned bombers – appeared only early in that decade.

Irrespective of whether nuclear strategy was a futile pursuit, it was an inescapable necessity. As their nuclear arsenals grew from the tens to the thousands, and eventually to the tens of thousands, the United States and the Soviet Union, followed by others, had to develop nuclear strategies (see Table 15.1). Furthermore, those strategies had to be tailored to the unique geostrategic situation of each state. Also, they were in constant need of amendment as the technologies of weapon design and delivery evolved. Most particularly, by the close of the 1950s the Nuclear Age had been joined, with synergistic effect, by the Missile Age.

Table 15.1 Nuclear stockpiles, 1945–89

Year	USA	USSR	UK	France	China	Total
1945	6					6
1946	11					11
1947	32					32
1948	110					110
1949	235	1				236
1950	369	5				374
1951	640	25				665
1952	1,005	50				1,055
1953	1,436	120	1			1,557
1954	2,063	150	5			2,218
1955	3,057	200	10			3,267
1956	4,618	426	15			5,059
1957	6,444	660	20			7,124
1958	9,822	869	22			10,713
1959	15,468	1,060	25			16,553
1960	20,434	1,605	30			22,069
1961	24,111	2,471	50			26,632
1962	27,297	3,322	205			30,824
1963	29,249	4,238	280			33,767
1964	30,751	5,221	310	4	1	36,287
1965	31,642	6,129	310	32	5	38,118
1966	31,700	7,089	270	36	20	39,115
1967	30,893	8,339	270	36	25	39,563
1968	28,884	9,399	280	36	35	38,634
1969	26,910	10,538	308	36	50	37,842
1970	26,119	11,643	280	36	75	38,153
1971	26,365	13,092	220	45	100	39,822
1972	27,296	14,478	220	70	130	42,194
1973	28,335	15,915	275	116	150	44,791
1974	28,170	17,385	325	145	170	46,195
1975	27,052	19,055	350	188	185	46,830
1976	25,956	21,205	350	212	190	47,913
1977	25,099	23,044	350	228	200	48,921
1978	24,243	25,393	350	235	220	50,441
1979	24,107	27,935	350	235	235	52,862
1980	23,764	30,062	350	250	280	54,706
1981	23,031	32,049	350	274	330	56,034
1982	22,937	33,952	335	274	360	57,858
1983	23,154	35,804	320	279	380	59,937
1984	23,228	37,431	270	280	415	61,624
1985	23,135	39,197	300	360	425	63,417
1986	23,254	40,723	300	355	425	65,057
1987	23,490	38,859	300	420	415	63,484
1988	23,077	37,333	300	410	430	61,550
1989	22,174	35,805	300	410	435	59,124

Source: Adapted from R. S. Norris and H. M. Kristensen, 'Global Nuclear Stockpiles, 1945–2002', *Bulletin of the Atomic Scientists*, 58 (2002): 103–4

Nearly everyone in the Western Alliance agreed on deterrence as the master concept for the new weapons, but there was scant agreement on how best to deter and how to keep a relationship of mutual deterrence stable. Strategic stability, regarded technically strictly in military terms, was deemed to reside in a context where neither side could secure a major advantage by striking first. In the contemporary jargon of defence analysis, a stable context was one in which the first-strike bonus was low or negligible. Such a context was said to be 'crisis stable'. The most popular thesis in the West was that strategic stability was ensured by the mutual ability of the superpowers to inflict unacceptable damage upon each other in any and all circumstances. This strategic – perhaps anti-strategic – condition came to be known as mutual assured destruction (MAD). The roles of society were to pay for the nuclear armed forces and to serve uncomplainingly as hostage to the prudent and sober behaviour of its political leaders.

The previous paragraph is the standard characterization of the Soviet–American nuclear stand-off during the Cold War. It is not so much untrue as misleading. Two aspects to superpower nuclear strategy need to be distinguished. First, there was declaratory policy and strategy, or what officials claimed to be the purpose and methods that would guide their nuclear forces in action. Second, both sides had operational nuclear strategies which might not bear much relationship to declaratory policy. Mutual assured destruction almost certainly would have been the result of an East–West nuclear war in the 1960s, 1970s or 1980s. Politicians may have spoken about the MAD context as though it were strategy, but of course it was not. Assured destruction, let alone mutual assured destruction, is a denial of strategy and, in action, could serve no conceivable political purpose.

It is reasonable to comment that the primary, possibly the sole, function of nuclear forces was to deter, and that therefore issues of nuclear strategy were all but irrelevant. Whatever the merit in that argument, it does leave open the question of the relationship between declaratory policy and operational strategy. How did states actually plan to employ their nuclear forces in the event of war? The evidence of deeds in defence preparation in the arms competition is overwhelming in pointing to the fact that neither the Soviet Union nor the United States was content with a context of mutual assured destruction. They may have struggled in vain to escape its logic and prospective reality, but struggle they did. Neither side was willing to abandon all hope of being able to employ nuclear weapons in search of strategic advantage. Politicians and commentators during the Cold War might characterize the contemporary nuclear stand-off in terms of MAD, and they were probably correct to do so, but defence professionals could not responsibly settle for a strategic context that guaranteed mutual suicide (Gray, 2006d: ch. 6; Jervis, 1989).

Mutual assured destruction was the reality of the superpowers' strategic nexus after the mid-1960s, but neither side selected it as strategy. Its public airing and explanation by Secretary of Defense Robert S. McNamara was declaratory, not action, policy and strategy. He presented it publicly for the purpose of capping America's build-up of long-range ballistic missiles and thereby limiting the size of the US nuclear arsenal. The policy had nothing worthy of note to do with actual strategy.

The Soviet Union would never concede as policy, or in strategy, its total vulnerability to nuclear attack. In fact, despite more than two decades of on–off–on negotiations on strategic arms control, by the end of the Cold War the superpowers still had not managed to agree on a common definition of 'strategic stability'. That rather telling point suggests that the Soviet Union was not fully on board for the contemporary US policy goal of a relationship of stable mutual deterrence. The ABM Treaty of 1972 permitted each side to deploy only one defensive site. In effect, it denied the signatories the option of seeking to defend actively the whole of their homelands. That treaty was widely interpreted in the West as proof positive that at last the Soviet Union had recognized the wisdom in Western strategic thinking and had endorsed the concept of mutual assured destruction. On balance, and with the benefit of hindsight and some post-Cold War revelations, it is reasonably clear that the Soviet Union signed up to the treaty not in order to freeze, or just recognize the grim reality of, a MAD condition, but rather for the purpose of slowing the pace of threatening American developments in defensive weapons technology (Odom, 1998: 71, 436 n.25).

To summarize the problems with mutual assured destruction: the Soviet Union never endorsed it, while the United States found it entirely unacceptable, indeed deemed it both absurd and irresponsible, as strategy. Americans worried that accidents and miscalculations could happen which might lead to nuclear war. In any of those dire events, what sense could there be in a nuclear war plan that offered only the single outcome of guaranteed Armageddon? For that was what mutual assured destruction meant. The threat to destroy Soviet cities and a large percentage of the Soviet people was both politically incredible, though technically easy to accomplish, and strategically valueless. How much destruction needed to be assured for the Soviet Union to be deterred from attacking the United States and its allies? According to McNamara, the answer was between 20 and 33 per cent of the Soviet population and 50–75 per cent of Soviet industry. The calculation was strictly material, a cost–benefit analysis; it had no basis in strategic theory or logic, let alone in historical experience.

From the moment when the Soviet Union demonstrated an atomic weapons capability in August 1949 until the end of the Cold War, the United States struggled to find a nuclear strategy capable of offsetting the inhibitions implicit in a mutuality of nuclear deterrence. The geopolitical and geostrategic context was classically asymmetrical. Superior Soviet conventional forces menaced America's friends and allies in Western Europe. But the United States extended deterrence to protect those friends and allies by means of technologically superior, and more numerous – until the 1970s – nuclear forces. The story of US nuclear strategy throughout the Cold War is keyed to the twin issues of credibility and, increasingly over time, the possible limitation and control of a nuclear war. The United States was an ocean away from NATO–Europe, and it was believed to be difficult to persuade a determined, perhaps a desperate, Soviet adversary that Americans would be willing to hazard US cities on behalf of Europeans or Asians.

For nearly forty years, American nuclear strategy sought to offset the inconvenient facts of strategic geography. The United States needed to persuade the Soviet Union that it might use nuclear weapons first in response to a conventional invasion of Western Europe. Furthermore, it had to appear capable of dominating a subsequent process of nuclear escalation. In the late 1940s the United States enjoyed a nuclear monopoly for four years, and through the 1950s and well into the 1960s it was plainly superior in nuclear forces, notwithstanding periodic alarms about falsely predicted bomber and missile 'gaps'. But how could extended deterrence be maintained once the Soviet Union achieved strategic parity in the late 1960s? What could the United States substitute for its previous nuclear superiority? The condition of strategic parity seemingly was conceded by Washington on 26 May 1972 with the SALT I Interim Agreement on Certain Measures with Respect to the Limitation of Strategic Offensive Arms.

There were four possible answers to America's, and therefore NATO's, credibility problem with nuclear deterrence. First, the British and especially the French national nuclear deterrents, which admittedly were more (Britain) or less (France) dependent upon US assistance, might take up any slack in the needful quantity and quality of deterrence. It might not be judged in Moscow to be likely that Americans would risk their country for European allies, or even for American forces in Europe, but the willingness of the French and the British to employ nuclear weapons if they were threatened with invasion, or with Soviet nuclear use, ought to be high. Unsurprisingly, this logic did not appeal to the United States. Washington was not at all keen on the idea of being precipitated into a nuclear war catalysed by an ally of its own volition.

Second, the United States might seek to restore some credible usability to its nuclear forces by recovering a measure of strategic superiority through the addition of active missile defence of its homeland. This distant possibility was abandoned in the ABM Treaty of 1972, though it did return with maximum political impact when President Reagan surprised friends and rivals alike with his announcement on 23 March 1983 of a Strategic Defense Initiative (SDI), promptly pejoratively labelled 'Star Wars' by Senator Edward Kennedy. Effective missile defence was not technically feasible during the Cold War decades. However, it was a not completely implausible technological possibility and, as a consequence, prudent Soviet policy-makers dared not dismiss the prospect out of hand.

Third, the United States could seek to restore credibility to its ever more evenly matched strategic nuclear forces by refining its nuclear doctrine and operational plans. In practice, this was the dominant US answer to the challenge posed by Soviet strategic parity. From the early 1960s until the end of the Cold War, US nuclear doctrine and plans sought to achieve flexibility in order to provide options for the National Command Authorities (NCA). It might not be credible to threaten total catastrophe, action that must end in mutual nuclear suicide, but, so the reasoning proceeded, it should be possible to restore credibility and retain some control of events by limiting nuclear strikes. Of course, the control of a nuclear war by flexibility of response would require cooperation on the part of the enemy. On the basis of the admittedly unreliable evidence available, there are grounds for scepticism over the ability and willingness of the Soviet Union to wage a limited nuclear war. After the mid-1960s, only by reciprocated restraint in nuclear targeting could damage in a World War III have been limited. The Soviet Union had both strategic cultural and practical military objections to the American liking for 'limited nuclear options'. If flexible response – or, more accurately, limited first and subsequent use – was the principal safety net against the Cold War concluding with Armageddon, then the world was in a most perilous condition. Unfortunately, regarded technically, Soviet–American strategic relations were in precisely such a condition in the 1970s and 1980s.

The fourth US answer to the Soviet attainment of strategic nuclear parity would be to return to its policy and strategic logic of 1950. In a high-level study, NSC-68, dated 14 April 1950, American officials had reasoned that in response to the Soviet breaking of the previous US atomic monopoly, the United States and its allies should build conventional forces capable of defending Europe against the Red Army (Etzold and Gaddis, 1978: 433–4). The burden of nuclear credibility, the credibility of first nuclear use, would be transferred from the United States to the Soviet Union. In practice, if never quite explicitly in policy, in the 1980s the United States came close to realizing the 1950 vision of a NATO able to withstand a Soviet conventional assault. By exploiting new information technologies, the United States developed, or threatened credibly to develop, 'smart conventional' munitions capable of massacring Soviet armour at a distance. The key technology programme was a project lethal to Soviet armoured fighting vehicles labelled 'Assault Breaker'. Soviet officials were appalled, and suitably worried that their recent massive investment in the comprehensive modernization of their ground forces was about to be negated.

Fortunately, there is no way of knowing which, if any, of the ideas and programmes just outlined would have fared well under the pressure of wartime events. Also, there is no way of knowing which ideas had more or less utility for deterrence. Although the nuclear revolution and its manifestation in rival arsenals was an expression of political hostility, somehow the political meaning of the nuclear arms competition could all but vanish from sight. The nuclear arms race seemed to take on a life, and follow a logic, of its own. This was not really the case, but it certainly appeared so. How did the nuclear revolution relate to the course and outcome of the Cold War?

The nuclear arms competition

The nuclear arms race, far from being a likely cause of war from the late 1940s until 1989, was a partial substitute for actual hostilities. Since nuclear arms were not obviously usable as weapons, and given that they had the effect of freezing geopolitical lines of demarcation, the arms competition was the principal safe way in which the superpowers could prosecute their rivalry. In times past, even as recently as the 1930s, international competition between great powers could be pursued by the acquisition of allies as well as by the unilateral development and amassing of armaments. But in the Nuclear Age, with the possible course of conventional warfare inevitably overshadowed by nuclear dangers, the addition or subtraction of allies was of little strategic importance. At least, that is how it seemed during the Cold War. However, this is not to deny the strategic importance of the Chinese defection from the Soviet camp in the early 1960s, and its eventual informal strategic alliance with the United States from 1972 until the end of the 1980s.

Although the nuclear arms race was not dangerous in itself, and on balance may have acted as a safety valve, it was inevitably a source of anxiety to both sides. Politicians seemed to understand that nuclear weapons were radically different from other kinds of armament, and that they had strategic utility only in non-use (Brodie, 1973: ch. 9). But the defence professionals of East and West had no choice other than to assume that nuclear weapons truly were weapons that might be used. As the nuclear arsenals grew in number and sophistication, and as the Missile Age joined the Nuclear Age, the rival military establishments were obliged to devise doctrines to guide planning for nuclear use. The fact that nuclear weapons are so destructive that they ought not to be used except as an instrument with which to threaten for deterrence is no guarantee that they will not be used. Nuclear war was an ever-present, if generally remote, possibility throughout the Cold War.

Both the United States and the Soviet Union succeeded in designing and implementing systems for the command and control of nuclear forces which accomplished contradictory functions. On the one hand, nuclear forces had to be so ready for use that they could not be destroyed in a surprise attack. This challenge was greatly eased by the allocation of a major fraction of the retaliatory mission to SLBMs carried by SSBNs (nuclear-powered ballistic missile-firing submarines), weapons which need not be launched in haste on warning in order to survive, provided the boats were at sea. On the other hand, the nuclear forces, while always ready to be launched, had to be kept under such tight control that they could never be launched by accident or by unauthorized local military initiative. Although the Cold War years registered many accidents and much miscalculation based on ignorance, the historical record tells us unambiguously that the safety procedures of both sides obviously were good enough because there was no nuclear war.

Conclusion

It is tempting to believe that the theory and practice of deterrence as rediscovered, practised and subsequently taught by the United States in the Cold War was a great success. It is hard to contradict such a claim, with its apparent supporting evidence of a no-war outcome to the Cold War. There can be no question but that American and Soviet nuclear doctrines proved to be compatible with an absence of war. But was there a causal relationship? We do not know. An ocean of ink and a small forest of paper were expended in protracted and repeated debates over nuclear strategy (Freedman, 2003). However, whether the peace was kept because of US and Soviet mastery and implementation of strategic ideas for the prudent governance of nuclear weapons must forever remain a mystery. It is possible that the human race survived the Cold War without suffering a nuclear cataclysm *despite*, rather than because of, the authoritative strategic theories and doctrines of the period.

The American and Soviet defence establishments were obliged as a matter of elementary prudence to assume that the rival might succeed in developing a weapon or weapons that would yield a militarily useful advantage. Eventually it was clear enough to both sides that nuclear weapons could not be used to threaten for the purpose of gain. Their utility was strictly for defence. However, that strategic revelation did not occur until the 1960s. In the 1950s, neither Washington nor Moscow knew what the limits of nuclear diplomacy were. Only experience could reveal the answer. In the 1950s, with nuclear weapons having been employed in anger as recently as 1945, there seemed good reason to believe that they would be used across a wide range of warfare in the future. The Cold War years, particularly those from 1950 to 1962, provided education in the meaning and implications of the nuclear revolution. But the lessons that could be learnt from negative evidence were inherently ambiguous.

Key points

1. Nuclear weapons were developed in an Anglo-American crash programme from 1942 to 1945, out of anxiety lest the Germans should be the first to acquire 'the bomb'.

continued

2. For a long while after Hiroshima and Nagasaki in 1945, the United States did not have a strategy for its growing nuclear arsenal.
3. The nuclear revolution occurred in two stages: first, the development of atomic weapons in the early 1940s; then, the development of thermonuclear, or hydrogen, weapons in the early 1950s.
4. Nuclear weapons raised the political threshold for the resort to force in relations between nuclear-armed states.
5. The Soviets did not agree with the American concept of stable mutual deterrence achieved by capabilities for mutual assured destruction (MAD).
6. The history of US nuclear strategy in the Cold War is the history of the search for credible nuclear threats and options for use, in order to extend deterrence over distant allies.
7. Strategic history cannot reveal whether World War III was avoided because of nuclear strategy, or despite it.

Questions

1. Is the concept of 'nuclear strategy' a contradiction in terms?
2. What was the strategic value of nuclear weapons in the Cold War?
3. How was nuclear deterrence supposed to work?
4. Did nuclear weapons keep the Cold War cold?

Further reading

B. Brodie *Strategy in the Missile Age* (Princeton, NJ: Princeton University Press, 1959).
—— *War and Politics* (New York: Macmillan, 1973).
—— (ed.) *The Absolute Weapon: Atomic Power and World Order* (New York: Harcourt, Brace, 1946).
G. J. DeGroot *The Bomb: A Life* (London: Jonathan Cape, 2004).
L. Freedman *The Evolution of Nuclear Strategy*, 3rd edn (Basingstoke: Palgrave Macmillan, 2003).
—— *Deterrence* (Cambridge: Polity Press, 2004).
D. Holloway *Stalin and the Bomb: The Soviet Union and Atomic Energy, 1939–1956* (New Haven, CT: Yale University Press, 1994).
R. Jervis *The Meaning of the Nuclear Revolution: Statecraft and the Prospect of Armageddon* (Ithaca, NY: Cornell University Press, 1989).
F. Kaplan *The Wizards of Armageddon* (New York: Touchstone, 1983).
R. Rhodes *The Making of the Atomic Bomb* (New York: Touchstone, 1986).

16 War and peace after the Cold War

An interwar decade

Reader's guide: The 1990s as an interwar period. A unipolar world. The 'new wars' thesis. The bloody conflicts of the decade.

Introduction: the interwar thesis

It is useful to think of the 1990s as an interwar decade, though it is a controversial thesis (Gray, 1994). This latest interwar period dates from November 1989, when the Wall came down in Berlin, to 9/11 (i.e., 11 September) 2001, when the global political and strategic contexts were dramatically altered. What happened on 9/11 was the equivalent of the Wall Street Crash of 29 October 1929. Just as understanding of the 1920s and 1930s is organized into the periods before and after the Crash and the subsequent Depression, so the post-Cold War period should be divided into the years pre- and post-9/11.

An important reason why some commentators have not been attracted to the thesis that the post-Cold War years have been an interwar period is because they are convinced that the era of great interstate conflicts has passed (Mandelbaum, 1998–9; R. Smith, 2005: 1–26). Allegedly, that era was eroded and retired by a combination of nuclear weapons, which rendered warfare impractical; by economic globalization, the logic of which finds no place for war; and by the decline in the authority and autonomy of the state, through both globalization and a decline in national feeling. General Rupert Smith argues that a new paradigm of war has succeeded the old paradigm of combat between regular armies. The new paradigm is of war 'amongst the people' (Smith, 2005: xiii).

The interwar thesis comes in two principal variants. First is the proposition that there is another great power conflict waiting to occur in the future, most probably organized around the United States and China as competing poles. Second, one can break away from the traditional focus on great interstate struggles and instead endorse the official American view which holds that 'America is a nation at war' (Rumsfeld, 2005: 1). In that view, 9/11 ended the latest interwar period. It produced a strategic context wherein the sole global superpower, the United States, is at war with Islamic extremists who resort to violence. Officially, America is at war with 'terror', but that is an impossibility. In practice, it is really at war only with the Islamic fundamentalists who have declared war upon both the West and allegedly apostate Islamic regimes, which is to say those that have fallen away from the 'true faith'.

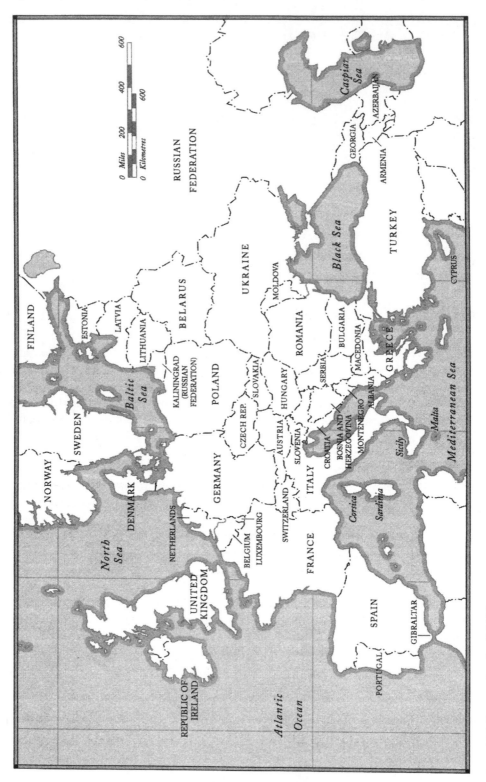

Map 16.1 Europe after the Cold War

The interwar issue is of high importance. Is the master strategic narrative of the 1990s and 2000s primarily to be regarded: (1) as a time-out from great power conflict, pending the return of that cyclical phenomenon; (2) as witnessing the emergence of a new strategic context wherein interstate warfare, particularly of the greater variety, is obsolescent and even obsolete; or (3) as the period when a radically asymmetrical kind of threat, religiously motivated terrorism and insurgency, came to take centre-stage as the leading force in global conflict? There is some merit in each of these perspectives.

The early 1990s were in some ways historically exceptional, while in others they were all too familiar. With respect to the exceptional and unfamiliar, there was no precedent in the past two centuries for a single state to be so dominant after a great conflict that it was unchallenged, and indeed unchallengeable, at least in the military–strategic dimension of power. This was, and thus far has remained, the American condition. In 1815, 1919 and 1945, no great power was so mighty as to be beyond discipline by other powers. Even if war had destroyed previous balances of power, new ones appeared in their aftermath. In fact, new balances emerged as vital contributors to the terms of the post-war settlements. Although France was unchallengeable on land in Europe in the 1920s, its overall strategic standing was balanced by Britain. But in 1989–91, as the Soviet imperium, then the Soviet Empire, then even the Soviet Union itself, melted down, the United States was left as the only superpower.

It has been a recurring phenomenon that in the aftermath of each great struggle, efforts are made to institutionalize a new approach to international security. Liberal optimists proclaim that the world has changed, is changing or may well change radically for the better. Alas, to date, they have always been disappointed. (This matter is discussed in Chapter 19.) Perhaps because of the unusual way in which the Cold War ended, the post-war (here labelled interwar) period was not launched with the historically usual institutional innovations.

Consider the circumstances of 1989–91. Quite suddenly, between 1987 and 1989, the Cold War ended. It faded away virtually to nothing, except for residual suspicions. Unquestionably, the Soviet Union had lost and was set on an eccentric path of uncontrollable reform and change. It was, however, still in the field as a functioning polity. It had a central government and it remained heavily armed in all categories. In those circumstances, understandably, there was no peace treaty; nor was there even some rough facsimile of such. Abruptly, after nearly forty-five years of Soviet–American, East–West Cold War, the principal organizing axis of global security was no more. This posed a challenge, provided an opportunity, but above all set a puzzle. How would security be managed and policed in the post-Cold War world? Perhaps more to the point, which security problems would be in need of management and policing?

A unipolar world

The 1990s should have been a decade of American self-confidence. It might even have been a decade of innovation in norm promotion and institution-building. America had responded with imagination and energy to the challenge it perceived from Moscow in the late 1940s. So, one could argue, in the early 1990s it needed to rise to the unique opportunity offered by the demise of the Soviet Union. It had to direct and manage the transition from Cold War to a more cooperative international political context. But how should that be attempted?

The decade opened with three triumphs for the United States, ranging from the minor, through the substantial, to the monumental. First, from 20 to 25 December 1989, General Manuel Noriega was forcibly removed from presidential office. America thereby solved its problem with Noriega's drug smuggling in Panama swiftly and efficiently.

Second, the United States unquestionably was the victor in the Cold War. It is true that the Soviet rival imploded, much as the diplomat George Kennan had predicted it would in his 1946 'Long Telegram' from the US Embassy Moscow (Etzold and Gaddis, 1978: 50–63). But the steadiness of the US performance as a strategic competitor was an important element leading to the Soviet demise. American willingness and ability periodically to compete more energetically in grand-strategic ways, and not only militarily, made a significant contribution to the impoverishment of the Soviet civilian economy. For the Soviet Union, the United States was the rival from hell. It could not be eliminated militarily because of the nuclear fact. Because of Moscow's Marxist ideology, it could not be transformed from an enemy into a friend, except as a matter of temporary tactical expediency. And the extraordinary effort to compete well enough with the United States in the military sphere ensured, grand-strategically, that the Soviet Union must lose the competition in living standards. It is true that Moscow's dysfunctional ideology and system of government were the prime causes of Soviet failure, but it is also plausible to claim that US policy was a significant reason why those systemic Soviet weaknesses proved fatal. The Soviet Union unquestionably lost the Cold War. It would be churlish to deny the United States some credit for that result.

The final American triumph of the period was the ejection of Iraqi forces from Kuwait in a 100-hour ground war launched on 24 February 1991. A precursor air campaign had opened on 17 January. So now, in less than two years, the United States had wielded its sword and disposed of its Panamanian problem; it had outlasted the 'evil empire' of the Soviet Union and encouraged it to self-destruct; and it had taught the murderous dictator in Baghdad, Saddam Hussein – a recent American friend, one must add, during the eight-year Iraq–Iran War – a painful and, hopefully, embarrassing lesson in acceptable international behaviour. The sun was shining on the United States in 1989–91. At least, that was how it seemed at the time.

The Soviet Union in 1989–91, like Britain in 1945–7 or France in the 1920s, proved to be far weaker than had been assumed. Although still viewed with some suspicion, and treated with much caution, by the administration of George Bush Snr, it slowly became unmistakably apparent that the Soviet decline truly was a terminal collapse. In 1991 all fourteen of the non-Russian republics of the USSR chose to secede; while on 25 December the Union itself was formally dissolved. The USSR was replaced by fifteen new states.

Good news in strategic history has a way of being a source of bad news, too. The sudden end of the Soviet Union, with its extensive foreign ties and influence, was by no means wholly a blessing, especially in the Balkans and Transcaucasia. The good news for Washington could hardly have been better. Now it stood alone as the only superpower, while its former rival descended through decline to actual fall. But what did this momentous event mean for America's role in the world? How should the sole superpower behave? President Bush spoke briefly of a 'new world order', ironically initially on the very day that Iraq invaded Kuwait. But he was not a man much enthralled by what he referred to dismissively as 'the vision thing'. His administration was cautious, businesslike, but emphatically not well peopled with potential political engineers for the construction of a new world order. The Cold War was no more, though Russia's future remained uncertain, but peace had not exactly broken out all over. Quite the contrary.

As will be discussed more fully in the next section, the 1990s were blighted bloodily by a series of wars. In the Balkans, the Wars of Yugoslavian Succession marred the entire decade. A book such as this focuses near-exclusively upon the major currents of strategic history, and particularly upon the principal conflicts and their consequences. However, there are nearly always lesser wars in the turbulent wake of a great war. So massive is the social and political upheaval created by a major war, and so radical a shift in the strategic context is wrought by its conclusion, that opportunity knocks for a host of actors who seek to exploit what they believe is their strategic moment. For example, more people died in the wars that immediately succeeded World War I, some of them ironically called 'civil', than had perished in the Great War itself. The 1990s, similarly, was not to be a peaceful decade.

The United States alone had a convincing global military reach, though the British and French could, and did, manage interventions on a minor scale. But with the Soviet Union, now Russia, off the gaming board of global politics, why and where should America intervene? Global reach is nice to have, but to what purpose? Without a Soviet enemy, indeed without any significant foe, US foreign policy and its military backstop were suddenly bereft of navigational guidance. The post-Cold War world was distressingly populated with outbreaks of organized violence, mainly of a character internal to states and would-be states. But none of those eruptions of warfare, in the Balkans and Africa pre-eminently, touched upon American vital interests. In the absence of a context of Cold War, virtually no local quarrel had the potential to ignite a perilous powder trail to a World War III. It was paradoxical that at the very moment in history when the American superpower enjoyed the utmost discretion over its potential resort to force, it was also maximally disinclined to exercise its unique military prowess. This was because there were hardly any violent disputes about which Americans really cared.

This text has already commented upon the injustice of hindsight. The facts of American political and strategic behaviour in the 1990s are not in any way remarkable. It is easy to argue that the victor, or maybe simply the superpower survivor, of the Cold War ought to have had a vision of a new world order. With knowledge of 9/11 and what followed, it is tempting to apply retrospective wisdom and identify steps that should have been taken in the 1990s but were not. If those steps had been taken, al Qaeda might well have been stifled early in its career. Readers must judge for themselves whether the Bush Snr era (1989–93) and, especially, the eight years of the Bill Clinton administration (1993–2001) should be regarded as periods of lost opportunity.

A political vision of a new world order requires a political visionary, and the United States was not governed by a political visionary in the 1990s. More to the point, events were not sufficiently challenging to produce the man or woman who could rise to the challenge presented by an hour of high peril or high promise. Plainly, the demise of the Soviet Union did not qualify as an event that provided such a challenge. Given the fact that Russia remained politically intact and heavily nuclear armed, it is understandable why prudent politicians in Washington were disinclined to rush to the drawing board – or, increasingly, to the computer – for the purpose of designing a new world order.

President Bush Snr was expert, and interested, in foreign affairs, but he and his senior advisers were mechanics of diplomacy, not designers of grand schemes. His successor, Bill Clinton, was neither knowledgeable about, nor much interested in, issues of national and international security. The motto for his successful 1992 election campaign was 'It's the economy, stupid!' Nothing in the outside world seemed to matter very much to post-Cold War America. The United States intervened for humanitarian reasons in Somalia in 1993 (see the next section for full details), but retreated with almost indecent haste when some of its soldiers were killed. In a replay of the last period of interwar history, the following year American forces – 20,000, to be precise – intervened in Haiti. Their mission was to restore Jean-Bertrand Aristide to power and, hopefully as a consequence, choke off the flow of Haitian America-bound refugees. The subsequent sad history of Haiti demonstrates the practical limits upon America's ability to enforce democratic practices in a non-permissive political context. In the former Yugoslavia the United States took action when it was all but obliged to as a consequence of the failure of other agencies, notably the UN and the European Union. In 1995, US air power was wielded to coerce the Bosnian Serbs; then, again belatedly and reluctantly, in 1999 it was employed against Serbia itself over its mistreatment of the Albanian majority in its province of Kosovo.

So, as can be seen from the above examples, the United States was hardly inactive on the world stage in the 1990s, but its behaviour generally was reactive, episodic and not especially determined in the face of any opposition. It favoured and sponsored NATO's eastward expansion, contrary to Secretary of State James Baker's explicit promise to Mikhail Gorbachev in 1989. But the reasons behind this policy were never explained clearly and coherently. Clinton wanted America to be a force for good in the world. After all, he was the contemporary banner-carrier for American values. He favoured human rights, international cooperation, multilateral rather than unilateral international action, freer trade and the spread of democracy. However, in the 1990s the rhetoric of the national security policy of the world's only superpower was quintessentially vague. Appropriately enough, the strategy of the Clinton administration bore the official, if rather opaque, title 'Engagement and Enlargement' (Clinton, 1994). To be fair, that vague American strategy was entirely appropriate to the way in which people at the time, and not only Americans, regarded the decade. Those years were known as the post-Cold War era, which is a no-name label. In other words, the 1990s were identified and characterized negatively, for what they were not – years of Cold War. Only an American political leader of extraordinary vision and energy might have succeeded in engaging the country in a serious bid to build a new world order. Moreover, such a bid probably would have failed anyway. As it happened, no such person was at the helm of US policy in the 1990s. For that policy to register a radical shift, the political and strategic contexts had to change markedly. They did with 9/11, which brought the post-Cold War era to an explosive conclusion.

'New wars' and 'old wars': a bloody decade

Active great power rivalry may have taken a vacation in the post-Cold War decade and beyond, but strategic history was all too busy. Peace did not reign supreme around the world. In point of fact, the 1990s was among the bloodiest decades of the twentieth century, at least with regard to warfare other than that between great powers. The new Russia was both understandably self-absorbed and materially unable to exercise much influence abroad, even in the near abroad of the 'lost' republics of the former USSR. It struggled against an irregular enemy in Chechnya, a would-be secessionist region. Russia did not accept a Chechnyan declaration of independence in 1991, and Moscow launched two campaigns to subdue the region: in 1994–6, which was a complete failure; and from 1999 to the present, which remains inconclusive. Russia created the Commonwealth of Independent States (CIS) in 1991 in an effort to preserve or restore some of the former authority of the USSR, but as an experiment in imperial re-engineering it proved an abject failure. Comprising twelve former republics of the USSR, the CIS was intended to provide a unified military command and to develop a common market. Headquartered in Minsk, Belarus, it foundered on the clashes of interests among its members (Armenia, Azerbaijan, Belarus, Georgia, Kazakhstan, Kyrgyzstan, Moldova, Russia, Tajikistan, Turkmenistan, Ukraine and Uzbekistan).

For its part, the United States was strongly disinclined to military intervention, especially after its disastrous humanitarian venture in Somalia in 1993. US forces, as part of a multinational effort under UN aegis (the United States initially provided 28,000 of the 37,000 UN troops), were obliged to effect a 'mission creep' in order to attempt to enforce order for security in the Somali capital, Mogadishu. The Americans concluded that progress towards security could not be made until the dominant clan warlord in Mogadishu, Mohamed Farah Aidid, was neutralized. However, on 3–4 October 1993 a US effort to capture Aidid and his senior lieutenants went catastrophically wrong: eighteen American soldiers were ambushed and killed, and some were displayed in gory detail and in an insulting manner, for the video entertainment of a global audience. The new Clinton administration, recognizing that the US military commitment in Somalia was a poisoned chalice bequeathed by the outgoing Bush presidency, hastened to terminate America's participation in that UN exercise. Operation Restore Hope, as the US project in Somalia had been called with inadvertent irony, was swiftly abandoned. The UN operation as a whole similarly was terminated in March 1994. The grisly experience in Somalia reinforced the dominant American view that peacekeeping, post-conflict stabilization and humanitarian intervention, let alone peace enforcement, were not suitable missions for a superpower. To quote a saying of the period, 'a superpower doesn't do windows'. The truth was, and indeed remains to this day, that the United States generally is less competent in combating irregular enemies than it is in dealing with regular ones. Even narrowly, in the military dimension of grand strategy, US behaviour in Somalia in 1993 affronted most of the traditional principles of war.

It is in the nature of multinational military operations, be they prosecuted under UN or NATO auspices, that the time-honoured Principles of War are apt to fall early victim to politics. The protracted strategic incompetence of the UN's multinational mission to Bosnia-Herzegovina, UNPROFOR (the United Nations Protection Force), was to reveal the inherent limitations of collective security. That ambitious concept requires states to contribute to a common security mission, irrespective of whether their own national interests are seriously at risk. But for a peacekeeping mission to succeed there has to be a peace to keep. Alas, there was no such peace in the former Yugoslavia in the 1990s. In 1999, NATO intervened with air power alone to coerce Serbia into halting its oppression of the Albanian majority in Kosovo. Notwithstanding its ultimate success, that lengthy bombardment demonstrated yet again the problems distinctive to multinational military operations.

The United States generally was unwilling to act unilaterally to enforce order in the 1990s. It followed that disorder in its many bloody forms either proceeded according to its own dynamics, unhampered by foreign intervention, or was policed ineffectually by multinational military missions, typically under the UN flag. The excellent book (and subsequent movie) *Black Hawk Down*, by Mark Bowden, reveals the costs of multi-nationalism to military, and hence strategic, effectiveness, in Somalia in 1993 (Bowden, 1999). No less penetrating, if not as dramatic, is Rupert Smith's memoir of command of UNPROFOR in Bosnia in 1995 and again from 1998 until 2001, *The Utility of Force* (Smith, 2005). UN forces generally were bystanders to the complex of wars under way in the former Yugoslavia. They lacked clear political purpose, they had no strategy and their principal concern swiftly became self-protection. The story told by General Smith does not make agreeable reading, and it is particularly discouraging for those who were hopeful that the new activism of the United Nations in peacekeeping – strongly advocated by the ambitious Secretary-General Boutros Boutros-Ghali – marked a major change in the organization's significance as an active contributor to international order and security. That activism was, of course, enabled by the end of the Cold War and the consequent unfreezing of a Security Council no longer paralysed from endorsing possibly controversial military interventions by the veto power of one or more of its five permanent members (the USA, Russia, the UK, France and China).

To complete a trilogy of cases which illustrate the strong tendency of multinational military efforts to deny strategic logic and decline to a lowest common denominator of commitment, one can cite the sad example of General Wesley Clark of the US Army, NATO's SACEUR (Supreme Allied Commander, Europe). In 1999, General Clark had the unenviable task of coordinating and securing the prompt coercion of Slobodan Milosevic, the President of Serbia, who was in the process of ejecting and otherwise oppressing the ethnic Albanians in Kosovo. The NATO air campaign, which had been anticipated to be very brief, in practice was compelled to persist for an embarrassing seventy-eight days. Although Milosevic eventually did concede, it is uncertain whether the principal reason for his defeat was NATO's air campaign, or, eventually, the credible threat of a ground-force invasion by NATO to be launched from Macedonia, or his belated realization that no Russian support was forthcoming. The Americans took from this strategic – but in practice almost anti-strategic – experience of multinational (NATO) campaigning the clear lesson that strategic effectiveness requires a simple, single, national and strictly American chain of command. Allies are beneficial for political comfort, but as active, or more usually semi-active, military partners they are likely to be more trouble than they are worth. The American preference for unilateral action which post-dated Kosovo was not so much a reflection of imperial hubris or cultural preference but pre-eminently a recognition that divided counsels and conflicting interests produce poor strategy. General Clark's tale of woe as the NATO commander for Kosovo, which included problems with the Clinton administration and the US Joint Chiefs of Staff, as well as with the European NATO allies, is well told in his book *Waging Modern War* (Clark, 2002).

What was the character of the strategic history of the post-Cold War decade? As the title of this section suggests, the strategic violence of the 1990s and beyond was tied by some scholars into a master narrative which postulated two kinds of war, the 'old' and the 'new' (Kaldor, 1999; Duyvesteyn and Angstrom, 2005). Broadly understood, the thesis was that old wars were those between states and their Industrial Age regular armed forces. The Gulf War of 1991 to liberate Kuwait was a classic example of an old war. The regular armed forces of both sides were organized and equipped in a manner not greatly dissimilar from their predecessors in World War II. The new wars of the post-Cold War era, in contrast, were expected to be principally internal to states, possibly transnational, and at least one of the belligerents would not carry state authority. It followed that the character of warfare waged by non-state entities most likely would be irregular. The thesis that the world was moving into a period of new wars was keyed logically to the popular belief that the modern state was in decline. Several processes of globalization were held to have reduced dramatically the ability of nominally sovereign states unilaterally to provide security in its many forms (political, socio-cultural, economic, military, individual human) for their citizens.

The new wars thesis found Clausewitz obsolete. Some theorists argued that the Prussian had theorized solely about and for war among states. Supposedly, his remarkable, or paradoxical – depending upon which translation one is using – trinity, the core of his theory of war, comprised the people, the army and its commander, and the government (Van Creveld, 1991: ch. 2; Honig, 1997). This, though, was a serious misreading of *On War*. As was explained in Chapter 2, Clausewitz wrote that war is the product of the inherently unstable relations among violence and passion, chance and genius, and reason or policy (Clausewitz, 1976: 89). It is true that he associated the three elements primarily respectively with the people, the army and the government, but that association was a matter of no essential consequence for his argument. Clausewitz's primary trinity – passion, chance and probability or genius, and reason or policy – is valid for wars of all kinds and for warfare of any character. This apparent digression into strategic theory is of great importance because it bears directly upon a major issue of the 1990s. Did most of the politically motivated violence of that decade comprise a new phenomenon? Did the world witness examples of new wars or of a new paradigm of warfare? Without denying the prevalence of intrastate and irregular warfare in those years and since, the new wars thesis has been criticized by scholars who argue that war is war (Gray, 2005: 139–45). There are no old wars or new wars, at least not with respect to their nature. But assuredly the character of warfare periodically is transformed by socio-cultural, political and technological change. However, it would be a mistake to endorse an unduly neat, linear view of strategic history. At any one time there will be a wide variety of modes of warfare waged by different kinds of belligerent political entities for diverse sets of motives.

To return to the question posed above, what was the character of the strategic history of the post-Cold War decade? Did it reveal a true transformation of war, as the Israeli strategic theorist Martin van Creveld asserted in his brilliant and influential book *The Transformation of War* (Van Creveld, 1991)? (The title revealed the whole of the plot.)

Or was the strategic history of the 1990s actually more complicated than a simple, albeit elemental, shift in the character of war? And even if war in that decade was transformed from its erstwhile Industrial Age, interstate form into a phenomenon marked pre-eminently by Intra-societal struggle and Irregular combat, was that perceived transformation to be permanent or merely transient? The clearest, least ambiguous claim for the transformation of war has been advanced by Rupert Smith, who was cited earlier in connection with the sad story of UN ineffectiveness in Bosnia. He begins *The Utility of Force* with an uncompromising claim, and is worth quoting at some length:

> War no longer exists. Confrontation, conflict and combat undoubtedly exist all round the world – most noticeably, but not only, in Iraq, Afghanistan, the Democratic Republic of the Congo and the Palestinian territories – and states still have armed forces which they use as a symbol of power. None the less, war as cognitively known to most non-combatants, war as battle in a field between men and machinery, war as a massive deciding event in a dispute in international affairs: such war no longer exists . . .
>
> It is now time to recognize that a paradigm shift in war has undoubtedly occurred: from armies with comparable forces doing battle on a field to strategic confrontation between a range of combatants, not all of which are armies, and using different types of weapons, often improvised. The old paradigm was that of interstate industrial war. The new one is the paradigm of war amongst the people.
>
> (Smith, 2005: 1, 3)

General Smith is justified in the emphasis he places upon irregular warfare among non-state entities. But, one should ask, is such warfare new? And is it plausible to claim that the paradigm of 'war amongst the people', as the general himself witnessed in Ireland, Bosnia and elsewhere, has superseded interstate war? These are questions with profound practical implications for the defence policies, strategies and force postures of states.

As has been emphasized, the 1990s were a bloody decade. Warfare was frequent and widespread in the former Yugoslavia, the Caucasian former republics of the USSR, South Asia, the Middle East and, most abominably of all, sub-Saharan Africa (plus Algeria). What follows is a discussion of three of the highest, or perhaps lowest, points in the all-too-ample strategic history of the post-Cold War decade.

The First Gulf War, 1991: America triumphant

With some reluctance, and preceded by a lively domestic political debate, the United States assembled and led a global coalition for the UN-blessed mission of ejecting Iraqi forces from Kuwait. With the Soviet Union in its political death throes, and in the context of clear-cut Iraqi aggression, the only real issue proved to be how extensive a victory the coalition desired. For reasons of anticipated Arab sensibilities, the limited nature of the UN licence (it did not include regime change) and anxiety over the difficulties of urban combat and subsequent control, the United States was content with the simple liberation of Kuwait and the imposition of serious losses upon the Iraqi armed forces. Somewhat after the fashion of British reasoning in 1814–15 and 1919 towards France and Germany, respectively, American policy-makers did not want a totally prostrate Iraq in 1991 because they needed Iraq to balance Ayatollah Khomeini's fundamentalist Iran in the Gulf.

The first Gulf War proved to be the source of much American overconfidence. It appeared to vindicate the efficacy of America's somewhat new way of war, favouring airborne bombardment, and the strategic promise in what was widely judged to be an emerging revolution in military affairs, keyed to the ability to deliver firepower with extraordinary precision. From being 'the gang that could not shoot straight' in the 1970s and 1980s, at least as viewed from abroad, rather abruptly American soldiers assumed the mantle of winners. However, the diplomatic and military triumph of 1991 against Iraq was contextually conditioned. The several contexts of war were all in America's favour in 1991. That unusually benign reality would not be repeated in the remainder of the decade.

The Wars of Yugoslavian Succession

One could argue that the Yugoslavian Federation created in 1919 as thin cover for the reality of a Greater Serbia was always a domestic disaster waiting to happen. The country originally called the Kingdom of the Serbs, Croats and Slovenes, then officially Yugoslavia from 1929, was culturally and geopolitically artificial. It was created by the post-World War I peace settlement, specifically by the settlement with Austria-Hungary, which was dismembered by the Treaty of Saint-Germain of 10 September 1919. Serbia's ambitions were rewarded as some recompense for its heavy sacrifices in the war. Also, the idea of a great southern Slav polity was a notion that had strong appeal to some influential academic advisers to the British government, in particular. The history of Yugoslavia was 'nasty, brutish, and short', to quote Thomas Hobbes. Violence was endemic in the country's dynamic ethnic mix, as well as in the cultures of those ethnicities. The interwar decades were only moderately bloody, but the German conquest in 1941 released passions and created opportunities which no one seemed inclined to resist. From 1941 until 1945 there were half a dozen armies of domestic origin contending for power in German- and Italian-occupied Yugoslavia. The only period of effective central governance the country enjoyed was when the Croat Joseph Broz Tito and his largely Serbian communist forces shot their way to national control in 1944–5. From then until Tito's death on 4 May 1980, the country was stable and largely untroubled by internal disorder.

Tito may have ruled with an iron fist, but he did so skilfully. Following his death, it was only a matter of time before chance events, or unscrupulous politicians with ethnically exclusive ideologies, triggered a process of national disintegration. In 1989 a person who virtually defines the meaning of 'unscrupulous politician', Slobodan Milosevic, succeeded in securing the presidency of Serbia. His political platform was the promise to be the saviour of the Serbian nation; to be its protector from the threats posed by the country's other ethnicities. Since the Croats were blessed with their own version of the Milosevic phenomenon in the person of the decidedly fascistic Franjo Tudjman, the stage was set for serious bloodletting in the 1990s. The principal belligerents were the Serbs in Serbia, ruled by Milosevic; the Croats in traditional Croatia; the Serbs and Croats in Bosnia-Herzegovina; the largely Muslim Bosnians (or Bosniacs); and the Albanian Kosovars, who were numerically dominant in the historically iconic (for Serbians) province of Kosovo. There were many minor players, too: the Slovenes, who wisely bade farewell to the Yugoslavian Federation in 1990; the Macedonians, who bailed out of the country in September 1991; and the Montenegrins, who stayed with the Federation, and then with Serbia, until 2006.

Milosevic's aggressive Serbian nationalism unleashed all of the particularist desires of this multi-ethnic, multinational country. In simple self-defence, but also to seize a historic opportunity to escape rule from Belgrade, Yugoslavia's major ethnic communities declared their independence and proceeded to fight over the body of the prostrate Federation. The whole decade of the 1990s was marred by a series, and sometimes the parallel occurrence, of wars of Yugoslavian succession. The violence began in earnest in 1991 between the new Croatia and Serbia, triggered by Croatian 'ethnic cleansing' of its Serbian minority in the Krajinas region. It was all downhill from there. The main prize in contention was largely Muslim Bosnia-Herzegovina. Atrocities in that large province – especially on the part of Bosnia's indigenous Serbs, led by the formidably murderous General Ratko Mladic – prompted belated and ineffectual UN intervention in the form of UNPROFOR. The latter's problem in Bosnia was that it was condemned by law, politics and capability limitations largely to be a witness to, and hence to acquiesce in, inter-ethnic violence of all kinds. It was utterly helpless; truly a forlorn hope. In the former Yugoslavia generally there was no context of peace, but a fragile peace of sorts for Bosnia was negotiated by the United States in 1995 in a diplomatic process that produced the famous Dayton Peace Accords. That process had been assisted contextually by a distinctly belated but vigorous NATO (i.e., US) bombing campaign against the Bosnian Serbs. The Accords still hold today, more or less.

Violence in Yugoslavia served as historical 'bookends' for the 1990s. The decade that opened in 1991–2 with warfare, atrocity and counter-atrocity between Croats and Serbs in the north of the country closed in 1999 with violence in the south. Serbia initiated a process of violent ethnic cleansing of its Albanian citizens in Kosovo. Eventually NATO, not the UN, intervened with air power to coerce Milosevic into ceasing the oppression. The bombardment was generally unsuccessful tactically in its efforts to destroy the dispersed Serbian Army in Kosovo, but, contrary to historical precedents, when it was applied against strategic targets in Serbia proper, the resultant economic and political pressure eventually secured a result. Indeed, so gleeful were some American devotees of air power as a great persuader that they hung banners upon a US Air Force building which read, 'Douhet Was Correct!' (Giulio Douhet, it will be remembered, was the Italian theorist who had argued in the 1920s for victory through strategic air power (Douhet, 1972).) At long last, ninety-six years into the Air Age, air power appeared to have won a war on its own. However, there is no way of knowing for certain whether Milosevic's climbdown over Kosovo was prompted by domestic discontent fuelled by NATO's strategic air campaign (historically, such a campaign usually hardens rather than weakens the public's will to resist coercion) or by the menace of a NATO invasion of Kosovo. Alas, the Kosovan conflict is not yet concluded. NATO succeeded in halting Serbian oppression, but at the cost of enabling Albanian Kosovar revenge against the Serbs who remained in the province.

The Wars of Yugoslavian Succession were the premier examples of 'new wars' in the post-Cold War decade. Certainly, they were the ones which attracted the most attention in Europe. Thus far, this chapter has told the story in a rather bloodless way, but it is necessary here to mention the atrocities committed by all sides, though especially the Serbs, in the former Yugoslavia, the like of which had not been seen in Europe since 1945. Every possible horror was visited upon the innocent: mass murder, systematic rape as policy, and torture were all commonplace. And the international community, that fictional body, did nothing effective to prevent or arrest it, even though it was present at the scene of the crimes in the form of UNPROFOR. The exemplar of the beastliness was the cold-blooded massacre by Bosnian Serbs of 7,000 male civilian Bosniacs in Srebrenica in 1995, while a battalion of Dutch UN troops stood by helplessly. The Dutch soldiers' rules of engagement – like those of the rest of the UN mission – forbade them from fighting, except in self-defence.

African anarchy

If the post-Cold War Balkans were disorderly and bloody, post-Cold War Africa was much worse. Whereas the conflicts in the former Yugoslavia produced fatality lists in the tens of thousands, at least two of the conflicts in Africa yielded fatalities in the millions. Journalist Robert D. Kaplan best captured the nature of the problem in the continent with an article first published in February 1994 and prophetically titled 'The Coming Anarchy' (reprinted in Kaplan, 2000: 3–57). It is important not to exaggerate the anarchy in 1990s Africa. Of course there were islands of stability and some major examples of multi-ethnic toleration, even reconciliation and progress. The political transformation of South Africa under the inspired leadership of Nelson Mandela was a historic event. Unfortunately, though, that beacon of hope was not matched widely elsewhere on the continent. This strategic history will not dwell on Africa's galloping health crisis, but it must take note of the fact that many African societies have been devastated, literally decimated or worse, by the spread of HIV/AIDS. Also, much of the continent, especially in the north-east, has been assaulted and further impoverished by the effects of protracted and repeated droughts. But the principal focus here must be upon the violence that people have visited upon each other.

In the 1990s and subsequently, there was 'warfare', to stretch the term somewhat, almost everywhere in Africa. By and large, that warfare was internal and irregular in character, but it also occurred between states, frequently across Africa's artificial and arbitrary international frontiers. This narrative will take special note of just three geographical seats of conflict in the continent. The world noticed the first, in Rwanda in 1994, albeit belatedly and to no useful consequence. The second, in the Democratic Republic of Congo from 1998 to the present day, has rumbled on, overshadowed for the West by 9/11 and the subsequent 'global war on terror'. The third area of conflict is West Africa as a whole, though especially Liberia and Sierra Leone. These countries, speaking loosely, in common with such other troubled states as the Congo, Somalia, Angola, Sudan, Ethiopia, the Ivory Coast, Guinea-Bissau and Mozambique, suffer from endemic social and political disorder. Some of this disorder does not fit comfortably into a Clausewitzian frame of analysis. While Clausewitz insisted that war 'is an act of policy' (Clausewitz, 1976: 87), in Africa, and sometimes in the former Yugoslavia, the violence often has been casual, even spontaneous and recreational, rather than politically motivated. Some of the massacres that Africa has registered since 1990 have appeared more like lethal, contagious hooliganism than calculated strategic behaviour.

In 1993 the Tutsis staged a coup in Burundi and slaughtered 100,000 of their rival Hutus. The following year the Hutus achieved a monster of a revenge when they too staged a coup, this time in neighbouring Rwanda, an event they celebrated in the traditional manner by attempting genocide against the Tutsis. Estimates vary wildly, but it is claimed confidently by those who have studied the grisly matter that between 600,000 and 1,000,000 Tutsis were killed. The higher figure is probably closer to the truth. When one bears in mind the geopolitics of Central Africa, it becomes obvious that severe strife in the tiny statelets of Burundi and Rwanda is bound to have ripple effects in neighbouring countries (Uganda, Tanzania and Sudan). And it must have an influence in the north-east of the Democratic Republic of Congo (DRC), a polity that for several decades, and increasingly, has been virtually synonymous with the idea of an 'ungoverned space', as the contemporary official American euphemism has it.

For thirty-two years, Mobutu Sese Seko ruled the DRC as a personal kleptocracy. He was deposed at last in 1998 by Laurent Kabila, but the new leader committed the serious error of turning on his erstwhile allies, seeking to disarm them. This fatal and hopeless mission triggered warfare between pro- and anti-Kabila parties among neighbouring states (Burundi, Rwanda and Uganda were 'anti', while Zimbabwe, Angola, Chad and Namibia were 'pro'), and between every group that saw advantage in organized violence in the vast DRC itself. Everyone accepts the estimate that at least 4 million people have died since 1998 for war-related reasons. Where they disagree is on just how great is the 'at least'. Kabila was assassinated in 2001, but that did not magically produce peace in the DRC. Warfare there continues.

In the 1990s, Sierra Leone and Liberia both descended into local rule by heavily armed and well-drugged gangs. These gangs, sometimes on the scale of small armies, were organized and led by ambitious petty warlords of the type that most societies throw up when the opportunities provided by anarchy beckon. Thanks to the reporting of people like Robert Kaplan, the world at large noticed that a significant segment of West Africa was in a state of chaos. Casual, as well as calculated, atrocities were commonplace, and gang leaders played the game of revolving presidents. However, given the contemporary warfare in the Balkans, in Ireland (for the British) and, as always, in the Middle East, especially between Arabs and Israelis, as well as in the Gulf between what remained of the grand coalition of 1990–1 and Iraq, West Africa was not exactly a matter of high international priority.

Conclusion

Discussion of Russia's two disastrous wars with its would-be breakaway region of Chechnya has been largely omitted from this narrative, as has comment on the continuing violent disorder in Somalia and Sudan. In fact, so many and so varied have been the 'wars', or at least the warfare, since the end of the Cold War that merely to list them would place a heavy burden upon this chapter. To illustrate the point that peace was a rare condition in many parts of the world in the 1990s, it is helpful to offer a listing that is by no means comprehensive of cases of warfare for just two years in the decade. The years have been selected more or less at random from an appalling accounting provided by Colin McInnes (2002: 162). The general story is the same, regardless of the years chosen.

In 1995 there was intrastate conflict in Croatia, Russia (Chechnya), Iran, Iraq, Israel, Turkey, Afghanistan, Bangladesh, Cambodia, India, Indonesia, Myanmar, the Philippines, Sri Lanka, Algeria, Angola, Liberia, Sierra Leone, Somalia, Sudan, Colombia, Guatemala and Peru. In addition, there was warfare between Bosnia-Herzegovina (and Croatia) and the Bosnian Serbs. Moving on to 1999, there was interstate conflict between Ethiopia and Eritrea, and between NATO and Yugoslavia. The intrastate conflict column was well populated, as usual. In that category, one takes note of warfare, at least of politically motivated violence, in Guinea-Bissau, Iran, Iraq, Bangladesh, Cambodia, Indonesia, Myanmar, Uganda, Sri Lanka, Algeria, Sierra Leone, Sudan, Angola, Colombia and Yugoslavia (Kosovo). Also, the Democratic Republic of Congo was in a condition of bloody anarchy.

For the first time in this book, the discussion has strayed seriously from what one might call the master narrative of contemporary strategic history. That is to say, these pages have not cited and analysed the decisions and behaviour of the world's major strategic players. The reason is not in order to help correct an imbalance between the attention paid to the great and the much less great. Rather, the intention is to suggest that the master strategic narrative that has carried this history along from the end of the eighteenth century to the demise of the USSR was resting in the 1990s. Political, criminal and even recreational violence were widespread in the post-Cold War decade, but that violence generally lacked strategic or political meaning beyond the local. However, there was an exception to that condition to which this book now must turn: religiously motivated irregular warfare, especially in the form of catastrophe terrorism.

Key points

1. The 1990s were an interwar decade.
2. Uniquely in modern history, the world of the 1990s was unipolar: the United States was the sole superpower.
3. Also uniquely in modern history, after the great virtual war that was the Cold War, no attempt was made to institutionalize a new vision of world order.
4. Both scholars and practitioners speculated that an era of 'new wars' had dawned, wars that were largely intrastate and irregular in character.
5. Conflict and actual warfare were widespread and exceptionally bloody, especially in Africa.
6. In the absence of an obvious dominant threat to national security, US policy and strategy lacked focus and urgency.

Questions

1. **Were the 1990s a time of lost opportunity to construct a new world order?**
2. **What problems did the demise of the Soviet Union set for American policy and strategy?**
3. **Did the end of the Cold War contribute to a proliferation of wars in Europe, Asia and Africa?**

4.   **Did the 1990s witness 'the transformation of war', as was argued by Martin van Creveld?**

Further reading

M. Bowden *Black Hawk Down* (London: Bantam Press, 1999).

W. K. Clark *Waging Modern War: Bosnia, Kosovo, and the Future of Conflict* (New York: Public Affairs, 2002).

M. R. Gordon and B. E. Trainor *The Generals' War: The Inside Story of the Conflict in the Gulf* (Boston: Little, Brown, 1995).

D. Halberstam *War in a Time of Peace: Bush, Clinton and the Generals* (London: Bloomsbury, 2003).

M. Kaldor *New and Old Wars: Organized Violence in a Global Era* (Cambridge: Polity Press, 1999).

R. D. Kaplan *The Coming Anarchy: Shattering the Dreams of the Post Cold War* (New York: Random House, 2000).

H. Münkler *The New Wars* (Cambridge: Polity Press, 2005).

R. Smith *The Utility of Force: The Art of War in the Modern World* (London: Allen Lane, 2005).

M. van Creveld *The Transformation of War* (New York: Free Press, 1991).

17 9/11 and the age of terror

Reader's guide: The impact of 9/11 on strategic history. The 'war on terror' as World War III? Warfare in the Information Age.

Introduction: the return of a master narrative

What was missing from the 1990s was the serious engagement of a great power, especially the American superpower, with a major enemy. So superior was the United States to all other states on the standard indices of strategic power that the potential appearance of a 'peer competitor' was not anticipated officially for fifteen to twenty-five years. But on 11 September 2001 a worthy foe made its existence and intentions crystal clear, even though it bore no relation to standard notions of a 'peer competitor'. With al Qaeda in the field as a self-declared enemy of the United States – in fact, an enemy of all 'Zionists and Crusaders', as Osama bin Laden's fatwas labelled al Qaeda's enemies – strategic history was back up and running with a master narrative. Violent Islamic fundamentalism would define the political and strategic contexts of the early twenty-first century. At least it would do so for the United States, for South Asia and for Europe, though to a lesser degree in the last case. Just how long this new 'age of terror' would last was a distinctly open question. It related intimately to the issue of whether future warfare would primarily be irregular. In common with death and taxes, terrorism will always be with us, just as it always has been. The strategic issue is how important will be its residual presence?

9/11: World War III?

After a decade wandering in the strategic wilderness, bereft of a dominant threat of sufficient potency to concentrate American minds, 9/11 returned the US superpower to the mainstream of strategic history, and did so explosively, one might add. America proclaimed that it was 'a nation at war', and those words from 2005 were amended a year later in the *Quadrennial Defense Review Report*: 'The United States is a nation engaged in what will be a long war' (Rumsfeld, 2006: v). At last, the Soviet threat, which had provided coherence to US policy and strategy, as well as to much of world politics for forty-five years, had been replaced. Terrorism, particularly when religiously motivated and devoted to inflicting catastrophic levels of casualties and damage, became the defining threat of the era, which is to say of the present day and the anticipated future.

Most of the world's armed forces are not well designed, doctrinally prepared, trained and equipped to wage war against elusive handfuls of religious fanatics. Rather, they are raised and maintained to fight regular enemies who would be approximate facsimiles of themselves. If states prepare primarily for warfare with other states, do they thereby condemn themselves to impotence in combat against irregular foes? Dare states, especially the sole superpower, transform their armed forces in a search for excellence against irregular enemies when there might still be regular interstate warfare to conduct in their future?

Notwithstanding their elusiveness, even terrorists with no fixed abode must have a territorial dimension to their existence and preparations. They require safe havens for training, for rest and recovery, and for planning. Regular armed forces can threaten those sanctuaries. A popular American metaphor in the wake of 9/11 was that 'we need to drain the swamps' where terrorists lurk. Immediately after 9/11, it appeared as if the United States could organize a global coalition against Islamic terrorism. Americans talked about a 'war on terror', but that enterprise was as impractical as it was conceptually impossible. The 'war' that America was committed to fight was against al Qaeda, its franchised branches, its associates and its imitators. There is a rough approximation to a 'terrorist international', and that shadowy association (one cannot call it an organization) has intimate connections with international, even global, criminal syndicates. But the US focus was, and remains, emphatically upon those who perpetrated 9/11.

Afghanistan was all but self-selected to be the first swamp in need of drainage in the new master narrative of strategic history. That unfortunate country, which has always contained ungoverned space to a greater or lesser extent, has had a history of almost constant warfare. When the USSR departed, defeated, in 1988, the Soviet-nominated President, Mohammed Najibullah, survived only until 1992. The country essentially dissolved into a complex civil war, a contest eventually won in large measure by the Islamic fundamentalist Taliban movement in 1996. (One must say 'in large measure', because the Taliban never had control of the north of the country.) Since the Taliban had provided sanctuary for al Qaeda, and had permitted it to run training camps for aspiring terrorists and insurgents, probably on the scale of 30,000–50,000 in total, Afghanistan was uncontroversial as the first target in the 'war on terror'. This was accomplished with some dexterity in October–December 2001. US strategic theorists and commentators proclaimed and celebrated an allegedly 'new American way of war', which, appropriately enough, they called 'the Afghan model' (Boot, 2003).

The Taliban was defeated decisively, but, as later history was to show, not by any means conclusively. The agents of its demise were, on the one hand, a combination of US air power directed for precision bombardment by handfuls of special forces soldiers on the ground engaged in target-spotting; and, on the other, old-fashioned ground combat conducted by the Taliban's local enemies, and hence allies of the United States, the tribal warlords of the 'Northern Alliance'. Unfortunately, although regime change was effected with relative ease, albeit at the cost of needing to reward its tribal allies of convenience, the United States was able to do serious damage to al Qaeda only in Afghanistan. Many of its leaders escaped over the mountains and into the all but independent frontier tribal area of Pakistan. Notably, the most charismatic of al Qaeda's leaders, Osama bin Laden, escaped to remain a thorn in America's flesh. Also, despite the success of the 2001 campaign to impose regime change in Kabul and deprive al Qaeda of its country-wide safe haven, the Taliban proved to be akin to a weed that is resistant to forceful efforts at eradication. At present it is alive and well, and is prospering in its areas of traditional strength in the south and east of the country.

George W. Bush's administration had Iraq on its mind even while Afghanistan was the swamp of the moment. But to invade Iraq and compel regime change would prove as controversial as the action in Afghanistan had been met with general international approval, nominally at least. (One must offer the qualification because many states were troubled by the new assertiveness, even what they perceived as aggressiveness, in American policy long before the invasion of Iraq.) Although the United States had been enjoying its protracted unipolar moment since the demise of the Soviet Union, it had not really behaved as one might expect a hegemonic or imperial power to act. Until 9/11, that is. Following that dire event, the United States made haste to make up for lost time in asserting itself as the active global leader in a war, almost a crusade, to extirpate violent Islamic extremism.

The events of 9/11 acted as a wake-up call to the United States, as well as to some of its friends and allies in Asia and Europe. If al Qaeda's intention was to stir America into responsive action that could prove self-defeating, it could hardly have been more successful. Assuming that Osama bin Laden's real enemies are in the realm of Islam and not in the West, it was notable that he and his confederates chose to attack targets in the media capital of the world. Moreover, the attacks were visually so dramatic that they give the idea of 'propaganda of the deed' a whole new meaning. Most particularly, though, on 9/11 al Qaeda took action that its leaders probably calculated would place them in a win–win situation. If the US response was feeble, as it had been throughout the 1990s, then that would encourage potential jihadists, and discourage America's allies and other moderate and even secular governments in the land of Islam. But if America reacted strongly and violently, and took direct military action, the intrusion should arouse the Islamic world and motivate many new recruits for al Qaeda in the holy cause of the defence of their religion and its holy territory.

The precise reasoning behind 9/11 is unknown, but its consequences are an open book. This illustrates a general truth of strategic history. Causes are often endlessly debatable, whereas outcomes are far more certain. The principal immediate effect of 9/11 was to prompt a radical shift in US national security policy and strategy. From being disinclined to intervene abroad, even for noble humanitarian reasons or to advance democracy and other American values, the United States quite suddenly assumed a vigorously proactive stance. It declared war on terror, terrorists and those who gave them comfort and support. The Bush administration reasoned that American quiescence in the 1990s, despite the ample evidence of a growing Islamic terrorist threat, had contributed decisively to the maturing of al Qaeda and hence to 9/11.

It was true that al Qaeda did not reveal itself out of the mountains and desert wastes in 2001 as a complete surprise. With the benefit of hindsight, ever the best friend of the strategic historian, the incident trail leading to the Twin Towers and the Pentagon is all too apparent. Following its founding in Afghanistan in 1988, al Qaeda, basking in the glory of victory over the hated Russian infidel, was responsible for a string of atrocities.

It was behind the failed attempt to blow up one of the towers of the World Trade Center on 23 February 1993 (had this succeeded, it would have killed approximately 30,000 people, not the 3,000 of 9/11). Next, it could have claimed credit for the successful assault on American soldiers in Khobar Towers in Saudi Arabia in 1996, but it did not do so. (At that time, it did not wish to attract the wrath of the Saudi government.) Then, in 1998, it organized the lethal bombings of the US embassies in Kenya and Tanzania. Finally, it was responsible for the deadly seaborne bomb attack on the USS *Cole* in the port of Aden in Yemen in 2000. Only with hindsight, however, did the scale and true quality of the menace of al Qaeda become fully apparent. On 9/11 it was finally recognized as the principal threat of the era.

The American response, and the international reaction to that response, has dominated world politics since 2001. Whatever the precise combination of American motives, American behaviour has been undeniably hegemonic in character and in declared intent. The battle space, both as a focus of debate and literally for combat, shifted rapidly from Afghanistan in 2001–2, to Iraq. Saddam Hussein's Ba'athist regime had long been a supporter of international terrorism, although it had little if any known connection with al Qaeda. For a decade, however, it had flouted UN rulings, and its own legal under-takings, with respect to the development and deployment of weapons of mass destruction (WMD). It had also murdered its own people, and viciously oppressed Iraq's Shi'ite majority and Kurdish minority. The United States, with British and Australian backing, plus a few others, determined to flex its hegemonic muscles and demonstrate that the global sheriff was on the job, regardless of whether the world as a whole approved. In the face of considerable international disapproval, and in the absence of a UN Security Council resolution explicitly authorizing the use of force, the United States and Britain invaded Iraq on 20 March 2003.

The American superpower was acting precisely as a responsible hegemon should act, or so one could argue. It was taking decisive action to remove a dangerous regime, one that most people believed was in possession of WMD, and which had a record of attacking its neighbours (Iran in 1980 and Kuwait in 1990). The invasion was consistent with a major policy shift in Washington: the superpower was now committed to reaching far abroad to touch with deadly force threats to Americans, and others, before those threats had time to be realized. In other words, the United States was assuming a willingness to take pre-emptive, or even preventive, military action. This entails shooting first, on suspicion, which will always be controversial. It is especially controversial in the eyes of those who believe that any discretionary use of force must be authorized explicitly by the UN Security Council. By its actions in 2003, the United States was saying that it would do what it believed it must for the security of Americans, and also on behalf of world order, and while it preferred to take action with the blessing of the international community, if need be it would act in its absence. In case the full scope of the shift in American policy and strategy had not been registered with sufficient clarity, the most authoritative policy document of the Bush administration, *The National Security Strategy of the United States of America* (September 2002), could hardly have been more explicit.

> We will disrupt and destroy terrorist organizations by . . . defending the United States, the American people, and our interests at home and abroad by identifying and

destroying the threat before it reaches our borders. While the United States will constantly strive to enlist the support of the international community, we will not hesitate to act alone, if necessary, to exercise our right of self-defense by acting pre-emptively against such terrorists, to prevent them from doing harm against our people and our country.

(Bush, 2002: 6)

The principle was unremarkable. However, it is plausible to speculate that much of the international hostility to the US and British invasion of Iraq had more to do with unease at America's near-unilateral exercise of force than with disagreement over the case at issue. The events of 9/11 had the consequence of awakening the world at large to two major, equally unwelcome, facts. First, it was obliged to recognize the reality of an extraordinary, relatively novel and apparently global terrorist menace driven pre-eminently by religious motivation. Second, the existence of a hegemonic superpower could no longer be disputed. And that hegemon was ready, willing and arguably able to take forceful action globally at its own discretion in defence of its own definition of the requirements of international security. Welcome to a new world order.

The United States government was warned, by its own Secretary of State, Colin Powell, no less, that if one invades a country, liberates its people and deposes the sitting regime, in effect, however briefly, one owns that country and must assume responsibility for its future. The full implications of this eternal truth were not sufficiently appreciated by the invaders in 2003. Suffice it to say that the task of the would-be liberator is rarely easy, particularly if understanding of local culture and politics is lacking. At the time of writing, the strategic story of the US-led venture in Iraq is not over. Even the victory in Afghanistan in 2001 appears less complete today, as much of the south of the country has reverted to Taliban control and local warlords pursue their traditional criminal activities.

By the middle of the first decade of the twenty-first century, several questions pertaining to the structure and functioning of world politics beg for the strategic historian's attention. The perilous activity of prediction is postponed until Chapter 20 of this text, but for now it is important to identify some of the greater uncertainties, the resolution of which must shape the decades ahead.

Will the United States tire of an interventionist policy and strategy? 'No more Iraqs' could well become a popular phrase, directly reminiscent of the former bumper sticker demand: 'No more Vietnams'. If the United States should decline to behave as a hegemon, which is to say as a leader as well as a servant of that elusive entity, the international community, who, if anyone, will do the controversial heavy lifting for world order? Strategic history is made by societies and cultures, not, certainly not only, by strategic logic.

Next, have the years since the collapse of the Soviet Union seen the definitive end of active great power rivalry, with its potential for interstate warfare on a major scale? Or has such rivalry simply been temporarily in abeyance? Is world politics just awaiting the arrival of a state, or states in coalition, ready and willing to challenge American primacy? The answer to this question bears strongly on judgements about a prudent defence posture for the twenty-first century. If all one's enemies in the future are going to be non-state and irregular in character, or relatively minor local powers at most, that is one thing.

But if the United States, and possibly NATO, should anticipate conflict, including the possibility of warfare, with a superpower China and its allies (which might include Russia), that is quite another.

Finally, did 9/11 herald World War III, as Lawrence Freedman (2001) has speculated? The United States, though not its European allies, appears to have decided that it did. Is the master narrative of the strategic history of this century going to be the global struggle against Islamic terrorism and insurgency, a struggle which is mainly about the future of the Islamic world? Or is that conflict likely to be sidelined either by its own lack of staying power or by its replacement for prime international attention by a return of great power political rivalry, probably in the form of a new bipolarity on a Sino-American axis of dangerous antagonism? One cannot know, but the question, and its possible answers, could hardly be more important for future international security.

If the topics just outlined were insufficiently troubling, readers might consider the possible and probable consequences of rapid climate change for civility among states and societies. As the material resources most vital for the sustenance of life itself come under growing pressure from environmental change, a whole new master narrative of violent strategic history may well be born, alas.

Warfare: from the Industrial Age to the Information Age

For a book on strategic history, this chapter and the previous one have said very little directly about the evolution of, or revolution in, warfare since the end of the Cold War. This apparent dereliction of duty reflects a suspicion that the often intense, and certainly protracted, debate about a revolution in military affairs was nowhere near as significant as many people assumed. This topic, which so obsessed American defence analysts and theorists in the 1990s, generally was treated somewhat autistically. It is difficult to have a strategy in the absence of an enemy, and it is no less difficult to carry through an RMA in the absence of strategic policy guidance. That difficulty disappears, of course, if it is simply assumed that one sort of military prowess will fit all strategic needs. In Iraq the United States has learnt, yet again, that regular and irregular warfare are fundamentally different, and that one kind of military competence most definitely does not suit all cases.

When one reviews the military dimension to the strategic history of the post-Cold War years, the first thing one ought to notice is the acute shortage of useful, let alone conclusive, evidence. How has the art and science of warfare advanced since the Berlin Wall came down in 1989? Certainly, US-led forces won swift and, for Americans and their allies, all but bloodless victories over Iraq in 1991 and 2003, Yugoslavia in 1999 and Taliban Afghanistan in 2001. But in each of those cases the enemy as a regular military opponent was so feeble that the United States would have had to try very hard in order to be frustrated, let alone to lose. (In fact, in 1999 over Kosovo, the Serbians did somewhat embarrass NATO by managing to conceal most of their military equipment so as to evade the air campaign.) Advances in the grammar of war achieved by the United States since the end of the Cold War have appeared impressive, but it was so easy to appear impressive when fighting Saddam Hussein's Iraq that nothing of much consequence can be learnt from it. One's military prowess is flattered when the enemy is grossly incompetent, or grossly overmatched in material and method, or both. It is well worth noting that although American and American-led forces were militarily victorious in each of the four campaigns just cited, having won the battles the United States discovered that warfare and criminal violence continued, albeit in different forms. Peace worthy of the name, which is to say political peace, did not break out in any of the four cases.

A large body of defence theorists argue that the master strategic narrative of the post-Cold War period, to the present day and well beyond, is a process of transition from Industrial Age warfare to a new chapter of warfare shaped and driven by the technologies of the Information Age (Benbow, 2004; Gray, 2006c; Hammes, 2004; Keaney and Cohen, 1995; Owens, 2000). For the better part of the 1990s, American analysts were debating the proposition that an RMA was under way. Although early evidence of its coming had been visible late in Vietnam with the introduction of laser- and radar-guided bombs, unmistakable signals of major change were provided by the air campaign (17 January–24 February) that preceded the 100-hour ground war against Iraq in 1991. Coalition 'briefers', led theatrically by the Allied Commander, the charismatic General Norman Schwarzkopf, made effective propaganda use of video footage of the discrete destruction wrought by smart precision-guided munitions (PGMs). It so happens that only 10 per cent of the aerial munitions employed in 1991 were precision guided, but the general impression given was that something momentous had changed in the conduct of warfare. In 2003, by contrast, precision guidance assisted as much as 70 per cent of the aerial firepower directed against Iraqi forces and other targets. There is no doubt that a military-technical revolution (MTR), at least, was well in train, if not necessarily a process worthy of being called an RMA.

Since the early 1990s the US armed forces in particular have been able to exploit the tools granted them by the Information Age to change the way that they fight. The great enabler of this MTR/RMA has been the computer, of course. The United States set its planning sights on three necessary achievements: information dominance, or dominant battle-space knowledge; the internetting of forces so as to exploit that information dominance; and precision strike. To date, the US armed forces would appear to have succeeded impressively in making major progress towards their tactical goals, but, to repeat the vital caveat, they have yet to fight a sophisticated regular enemy. As a result, one cannot be sure that America's information-led forces do not suffer from some fatal weaknesses. One of the lessons of strategic history is that RMAs are eventually always emulated, offset or effectively evaded. There is no final move. In the current case of America's exploitation of advanced electronics, the Russian military professes a contingent intention to achieve its neutralization by the delivery of low-yield nuclear weapons. The electromagnetic pulse (emp) generated by a nuclear explosion is deadly to unshielded electronic equipment. This would be a brute force approach, crude and dangerous, but probably highly effective.

Arguably, over the past fifteen years the United States has effected an RMA with reference to the waging of regular warfare. The US superiority in C^4ISTAR (Command, Control, Communications, Computing, Intelligence, Surveillance, Targeting And Reconnaissance) is so marked, at least at present, that no enemy could engage America in regular warfare with any prospect of success. The United States is unquestionably king of the regular battle space in most geographical environments. Through precision firepower delivered from altitude by aircraft, cruise missiles or unmanned aerial vehicles

(UAVs), the United States currently owns regular warfare. But this happy condition for Washington has its limitations. First, American domination of regular battle in the Information Age obliges prudent enemies to decline to fight on America's terms. In other words, the US armed forces are developing an excellence in aggressive decisive manoeu vre assisted by precision fire from the overhead flank that they are not likely to be able to exploit fully. As Clausewitz insisted, and as we must keep reminding ourselves, 'War is nothing but a duel on a larger scale' (Clausewitz, 1976: 75). Second, in the wars that America is waging currently in Iraq and Afghanistan, the technical tools provided by the Information Age are of only limited value. Decisive manoeuvre is generally impractical against an irregular enemy who declines to stand and fight. Furthermore, the ability to deliver firepower with great precision is useful only if one has equally precise political intelligence as to the identity of the enemy, an enemy who, as often as not, is hiding 'amongst the people' (R. Smith, 2005: Part 3).

This commentary on the state of the art in regular warfare, which is to say the American way of warfare as it has evolved since the end of the Cold War, is not intended to be wholly critical. The United States seems to have succeeded in achieving a new level of excellence in regular warfare – although, as noted above, it is hard to be certain in the absence of combat experience against a competent enemy. However, the largely technological RMA that the US forces have been pursuing, a process more recently described as one of transformation rather than revolution, does prompt a basic sceptical question. Is the *right* transformation being sought?

If one grants the utility of the sole superpower's enhanced prowess in regular warfare, next one must ask whether that expensive project has been pursued with inadequate attention paid to the challenges posed by irregular enemies. From the evidence of Iraq and Afghanistan in the 2000s, one might argue that the United States – the hegemon (and guardian), by default, of the contemporary world order – has a shortfall in grand-strategic competence in combating irregular foes. The US Army, in particular, is more in need of a transformation that privileges counter-insurgency and counter-terrorist skills than one which enables it to rise to yet greater heights of proficiency in regular warfare.

The last word in this historical discussion must pertain to the unprecedented significance of the now global media, particularly the electronic visual media. The technologies of the Information Age probably are having more influence upon warfare through their enabling of almost real-time media monitoring than by their enhancement of fighting power. For soldiers in warfare of any kind, regular or irregular, today there is no escape from media scrutiny. The details of a lethal incident in Basra can be shown world-wide, thanks to satellite video links, before they are known to, let alone assessed by, local military commanders. This is something new in strategic history. Some scholars believe that over recent decades this development has led to a transformation in public attitudes towards both the military and war itself, a shift towards a less permissive view of the use of force (Kurth, 2003).

Conclusion

War has a dominant political context, but it also has a socio-cultural context which will constrain, or sometimes energize, the political context. States can be slow to recognize and act upon the reality of the pervasively political character of warfare. They may tend to regard war and politics as separate realms. Similarly, the significance of war's socio-cultural context frequently has not been sufficiently appreciated. If this is now an 'age of terror', or at least an age wherein terrorists and insurgents pose the most immediate dangers to world order, there is no alternative to treating the socio-cultural context of warfare with the utmost care. This is because the struggle in irregular warfare is always for the allegiance, or acquiescence, of people. Since irregular warfare is about the will of people, the social and cultural dimensions of strategy have to take pole position among the needed strategic competencies.

Thus far, this book has discussed terrorism and irregular warfare principally in historical context. It is necessary now to turn from the strategic historical narrative to a more analytical examination. Chapter 18 explores the nature, purpose and changing character of irregular warfare, including terrorism.

Key points

1. The events of 9/11 provided the dominant threat to international security that US policy and strategy had been missing since 1989.
2. Regular armed forces are not usually proficient in combating highly irregular enemies.
3. Al Qaeda caught the world by surprise on 9/11, despite its history of terrorist acts.
4. The events of 9/11 galvanized the United States into behaving vigorously and proactively as the hegemonic power.
5. The information-led RMA of the 1990s and beyond was not especially helpful in waging the 'war on terror'.
6. The global electronic media are now a major factor in the waging of warfare.

Questions

1. **What were the consequences of 9/11 for world politics?**
2. **How effective has the US-led 'war on terror' been so far?**
3. **Why is the American policy of forcible pre-emption and prevention so contro-versial?**
4. **What military benefits are claimed to flow from the information-led RMA? Are those claims justified?**

Further reading

A. J. Bacevich *American Empire: The Realities and Consequences of US Diplomacy* (Cambridge, MA: Harvard University Press, 2002).
—— *The New American Militarism: How Americans are Seduced by War* (New York: Oxford University Press, 2005).
T. Benbow *The Magic Bullet? Understanding the Revolution in Military Affairs* (London: Brassey's, 2004).

K. Booth and T. Dunne (eds) *Worlds in Collision: Terror and the Future of Global Order* (Basingstoke: Palgrave Macmillan, 2002).

L. Freedman 'The Third World War?', *Survival*, 43: 61–88 (2001).

—— *The Transformation of Strategic Affairs*, Adelphi Paper 379 (Abingdon: Routledge for the International Institute for Strategic Studies, 2006).

M. Gordon and B. Trainor *Cobra II: The Inside Story of the Invasion and Occupation of Iraq* (London: Atlantic Books, 2006).

C. S. Gray *Another Bloody Century: Future Warfare* (London: Weidenfeld and Nicolson, 2005).

—— *Irregular Enemies and the Essence of Strategy: Can the American Way of War Adapt?* (Carlisle, PA: Strategic Studies Institute, US Army War College, 2006).

R. Gunaratna *Inside al Qaeda: Global Network of Terror* (New York: Columbia University Press, 2002).

C. McInnes *Spectator-Sport War: The West and Contemporary Conflict* (Boulder, CO: Lynne Rienner Publishers, 2002).

W. Murray and R. H. Scales, Jr *The Iraq War: A Military History* (Cambridge, MA: Harvard University Press, 2003).

18 Irregular warfare

Guerrillas, insurgents and terrorists

Reader's guide: Regular and irregular warfare. Guerrilla warfare, insurgency and terrorism. The nature and varied character of irregular warfare. Terrorism and counter-terrorism. Al Qaeda and the 'New Terrorism'.

Introduction: two kinds of warfare

It is both useful and historically justifiable to divide the experience of warfare into two broad categories: regular and irregular. The former is warfare between the regular, armed forces of states, while the latter is warfare between those forces and the irregular armed forces of non-state political entities. Irregular warfare is asymmetrical: the opponents are certain to be very different. Also, the warfare may well be transcultural. It follows that such belligerency must pose unusual, and unusually severe, challenges to the regular side. An army justly proud of its military effectiveness in regular warfare is apt to discover that irregular combat, with the absence of large-scale open combat, prices its strength at a heavy discount. To be outstanding at regular warfare does not mean that one will even be competent, let alone good, at warfare of an irregular kind. To employ a vital Clausewitzian concept, the 'grammar' of irregular warfare is radically different from that of regular warfare (Clausewitz, 1976: 605).

Thus far in this book, only in Chapter 17 did irregular warfare assume centre-stage. The reason for the apparent neglect of such warfare through most of these pages is that it has not played a sufficiently significant role in the master narrative of strategic history to warrant being accommodated in an already substantial text. To explain: over the past two centuries, irregular warfare has been widespread, frequent and typically extremely bloody; however, until recent years such warfare, in its several variants, has never been the dominant category of politically organized violence in the mainstream of strategic history. Only in the twenty-first century, following 9/11, has the principal plot line of world strategic history privileged irregular warfare. Never before in those 200 years have the major powers elevated irregular hostilities to the status of the main strategic activity of the era. This condition may not long endure. There could be a return to dominant significance of the plausible threat of regular warfare between states, including major powers. But, for the present at least, irregular warfare is the cutting edge of strategic history.

The purpose of this chapter is not historical explanation. Contemporary terrorism was discussed in Chapter 17. Rather, the intention here is to explore the character of irregular warfare, to identify and distinguish among its several forms, and to analyse its strategic advantages and disadvantages. Nearly every chapter up to now has described and discussed regular warfare. Here, a modest corrective is provided to that deliberate imbalance.

Guerrilla warfare, insurgency and terrorism

Historically, it is easily justifiable to define irregular warfare essentially politically. But, more strictly viewed, irregular warfare simply encompasses military organization, tactics and styles in combat. It need imply nothing about the political character and purposes of the belligerents. Even a state may find itself obliged to fight an irregular style of war. In addition, to risk muddying the water further, many states, including super- and great powers, have developed and now maintain regular forces trained to fight irregularly. Those soldiers are members of what are called special forces. Britain has its SAS (Special Air Service) and SBS (Special Boat Squadron), the United States its Delta Force and Navy SEALs (Sea, Air and Land) and Army Green Berets, and Russia its Spetsnaz. Most countries have found a strategic need for necessarily small, elite, commando-type units that are created for, and are prepared to undertake, missions of a kind far removed from the mainstream of behaviour in regular warfare. One might comment that special forces are guerrillas, even terrorists, in uniform. However, sometimes they dispense with the uniforms, even though they need them in order to claim protection under the laws of war. Few wholly irregular belligerents know or care about such civilized niceties, though.

It is almost a definitional truth to claim that regular forces are much stronger than irregulars in combat. If that were not the case, the irregular side would rapidly shift to fighting in a regular mode in order to bid for clear-cut victory. Regular forces typically have advantages in numbers, equipment, training and discipline. Because of the dramatic asymmetry between regulars and irregulars, the latter are compelled to wage a style, or styles, of warfare that favours their distinctive strengths, and disadvantages the regular enemy. Irregulars fight irregularly because they cannot succeed, or even survive, in any other way.

Irregular warfare comes in different modes and has been known by many different names. The most popular of those names has been guerrilla warfare, a title borrowed from the Spanish for 'little war'. Spaniards waged irregular warfare, in guerrilla mode, with their popular resistance to French occupation from 1808 to 1814. Spanish regular forces generally could not stand against the French, though they did win one notable battle at Baylen on 19 July 1808, when a French army 20,000 strong was compelled to surrender. To lose in Spain was always bad for the health of French soldiers. Many of the 20,000 prisoners taken at Baylen were promptly massacred, contrary to the terms of surrender as well as to the standard practice of the time. Most of those who survived the immediate fury of the Spaniards expired subsequently on prison hulks.

Cruelty and brutality unmodified by rules of war are basic and enduring characteristics of irregular warfare. Not for nothing did Clausewitz, in his famous trinity of elements that is the heart of his theory of war, associate violence and passion most closely with 'the people' (Clausewitz, 1976: 89). From the Napoleonic Wars to the former Yugoslavia and Chechnya in the 1990s, and Iraq and Afghanistan in the 2000s, irregular warfare has carried the stamp of extreme violence. The laws of war that proliferated in the twentieth century made little or no impact upon the conduct of either side in irregular warfare.

Terrorism is a mode of irregular combat, and it may or may not accompany guerrilla warfare. It is simply a tactic, as is guerrilla fighting. Strategic irregularity is proof of relative weakness. To choose to fight in irregular modes, with guerrilla warfare and terrorism, is always a forced choice. Those tactical modes are selected because their practitioners are unable to compete in regular combat. The belligerent that is short of fighters and equipment must wage war stealthily, and strictly on its preferred terms, if it is to endure. If their cause prospers, terrorists will become insurgents. Should they continue to gain in strength they will mutate from insurgents into regular soldiers able to confront the forces of the state in open battle. Because of the political context of irregular warfare, one needs to be careful in the use of terms, all the while recognizing the subjectivity of characterization of irregulars.

Terrorists, a pejorative label, are regarded and discussed here as soldiers. Since terrorism is a mode of warfare, this choice is logical. However, all states, and many experts, prefer to define terrorists as criminals. This is an important matter. If terrorists are soldiers, or warriors, they are irregular combatants who, under recent developments in the international law of war (in the 1977 Second Protocol to the Geneva Conventions of 1949), have combatant rights and duties. They enjoy legal status and, as a consequence, they are granted a political standing that governments will resist (Roberts and Guelff, 2004: 22–5). Irregular warfare is about the relative political strength of the belligerents. No government is willingly going to concede combatant status to its domestic enemies, thereby gratuitously according them political legitimacy. It has been a cardinal principle of the international political system since the middle of the seventeenth century that the state should have a monopoly on the legitimate use of force. The days of private armies passed into history after the horrors of the Thirty Years War (1618–48). So, for political reasons, the state must treat the domestic exponents of irregular violence as criminals. In principle, at least, this means that terrorists have to be afforded the protections of the criminal law. In practice, those protections often are anything but robust.

There is an important difference between terrorism and an insurgency that employs terrorism. Strategically viewed, the former should never be able to defeat established authority, unless that authority panics and overreacts, or loses the political will to stand firm. The tactic of occasional violence to promote fear (terror) is, in and of itself, nearly always strategically hopeless. But if terrorism is handled poorly by the state, the official response will enable, perhaps trigger, mass mobilization of the public. The result will be the creation of a popular insurgency, probably accompanied by terrorism. Unlike the terrorist, the insurgent poses a potentially deadly threat to established authority. An insurgency can even grow in strength to the point where it is able to defeat the regular forces of the state. Government overreaction to terrorism may even inadvertently aid recruitment to the terrorists' cause.

Irregular warfare is so different from the regular kind that the armed forces of states have to discard their standard doctrinal manuals if they are to wage it competently. They still require the classic military virtues of morale, training, discipline, leadership and so forth. But with respect to 'how to fight', the subject of tactical and operational military doctrinal manuals, the demands of irregular warfare are virtually a reversal of sound practice in regular combat. To effect such a radical change while still retaining a core competency in regular warfare is a major challenge which few regular military establishments succeed in meeting satisfactorily. The regular soldier engaged in irregular warfare finds that the enemy has no obvious 'centre of gravity' (Clausewitz, 1976: 595–7), no capital city and probably no fixed lines of communication; looks identical to the civilian population; and refuses to stand and fight, except at times and in places of its own choosing, or when it is trapped and has no choice. As a general rule, regular soldiers trained to fight other regulars are out of their military depth when the enemy is irregular. This is an ancient phenomenon. Chechnya, Iraq and Afghanistan are simply the most recent examples of a thread that runs through all of strategic history. How to counter an insurgency is no great mystery. The difficulties lie in translating and adapting theory for effective practice in particular historical instances.

Because of the significance of the differences among the handful of terms key to this discussion, Box 18.1 provides a convenient collection of the essential definitions.

Box 18.1 Irregular warfare: definition of key terms

> The primary purpose of any theory is to clarify concepts and ideas that have become, as it were, confused and entangled. Not until terms and concepts have been defined can one hope to make any progress in examining the question clearly and simply and expect the reader to share one's views.
>
> (Clausewitz, 1976: 132)

Clausewitz is correct, but the key terms and concepts that bear upon irregular warfare are exceptionally vague and contestable. For a classic example that has become a cliché, one person's 'terrorist' is another person's 'freedom fighter'. To some people, terrorists are soldiers; to others they are criminals. Opinion is apt to depend upon political and moral judgement about the stakes in the conflict at issue. One cannot evade these difficulties entirely when offering definitions, but by following the minimalist rule that less is more, one can at least avoid some of the traps.

1. *Irregular warfare:* '[A small war] may be said to include all campaigns other than those where both the opposing sides consist of regular troops' (Callwell, 1990: 21). Callwell, writing a century ago (1906, 3rd edn), referred to 'small wars' rather than irregular war, but the terms are identical in meaning. '[Small war] is simply used to denote, in default for a better, operations of regular armies against irregular, or comparatively speaking irregular, forces' (Callwell, 1990: 22).
2. *Guerrilla warfare* is the character of warfare waged of necessity by irregular belligerents. Its hallmarks are surprise and the avoidance of large-scale open combat. It is a technique in the waging of war that any group or army, regular or irregular, can learn. But to be conducted successfully, guerrilla warfare

generally requires a friendly, or at least acquiescent, civilian context. The most eloquent, as well as the briefest, explanation of the theory of guerrilla warfare was written by T. E. Lawrence (of Arabia). Lying sick in his tent, he expounded the first principles of this form of warfare:

> [S]uppose we were (as we might be) an influence, an idea, a thing intangible, invulnerable, without front or back, drifting about like a gas? Armies were like plants, immobile, firm-rooted, nourished through long stems to the head. We might be a vapour, blowing where we listed. Our kingdoms lay in each man's mind; and as we wanted nothing material to live on, so we might offer nothing material to the killing. It seemed a regular soldier might be helpless without a target, owning only what he sat on, and subjugating only what, by order, he could poke his rifle at.
>
> (Lawrence, 1991: 192)

Lawrence's memoir of the Arab revolt against the Turks in World War I, *Seven Pillars of Wisdom: A Triumph*, is mandatory reading today in counter-insurgency communities around the world, as well as, one suspects, among guerrillas.

3. *Insurgency:* 'An insurgency is a protracted struggle conducted methodically, step by step, in order to obtain specific intermediate objectives leading finally to the overthrow of the existing order' (Krepinevich 1986: 7). This is good enough, but it does understate the importance of contingency. Methodical conduct frequently has to effect a U-turn if the regular enemy proves to be competent at counter-insurgency. Also, insurgents must employ irregular tactics, which is to say those of the guerrilla, as long as they are seriously inferior in combat strength to their regular enemy. In its final stage, a successful insurgency will transition to regular warfare.

4. *Terrorism* is the deliberate creation and exploitation of fear through the use, or the threat, of violence for political ends. This is an amended version of the definition provided by Bruce Hoffman (1998: 43).

The part of the spectrum of irregular violence that is of concern to this strategic history is defined by the dominance of political motives on the part of belligerents. However, beyond the orderly and neatly categorized conceptual world of the strategic theorist, there are other forms of irregular violence. There is criminal violence and, for want of a more apt concept, what one might call violent and often imitative or 'copycat' hooliganism. The latter occurs in a social context of disorder. It is unlikely to have serious political motives, or indeed any political motives at all. Expressive violence by bored and undisciplined people occurs all over the world. There may or may not be significant grievances on the part of the hooligans, but they are as likely to be an excuse for the enjoyable creation of mayhem as a set of issues that the rioters demand be addressed. A strategic context of insurgency encourages violent hooliganism because it weakens the bonds of social discipline and the norms of civility. Also, it provides favourable opportunities for well-organized criminal violence. Many an insurgent movement has been dependent upon working alliances with criminal organizations for reason of logistic needs. Since most states regard insurgents as criminals, especially when they function in terrorist mode, it can be difficult to identify the dividing line between irregular warfare and criminal violence. In theory, the distinction is crystal clear: to be classed as warfare, violence must be motivated by politics, not profit, as is the case with criminal behaviour. In practice, though, the political and the criminal tend to merge. For one example, the unquestionably political irregular war waged by Nationalist and Unionist secret armies in Northern Ireland was conducted in tandem with organized crime. In operational terms, crime and guerrilla warfare are near-perfect partners.

Guerrilla warfare and terrorism are simply military techniques that anyone can learn. Insurgency, in contrast, is not a military technique. While military competence is essential, it is but a minor aspect to the process. A similar judgement necessarily applies to counter-insurgency. In small – but again essential – part, it requires military prowess, but the skills that matter most contribute to public safety, good governance and cultural empathy. For a clear example of a historical insurgency, consider the campaign waged in South Vietnam by the Viet Cong (under North Vietnamese direction) in the 1960s. The Viet Cong insurgents engaged in bloody and brutal acts of terrorism; they waged guerrilla warfare; and occasionally they resorted to open regular warfare when the military context was highly favourable. As categories of warfare, regular and irregular sound neat and exclusive. But in practice, insurgent movements shift back and forth between guerrilla and conventional tactics. The best explanation of the tactical flexibility needed by insurgent strategy is to be found in the writings of Mao Tse-tung. In a classic manual, he explained that

> This protracted war will pass through three stages. The first stage covers the period of the enemy's strategic offensive and our strategic defensive. The second stage will be the period of the enemy's strategic consolidation and our preparation for the counter-offensive. The third stage will be the period of our strategic counter-offensive and the enemy's strategic retreat.
>
> (Mao, 1963: 210–11)

Mao was careful to emphasize the need for tactical flexibility in the face of a changing strategic context. Also, he warned explicitly against regarding the resort to guerrilla warfare as being anything other than an instrumental necessity. In China, as elsewhere, many guerrilla fighters forgot that guerrilla tactics were simply an expedient means to a political end: they had no merit in and of themselves. Mao could hardly have been more direct on this matter:

> The concept that guerrilla warfare is an end in itself and that guerrilla activities can be divorced from those of the regular forces is incorrect. If we assume that guerrilla warfare does not progress from beginning to end beyond its elementary forms, we have failed to recognize the fact that guerrilla hostilities can, under specific conditions, develop and assume orthodox characteristics.
>
> (Mao, 1961: 55–6)

In other words, an insurgency can grow from a period of preparation with political agitation, some guerrilla activity, and terrorism; through a period of intense guerrilla warfare and some mobile (conventional) operations – a time of rough strategic balance, or even stalemate; to a period of offensive conventional operations. In the context of steady strategic direction and political purpose, tactical and operational flexibility is the hallmark of a competently conducted insurgency.

Just as guerrilla warfare is no more than an expedient tactical means to a political end, so is terrorism. Both forms of irregular warfare are employed strictly for their strategic effect. If either begins to yield negative returns, it must be halted. For example, guerrilla activity may attract an official response that bears down heavily on local people, and many of those people might blame the guerrillas rather than the government for their misfortune. With respect to terrorism, rather than delegitimizing the government for its evident inability to protect innocent citizens, terrorist outrages against blameless civilians can provoke feelings of moral revulsion at the callous brutality of the terrorists. The irregular strategist cannot afford to become overly fond of one military tactic, regardless of evidence suggesting that it has become counter-productive. It is important to note that the theory of war and strategy presented by Clausewitz in *On War* (see Chapter 2) applies to both sides in irregular warfare. Mao was an admirer of Clausewitz (Mao, 1961: 49). Regular and irregular warfare differ only in tactical character. Because both are categories of a common activity, warfare, and both require direction by strategy, they share the need to be obedient to the general lore of war and strategy.

Irregular warfare in the forms of guerrilla operations or terrorism (or both) is the forced choice of the weaker side. As a preference, guerrillas and terrorists would rather fight in a regular army, engage in decisive manoeuvre and seek swift battlefield victory.

Guerrilla warfare and terrorism are instruments of protracted war, as Mao emphasized explicitly. He delivered a series of lectures in May and June 1938 collectively titled 'On Protracted War' (Mao, 1963: 187–266). In them he explained why the war against the Japanese invader had to have a protracted character if it were to be waged successfully. Strategic effect and political effect accumulate only slowly as a result of the generally small-scale actions in irregular warfare. The conduct of protracted warfare requires patience, a high measure of discipline and therefore leadership of outstanding quality. Irregular fighters face a life of great hardship and need to be able to sustain faith in their cause, even when victory is nowhere in sight. It follows that morale is of the utmost importance, a condition shared by regular and irregular combatants.

It is rare for an irregular campaign alone to suffice to bring victory. At some point the irregular side needs to shift combat mode from guerrilla to regular warfare in pursuit of a definitive strategic and political success.

The skilful insurgent will conduct guerrilla and regular operations simultaneously, or at least will threaten convincingly to do so. From Spain and Portugal in 1808–14 to Indo-China from 1945 to 1975 (with a pause from 1954 to 1960), the story is much the same. If an irregular force can pose both a dispersed guerrilla menace and a threat of concentrated military power, or if its operations are coordinated with those of friendly regular forces, the regular army of the enemy is caught on the horns of an operational dilemma. If the regular enemy masses troops to meet the regular style of threat, it must leave most of the civilian population unprotected. But if it disperses troops in order to provide protection in many locations, it all but invites the irregular enemy to concentrate its forces against isolated garrisons and destroy them in detail, one by one.

As always in strategic history, the contexts of a particular war are of vital importance. However, just as there are general principles of advice for irregulars, so there are well-established principles for the guidance of the authorities who must oppose the insurgents. Although every historical case of insurgency is distinctive, it will share sufficient characteristics common to all such conflicts for a set of general principles to be relevant. The extensive historical experience of many countries can be summarized in a short-list of essential 'dos' and 'don'ts'. There is a grand-strategic, which is to say not only a military, approach to counter-insurgency (COIN) and counter-terrorism (CT) which approximates best practice. It will not always succeed. Principles cannot reliably be applied in practice, and sometimes the military, or the socio-cultural, or the political contexts are just too unfavourable for any COIN efforts to succeed. Nevertheless, historical experience does suggest how COIN should be approached. The following are the most important principles:

1. *The civilian, not the military, authorities must be in overall charge.*
2. *There must be unity of command and therefore of effort over civilian and military authorities.*
3. *The people have to be protected.* This is job one in COIN. The allegiance of the civilian population is the stake in the conflict.
4. *The regular belligerent must behave lawfully.* A significant part of the official story is that the established authorities represent order over disorder, due process for justice rather than arbitrary behaviour, and respect for people as contrasted with disdain for them.
5. *Intelligence is king.* An irregular force will be defeated only if it is betrayed by people close to it, or if the regular belligerent is able to infiltrate its ranks, though such infiltration is typically difficult for physical and cultural reasons. Irregular warfare is also significantly transcultural (Strachan, 2006), as in Iraq and Afghanistan in the 2000s.
6. *Take ideology seriously.* Every insurgency mobilizes around a big idea, a cause, an ideology. It will always be political, though it may be clothed in religion. Strictly speaking, in Islam there is a unity of the political and the religious. Since morale is a key to the fate of an irregular, or regular, force, loss of ideological conviction must have devastating consequences.
7. *The irregular enemy is not the target in COIN; the minds of the people are the zone of strategic and political decision.* If the people can be protected well enough for them to support the COIN effort, or at the least to acquiesce in its behaviour, the insurgents must lose. Modern irregular warfare is all about the allegiance, or tolerance, of the civilian population. Regular troops tend to rush about the country chasing elusive guerrillas. They do not always understand that high body counts of irregular fighters are likely to be strategically irrelevant, because COIN cannot usually achieve a military victory. It is far more important to protect civilians than it is to kill insurgents. If the latter are isolated from the sympathy of the former, they are doomed to fail.
8. *Cultural understanding is highly desirable, even essential.* It will be perfect, or

nearly so, only if the COIN effort is directed at an irregular enemy with which it shares public and strategic cultures, as in some civil wars. But when a foreign power undertakes a campaign against an irregular foe, it is bound to be more or less ignorant of the cultural context of the struggle into which it is intruding.

9. *Deny the irregular enemy sanctuaries and external support.* Every insurgent force requires a safe base area in which to rest, recover, train, indoctrinate, and wait for opportunities to strike. While it is important to try to deny sanctuaries and foreign support to insurgents, even considerable success in those endeavours is only of secondary strategic importance. If the COIN strategy succeeds in winning the minds of a sufficient number of civilians, it will not much matter whether the irregulars have secure sanctuaries.

10. *Time is a weapon.* Of all the dimensions of war and strategy, time is the least forgiving. Mistakes committed in every other dimension can be corrected, in theory at least. But time passed is strictly irretrievable. As Mao argued in his lectures 'On Protracted War', an initially militarily weaker insurgent has to use time as an ally. By prolonging a conflict, the irregular tests the patience of the regular enemy, and especially that of its domestic public.

11. *Undercut the irregular enemy politically.* This will not always be possible, but it is still vital. In Algeria the French Army was expert in COIN. It believed it had mastered the military-technical conduct of what it termed 'modern war' (Trinquier, 1964). But although it knew from its bitter recent experience in Indo-China that irregular warfare was a thoroughly political undertaking, it was trapped in a non-permissive political context. France simply did not have a political story to offer its Muslim citizens in Algeria that they found attractive. As a result, although the French Army won the warfare, France lost the war.

These principles do not comprise the golden key to certain victory against irregular enemies. Every historical case, past, present and future, is different, so the advice may not be practicable in the circumstances of a particular insurgency. However, if a COIN campaign is to have any prospect of success, it needs to be founded upon an understanding of these principles. Once they are well understood, they can be adapted to fit local conditions.

Irregular warfare: an overview

For the same strategic reason that warfare between a continental and a maritime power is liable to stalemate, so warfare between regulars and irregulars is also prone to deadlock. This is because neither side can exercise decisive strategic leverage against the other. In both cases, there is a contrast in dominant military cultures. A country supreme on land may well be weak at sea. An unbeatable navy is likely to coexist with a second-class army (in quantity if not necessarily in quality). Historical examples are not in short supply: Athens and Sparta, Rome and Carthage, Britain and France, Britain and Germany in 1940, to cite but a few. The arrival of mature air power, long-range missiles and nuclear weapons has altered the terms of a strategic stand-off in some cases, but the dilemma in question here still remains. Strategically regarded, irregular warfare is as liable to stalemate today as it was a century ago, and for the same reason: neither side is able to reach the main strength of the other to compel a military decision. On the one hand, the irregular army cannot risk itself concentrated in open battle against its regular foe. On the other, the regular army cannot locate insurgent forces in large numbers so that they can be pinned down and destroyed. In other words, neither side has any realistic prospect of achieving an approximation to victory while it fails to score heavily in the true strategic currency of this kind of warfare. That currency, to repeat, is the will of the civilian population, the true battle space in irregular warfare. Of course, there have been circumstances wherein a long war is waged by both irregular and regular methods, as in Vietnam from the early 1960s until 1975. In the latter year, South Vietnam was defeated militarily by the regular North Vietnamese Army, so the will of South Vietnamese civilians in the spring of 1975 was irrelevant.

A century ago, Colonel Charles E. Callwell of the British Army wrote in his classic manual on irregular warfare, *Small Wars*, that the fundamental military problem for the regular side was to find ways to bring the irregular enemy to battle (Callwell, 1990: ch.3). An obvious answer is to threaten something that the irregulars would be compelled to mass and stand to defend: their homes, families and animals are all possibilities. But if the irregulars of the period do not have fixed abodes, with families, granaries and the like, the regulars face a problem. So how can insurgents be compelled to fight in such a manner that they can be defeated in open battle? In principle, it is necessary to argue that today the contexts of irregular warfare are radically different from those dominated by the apolitical assumptions that underlay Callwell's magnificent treatise on colonial warfare. As Ian Beckett has pointed out, the politicization of guerrilla warfare and insurgency was largely a phenomenon of the post-1914–18 world (Beckett, 2001b: viii). Irregular warfare could no longer be treated as a challenge to military and diplomatic techniques. Callwell was interested in deterring, and if need be defeating, or at least punishing, tribal-based violence. The need to win 'hearts and minds' was not a commandment in his playbook. However, the colonel did emphasize the need to study the irregular enemy carefully (Callwell, 1990: 33).

Because of the changes in the character of irregular warfare, especially its routine acquisition of revolutionary political purpose, strategy for its suppression or containment has had to alter. Contrary to the argument Callwell advanced, the difficulty of bringing the irregular enemy to battle is no longer the primary challenge. Rather, the central problem today is the protection of the civilian population. They are the battleground. If a regular force achieves some success hunting guerrilla units in remote parts of a country but neglects to protect the bulk of the civilian population, it will fail in the war. Irregular warfare today is about the will of the people, not about dead guerrillas and captured weapons. Those corpses and weapons are likely to be easy to replace.

For the irregular combatant, the strategic challenge is how to behave, or trap the enemy into misbehaving, so as to shift the net balance of advantage in its favour. That challenge can only be met politically. While all warfare is an expression of politics, none is more pervasively so than irregular conflict. The irregular side, most probably employing a mixture of guerrilla tactics and terrorism, will seek favourable political effect from several courses of action. There are three especially productive tactics for irregulars to adopt. First, they can inflict painful and humiliating isolated military defeats on the regulars. This undermines the government's prestige and diminishes public confidence in the ability of the army and other security forces to protect them. Also, perhaps most damaging of all, such defeats cause civilians to doubt that the government will prevail. As a matter of prudence for personal survival, civilians are inclined to support the side that they believe ultimately will win. As a result, the public will withdraw its support from official COIN efforts.

Second, the irregular side will hurt civilians deliberately even though their allegiance is strategically crucial. By doing this, the irregular offers undeniable proof of the inability of the government to meet its primary obligation, the protection of its people. Also, to kill and maim civilians teaches the plain lesson that the irregular is able to reach and hurt those who oppose it.

Third and finally, the irregular will attempt to goad the regular enemy into tactics that should prove self-defeating. Since the contest is about rival claims to legitimacy, each side must strive to provoke the enemy into behaviour that contributes to its delegitimization in domestic public, and perhaps foreign, perception. Insurgents are often only part-time warriors, indistinguishable from civilians for most of the time. It follows that it is all too easy for regular troops to err by treating everybody in a neighbourhood, for example, as being by and large guilty. If the regulars overreact and behave with scant discrimination, inadvertently they aid recruitment for the irregulars' cause. An attitude of 'shoot on suspicion' is fatal for a COIN and CT campaign.

Irregular warfare has been a permanent feature of the strategic history of the two centuries covered in this book. American colonists of both political persuasions showed the way in the 1770s and 1780s, while Spanish and Portuguese guerrillas brought irregular conflict to a high and brutal pitch of effectiveness. Before the French Empire triggered irregular resistance in the Tyrol in 1808, in the Iberian peninsula in 1808–14 and in Russia in 1812, its Republican predecessor had struggled bloodily against domestic guerrilla fighters. The irregular warfare in 1793–6 in the Vendée region of western France, conducted to suppress a Catholic insurgency, matched in atrocity and counter-atrocity anything to be found in the French conduct of irregular combat abroad. At least 400,000 people died in that COIN campaign. Civil wars tend to extremes of violence. The issues are more immediate and therefore personal. The passion of the people is aroused, with dire consequences for the prospects of moderation in behaviour.

The nineteenth, twentieth and now twenty-first centuries have recorded dozens, probably hundreds, of insurgencies, great and small. Until the fourth quarter of the twentieth century those insurgencies were primarily anti-colonial in context and motivation. They were largely rural in origin and popular strength, though not in leadership, and many were armed with an ideology that mingled nationalism with a local or borrowed variant of Marxism. Needless to say, twentieth-century Marxists had to turn the master's theory of historical change on its head. They needed to explain how proletarian revolution could occur in countries that scarcely had a proletariat. Mao Tse-tung showed the way to succeed with his theory and practice of people's revolutionary war in a rural context. (This was formulated after a disastrous attempted urban insurgency in the 1920s.) But an irregular party does not have to resort to violence. Mahatma Gandhi's challenge to the legitimacy of British rule in India was deadly in its non-violence. Gandhi, demonstrating Machiavellian cunning based upon deep cultural understanding of both the British and his own people, tempted the former to offend against their own values and principles. He achieved a moral ascendancy for his highly irregular campaign of non-violent resistance. That ascendancy was politically priceless. Indeed, the ability to seize and hold the moral high ground is one of the most valuable sources of strategic effectiveness in irregular warfare in all cultural and geopolitical contexts.

The regular soldier tends to abhor irregular warfare. The enemy is elusive, anonymous in a crowd of civilians, and generally inaccessible to application of the mailed fist. As a result, it is tempting to try short cuts to success, particularly military success. The regular is ever liable to forget that irregular war is deeply political and has no strictly military dimension. In their frustration, regulars engage in energetic and violent sweeps of 'bandit country'. They harass suspect communities, and generally do what energetic, career-minded soldiers are supposed to do: they take the offensive, try to seize the initiative, and display much activity. However, none of this is strategically very helpful. In order to succeed against an irregular enemy, regular soldiers have to discard old doctrine manuals and write new ones. The merit in this view is recognized today. For example, on 25 June 2006, Sergeant Jonathan Mayville, US Army, said, 'All of our army regulations, all of our training manuals, are completely changed.' Speaking on the same day and at the same location (Pinon Canyon Maneuver Site, Colorado, USA), Command Sergeant Major Terrance McWilliams also emphasized the extent of the US Army's effort at cultural and tactical transformation for greater effectiveness in irregular warfare: 'This is no longer the old Army where you see a bad guy, you automatically shoot them. You're trying to maintain the calm with the villagers and at the same time weed out the insurgents' (both quoted in Squires, 2006).

Terrorism and counter-terrorism

Terrorism is exemplary violence executed primarily for the purpose of inducing fear among the general public. It can be targeted against either innocent civilians or agents of the state, military or bureaucratic. In the latter case, the intention is to promote demoralization. Definitions that require terrorist action to be directed at civilians are too restrictive. The particular targets of terrorist assault are not usually inherently important, even when they are of high symbolic or economic significance, though the destruction of the Twin Towers of the World Trade Center in New York was an exception to that rule. Terrorists do not seek to inflict material damage or casualties as tactical ends in themselves. They are not engaged in materially attritional warfare, but rather in warfare to erode the will of the enemy. They can never inflict sufficient damage upon their enemies to be able to win by force, probably not even if they employ a weapon of mass destruction (e.g., a nuclear device). Terrorists can win only politically, if they can win at all. Generally, they do not win. However, it is important to note that the 'new terrorism' executed by al Qaeda does seem to be attempting a strategy of economic warfare. Al Qaeda may have calculated that a series of blows such as those on 9/11 would have such expensive consequences for its enemies that they would be compelled to accept defeat.

Terrorism occurs in one of two forms: as a strategic, stand-alone technique of warfare; or as an adjunct to guerrilla operations. In the latter case it may be employed early in a conflict when insurgent numbers are small, with the hope being that the official response will be so mishandled that a popular insurgency can be mobilized. In the case of stand-alone terrorism, executed in no expectation of its leading to an insurgency, the strategy will be one of political and psychological attrition. The terrorists will be an expensive nuisance and a political embarrassment. As that situation persists, the state might lose its nerve, have a failure of political will, and, in effect if not formally, offer a political deal. All governments have a declaratory stance of never negotiating with terrorists, whom they categorize and denounce as criminals. But in practice, governments do negotiate, though typically indirectly, through third-party agencies, and therefore somewhat deniably.

When one compares how terrorism and counter-terrorism can win strategically, the answers are mirror images of each other. And that is true despite the dramatic asymmetries between the two sides. Victory or defeat (admittedly two terms in need of careful definition with regard to terrorism and CT) depends critically upon who can win the struggle for perceived legitimacy. The terrorist branch of irregular warfare is very much a moral and psychological, which is to say a cultural, struggle, not a material one.

Usually, the terrorist can win only if the government's CT efforts include heavy-handed overreaction. If they entail the use of disproportionate and indiscriminate violence against civilians, they will produce recruits for the terrorists. A clumsy, over-reacting CT campaign can transform a terrorist nuisance into a small-scale guerrilla war, which might escalate into a full-fledged popular insurgency. Strategically, the CT side will have delegitimized itself politically. The dominant issue in the conflict will no longer be whatever is motivating hard-core terrorists but the government's alleged crimes against the people.

For the government, a prime strategy for success in CT is to try to trap the terrorists into delegitimizing themselves in the eyes of the public. The official response needs to be restrained, obedient to the principle of minimum force, and respectful of the rights and feelings even of suspect communities within the state. In that context, the terrorists have a strategic problem, even a crisis, on their hands. Since the government is not overreacting in response to terrorist outrages, the temptation is to raise the stakes and strive for ever-bigger and more shocking atrocities. But that path is fairly certain to lead to a dramatic loss of public sympathy, always assuming that such sympathy had been enjoyed previously. The political and moral issue then ceases to be the merit or otherwise in the terrorists' cause but rather their culturally intolerable misbehaviour. If the government's CT efforts continue to be low key, some terrorists, and especially many potential recruits, should suffer a devastating loss of morale. Terrorism will seem hopeless, a path to nowhere, and few people will be attracted to an organization staffed by what are judged to be inevitable losers.

In its pure (if one dare use the term) form, which is to say as stand-alone behaviour, terrorism is rarely successful. Recall that unlike an insurgency, which by definition requires a mass movement directed towards regime change, terrorism itself has no capacity to seize state power. The terrorist wins only if the government is intimidated, coerced and thereby humiliated into offering political concessions – or if the government panics, overreacts and inadvertently fuels an insurgency out of what had been only an isolated terrorist campaign. In order to gain power, irregular fighters have to evolve from terrorists into insurgents. Terrorism is always a high-risk tactic, one liable to blow back negatively on the terrorists themselves. The public is at least as likely to turn on the terrorists for their outrages against the innocent as it is to be mobilized in hatred of official misdeeds.

The normal language of military analysis, as well as popular commentary, does not fit comfortably the context of terrorist–CT struggle. Officials talk of victory and defeat, and success and failure, but what do these commonplace concepts mean in irregular warfare against terrorists? The ever-essential Mao advises that 'There is in guerrilla warfare no such thing as a decisive battle' (Mao, 1961: 52). His maxim applies no less to terrorism. As a general rule, CT is a protracted attritional struggle of political wills. It is waged pre-eminently by the police and other security services, with the military typically in reserve. And the most important weapon in the arsenal of the counter-terrorist is information.

All terrorist organizations eventually come to the end of their strategically unnatural lives. They may persist for decades, but generally they do not remain a potent force for very long. Usefully, Christopher Harmon has identified six reasons why terrorist movements end (Harmon, 2006: 232–7):

1. The regime strikes back with overwhelming force and crushes the movement.
2. The regime suppresses the terrorists by means of comprehensive, hard measures.
3. The regime arrests or kills 'the individual who is its centre of gravity', its charismatic, or at least its key, leader. The terrorist organization is thus decapitated.
4. The terrorist movement simply fades away through sheer fatigue. Once dedicated and apparently selfless terrorists can suffer a terminal 'failure of will'.
5. The terrorists may be absorbed into normal politics or civilized life. In other words, they go legitimate and join the political mainstream. This has happened many times. The contemporary political history of Northern Ireland has registered the phenomenon of former terrorists, or at least organizers of terrorism, in government.
6. Finally, the terrorists might 'win'. In the twentieth century, many irregular belligerents who employed terrorism extensively seized or otherwise achieved state power. Leading examples include the Bolsheviks, the Maoists, the Castroites, the Algerian FLN and the Khmer Rouge.

The question 'What is success?' for a terrorist organization does not lend itself to a simple answer. Some terrorists seek state power: they want to govern, even though their way of life as terrorists should disqualify them from doing so. Terrorists aspiring for high office have a way of continuing to behave like terrorists when in such office. Others are content just to help the march of history proceed in what they perceive as the right direction. Yet others may be satisfied with the conviction that they are instruments of righteousness, however defined. Their atrocities are strictly cases of expressive violence.

As usual in strategic history, one size of theory does not fit all situations. For the CT side, although total eradication is the nominal aim, and is even achieved occasionally, in practice a more modest aim must define success. Pragmatically, a government will tend to be satisfied if it is able to contain and reduce terrorist outrages to a level that is politically and socially tolerable. That may sound callous, but it is realistic and practical. And strategy is nothing if it is not practical. The prudent CT strategist will strive for victory in traditional military understanding, with the last terrorists emerging from their hiding-place with their hands in the air, or remaining in their hideout permanently, suitably riddled with bullets. But, pragmatically, a CT campaign will have succeeded well enough if it manages to scale down the atrocities to a very low rate of occurrence. They will continue to be a nuisance, and certainly a tragedy in their human consequences, but they will cease to be a political factor of much significance.

Al Qaeda and the 'new terrorism'

The 1990s saw the emergence and rise of what has come to be known as the 'New Terrorism' (Laqueur, 1999). It is distinguished in its motivation, goals and methods from what, of necessity, is now called the 'Old Terrorism'. Terrorists of the old school were, indeed still are, motivated by political ideology. They had specific, geopolitically limited objectives, and, in theory, one could negotiate with them. In some respects at least, old-style terrorists, such as the members of the IRA (Irish Republican Army) and ETA (Euskadi Ta Askatasuna, or Freedom for the Basque Homeland), inhabited the same strategic cultural universe as did the forces of law and order, the counter-terrorists. They comprised an irregular and, of course, a materially and culturally asymmetrical enemy, but their strategic behaviour was both familiar and easy to understand. To counter them effectively was, naturally, rather more difficult. The prototype of the Old Terrorism in recent times was the Palestine Liberation Organization, led by Yasser Arafat, in the late 1960s and the 1970s. It became the model for many imitators and rivals. Unlike practitioners of the New Terrorism, the PLO and most of the other anti-Israeli terrorist groups were essentially secular, political and focused on a single dominant issue. In principle, the PLO and the others (e.g., Hamas, now in power in Gaza; and Hezbullah, supported by Iran and based in Lebanon) pursued a political agenda that could be discussed, if not satisfied, diplomatically.

The New Terrorism of today has features in stark contrast to its immediate predecessor. So-called new, post-modern or apocalyptic terrorists (Peters, 2002: 22–65) have a religious motive, at least religious inspiration and sanction, albeit one with a political subtext, and are not focused narrowly on a particular issue or two in a limited geopolitical context. Moreover, they are not careful of human lives; indeed, quite the contrary. As a matter of political expediency, governments talk about waging a 'war on terror'. What they mean is a war on violent Islamic extremists. The root problem is with Islam and the Islamic world, the Dar ul Islam (the House of Islam). The global struggle, the irregular warfare now under way between al Qaeda and its many official and other enemies, is a war about the future of the Islamic religion and, in particular, about the modernization of the Dar ul Islam. Al Qaeda has recruited from the ranks of those many Islamic young people who have sought security of identity and a sense of worth and purpose in the embrace of religion.

As the tip of the spear of the New Terrorism, al Qaeda, generically, is a historically familiar phenomenon. It is a backward-looking movement. It rests its authority and its promise upon the purported blessings that must flow from the strictest adherence to a particular, extreme interpretation of Islam's holiest texts. In historical context it can be understood as a product of victory over the atheistic Soviets in 1980s Afghanistan. In addition, as just indicated, it is a response to the crisis of identity and self-regard that besets much of the Islamic realm.

Al Qaeda has declared war on the West, but its true enemies lie in the Dar ul Islam itself. The United States and other Western countries have been targeted only because they support what al Qaeda regards as apostate regimes in the land of Islam. Al Qaeda has no serious quarrel with the West. It is the West's behaviour in, and towards, nominally Islamic countries that is the source of the antagonism. The movement's goals are quite rational. The problem is that those goals happen to be wildly unreasonable in the view of other cultures. It is true to claim that its objectives are so radical as to be non-negotiable, but it is incorrect to argue that it has no real political agenda. Led by the charismatic Osama bin Laden, al Qaeda demands the removal of allegedly apostate Islamic regimes; the restoration of the Caliphate as the source of supreme Islamic authority over the whole of the Dar ul Islam (it was abolished by Kemal Atatürk in 1924 as a necessary step in his creation of a modern, secular Turkey); and the elimination of Western non-, even anti-, Islamic influence and practices from the Middle East. As said, in practice these demands are thoroughly non-negotiable. Indeed, they are too general in character to serve even as a basis for negotiation. In other words, even if al Qaeda's enemies would like to seek a compromise settlement, the movement's ideologically driven agenda is not of a kind that lends itself to a process of give and take. Unlike Irish or Palestinian terrorist organizations, al Qaeda, claiming religious sanction for its absolute demands, cannot be bribed to the conference table and offered some fraction of its demands.

The New Terrorism is novel in several important respects. As befits a creation of the Information Age, it is organized as a network, not a hierarchy. It is indifferent to the loss of human life. Those whom it kills, or murders, as well as those who sacrifice themselves as its shock troops, serve the will of Allah, consensually or otherwise. And it has the potential to graduate from terrorism, through guerrilla warfare, to a full-scale insurgency in especially vulnerable Islamic countries. At present, al Qaeda is not a popular insurgency anywhere, but that situation could alter for the worse. The insurgents in Iraq and Afghanistan have many motives, with al Qaeda's brand of jihad figuring in them only modestly. But it is well to recall that before they were forcibly eliminated, al Qaeda's training camps, pre-eminently in Taliban Afghanistan, graduated some 30,000–50,000 recruits. They comprise a reserve army of potential jihadists, including suicide bombers. Today, novice jihadists can receive on-the-job training under fire in Iraq and Afghanistan.

As an irregular menace, al Qaeda's New Terrorism poses an extraordinary strategic problem. To cite the leading elements in that challenge from the perspective of CT endeavours, al Qaeda:

1. is culturally very hard to penetrate;
2. is experienced in the conduct of irregular warfare;
3. enjoys the prestige that flows from a tradition of victory;
4. is ever changing in its organization and methods – it is a highly adaptive movement, perhaps not really an organization at all, but rather both an inspiration and a source of practical advice and support to disparate groups;
5. seeks to punish, inflict pain and wreak destruction, all sanctioned by the will of God, as interpreted;
6. favours the employment of suicide bombers, a tactic that renders the CT task unusually difficult – the greatest challenge to the would-be terrorist has always previously been the problem of escaping safely after an outrage is committed.

In due course, al Qaeda will decline and fall, but already it has demonstrated the ability to conduct irregular warfare so successfully that it has all but transformed the character of contemporary international politics, and it is unquestionably the defining threat of this era. Before al Qaeda and its imitators and successors fade away, they have the potential to wreak immeasurable harm in the world of Islam and, as a direct consequence, upon the global economy through the agencies of oil supply and general economic confidence. In addition, there is a real possibility, even a probability, that the New Terrorism will acquire some weapons of mass destruction. In sharp contrast to nuclear-armed states, a nuclear-armed al Qaeda could not be deterred, even in theory (Allison, 2004).

Conclusion

There are two principal reasons why a healthy future can be predicted for irregular warfare. The first is uncontentious; the second is controversial. First, there will always be conflicts, primarily domestic, wherein the belligerents are grossly asymmetrical according to standard measurements of military power. In those contests the much weaker side is able to survive strategically only by behaving as a terrorist, guerrilla or insurgent. Open, regular warfare would be suicidal. The second reason why irregular warfare currently is on a rising curve of popularity is the alleged decline in the authority of the state under the pressures of globalization. Rephrased, it is claimed that the state is less powerful than it used to be. This condition serves as an invitation to armed insurrection by groups that sense a historic opportunity to shoot their way to a local victory for their dreams, ambitions and interests. There is little doubt that the processes of globalization have weakened the ability of most states to serve the vital interests of their citizens unilaterally. But whether this relative decline is of a significance great enough to tempt dissidents to resort to organized violence is debatable.

In the first decade of the twenty-first century the United States has declared that it is a 'nation at war'. But commitment to irregular warfare with a global domain against Islamic jihadists is not a strategically promising undertaking. The reasons lie in those contexts identified as vital back in Chapter 1. Of the seven contexts identified (political; socio-cultural; economic; technological; military-strategic; geographical; and historical), at least three intrude upon, even dominate, the West's struggle against Islamic irregulars. Specifically, Islamic terrorists and insurgents cannot be defeated by military means, and especially not by non-Islamic arms. The irregular campaign advertised so dramatically on 9/11 will be defeated, which is to say contained and slowly reduced to irrelevance, only as a consequence of effective measures taken by Islamic governments and societies. The Islamic world needs to reform itself, cope better with the problem of gross maldistribution of wealth, and come to grips with the need to accommodate a proper respect for religion within a modernizing society. If that formidable agenda were addressed fairly successfully, the political fuel for al Qaeda and other violent groups and movements would diminish markedly.

Irregular warfare has been discussed separately in this chapter strictly as a matter of convenience. Because the strategic history of the past 200 years has been driven forward overwhelmingly by interstate conflict, this book is obliged to reflect that fact. However, warfare as conducted by irregulars has been an ever-present strategic reality. It featured especially in resistance to the growth of European empires, and then in efforts to speed their decline and collapse. Irregular warfare is not owned by any particular creed or interest but is simply a tool kit of military techniques to which the materially inferior side must resort if it wishes to take up arms.

The fact that irregular warfare is treated separately here implies nothing about its nature and functioning. It has not competed hard for space in previous chapters because its strategic importance has long been overshadowed by regular warfare between states. But war is war, warfare is warfare, and strategy is strategy. It does not matter whether the war, warfare or strategy in question is regular, irregular or a combination of the two. As Stuart Kinross (2004) has argued, Clausewitz's theory of war and strategy applies no less to irregular than to regular warfare.

Key points

1. Only after 9/11 has irregular warfare been the principal plot line in modern strategic history.
2. It is useful to distinguish regular from irregular warfare. Choice of the latter signifies weakness.
3. All war is political, but none is more so than the irregular kind (terrorism, insurgency and guerrilla warfare).
4. Irregular warfare differs radically from regular warfare tactically and operationally, but not strategically.
5. Terrorists and counter-terrorists struggle to induce each other to delegitimize themselves politically and culturally.
6. Violent Islamic extremists can be defeated only by other Muslims. The issue in contention is how to reconcile the modernization of society with religious values.

Questions

1. **How do regular and irregular warfare differ?**
2. **In waging irregular warfare, what are the distinctive tactical and strategic problems for the regulars and the irregulars?**
3. **How can terrorism and counter-terrorism succeed or fail strategically?**
4. **How does the 'New Terrorism' differ from the 'Old Terrorism'?**

Further reading

R. B. Asprey *War in the Shadows: The Classic History of Guerrilla Warfare from Ancient Persia to the Present*, rev. edn (Boston: Little, Brown, 1994).
I. F. W. Beckett *Modern Insurgencies and Counter-insurgencies: Guerrillas and Their Opponents since 1750* (London: Routledge, 2001).
A. K. Cronin 'How al-Qaeda Ends: The Decline and Demise of Terrorist Groups', *International Security*, 31: 7–48 (2006).
R. Gunaratna *Inside al Qaeda: Global Network of Terror* (New York: Columbia University Press, 2002).
B. Hoffman *Inside Terrorism* (London: Victor Gollancz, 1998).
A. F. Krepinevich Jr *The Army and Vietnam* (Baltimore: Johns Hopkins University Press, 1986).
W. Laqueur *Guerrilla Warfare: A Historical and Critical Study* (New Brunswick, NJ: Transaction Publishers, 1998).

—— *The New Terrorism: Fanaticism and the Arms of Mass Destruction* (New York: Oxford University Press, 1999).

—— *No End to War: Terrorism in the Twenty-first Century* (New York: Continuum, 2003).

T. E. Lawrence *Seven Pillars of Wisdom: A Triumph* (New York: Anchor Books, 1991), esp. ch. 33.

Mao Tse-tung *On Guerrilla Warfare*, trans. B. Griffith (New York: Praeger, 1961).

—— *Selected Military Writings* (Beijing: Foreign Languages Press, 1963).

J. Stern *Terror in the Name of God: Why Religious Militants Kill* (New York: HarperCollins, 2003).

19 War, peace and international order

Reader's guide: Optimism, pessimism and the future of war. The meaning and requirements of world order. Two hundred years of new world orders. Understanding peace.

Introduction: war–peace cycle

There are two principal views of war in history. People can be classed either as optimists or pessimists. Alternative labelling contrasts idealists with realists, or believers in progress with sceptics. It is difficult to select words that do not carry pejorative baggage. Optimist-idealists believe in progress. In the context of strategic history this means progress towards the eventual abolition, at least the major amelioration, of warfare. In contrast, pessimist-realists believe in constancy and continuity in the challenges to, and responses of, statecraft. The pessimist-realist is not convinced that the future strategic history of humankind will produce anything other than a repeat of past history, albeit in different contexts. Optimist-idealists hold that the human race is improving in its strategic behaviour, that it has learnt from past mistakes. They point to the growth of norms, laws and institutions that both flag up and contribute to the taming of politically motivated violence. In this view, today is the highest point humans have attained in the long journey towards a war-free world. The contrasting view of pessimistic realists holds that human behaviour, including behaviour of the political and strategic kinds, does not change, though it is reshaped by, and adapted to, dynamic circumstances. Peace and war succeed each other in an endless, though irregular, cycle. Optimist-idealists believe that war is a problem that could, should and one day will succumb to assault by the proper weapons. Some conceive of war as a disease that can be eradicated by application of the right treatment. There is no shortage of optimist-idealist weapons for the vanquishing of war-proneness, including disarmament; arms control; globalization; democracy; law; the erosion of nationalism; and the growth of a true global community. The contrasting view of the pessimist-realist is that war is not a single problem but countless problems, all unique to particular conflicts. It follows, in this perspective, that there can be no general solution to the 'problem of war', because to frame the issue in that way is to misunderstand its nature.

Readers must choose for themselves whether to regard the two centuries of strategic history analysed here as a journey towards a less war-prone world. Or have those 200 years simply registered enormous changes in many of the contexts for statecraft but no changes of significant note in the fundamentals of strategic history? Change is not synonymous with progress, understood to mean ethical and political advance. Is history more cyclical than arrow-like, or vice versa? It is tempting to try to impose scholarly discipline upon the two centuries by means of working backwards from today. One might seek to demonstrate how, faltering step by faltering step, with many painful falls along the way, humankind has struggled to improve its conduct of international relations. Conflictual domestic relations are another class of challenge. As Chapters 17 and 18 explained, the prospects for peace, order, justice and general good governance are none too bright in many parts of the world, especially in Africa, the Middle East and South and Central Asia.

This book has adopted only one concept to serve as a working approximation to that highly suspect, though convenient, scholarly weapon, the master narrative. That concept is strategic history. This text rests upon the proposition that force and the threat of force have had a greater impact upon the many contexts for human behaviour than has any other source of influence. This view is undoubtedly pessimistic-realistic, although it is open minded about the future. Above all else, this venture in strategic history does not postulate a predetermined destination for human endeavours. It is hostile to historical narratives that fail to allow contingency a major role.

This chapter reviews the whole of the historical domain that has been discussed. The focus is upon the relationship between peace and war, and, no less important, war and peace. A condition of peace with security generally is held to be the product of an international order characterized by justice, or tolerable injustice; by widely shared norms for acceptable international conduct; by processes and possibly institutions for the resolution or amelioration of disputes; and, last but not least, by a policing mechanism and a policeman or two, or three, or more. What does the strategic history of the past two centuries reveal? How well did statesmen and soldiers cope with the challenges they had to face? The period covered here saw four great, or general, wars (three actual and one mercifully only potential, though potentially that was the most awesome and awful of all). These were the conflicts (or, in the final case, non-conflict) of 1792–1815, 1914–18, 1939–45 and 1947–89. A subject of prime interest to the strategic historian is how well international order was organized and maintained in the interwar periods, though that phrasing exaggerates the role of purposeful design and behaviour geared to system stability.

The core concern here is to review how great wars emerged, or erupted, from the preceding period of peace, and also how particular conditions of peace succeeded wars. (The latter is a topic much neglected by scholars.) The chapter concludes with an examination of the deceptively simple concept of peace.

New world orders

Strategic history is not only about the consequences of the use and threat of organized force for political reasons. It is also deeply interested in the slippery, and much contested, concept of order, both international and domestic. The wars discussed in this book all had their origins, though not always their profoundest roots, in the interwar periods from which they emerged. Efforts to establish and sustain a stable international order and the fate of those endeavours are integral to strategic history. Chapter after chapter has had much to say about the pre and post-war contexts of conflicts. Not until the nuclear revolution radically altered the cost–benefit ratio of warfare were peace and order synonymous. The great general wars of 1792–1815, 1914–18 and 1939–45 were all waged by one side, at least, with the restoration of a stable and tolerable international order as the principal motive. Order and war have not only been compatible; sometimes the former has been judged widely to require the latter.

What is the meaning of the obviously important, but somewhat opaque, concept of international, even world, order? It can be understood to refer to a stable pattern in the relations among states, with that pattern expressing interests, values and norms that the major states find acceptable. One could tinker with the definition for a better historical fit with particular periods, but the bare definition just offered holds no less for the 2000s than it did for the 1820s or 1920s. International order has to be understood in three ways. First, it is simply descriptive: what is, or was, the international order? Second, it is a normative concept: what should it be? Third, it can be employed prescriptively: how might it be improved?

With just a single exception, after every great war in modern history there has been a conscious effort to construct a world order that should be an improvement upon that which preceded the period of conflict. Those construction efforts always involved institution-building. Their successes and failures, time after time, depended upon the same factors. An international order is relatively stable when its rules, norms, and distribution of rights and duties are broadly in accord with the interests and values of the major state, and other essential, players. Not until the 1990s was the structure of world order in modern history dominated by a single state, the American superpower. From the 1790s until the 1980s the architecture of world order was either multipolar, typically with five great powers of variable strength, or briefly bipolar, as from 1945 to 1989. The 1990s were also historically unique in the period covered by this analysis in that they were the only post-war–interwar period that did not witness a purposeful effort to construct a new world order. One can speculate as to why that was the case, and focus upon lack of political vision and leadership, but it is probably more plausible to suggest that the unusual and unexpected manner of the termination of the Cold War was the principal element shaping the post-war environment. The Cold War did not conclude officially, any more than it had begun officially. There could be no peace treaty, and as a result there was no conference to debate the issues of the era. In the 1990s there was no replay of Vienna in 1814–15, or Versailles in 1919 or even Yalta and Potsdam in 1945.

Before providing a summary of the historical record of ordering efforts from the 1810s until today, it is necessary to emphasize the nature of the subject at issue. Order does not necessarily mean peace, at least not directly. International or world order, understood normatively rather than just descriptively, can be said to be in place and functioning well enough when the essential state and any other players are able to pursue and protect their interests in ways and to a degree that all, or most, find acceptable. Power is balanced, albeit only approximately. Should a state or coalition threaten to destabilize the international order, then sooner or later the other great powers in the system would combine to contain, and if need be materially reduce, it by force. World order is about the partial control of the possibility of war but also about the use of war as an instrument to discipline rogue behaviour. Since peace is a concept with several meanings (see the later discussion), a focus on international order reflects appreciation of the fact that people, societies and states do not simply favour an unqualified peace. After all, strategic history might offer them the peace of the grave or the peace of slavery. Those were the practical options open to non-Jewish Poles from 1939 to 1945. People want the kind of peace that provides security, and for that they need the contextual discipline of a functioning international order.

The analysis now will briefly review the historical record of efforts to provide for international order over the past two centuries. This entails revisiting the four principal post-war–interwar contexts: those succeeding the Wars of the French Revolution and Napoleon; World War I; World War II; and the Cold War. The interwar periods were discussed in detail in the relevant chapters. However, the intention here is to consider the whole enterprise of containing, controlling and occasionally resorting to war, through the institutions, practices and norms of what is known as international or world order.

Vienna and Concert diplomacy

After the Congress of Vienna of 1 September 1814 – 9 June 1815, the 'gang of four' – Russia, Prussia, Austria and Britain (later five, when France was readmitted to the top table in 1823) – established a novel process of Congress diplomacy. The most vital operating principle was that no great power should take action unilaterally that would impinge negatively upon the interests of another great power. At least, it should not take such action without first advising the other interested great power of its intentions. The Congress System rapidly broke down, primarily because of the ideological cleavage between liberal Britain and profoundly conservative Russia, Prussia and Austria. Nevertheless, the Vienna Settlement was by no means a failure. It is a fact that Europe did not suffer a general war for almost a century, 1815 to 1914. That strategic historical fact was determined by the play of several factors, but it is necessary to allow some credit to those who designed and sometimes practised Congress and later Concert diplomacy.

In three particulars at least, the Congress/Concert System can claim some credit for promoting a stable international order. First, it obliged the great powers to consider the systemic effects of their behaviour. No longer were issues of war and peace strictly matters for unilateral calculation and decision. State policy was considered in the context of the stability of the international, which is to say the European, order. Of course, that principle was not always followed, but it was still an enduring part of the normative bequest of the Vienna Settlement. Second, summit and foreign ministers' conferences were inaugurated. These rapidly declined in frequency after the early 1820s, but they remained as an occasional acceptable convenience in the diplomatic arsenal. At the Congress of Berlin in 1878, Bismarck succeeded in depriving Russia of much of the advantage it had gained in its recent war with Turkey. Fast-forward to 1986, to the Reagan–Gorbachev summit at Reykjavik where important common ground on nuclear disarmament was discovered, to the surprise of the principals. Both episodes provided evidence of the distant legacy of the Vienna Settlement's Congress System. Top-level meetings had become an occasionally necessary part, albeit not a regular feature, of the struggle for international order. The third claim one can advance in praise of the

Congress/Concert System was that it could, and did, tolerate warfare that served to adjust relations among the great powers. An international order is not a static structure; it has to be dynamic, able to accommodate changing contexts and the rise and fall of states. In the sharpest of contrasts to the great power wars of the twentieth century, those of the nineteenth, concentrated in the sixteen years between 1854 and 1870, did not escalate to engulf the whole of Europe.

It is commonplace to argue that the Congress System died as early as the 1820s, while its normative features in the form of the Concert System did not survive beyond mid-century. There is some merit in that view, but overall it is too harsh. As reluctant chairman of the Berlin Congress in 1878, Bismarck gave voice to a distinctly systemic view of the purpose of the proceedings when he said, 'We are not here to consider the happiness of the Bulgarians [who, as Russia's clients, had just been awarded huge territorial gains by the soon to be annulled Treaty of San Stefano] but to secure the peace of Europe' (quoted in Bartlett, 1996: 105). Would that a similar congress could have been convened in July 1914. But high-level diplomacy is hostage to many factors, not least the competence of the statesmen involved, and the measure of discretion they are allowed by their domestic contexts.

Versailles, the League and collective security

In 1919 the victorious Allies and their associates tried a new approach to international order: collective security through the agency of a League of Nations. Whereas the post-1815 Congress of Europe had been an exclusive club of the recognized great powers, the League was to embrace all states in good standing (e.g., Germany and the new Bolshevik Republic in Russia were not invited to join at first), those who, in the language of the time, 'abided by the standards of civilization' (Gong, 1984). The League did have a premier class in the form of a permanent council, so it bore more than a casual resemblance in practice to the Congress System. However, the later institution's founding fathers intended that it should introduce a radical change in the way international relations were conducted. Those founders were primarily American and British, with President Woodrow Wilson well out in front as advocate. The French contributed to the extensive planning for the League, but their political culture and their geostrategic concerns were not as friendly to idealistic schemes for the wholesale reformation of international politics as were those of the more liberal, optimistic and geostrategically disengaged Americans and British.

To be fair to the statesmen of 1919, one must recall their historical context. More than 9 million men had just died in battle. The greatest war in history had terminated less than a year previously. Moreover, unwisely but inevitably, the peace conference was convened, bereft of participation by the defeated states, in and close by the capital of the principal Allied power. France was the state that had suffered the most from German aggression, so Paris was not a political environment especially conducive to the shaping of a post-war order that would be generous towards the defeated. There was a certain euphoria in the air at the time, and understandably so. Recent events had been so terrible that they were held both to necessitate and to license a revolution in diplomatic and strategic behaviour. The general publics in France and Britain simultaneously seemed ready to believe that the League could deliver eternal peace, while demanding that the guilty enemy must be punished. In those circumstances, the wonder is not that the Versailles Settlement and the succeeding treaties with Germany's allies were decidedly imperfect. Rather, it is remarkable that the settlement was as moderate as it was. That, of course, is a subjective judgement, delivered with the benefit of hindsight. The problem was that to most Germans at the time, and for the next two decades, Versailles was iconic as the symbol of an injustice imposed by vengeful victors. Moreover, in the opinion of too many Germans, those foreign victors had not really won the war militarily. In short, the political context of 1919 was far from ideal for the reformation of world politics. But one might well be moved to comment that if radical change in state practices could not be introduced in the immediate aftermath of arguably the greatest tragedy in history, when could it be? Not only was it entirely reasonable that the victorious Allies should attempt to reform the conduct of international relations, but it was inevitable that they had to try.

The Versailles Settlement was founded, or was declared to be founded, upon five guiding principles: the self-determination of nations; democratization (German, or Prussian, authoritarianism was held to be guilty of a cultural militarism that led to policies and behaviour that produced war); open diplomacy, no secret treaties (unlike those negotiated by all the Allied powers before and during World War I); disarmament (since many people believed that the war had been caused by the cunning machinations of evil arms manufacturers, the so-called merchants of death); and collective security. There are two contrasting opinions about the main problem with the settlement. The first claims that it was too lenient on Germany, meaning that it would leave it both eventually strong and vengeful. The second suggests that it was too harsh: it was not well designed for Germany's re-entry into the ranks of the basically satisfied, responsible great powers. In other words, with respect to the latter argument, Versailles undermined the domestic legitimacy of the Weimar Republic and, as a consequence, lengthened the odds against the new Germany achieving an enduring political stability at home. What that would mean for international order and, ultimately, for peace in Europe would depend upon the changing contexts of future history. Unfortunately, those contexts were not permissive of long-term stability, either in Germany or in Europe as a whole. Bitter disputes among the Allies over many details of the settlement, typically with France opposed by Britain and the United States, subverted from the outset the legitimacy of the Versailles Treaty and the international order it created.

It is plausible to argue that with respect to major issues of war and peace, the League of Nations was constructed to give expression to two dominant concepts, both of which were unsound. It is not only hindsight that commands such a negative verdict. Experienced statesmen in 1919 should have known that the two concepts were fallacious. The ideas in question were, first, the moral force of world public opinion, and, second, collective security. The League was to provide a universal sounding chamber in, and from, which the global public would voice its opinion. This idea is not entirely ridiculous. There is no doubt that states can be embarrassed by a barrage of criticism voiced by a host of otherwise powerless polities in the forum of world diplomacy: then the League, now the United Nations. The fallacy lies in the belief that principled expressions of disapproval, often uttered by those who are thoroughly unprincipled themselves, can serve as powerful restraints upon the behaviour of states. When states are strongly motivated to pursue by force what they understand to be their vital interests, they are not readily influenced by the rhetoric of disinterested parties.

As for the principle of collective security, it falls at the first fence of strategic historical reality. The idea requires that a state declared by the League (or later by the UN) to be an aggressor should be opposed by the whole collectivity of states, by force if necessary, and regardless of the interest of individual polities in the case at issue. The trouble with collective security as the leading deterrent to aggression and the principal tool to restore international order is that it ignores the nature of the modern system of states. All states are self-regarding entities that act collectively only when the advantages of so doing outweigh the disadvantages. Only very rarely will states thoroughly indifferent to an international dispute be prepared to commit blood and money for the common good.

'[N]ew world orders . . . need to be policed,' according to historian Michael Howard (2001: 124). Every international order in every period requires that someone or something functions as a protector of the system. If there is no such protector or protective mechanism, then that particular international order cannot endure. The consequences of the absence of a capable and willing international policeman, or of a practical policing arrangement, inevitably is disorder, and disorder is a precursor to warfare. Rephrased, someone has to do the dirty and expensive work on behalf of international order if there is to be an order worthy of the title.

By the late 1930s, Germany had joined and left the League of Nations (1926–33), everyone was rearming and the principle of collective security was dead and buried. A condition of international disorder had returned to where it had been in the decade before 1914, only this time the political, socio-cultural, strategic and technological contexts were even less promising for a peaceful future. The reasons why can be summarized thus:

1. In the late 1930s, as in 1914, Germany was too powerful to be contained and balanced by its continental European neighbours. In 1914, Germany did not believe this, which is the principal reason why it manipulated a crisis in the Balkans as an excuse to launch a preventive war. In the late 1930s, Hitler believed that the other great powers would catch up with, and overmatch, Germany's rearmament by 1943. So, in an eerie replay of German reasoning in 1912–14, Nazi Germany believed that it had only a narrow historical window for victorious war-making.
2. Contrary to the 1914 context, Germany in the 1930s was set firmly and irrevocably on a course for war. Nazism was a quasi-religion that honoured, indeed required, war. And Hitler's bizarre ideological purpose was to establish by force a racially pure Aryan super-state. That was his dominant mission. Therefore, it was the destiny of his Germany to attempt to transform ideology into reality. Also, in a minor key, Nazi Germany had some old scores to settle from 1914–18. Revenge is a powerful non-strategic makeweight among motives for war.
3. In 1914, in theory at least, Germany and Austria-Hungary were overmatched materially by the Franco-Russian Alliance. In 1939, Russia was not playing for the anti-German team. Indeed, Stalin joined Hitler in a pact of temporary mutual convenience on 23 August of that year. Britain and France were confident of their ability to defeat Germany in a long and total war, a replay of 1914–18, but they had some fatal weaknesses in the short-war zone.
4. In 1914, Britain could worry almost exclusively about the danger posed to its interests by Germany. But in the 1930s London faced the strategic nightmare of possible war with three great powers simultaneously. And those three were

distributed geopolitically in the worst possible way for the security of Britain and its empire. Germany in Northern Europe, Italy in the Mediterranean on the main route to the Middle East and India, and Japan in the Far East equalled at least one enemy too many for Britain. And in the 1930s, France increasingly took its lead in foreign policy from Britain.

The 1930s was a decade separated from its predecessor politically, economically, socio-culturally and strategically by the consequences of the Great Depression. The history of the 1930s demonstrates what can happen when an international order, in this case that established by the Versailles Settlement, lacks a policeman. Someone or something has to keep the peace. The duty includes a necessary readiness to wage some warfare soon, lest a great deal more warfare might need to be waged later. In the 1930s, international order was at the mercy of the most unscrupulous and ambitious states. The issue of interest for this analysis is not international misbehaviour, but rather the historically attested importance of the need for the protection of order. It cannot be assumed that by some hidden hand of political and strategic necessity, aggressive revolutionary powers somehow will be deterred, and if need be defeated. Wars, great and small, regular and irregular, occur despite the presence of a willing and fairly able protecting agent, but at least the reality of such a policeman affords some prospect of a stable international, and domestic, order. The League of Nations failed in its primary mission, which was to prevent the recurrence of the Great War of 1914–18. In the 1930s there was no one willing or able, singly or in combination with others, to act forcibly to protect the international order. As a consequence of this failure, 53 million people died, more than 36 million of them civilians.

The Cold War order and the United Nations

The new world order envisaged by optimist-idealists in 1945 had as its centre of gravity the invention of the United Nations. It was created in wartime at a conference in San Francisco, and its permanent home was to be in New York City. President Roosevelt was determined to lock his country into a leading role in the UN, and by housing the organization in America he believed he could prevent much of the kind of domestic opposition that had thwarted Woodrow Wilson over US participation in the League. The UN was not wholly the product of optimist-idealists, though. Pessimist-realists made some useful contributions, too. Most notably, the UN, in common with its League predecessor, was to have what amounted to an executive committee in the form of the Security Council. The core of the Council would comprise five permanent members (the P5), each of which enjoyed a right of veto over all Security Council decisions. The veto has turned out to be a blessing for world peace, which was a virtue of no small importance during the Cold War. It meant that the Security Council could not achieve the unanimity necessary for action to be recommended or ordered, but, crucially, it also meant that the super- and great powers would not fight each other as a result of an ill-judged majority vote in the Security Council.

In practice, the UN performed a worthwhile function during the Cold War decades as a stage upon which otherwise unheard voices could assert their existence. In addition, it did useful work in such essentially non-political fields as health and disease, education, and providing assistance to refugees. But as the prime institution for the management of international order, the UN was stillborn. The lack of consensus among the P5 translated into paralysis of the organization on all important matters bearing upon international security. Some experienced statesmen who should have known better, including the tough-minded and fairly cynical politician Franklin D. Roosevelt, sincerely believed that the P5 would function as a working and workable continuation of the Grand Alliance that was winning World War II. It did not.

The UN as an institution and as a forum or theatre may have contributed little worth mentioning to world order during the Cold War, but that did not mean that international peace and security were much impoverished as a result. Since the East–West rivalry deprived the UN of a practical role in support of international order, the contending states made an alternative arrangement. The order that kept the peace, at least with respect to any direct clash of arms between the principals, was organized by a bipolar balance of power. That balance came to be ever more heavily, and mutually, nuclear in content. So, international order was simultaneously both menaced by the most awesome threats of destruction in all of history and protected robustly by those same awesome menaces. The nuclear stand-off, and the geopolitical lines of demarcation that it froze, made for an orderly world with regard to the mainstream of strategic history. There was disorder aplenty in the 1950s, 1960s and 1970s as the European colonial empires expired, but a nuclear World War III did not occur, contrary to the confident expectations of many people in the 1940s and 1950s.

It is necessary to mention the one occasion in those years when the UN was able to make a positive contribution to international order. The Soviet representative was absent temporarily from the Security Council in June 1950, in protest over the denial of the China seat to Mao Tse-tung's new People's Republic of China. This meant that the Western powers were able to arrange and see passed a 'Uniting for Peace' resolution in the General Assembly. That resolution declared North Korea to be an aggressor and licensed member states to come to the military assistance of South Korea. In 1950, as in 1990–1 over Iraq, the blessing of the UN carried useful moral authority. A significant reason why this was, and remains, so has much to do with the fact that the UN is the world's only institution with a security mission that has universal membership. It has all the faults of its members and of the typical workings of international politics, but, unfortunately, it is the only UN that is available. There is no alternative universal institution. Periodic attempts at reform are essayed, but if they are significant, they are certain to be opposed by strong vested interests. For example, moves to expand the P5 so as to include rising powers, or risen powers, as well as to provide better representation for Africa, South America and Asia, must negotiate an obstacle course of objections. To date, that obstacle course has defied all challenges.

When there is a consensus on the Security Council, the UN can play a significant role at the heart of efforts to protect world order. If that order should be menaced by the political and strategic consequences of climate change, the UN could function indispensably in providing the necessary forum for decisions of global scope. However, it is necessary to observe that any threat sufficiently grave as to open the possibility of global consensus is just as likely to drive the major state players into a ruthlessly selfish mode of behaviour.

The end of the Cold War and new world disorders

When the Soviet Union and its empire collapsed, more or less peaceably, between 1989 and 1991, in a descriptive sense a new world order was born. That order was characterized negatively by the absence of a working balance of power. By default, the American superpower was left in charge of any security problem that it chose to treat as worthy of its attention.

In 1990, President George Bush Snr spoke briefly, normatively, of a new world order, but one suspects that there was no deep thought, let alone clear purpose, behind the elevated language. The world order rhetoric was overtaken immediately by the protracted crisis triggered by Iraq's seizure of Kuwait. It is easy to be critical of the statesmen who have had to make peace out of war. The process has been hugely underexamined by scholars, in contrast to the attention that has been devoted to the transition from peace to war. The end of a great war may appear to be one of history's 'strategic moments', a brief period when bold new approaches to international order should be feasible, but in practice those moments can have fatally non-permissive contexts.

With respect to the post-war–interwar decade of the 1990s, the Bush administration (1989–93) faced daunting uncertainties. Had the Soviet Union really collapsed, definitively? What kind of a state would the new Russian Federation prove to be? Germany was abruptly reunited after forty-five years. Would it be a security problem again? There were pressures to extend NATO eastwards, despite the promise to the contrary made by Washington to the Soviet Union. What would, and should, be the roles of NATO in a Europe bereft of a Soviet threat? Did it have an important job to do in helping to lock the former Soviet satellites into the practices and values of the Western world? And, to cite the largest uncertainty of all, what should be the United States' role in the world? Suddenly, it was the only superpower, not balanced militarily by a rival or collection of rivals. But to what ends ought America to lend its strength? What did it truly care about?

In practice, the answer to the last of these questions was 'not very much'. The Clinton administration, like its predecessor, was more than content to leave international ordering duties to others. In the early 1990s, those others were a newly active UN, one liberated by the *de facto* disappearance of the threat of a Soviet veto, and the European Union (EU). But, as was explained in Chapter 16, neither the UN nor the EU (nor even NATO minus the United States) proved capable of imposing order, of making peace out of war in violently troubled places. The Clinton administration meant well. It wanted to advance the practice of Western-style democracy, to push for freer trade – always provided politically potent sectors of the US economy (agriculture, for example) would remain protected – and generally it wished to do good in the world. But the extensive and bloody disorder of the 1990s lacked a focus, a dominant challenge requiring firm discipline by the ordering power. Violence had become endemic in much of the former Yugoslavia, in Russia's 'near abroad' and would-be secessionist regions (such as Chechnya), and above all in Africa.

A new kind of fanatical, religiously motivated terrorism was recognized, tracked and occasionally assaulted. But, overall, America did not have a grand strategy for the prudent orchestration of the instruments of national power. That was hardly surprising, since it lacked a coherent policy keyed to a sense of duty to maintain international order.

One has to be somewhat sympathetic to the American policy-makers of the 1990s. They ruled the only superpower in an interwar period of unknowable duration. And that was a period blessedly innocent of any security threat of sufficient seriousness to mobilize US policy creativity and national energy. America is not especially gifted in putting out small-scale, but well-established, fires in culturally alien contexts.

9/11 and a hegemonic order

Only when provoked violently on 11 September 2001 did the lone superpower, the principal guardian of international order, put on its uniform and declare its intention to make the world a safer place, irrespective of whether the world approved. After 9/11, world order had a clearly defined meaning, in Washington at least. America committed itself to the thankless and predictably internationally unpopular task of behaving like a hegemonic power. Islamic terrorism and the spread of weapons of mass destruction – separately and, even more terrifyingly, possibly in tandem – were identified as the dominant threats of the new era. America now had a job to do. It had found a foe worthy of serious and sustained attention. In addition, it had come to identify its own national security closely with a world order that was very much the product of American ideas, practices and material effort.

The world order of the twenty-first century that the United States has volunteered to police does not rest upon an international consensus. US policing authority derives from its military and economic strength. The international community, a largely notional entity, makes its appearance on the stage of the UN in New York. With some exceptions among America's closest friends and allies, and those who feel themselves dependent upon the United States for their security (e.g., the Baltic States and others recently relieved of Soviet overlordship), the international community demands that America should act only with its blessing. This is not an endorsement of collective security. The context, rather, is one of asserted rights without responsibilities. Today there are two rival master principles vying for primacy for the maintenance or restoration of world order.

On the one hand, there is an insistence upon multilateralism and consensus. World order should be protected by behaviour agreed among all the major state players. Those willing and able to act should do so strictly under licence from the international community as represented at the United Nations. Given that three of the veto-armed P5 members of the Security Council (France, Russia and China) tend to be more concerned to constrain America than to solve challenges to world order, this consensual approach has obvious weaknesses from the perspective of order.

The second approach to maintaining world order is that which is extant. As the only possible executive agent of the international community, and by now wise in the ways of unhelpful but uncompetitive detractors, America takes such action as it judges necessary for world order. Support and endorsement are invited from the international community. Diplomacy is practised actively at the UN as well as bilaterally in capitals around the world. But in the event that international consensus proves elusive, especially among the rest of the P5, America, as self-appointed guardian of global order, is prepared to go into action anyway. This was the story of the invasion of Iraq in 2003 to impose a forcible change of regime.

The final judgement in this discussion is provided by the historian Donald Kagan. He comments, advises even, that 'What seems to work best, even though imperfectly, is the possession by those states who wish to preserve the peace of the preponderant power and of the will to accept the burdens and responsibilities required to achieve that purpose' (Kagan, 1995: 570). Unfortunately, as Kagan recognizes, that is not always feasible. More often than not in modern strategic history, power has been roughly in balance among major state players. In such a context, Kagan's principle would tend to spark a war that might easily spread far beyond its local origins. One thinks of the local Austro-Serbian quarrel in the summer of 1914 as a possible example.

There can be no single, all-contexts solution to the challenge of maintaining international order. There is, however, at least one maxim of enduring merit: international order needs to be policed by someone or something. From time to time, order is menaced by threats, great and small. Disorder looms as a potent possibility. Today, it is the menace posed by irregular warriors for an extreme variant of Islam, as well as by the threat of weapons of mass destruction in the hands of those motivated to employ them. In the future, international order may well be challenged primarily by the rise of a rival or two to American hegemony. In addition, climate change has the potential to create disorder on a global scale, as the geographies of population distribution, energy, and food and water resources move ever more severely out of balance. Disorder is a fuel of conflict and a context that favours violence and warfare.

Conclusion

'Peace' is a word with two principal meanings. On the one hand, it is a simple description of a condition of non-war. On the other, it can carry a normative judgement on political relations, as well as describing a non-war condition. In its second definition, 'peace' refers to a political relationship wherein war is all but unthinkable. For illustration: in 1938 and 2007 Britain was at peace with Germany. But in 1938 that peace was tenuous and, emphatically, strictly of the simple, non-war variety. In 2007, war between the two countries was unthinkable. And yet the same term is used in both cases.

Peace is a very high concept, bearing much emotional, normative and prescriptive content. The choice of words employed in strategic historical analysis can matter deeply. For example, were the years 1947–89 a period of Cold War or one of Long Peace (Gaddis, 2001: 32–3)? With hindsight, it was Long Peace, but to policy-makers in the 1950s and 1960s it did not look like that. They were obliged by the dictates of prudence to assume that the condition of non-war rested upon a delicate balance of power, especially strategic nuclear power (Wohlstetter, 1959). In retrospect, it is not difficult to explain why the Cold War really was the Long Peace. One can cite a lack of political motivation to go to war; the fear of nuclear war; and some skill in the interacting bilateral management of the consequences of the nuclear and missile revolutions. To those rational explanations one should add the vital factor of luck. In truth, there is no way of knowing for certain why the Cold War did not provide the context out of which World War III exploded. What is more, historical research will never yield a definitive answer.

If one asks, 'What causes peace?', the character of the peace referred to matters greatly. If one means simply peace as the absence of war, replies might include: a balance of power; a temporarily unchallengeable imbalance of power; mutual nuclear terror; and the absence of vital interests in contention. But if one wishes to promote a world order which, like an oil stain, spreads over a growing geopolitical domain wherein war is all but unthinkable, and is probably impractical as well, one needs to search for deeper reasons. For peace in the second sense – the peace that finds war unthinkable – to reign, two developments are necessary. First, war must cease to be perceived to be useful as an instrument of policy. No longer must it be the last resort of polities, anticipated to be able to resolve problems that would not yield to non-violent methods. Second, it has to be rejected culturally, which is to say normatively, by taboo even. No longer must war be socially acceptable. Politics and strategy tend to reflect and follow culture. At least, they will until, or unless, communities suffer extraordinary security shock.

Peace in both senses comprises a political context desired strongly, almost universally. But how does humankind both reinforce the simple state of non-war and best advance the prospects for the deeper peace, the kind that rests upon the cultural rejection of war? Is the question even sensible? Can peace be constructed purposively? Have not succeeding generations of statesmen for the past two centuries attempted to do this, and ultimately failed every time? Perhaps the wrong question has been posed, and therefore largely irrelevant answers have been devised. On a more positive note, the historical record of peacemaking and international ordering, though studded with awesome failures, has not been entirely negative. Organized political, and criminal, violence has been, and remains, widespread and is probably ineradicable. People will always fight about something. In Thucydides' immortal formula, they will fight for reasons of fear, honour (or culture) and interest, so the likelihood of politically motivated violence fading away entirely cannot be high. But one should not conclude the debate by insisting upon perfection, which is to say upon the total demise of the institution of war in all its manifestations, both regular and irregular.

How, if at all, can humankind improve its resistance to war? There is a literature which points out that an important part of the world already comprises a zone of stability wherein military strategic questions are of little, if any, policy significance (Singer and Wildavsky, 1993). In that zone, so the argument goes, war has been culturally rejected. EU Europe constitutes the core, the exemplar, of a zone of non-strategic, even anti-strategic, stability. If the whole world viewed war and warfare as do the older members of the EU, then challenges to international order would no longer include the possibility of disorder caused by warfare.

There is no denying that much of Europe (minus the Balkans, of course) has turned its back on war. But the cultural rejection of war by many Europeans is the consequence of special historical circumstances; not least, it is the product of the horrific, repeated experience of total war. Also, Europeans inhabit a pleasant realm of affluence, unlike most of the rest of the human race. A post-military EU Europe, with a declining population, can be viewed as an island of prosperity amid a sea of relative and absolute poverty. The greatest threat of disorder in the future, as indeed today, stems ultimately from grossly uneven development between regions. Today's international order includes modernized, partially modernized and unmodernized societies. Huge disparities in standards of living are visible to all via electronic media that now are near-universally accessible. This is not a prescription for an orderly international system. Strategic history, both international and domestic, suggests that prosperous and contented regions need to be defended against those who wish to join the feast. The fall of Rome in the fifth century to tribes that sought to share in, or seize, the good life is a story with a message for all periods, including our own (Heather, 2005).

What is known with confidence about this most vital, yet variable, condition known as peace? Strategic history suggests strongly that peace cannot be constructed by means of institutional engineering. Such construction can be useful to polities that wish to use it. Institutions and procedures that facilitate communication, perhaps improve mutual understanding, and provide mechanisms for interstate arbitration have roles to play on behalf of order. But those roles will be fulfilled only when the political players are prepared to negotiate and compromise. There is nothing magically transformative about participation in international institutions. States, as well as other security communities that generally are not represented in the UN, frequently prefer to act unilaterally, or with allies, in defence of their vital interests. In most of those situations, international political architecture and its norms and procedures can be of only limited value for international order. The existence of the UN facilitates multinational efforts to contain, limit and even halt a war, should the belligerent parties agree to be contained, limited and prevented from fighting to a finish. The story was the same for the Concert System in the nineteenth century and the League of Nations in the twentieth. The functioning of such institutions must reflect their political contexts. They have been as helpful for international order as their leading members would permit. An international institution constructed to advance the prospects for good order and peace can be used or abused on behalf of disorder and war. States can behave in the UN in such a way as to block decisions for collective action to suppress disorderly behaviour.

International institutions, with the UN as the prime example, cannot themselves contribute in a vital way to a more orderly world. Rather, they should be viewed as the faithful products of world order and disorder. States determined to cooperate will use the good offices and fora of those institutions. States determined upon conflict will use them as an arena for propaganda and coalition-building and, if need be, will employ their rules to paralyse the international community. Michael Howard explains why world peace cannot be constructed by the invention, or reform, of institutions:

> The establishment of a global peaceful order thus depends on the creation of a world community sharing the characteristics that make possible domestic order, and this will require the widest possible diffusion of those characteristics by the societies that already possess them. World order cannot be created simply by building international institutions and organizations that do not arise naturally out of the cultural disposition and historical experience of their members. Their creation and operation require at the very least the existence of a transnational elite that not only shares the same cultural norms but can render those norms acceptable within their own societies and can where necessary persuade their colleagues to agree to the modifications necessary to make them acceptable.
>
> (Howard, 2001: 105)

This is a fair summary of historical experience. Just as peace cannot be constructed by ingenious institution-building, nor can it be mandated by law, custom or norms. When obedience to those restraints is predicted to work towards results sharply contrary to states' national interests, they will be ignored.

Key points

1. There are two main and opposing views of strategic history. One holds that the human race is slowly making progress towards a warless world; the other believes that the strategic future will resemble the strategic past, though not in detail.
2. Great wars have been waged for the purpose of restoring or creating a favoured international order.
3. After every great war in modern times, except for the Cold War, an effort was made to institutionalize a new world order.
4. The repeated efforts to construct a new and improved world order were not wholly without value, but they all foundered on the rocks of the sovereign self-regard of states.
5. Peace has two principal meanings: war is not under way at present; and war is all but unthinkable and impossible.
6. A peaceful world order cannot be created by institutional engineering. It has to be the product of some shared cultural values and of common understanding of historical experience.

Questions

1. Can the human race make progress towards a more peaceful world? Has it done so since 1800?
2. What are the requirements for international order?
3. What were the strengths and weaknesses of the successive 'new world orders' attempted since 1800?
4. What is peace? How best is it achieved and maintained?

Further reading

C. J. Bartlett *Peace, War and the European Powers, 1814–1914* (Basingstoke: Macmillan, 1996).

M. E. Brown, S. M. Lynn-Jones and S. E. Miller (eds) *Debating the Democratic Peace* (Cambridge, MA: MIT Press, 1996)

M. E. Brown, O. R. Cote, Jr, S. Lynn-Jones and S. E. Miller (eds) *Theories of War and Peace* (Cambridge, MA: MIT Press, 1998)

I. Clark *The Hierarchy of States: Reform and Resistance in the International Order* (Cambridge: Cambridge University Press, 1989).

F. H. Hinsley *Power and the Pursuit of Peace: Theory and Practice in the History of Relations between States* (Cambridge: Cambridge University Press, 1963).

M. Howard *The Invention of Peace and the Reinvention of War* (London: Profile Books, 2001).

G. J. Ikenberry *After Victory: Institutions, Strategic Restraint, and the Rebuilding of Order after Major Wars* (Princeton, NJ: Princeton University Press, 2001).

T. L. Knutsen *The Rise and Fall of World Orders* (Manchester: Manchester University Press, 1999).

A. Williams *Failed Imagination? New World Orders of the Twentieth Century* (Manchester: Manchester University Press, 1998).

20 Conclusion

Must future strategic history resemble the past?

Reader's guide: Continuity and discontinuity in strategic history.

Because this is a strategic history, its dominant narrative comprises the consequences of the threat and use of politically motivated, organized force upon the course of events. Of course, there is more to history than its strategic dimension alone, and there is more to strategy than its military component. However, the assumption upon which this text is founded is only that the strategic thread is the most significant of the several engines of historical change, not that it is the sole driver. It is true that unmodified reference to strategy obscures the issue of whether one refers to grand strategy – that is, the purposeful employment of all of a state's or other political entity's assets – or only to military strategy.

Unless otherwise indicated, the abundant references to strategy in this book refer to military strategy. There are two reasons for this. First, the master narrative, the plot line, is about the role and consequences of force. Second, if military strategy is allowed to merge into grand strategy, the logic and perspective of strategic history can be lost, or at least weakened. The unique perspective that a (military) strategic historical narrative and analysis can provide would all but disappear. Grand-strategic history is unquestionably indistinguishable from history. Similarly, grand strategy is synonymous with the old-fashioned but still useful term 'statecraft'.

Just four broad claims conclude this discourse. Although this introduction to strategic history has conclusions, strategic history itself does not.

1. *Great wars of industrial mobilization, such as World War II, cannot occur any more.* They have been banished by two technological developments: nuclear weapons and information technology.
2. *The strategic thread in history has fluctuated in importance, but it always returns to pole position and, overall, it has lost none of its relative significance.* Two hundred years of history show repeatedly both evolutionary and revolutionary changes in warfare. The military-strategic context has been constantly in motion. Sometimes movement has been slow, while at other times – from 1916 to 1918, for example – it has proceeded at almost breakneck speed under the pressure of real-time necessity.

If history is a guide, some security communities will always have interests that they believe must be protected by force.

3. *In their natures and dynamics, war, warfare and strategy have not changed over the course of two centuries.* That is why the writings of Sun-tzu from the China of 400 BC and those of Carl von Clausewitz from the 1820s remain relevant to, indeed essential for, strategic education today. With the partial exception of the geographical, the details of the contexts specified in Chapter 1 (political, socio-cultural, economic, technological, military-strategic, geographical and historical) have altered beyond recognition over the course of two centuries. But it is only the detail that has changed. The nature of strategic challenges has not evolved. The task of the strategist is the same today as it was in 1800. It is to employ force, or the threat of force, for policy ends. Despite technological advances beyond counting, strategy is as difficult an undertaking today as ever it was in the past (Gray, 1999: 63–8). Also, Chapter 1 identified themes that run through the text. Those themes were as follows: the dialogue between continuity and discontinuity; the complex relations between war and peace, and peace and war; the often tense relations between soldiers and politicians; and the nexus between war and society. With the passage of time, those themes have lost none of their relevance to the course of strategic history.

4. *Because so many sources of continuity effectively are permanent, one can predict with confidence, though not with satisfaction, that history's strategic dimension is not in the process of fading away.* Independent security communities, each with their Thucydidean motives of fear, honour and interest, are, in the last resort, condemned to fend for themselves in what can be a rough and dangerous world. The persistence of this core condition suggests that humankind's strategic future is likely to resemble its past in important respects. The details will be different, but the grand narrative most probably will be painfully familiar.

Glossary

ABCD coalition: Coalition formed and led by America in 1940–1 to oppose further Japanese aggression in East Asia (America, Britain, China, Dutch East Indies).

Atomic weapons: Weapons that derive their energy from the process of nuclear fission.

CBO: The Combined Bomber Offensive conducted by the UK's RAF Bomber Command attacking Germany at night, and the US Army Air Forces attacking by day. Agreed at the Casablanca summit between Roosevelt and Churchill in January 1943.

C⁴ISTAR: Command, control, communications, computing, intelligence, surveillance, targeting and reconnaissance.

Clausewitz, Carl von *(1780–1831):* Author of *On War* (1832), the most widely respected work on the theory of war ever written.

COIN: Counter-insurgency.

Collective security: The principle that an aggressor state should be opposed by the entire international community.

Combined-arms warfare: The theory that every military asset fulfils its potential when employed in combination with other assets.

Concert System: The occasional nineteenth-century practice of summit-level, or near-summit-level, meetings by great powers, where they would concert efforts to maintain or restore international order.

Containment: The fundamental concept underpinning US foreign policy towards the Soviet Union during the Cold War.

Coup d'oeil: An instantaneous, perhaps instinctive, grasp of a complex and confused military situation.

CT: Counter-terrorism.

Culture: The beliefs, values, attitudes, habits of mind and preferred practices of a community.

Détente: The relaxation of tensions; a term first popular in the 1970s.

Extended deterrence: The extending of protection by (generally) nuclear deterrence over distant friends and allies.

First-strike bonus: The predicted military benefit that should accrue to the belligerent who attacks first with nuclear weapons.

Fleet train: The at-sea logistic fleet provided to support the combat navy.

Geopolitics: The political meaning of geography.

Globalization: The process of ever-greater global interaction among states, communities and economies.

Grand strategy: The purposeful employment of all the instruments of power available to a security community.

Great Depression: Collapse of much of international commerce following the Wall Street Crash of 29 October 1929, and its consequences in sharply reduced economic activity and high unemployment.

Great war: A war involving all, or at least most, of the world's great powers.

Guerrilla warfare: A style of warfare waged by the weaker belligerent, favouring surprise and small-scale engagements.

Hydrogen, or thermonuclear, weapons: Nuclear weapons that require the fusion of two isotopes of hydrogen. This is achieved by implosion effected by an atomic fission 'trigger'.

ICBM: Intercontinental ballistic missile of 4,000-mile range or more.

Insurgency: A popular uprising, probably employing the tactics of guerrilla warfare, initially at least.

International community: The notional collectivity of all humankind. The UN is its rough approximation.

Irregular warfare: Warfare in which at least one belligerent is not a state with regular armed forces.

Joint warfare: Warfare as a joint endeavour by two or more of the geographically specialized forces: army, navy and air force.

Jomini, Baron Antoine Henri de *(1779–1869):* The most influential military writer of the first half of the nineteenth century, especially with respect to strategy.

League of Nations: International organization established by the Versailles Treaty of 1919 for the purpose of keeping, or restoring, international order and peace.

Manoeuvre warfare: A style of combat dependent upon mobility; usually contrasted with attrition.

Military revolution (MR): Great change in the contexts of warfare that cannot be resisted. Examples include the Industrial Revolution, the nuclear revolution and the information revolution.

Military-technical revolution (MTR): A revolution in military affairs keyed to technological change.

Mutual assured destruction (MAD): A condition of mutual societal vulnerability to nuclear destruction.

Operations, operational art: The conduct of a campaign, requiring the employment of tactical engagements and other behaviour for their campaign-level effects.

Peer competitor: A country or coalition sufficiently powerful to be one's near equal.

Pre-emption, prevention: A strategy of pre-emption entails a commitment to strike first in the last resort. By contrast, a strategy of prevention entails a readiness to strike first in order to prevent the presumptive enemy from being ready to initiate hostilities on its terms.

Reconnaissance–strike complex: Soviet concept of the 1980s, subsequently more or less realized by the United States. It is a military system that, all but seamlessly, can locate enemy assets and strike them with great precision over a long distance.

Regular warfare: Open warfare between the uniformed armed forces of states.

Reparation: A bill for the recovery of costs suffered by the actions of the defeated belligerent in war.

Revolution in military affairs (RMA): A radical change in the character of warfare.

SALT (Strategic Arms Limitation Talks): Soviet–American arms-control process from 1969 to 1979. A SALT I package in 1972 included an interim agreement on offensive arms and the Anti-Ballistic Missile (ABM) Treaty. It led to a SALT II treaty in 1979, which was politically infeasible as the political context deteriorated sharply.

Schlieffen Plan: The German plan to defeat France in a six-week campaign. It was implemented as the Schlieffen–Moltke Plan (having been amended by Moltke the younger, Schlieffen's successor) in August–September 1914. It failed.

Sea lines of communication: Imaginary lines at sea which mark the most important maritime routes.

Special forces: Small elite units trained to undertake tasks beyond the scope of normal military competence.

Stability: A much-favoured quality in security politics. It refers to an absence of potentially dangerous change. Cold War strategic theory recognized crisis stability, deterrence stability and arms-race stability.

Strategic history: The history of the influence of the use, and threat of use, of politically motivated force.

Strategic moment: A particular short period of extraordinary strategic importance and opportunity.

Strategy: The use made of force and the threat of force for the ends of policy. It is the bridge that connects policy with military power.

Submarine-launched ballistic missiles (SLBMs): Missiles deployed under the sea that are effectively invulnerable to detection.

Tactics: The use of armed forces in combat.

Terrorism: The use of violence to induce fear for political ends.

Total war: War waged by all the resources of belligerent societies.

Triad: The strategic forces triad comprises ICBMs, SLBMs and manned bombers. Each 'leg' of the triad has distinctive tactical features.

Ungoverned space: Contemporary euphemism for 'bandit country', or territory that is not subject to effective governance.

Waffen SS: The 'fighting' SS, the private army of the Nazi regime, eventually thirty-six divisions strong.

War: Organized violence waged for political purposes.

Warfare: The waging of war; the fighting.

Weapons of mass destruction (WMD): These can be nuclear, radiological, chemical or biological.

Bibliography

Agawa, H. (1982) *The Reluctant Admiral: Yamamoto and the Imperial Navy*, New York: Kodansha International/USA.

Alger, J. I. (1982) *The Quest for Victory: The History of the Principles of War*, Westport, CT: Greenwood Press.

Allison, G. (2004) *Nuclear Terrorism: The Ultimate Preventable Catastrophe*, New York: Times Books.

Anderson, M. S. (2003) *The Ascendancy of Europe, 1815–1914*, 3rd edn, Harlow: Pearson Education.

Angell, N. (1911) *The Great Illusion: A Study of the Relation of Military Power in Nations to Their Economic and Social Advantage*, London: William Heinemann.

—— (1938) *The Great Illusion – Now*, London: Penguin.

Aron, R. (1970) 'The Evolution of Modern Strategic Thought', in A. Buchan (ed.), *Problems of Modern Strategy*, London: Chatto and Windus.

—— (1983) *Clausewitz: Philosopher of War*, London: Routledge and Kegan Paul.

—— (2002) *The Dawn of Universal History: Selected Essays from a Witness to the Twentieth Century*, New York: Basic Books.

Asprey, R. B. (1994) *War in the Shadows: The Classic History of Guerrilla Warfare from Ancient Persia to the Present*, rev. edn, Boston: Little, Brown.

Bacevich, A. J. (2002) *American Empire: The Realities and Consequences of US Diplomacy*, Cambridge: MA: Harvard University Press.

—— (2005) *The New American Militarism: How Americans are Seduced by War*, New York: Oxford University Press.

Barnett, C. (1991) *Engage the Enemy More Closely: The Royal Navy in the Second World War*, New York: W. W. Norton.

Barnhart, M. A. (1987) *Japan Prepares for Total War: The Search for Economic Security, 1919–1941*, Ithaca, NY: Cornell University Press.

Barry, J. M. (2005) *The Great Influenza: The Epic Story of the Deadliest Plague in History*, New York: Penguin Books.

Bartlett, C. J. (1996) *Peace, War and the European Powers, 1814–1914*, London: Macmillan.

Bayly, C. and Harper, T. (2004) *Forgotten Armies: The Fall of British Asia, 1941–1945*, London: Allen Lane.

Beckett, I. F. W. (2001a) *The Great War, 1914–1918*, Harlow: Longman.

—— (2001b) *Modern Insurgencies and Counter-insurgencies: Guerrillas and Their Opponents since 1750*, London: Routledge.

Belfield, E. (1993) *The Boer War*, London: Leo Cooper.

Bell, P. M. H. (1997) *The Origins of the Second World War in Europe*, 2nd edn, London: Longman.

Benbow, T. (2004) *The Magic Bullet? Understanding the Revolution in Military Affairs*, London: Brassey's.

Bessel, R. (2004) *Nazism and War*, London: Weidenfeld and Nicolson.

Best, G. (1982) *War and Society in Revolutionary Europe, 1770–1870*, London: Fontana.

Betts, R. K. (1997) 'Should Strategic Studies Survive?', *World Politics*, 50: 7–33.

Bialer, U. (1980) *The Shadow of the Bomber: The Fear of Air Attack and British Politics, 1932–1939*, London: Royal Historical Society.

Black, J. (2001) *Western Warfare, 1775–1882*, Bloomington, IN: Indiana University Press.

—— (2002) *Warfare in the Western World, 1882–1975*, Chesham: Acumen.

—— (2003) *World War Two: A Military History*, London: Routledge.

—— (2004) *Rethinking Military History*, London: Routledge.

—— (2005) *Introduction to Global Military History: 1775 to the Present Day*, London: Routledge.

Blanning, T. C. W. (ed.) (2000) *The Nineteenth Century: Europe, 1789–1914*, Oxford: Oxford University Press.

Boemke, M. F., Feldman, G. D. and Glaser, E. (eds) (1998) *The Treaty of Versailles: A Reassessment after 75 years*, Cambridge: Cambridge University Press.

Boemke, M. F., Chickering, R. and Förster, S. (eds) (1999) *Anticipating Total War: The German and American Experiences, 1871–1914*, Cambridge: Cambridge University Press.

Bond, B. (1996) *The Pursuit of Victory: From Napoleon to Saddam Hussein*, Oxford: Oxford University Press.

Boog, H. *et al.* (1998) *Germany and the Second World War*, Vol. IV: *The Attack on the Soviet Union*, Oxford: Clarendon Press.

Boot, M. (2003) 'The New American Way of War', *Foreign Affairs*, 82: 41–58.

Booth, K. and Dunne, T. (eds) (2002) *Worlds in Collision: Terror and the Future of Global Conflict*, Basingstoke: Palgrave Macmillan.

Boulding, K. E. (1962) *Conflict and Defense: A General Theory*, New York: Harper and Brothers.

Bowden, M. (1999) *Black Hawk Down*, London: Bantam Press.

Boyce, R. and Maiolo, J. A. (eds) (2003) *The Origins of World War Two: The Debate Continues*, Basingstoke: Palgrave Macmillan.

Bridge, F. R. and Bullen, R. (2005) *The Great Powers and the European States System, 1814–1914*, 2nd edn, Harlow: Pearson Education.

Brodie, B. (1959) *Strategy in the Missile Age*, Princeton, NJ: Princeton University Press.

—— (1973) *War and Politics*, New York: Macmillan.

—— (1976) 'The Continuing Relevance of *On War*', in C. von Clausewitz, *On War*, ed. and trans. M. Howard and P. Paret, Princeton, NJ: Princeton University Press.

—— (ed.) (1946) *The Absolute Weapon: Atomic Power and World Order*, New York: Harcourt, Brace.

Brown, M. E., Lynn-Jones, S. M. and Miller, S. E. (eds) (1996) *Debating the Democratic Peace*, Cambridge, MA: MIT Press.

Brown, M. E., Cote, O. R., Jr, Lynn-Jones, S. and Miller, S. E. (eds) (1998) *Theories of War and Peace*, Cambridge, MA: MIT Press.

Browning, P. (2002) *The Changing Nature of Warfare: The Development of Land Warfare from 1792 to 1945*, Cambridge: Cambridge University Press.

Buchan, A. (ed.) (1970) *Problems of Modern Strategy*, London: Chatto and Windus.

Bull, H. (1977) *The Anarchical Society: A Study of Order in World Politics*, New York: Columbia University Press.

Bush, G. W. (2002) *The National Security Strategy of the United States of America*, Washington, DC: White House.

—— (2006) *The National Security Strategy of the United States of America*, Washington, DC: White House.

Callwell, C. E. (1990) *Small Wars: A Tactical Textbook for Imperial Soldiers*, London: Greenhill Books.

Calvocoressi, P., Wint, G. and Pritchard, J. (1999) *The Penguin History of the Second World War*, London: Penguin.

Chandler, D. (1967) *The Campaigns of Napoleon*, London: Weidenfeld and Nicolson.

—— (ed.) (1998) *Napoleon's Marshals*, London: Weidenfeld and Nicolson.

Chickering, R. (1999) 'Total War: The Use and Abuse of a Concept', in M. F. Boemke, R. Chickering and S. Förster (eds), *Anticipating Total War: The German and American Experiences, 1871–1914*, Cambridge: Cambridge University Press.

Chickering, R. and Förster, S. (eds) (2003) *The Shadows of Total War: Europe, East Asia, and the United States, 1919–1939*, Cambridge: Cambridge University Press.

Clark, A. (1961) *The Donkeys*, London: Hutchinson.

Clark, I. (1989) *The Hierarchy of States: Reform and Resistance in the International Order*, Cambridge: Cambridge University Press.

Clark, W. K. (2002) *Waging Modern War: Bosnia, Kosovo, and the Future of Combat*, New York: Public Affairs.

Clausewitz, C. von (1976) *On War*, ed. and trans. M. Howard and P. Paret, Princeton, NJ: Princeton University Press.

Clinton, W. J. (1994) *A National Security Strategy for a New Century*, Washington, DC: White House.

Cohen, E. A. (2002) *Supreme Command: Soldiers, Statesmen, and Leadership in Wartime*, New York: Free Press.

Connelly, O. (1999) *Blundering to Glory: Napoleon's Military Campaigns*, rev. edn, Wilmington, DE: Scholarly Resources.

—— (2006) *The Wars of the French Revolution and Napoleon, 1792–1815*, London: Routledge.

Corbett, J. S. (1973) *England in the Seven Years' War: A Study in Combined Strategy*, 2 vols, repr. of 2nd edn of 1918, New York: AMS Press.

—— (1988) *Some Principles of Maritime Strategy*, Annapolis, MD: Naval Institute Press.

Cornwell, J. (2004) *Hitler's Scientists: Science, War and the Devil's Pact*, London: Penguin Books.

Corum, J. S. (1992) *The Roots of Blitzkrieg: Hans von Seeckt and German Military Reform*, Lawrence, KS: University Press of Kansas.

Crockatt, R. (1995) *The Fifty Years War: The United States and the Soviet Union in World Politics, 1941–1991*, New York: Routledge.

Cronin, A. K. (2006) 'How al-Qaeda Ends: The Decline and Demise of Terrorist Groups', *International Security*, 31: 7–48.

Dear, I. C. B. and Foot, M. R. D. (eds) (1995) *The Oxford Companion to the Second World War*, Oxford: Oxford University Press.

DeGroot, G. J. (2004) *The Bomb: A Life*, London: Jonathan Cape.

Doughty, R. A. (2005) *Pyrrhic Victory: French Strategy and Operations in the Great War*, Cambridge, MA: Harvard University Press.

Douhet, G. (1972) *The Command of the Air*, New York: Arno Press.

Dull, P. S. (1978) *A Battle History of the Imperial Japanese Navy (1941–1945)*, Annapolis, MD: Naval Institute Press.

Dupuy, R. E. and Dupuy, T. N. (1993) *The Collins Encyclopaedia of Military History: From 3,500 BC to the Present*, 4th edn, London: BCA.

Duyvesteyn, I. and Angstrom, J. (eds) (2005) *Rethinking the Nature of War*, London: Frank Cass.

Echevarria, A. J., II (2000) *After Clausewitz: German Military Thinkers before the Great War*, Lawrence, KS: University Press of Kansas.

Esdaile, C. J. (1995) *The Wars of Napoleon*, London: Longman.

Etzold, T. H. and Gaddis, J. L. (eds) (1978) *Containment: Documents on American Policy and Strategy, 1945–1950*, New York: Columbia University Press.

Evans, D. C. and Peattie, M. R. (1997) *Kaigun: Strategy, Tactics, and Technology in the Imperial Japanese Navy 1887–1941*, Annapolis, MD: Naval Institute Press.

Evans, R. J. (2005) *The Third Reich in Power*, London: Allen Lane.

Falls, C. (1959) *The Great War, 1914–1918*, New York: Perigee Books.

Feis, H. (1971) *The Road to Pearl Harbor: The Coming of the War between the United States and Japan*, Princeton, NJ: Princeton University Press.

Ferguson, N. (1998) *The Pity of War*, London: Allen Lane.

Finney, P. (ed.) (1997) *The Origins of the Second World War*, London: Arnold.

Förster, S. and Nagler, J. (eds) (1997) *On the Road to Total War: The American Civil War and the German Wars of Unification, 1861–1871*, Cambridge: Cambridge University Press.

Frank, R. B. (1992) *Guadalcanal: The Definitive Account of the Landmark Battle*, New York: Penguin Books.

Freedman, L. (2001) 'The Third World War?', *Survival*, 43: 61–88.

—— (2003) *The Evolution of Nuclear Strategy*, 3rd edn, Basingstoke: Palgrave Macmillan.

—— (2004) *Deterrence*, Cambridge: Polity Press.

—— (2006) *The Transformation of Strategic Affairs*, Adelphi Paper 379, Abingdon: Routledge for the International Institute for Strategic Studies.

Friedman, N. (2000) *The Fifty-Year War: Conflict and Strategy in the Cold War*, Annapolis, MD: Naval Institute Press.

Fursenko, A. and Naftali, T. (1997) *'One Hell of a Gamble': Khrushchev, Castro, Kennedy, and the Cuban Missile Crisis, 1958–1964*, London: John Murray.

Gaddis, J. L. (1982) *Strategies of Containment: A Critical Appraisal of Postwar American National Security Policy*, New York: Oxford University Press.

—— (1997) *We Now Know: Rethinking Cold War History*, Oxford: Clarendon Press.

—— (2001) 'On Starting All Over Again: A Naïve Approach to the Study of the Cold War', in O. A. Westad (ed.), *Reviewing the Cold War: Approaches, Interpretations, Theory*, London: Frank Cass.

—— (2006) *The Cold War*, London: Allen Lane.

Gat, A. (1989) *The Origins of Military Thought: From the Enlightenment to Clausewitz*, Oxford: Oxford University Press.

—— (1998) *Fascist and Liberal Visions of War: Fuller, Liddell Hart, Douhet, and Other Modernists*, Oxford: Clarendon Press.

Gates, D. (1997) *The Napoleonic Wars, 1803–1815*, London: Arnold.

—— (2001) *Warfare in the Nineteenth Century*, Basingstoke: Palgrave.

Glantz, D. M. and House, J. (1995) *When Titans Clashed: How the Red Army Stopped Hitler*, Lawrence, KS: University Press of Kansas.

Goldhagen, D. J. (1997) *Hitler's Willing Executioners: Ordinary Germans and the Holocaust*, London: Abacus.

Goldstein, E. (2002) *The First World War Peace Settlements, 1919–1925*, Harlow: Pearson Education.

Goldstein, E. and Maurer, J. (eds) (1994) *The Washington Conference 1921–22: Naval Rivalry, East Asian Stability and the Road to Pearl Harbor*, London: Frank Cass.

Gong, G. W. (1984) *The Standard of 'Civilization' in International Society*, Oxford: Clarendon Press.

Gordon, M. R. and Trainor, B. E. (1995) *The Generals' War: The Inside Story of the Conflict in the Gulf*, Boston: Little, Brown.

—— (2006) *Cobra II: The Inside Story of the Invasion and Occupation of Iraq*, London: Atlantic Books.

Gorlizki, Y. and Khlevniuk, O. (2004) *Cold Peace: Stalin and the Soviet Ruling Circle, 1945–1953*, Oxford: Oxford University Press.

Gray, C. S. (1994) 'Villains, Victims, and Sheriffs: Strategic Studies for an Interwar Period', *Comparative Strategy*, 13: 353–69.

—— (1999) *Modern Strategy*, Oxford: Oxford University Press.

—— (2005) *Another Bloody Century: Future Warfare*, London: Weidenfeld and Nicolson.

—— (2006a) 'Clausewitz, History, and the Future Strategic World', in W. Murray and R. H. Sinnreich (eds), *The Past as Prologue: The Importance of History to the Military Profession*, Cambridge: Cambridge University Press.

—— (2006b) *Irregular Enemies and the Essence of Strategy: Can the American Way of War Adapt?*, Carlisle, PA: Strategic Studies Institute, US Army War College.

—— (2006c) *Recognizing and Understanding Revolutionary Change in Warfare: The Sovereignty of Context*, Carlisle, PA: Strategic Studies Institute, US Army War College.

—— (2006d) *Strategy and History: Essays on Theory and Practice*, London: Routledge.

Griffith, P. (1994) *Battle Tactics of the Western Front: The British Army's Art of Attack, 1916–18*, New Haven, CT: Yale University Press.

—— (1998) *The Art of War of Revolutionary France, 1789–1802*, London: Greenhill Books.

Gunaratna, R. (2002) *Inside al Qaeda: Global Network of Terror*, New York: Columbia University Press.

Halberstam, D. (2003) *War in a Time of Peace: Bush, Clinton and the Generals*, London: Bloomsbury.

Halliday, F. (1983) *The Making of the Second Cold War*, London: Verso.

Halpern, P. G. (1994) *A Naval History of World War I*, London: UCL Press.

Hamilton, I. (1921) *The Soul and Body of an Army*, London: Edward Arnold.

Hamilton, R. F. and Herwig, H. H. (2004) *Decisions for War, 1914–1917*, Cambridge: Cambridge University Press.

Hammes, T. X. (2004) *The Sling and the Stone: On War in the 21st Century*, St Paul, MN: Zenith Press.

Handel, M. I. (2001) *Masters of War: Classical Strategic Thought*, 3rd edn, London: Frank Cass.

—— (ed.) (1986) *Clausewitz and Modern Strategy*, London: Frank Cass.

Harmon, C. C. (2006) 'What History Suggests about Terrorism and Its Future', in W. Murray and R. H. Sinnreich (eds), *The Past as Prologue: The Importance of History to the Military Profession*, Cambridge: Cambridge University Press.

Harris, J. P. (1995) *Men, Ideas and Tanks: British Military Thought and Armoured Forces, 1903–1939*, Manchester: Manchester University Press.

Harrison, R. W. (2001) *The Russian Way of War: Operational Art, 1904–1940*, Lawrence, KS: University Press of Kansas.

Heather, P. (2005) *The Fall of the Roman Empire*, London: Macmillan.

Heinl, R. D., Jr (1966) *Dictionary of Military and Naval Quotations*, Annapolis, MD: US Naval Institute.

Herrman, R. K. and Lebow, R. N. (eds) (2004) *Ending the Cold War: Interpretations, Causation, and the Study of International Relations*, New York: Palgrave Macmillan.

Herwig, H. H. (1997) *The First World War: Germany and Austria-Hungary, 1914–1918*, London: Arnold.

Heuser, B. (2002) *Reading Clausewitz*, London: Pimlico.

Hinsley, F. H. (1963) *Power and the Pursuit of Peace: Theory and Practice in the History of International Relations between States*, Cambridge: Cambridge University Press.

Hirst, P. (2001) *War and Power in the 21st Century: The State, Military Conflict and the International System*, Cambridge: Polity Press

Hitler, A. (2003) *Mein Kampf*, New York: Fredonia Classics.

Hoffman, B. (1998) *Inside Terrorism*, London: Victor Gollancz.

Holloway, D. (1994) *Stalin and the Bomb: The Soviet Union and Atomic Energy, 1939–1956*, New Haven, CT: Yale University Press.

Honig, J. W. (1997) 'Strategy in a Post-Clausewitzian Setting', in G. de Nooy (ed.), *The Clausewitzian Dictum and the Future of Western Military Strategy*, The Hague: Kluwer Law International.

Howard, M. (1981) *The Franco-Prussian War: The German Invasion of France, 1870–1871*, London: Methuen.

—— (1983) *Clausewitz*, Oxford: Oxford University Press.

—— (2001) *The Invention of Peace and the Reinvention of War*, London: Profile Books.

—— (2004) 'Military History and the History of War', in Strategic and Combat Studies Institute, *Contemporary Essays*, The Occasional [monograph], No. 47, Shrivenham: Strategic and Combat Studies Institute.

Howes, P. (1998) *The Catalytic Wars: A Study of the Development of Warfare, 1860–1870*, London: Minerva Press.

Hughes, D. J. (ed.) (1993) *Moltke on the Art of War: Selected Writings*, trans. D. J. Hughes and H. Bell, Novato, CA: Presidio Press.

Ikenberry, G. J. (2001) *After Victory: Institutions, Strategic Restraint, and the Rebuilding of Order after Major Wars*, Princeton, NJ: Princeton University Press.

Iriye, A. (1987) *The Origins of the Second World War in Asia and the Pacific*, London: Longman.

Jervis, R. (1989) *The Meaning of the Nuclear Revolution: Statecraft and the Prospect of Armageddon*, Ithaca, NY: Cornell University Press.

Jomini, Baron Antoine Henri de (1992) *The Art of War*, London: Greenhill Books.

Kagan, D. (1995) *On the Origins of War and the Preservation of Peace*, New York: Doubleday.

Kaldor, M. (1999) *New and Old Wars: Organized Violence in a Global Era*, Cambridge: Polity Press.

Kaplan, F. (1983) *The Wizards of Armageddon*, New York: Touchstone.

Kaplan, R. D. (2000) *The Coming Anarchy: Shattering the Dreams of the Post Cold War*, New York: Random House.

Kaufman, R. G. (1990) *Arms Control during the Pre-nuclear Era: The United States and Naval Limitation between the Two World Wars*, New York: Columbia University Press.

Keaney, T. A. and Cohen, E. A. (1995) *Revolution in Warfare? Air Power in the Persian Gulf*, Annapolis, MD: Naval Institute Press.

Keegan, J. (1989) *The Second World War*, London: Hutchinson.

—— (1995) *The Battle for History: Re-fighting World War Two*, London: Hutchinson.

——(1998a) *The First World War*, London: Hutchinson.

—— (1998b) *War and Our World*, London: Hutchinson.

Kennedy, P. (1987) *The Rise and Fall of the Great Powers: Economic Change and Military Conflict from 1500 to 2000*, New York: Random House.

Kershaw, I. (2000) *Hitler, 1936–45: Nemesis*, London: Allen Lane.

Kiesling, E. (1996) *Arming against Hitler: France and the Limits of Military Planning*, Lawrence, KS: University Press of Kansas.

Kinross, S. (2004) 'Clausewitz and Low-Intensity Conflict', *Journal of Strategic Studies*, 27: 35–58.

Kissinger, H. (1964) *A World Restored: Europe after Napoleon: The Politics of Conservatism in a Revolutionary Age*, New York: Grosset and Dunlop.

—— (1994) *Diplomacy*, New York: Simon and Schuster.

—— (1999) *Years of Renewal*, London: Weidenfeld and Nicolson.

Kitchen, M. (2000) *Europe between the Wars: A Political History*, Harlow: Pearson Education.

Knox, M. and Murray, W. (eds) (2001) *The Dynamics of Military Revolution, 1300–2050*, Cambridge: Cambridge University Press.

Knutsen, T. L. (1999) *The Rise and Fall of World Orders*, Manchester: Manchester University Press.

Krepinevich, A. F., Jr (1986) *The Army and Vietnam*, Baltimore, MD: Johns Hopkins University Press.

Kurth, J.C. (2003) 'Clausewitz and the Two Contemporary Military Revolutions: RMA and RAM', in B. A. Lee and K. F. Walling (eds), *Strategic Logic and Political Rationality: Essays in Honor of Michael I. Handel*, London: Frank Cass.

Laffin, J. (1988) *British Butchers and Bunglers of World War One*, Gloucester: Alan Sutton.

Lamb, M. and Tarling, N. (2001) *From Versailles to Pearl Harbor: The Origins of the Second World War in Europe and Asia*, Basingstoke: Palgrave.

Lambert, A. D. (1990) *The Crimean War: British Grand Strategy against Russia, 1853–56*, Manchester: Manchester University Press.

Laqueur, W. (1998) *Guerrilla Warfare: A Historical and Critical Study*, New Brunswick, NJ: Transaction.

—— (1999) *The New Terrorism: Fanaticism and the Arms of Mass Destruction*, New York: Oxford University Press.

—— (2003) *No End to War: Terrorism in the Twenty-first Century*, New York: Continuum.

Lawrence, T. E. (1991) *Seven Pillars of Wisdom: A Triumph*, New York: Anchor Books.

Leffler, M. P. (1992) *A Preponderance of Power: National Security, the Truman Administration, and the Cold War*, Stanford, CA: Stanford University Press.

Lewin, R. (1978) *Ultra Goes to War*, New York: McGraw-Hill.

—— (1983) *The American Magic: Codes, Ciphers and the Defeat of Japan*, London: Penguin.

—— (1984) *Hitler's Mistakes*, London: Leo Cooper.

Liddell Hart, B. H. (1967) *Strategy: The Indirect Approach*, London: Faber and Faber.

—— (1970a) *History of the First World War*, London: Pan.

—— (1970b) *History of the Second World War*, New York: G. P. Putnam's Sons.

Longerich, P. (2005) *The Unwritten Order: Hitler's Role in the Final Solution*, Stroud: Tempus.

McInnes, C. (2002) *Spectator-Sport War: The West and Contemporary Conflict*, Boulder, CO: Lynne Rienner.

Mc Ivor, A. D. (ed.) (2005) *Rethinking the Principles of War*, Annapolis, MD: Naval Institute Press.

Macksey, K. (1987) *Military Errors of World War Two*, Poole: Arms and Armour Press.

—— (1994) *Why the Germans Lose at War: The Myth of German Military Superiority*, London: Greenhill.

Mahan, A. T. H. (1965) *The Influence of Sea Power upon History, 1660–1783*, repr. of 1890 edn, London: Methuen.

Mahnken, T. G. (2002) *Uncovering Ways of War: US Intelligence and Foreign Military Innovation, 1918–1941*, Ithaca, NY: Cornell University Press.

Mandelbaum, M. (1998–9) 'Is Major War Obsolete?', *Survival*, 40: 20–38.

Mao Tse-tung (1961) *On Guerrilla Warfare*, trans. S. B. Griffith, New York: Praeger.

—— (1963) *Selected Military Writings*, Beijing: Foreign Languages Press.

Marks, S. (2003) *The Illusion of Peace: International Relations in Europe, 1918–1933*, 2nd edn, Basingstoke: Palgrave Macmillan.

Martel, G. (ed.) (1986) *The Origins of the Second World War Reconsidered*, London: Routledge.

Mastry, V. (1996) *The Cold War and Soviet Insecurity: The Stalin Years*, New York: Oxford University Press.

Maudsley, E. (2005) *Thunder in the East: The Nazi–Soviet War, 1941–1945*, London: Hodder Arnold.

Mearsheimer, J. J. (2001) *The Tragedy of Great Power Politics*, New York, W. W. Norton.

Medawar, J. and Pyke, D. (2001) *Hitler's Gift: Scientists who Fled Nazi Germany*, London: Piatkus.

Megargee, G. P. (2006) *War of Annihilation: Combat and Genocide on the Eastern Front, 1941*, Lanham, MD: Rowman and Littlefield.

Miller, E. S. (1991) *War Plan Orange*, Annapolis, MD: Naval Institute Press.

Millett, A. R. and Murray, W. (eds) (1998) *Military Effectiveness*, Vol. III: *The Second World War*, Boston: Allen and Unwin.

Mombauer, A. (2001) *Helmuth von Moltke and the Origins of the First World War*, Cambridge: Cambridge University Press.

—— (2005) 'Of War Plans and War Guilt: The Debate Surrounding the Schlieffen Plan', *Journal of Strategic Studies*, 28: 857–85.

Moran, D. (2002) 'Strategic Theory and the History of War', in J. Baylis, J. Wirtz, E. Cohen and C. S. Gray (eds), *Strategy in the Contemporary World: An Introduction to Strategic Studies*, Oxford: Oxford University Press.

Muir, R. (1998) *Tactics and the Experience of Battle in the Age of Napoleon*, New Haven, CT: Yale University Press.

Münkler, H. (2005) *The New Wars*, Cambridge: Polity Press.

Murray, W. and Knox, M. (2001) 'Thinking about Revolutions in Warfare', in M. Knox and W. Murray (eds), *The Dynamics of Military Revolution, 1300–2050*, Cambridge: Cambridge University Press.

Murray, W. and Millett, A. R. (2000) *A War to be Won: Fighting the Second World War*, Cambridge, MA: Harvard University Press.

—— (eds) (1996) *Military Innovation in the Interwar Period*, Cambridge: Cambridge University Press.

Murray, W. and Scales, R. H., Jr (2003) *The Iraq War: A Military History*, Cambridge, MA: Harvard University Press.

Nathan, J. A. (ed.) (1992) *The Cuban Missile Crisis Revisited*, New York: St Martin's Press.

Neiberg, M. S. (2005) *Fighting the Great War: A Global History*, Cambridge, MA: Harvard University Press.

Nooy, G. de (ed.) (1997) *The Clausewitzian Dictum and the Future of Western Military Strategy*, The Hague: Kluwer Law International.

Norris, R. S. and Kristensen, H. M. (2002) 'Global Nuclear Stockpiles, 1945–2002', *Bulletin of the Atomic Scientists*, 58: 103–4.

Nye, J., S. Jr (2002) *The Paradox of American Power: Why the World's Only Superpower Can't Go It Alone*, Oxford: Oxford University Press.

—— (2007) *Understanding International Conflicts: An Introduction to Theory and History*, 6th edn, New York: Pearson Longman.

Odom, W. E. (1998) *The Collapse of the Soviet Military*, New Haven, CT: Yale University Press.

Overy, R. J. (1981) *The Air War, 1939–1945*, New York: Stein and Day.

—— (1995) *Why the Allies Won*, London: Jonathan Cape.

—— (2000) *The Battle*, London: Penguin.

Owens, B. (2000) *Lifting the Fog of War*, New York: Farrar, Straus and Giroux.

Paret, P. (1976) *Clausewitz and the State*, New York: Oxford University Press.

—— (1992) *Understanding War: Essays on Clausewitz and the History of Military Power*, Princeton, NJ: Princeton University Press.

—— (ed.) (1986) *Makers of Modern Strategy: From Machiavelli to the Nuclear Age*, Princeton, NJ: Princeton University Press.

Parry, J. H. (1981) *The Discovery of the Sea*, Berkeley, CA: University of California Press.

Perret, G. (1990) *A Country Made by War: From the Revolution to Vietnam – the Story of America's Rise to Power*, New York: Vintage Books.

Peters, R. (2002) *Beyond Terror: Strategy in a Changing World*, Mechanicsburg, PA: Stackpole Books.

Pitt, W. (1915) *The War Speeches of William Pitt the Younger*, Oxford: Clarendon Press.

Powers, T. (1993) *Heisenberg's War: The Secret History of the German Bomb*, Boston: Da Capo Press.

Pratt, E. A. (1916) *The Rise of Rail-Power in War and Conquest, 1833–1914*, Philadelphia, PA: J. B. Lippincott.

Pry, P. V. (1999) *War Scare: Russia and America on the Nuclear Brink*, Westport, CT: Praeger.

Rathbone, J. (ed.) (1984) *Wellington's War: Peninsular Dispatches*, London: Michael Joseph.

Record, J. (2005) *Appeasement Reconsidered: Investigating the Mythology of the 1930s*, Carlisle, PA: Strategic Studies Institute, US Army War College.

Reid, B. H. (2002) *The Civil War and the Wars of the Nineteenth Century*, London: Cassell.

Reynolds, C. G. (1978) *The Fast Carriers: The Forging of an Air Navy*, Huntington, NY: Robert E. Krieger.

Rhodes, R. (1986) *The Making of the Atomic Bomb*, New York: Touchstone.

Roberts, A. and Guelff, R. (eds) (2004) *Documents on the Laws of War*, 3rd edn, Oxford: Oxford University Press.

Roberts, G. (2002) *Victory at Stalingrad: The Battle that Changed History*, London: Longman.

Rosen, S. P. (1991) *Winning the Next War: Innovation and the Modern Military*, Ithaca, NY: Cornell University Press.

Rothenberg, G. E. (1980) *The Art of War in the Age of Napoleon*, Bloomington, IN: Indiana University Press.

—— (1995) *Napoleon's Great Adversary: Archduke Charles and the Austrian Army, 1729–1814*, New York: Sarpendon.

Rumsfeld, D. H. (2005) *The National Defense Strategy of the United States of America*, Washington, DC: US Department of Defense.

—— (2006) *Quadrennial Defense Review Report*, Washington, DC: US Department of Defense.

Schelling, T. C. (1966) *Arms and Influence*, New Haven, CT: Yale University Press.

Schom, A. (2004) *The Eagle and the Rising Sun: The Japanese–American War, 1941–1943, Pearl Harbor through Guadalcanal*, New York: W. W. Norton.

Schroeder, P. W. (1994) *The Transformation of European Politics, 1763–1848*, Oxford: Clarendon Press.

Sheffield, G. (2001) *Forgotten Victory: The First World War: Myths and Realities*, London: Headline.

Showalter, D. E. (2000) 'Military Innovation and the Whig Interpretation of History', in H. R. Winton and D. R. Mets (eds), *The Challenge of Change: Military Institutions and New Realities, 1918–1941*, Lincoln, NE: University of Nebraska Press.

—— (2004) *The Wars of German Unification*, London: Arnold.

Shuster, R. J. (2006) *German Disarmament after World War I: The Diplomacy of International Arms Inspection, 1920–1931*, Routledge: London.

Singer, M. and Wildavsky, A. (1993) *The Real World Order: Zones of Peace/Zones of Turmoil*, London: Chatham House.

Smith, H. (2005) *On Clausewitz: A Study of Military and Political Ideas*, Basingstoke: Palgrave Macmillan.

Smith, R. (2005) *The Utility of Force: The Art of War in the Modern World*, London: Allen Lane.

Snyder, L. L. (ed.) (1981) *Hitler's Third Reich: A Documentary History*, Chicago: Nelson Hall.

Sondhaus, L. (2001) *Naval Warfare, 1815–1914*, London: Routledge.

Spector, R. H. (1985) *Eagle against the Sun: The American War with Japan*, New York: Free Press.

Squires, C. (2006) 'New War Demands New Training for Troops', *Guardian Unlimited*, <http://www.guardian.co.uk/worldlatest/story/O,,-5910352.00.html> (accessed 25 June 2006).

Standage, T. (1998) *The Victorian Internet: The Remarkable Story of the Telegraph and the Nineteenth Century's Online Pioneers*, London: Weidenfeld and Nicolson.

Steiner, Z. (2005) *The Lights that Failed: European International History, 1919–1933*, Oxford: Oxford University Press.

Stern, J. (2003) *Terror in the Name of God: Why Religious Militants Kill*, New York: HarperCollins.

Stevenson, D. (1988) *The First World War and International Politics*, Oxford: Oxford University Press.

—— (2004) *Cataclysm: The First World War as Political Tragedy*, New York: Basic Books.

Stone, N. (1975) *The Eastern Front, 1914–1917*, London: Hodder and Stoughton.

Strachan, H. (2001) *The First World War*, Vol. I: *To Arms*, Oxford: Oxford University Press.

—— (2005a) *The First World War: A New Illustrated History*, London: Pocket Books.

—— (2005b) 'The Lost Meaning of Strategy', *Survival*, 47: 33–54.

—— (2006) 'A General Typology of Transcultural Wars – the Modern Ages', in H.-H. Kortüm (ed.), *Transcultural Wars: From the Middle Ages to the 21st Century*, Berlin: Akademie Verlag.

Strassler, R. B. (ed.) (1996) *The Landmark Thucydides: A Comprehensive Guide to 'The Peloponnesian War'*, trans. R. Crawley, rev. edn, New York: Free Press.

Sun-tzu (1994) *The Art of War*, trans. R. D. Sawyer, Boulder, CO: Westview Press.

Taylor, A. J. P. (1969) *War by Time-table: How the First World War Began*, New York: American Heritage.

Terraine, J. (1996) 'The Substance of the War', in H. Cecil and P. H. Liddle (eds), *Facing Armageddon: The First World War Experience*, London: Leo Cooper.

Toland, J. (1976) *The Rising Sun: The Decline and Fall of the Japanese Empire, 1936–1945*, New York: Random House.

Tooze, A. (2006) *The Wages of Destruction: The Making and Breaking of the Nazi Economy*, London: Allen Lane.

Townshend, C. (ed.) (2005) *The Oxford History of Modern War*, Oxford: Oxford University Press.

Trachtenberg, M. (1999) *A Constructed Peace: The Making of the European Settlement, 1945–1963*, Princeton, NJ: Princeton University Press.

Trinquier, R. (1964) *Modern Warfare: A French View of Counterinsurgency*, New York: Praeger.

Tucker, S. C. (1998) *The Great War, 1914–18*, London: UCL Press.

—— (2004) *The Second World War*, Basingstoke: Palgrave Macmillan.

US Army (2001) *Field Manual FM3-0, Operations*, Washington, DC: HQ, US Army.

Utley, J. G. (1985) *Going to War with Japan, 1937–1941*, Knoxville, TN: University of Tennessee Press.

Van Creveld, M. (1985) *Command in War*, Cambridge, MA: Harvard University Press.

—— (1991) *The Transformation of War*, New York: Free Press.

—— (1997) 'What is Wrong with Clausewitz?', in G. de Nooy (ed.) *The Clausewitzian Dictum and the Future of Western Military Strategy*, The Hague: Kluwer Law International.

Van Evera, S. (1999) *Causes of War: Power and the Roots of Conflict*, Ithaca, NY: Cornell University Press.

Vat, D. van der (1991) *The Pacific Campaign: World War II, the US–Japanese Naval War, 1941–1945*, New York: Simon and Schuster.

Wawro, G. (1996) *The Austro-Prussian War: Austria's War with Prussia and Italy in 1866*, Cambridge: Cambridge University Press.

—— (2000) *Warfare and Society in Europe, 1792–1914*, London: Routledge.

—— (2003) *The Franco-Prussian War: The German Conquest of France in 1870–1871*, Cambridge: Cambridge University Press.

Weinberg, G. L. (1994) *A World at Arms: A Global History of World War II*, Cambridge: Cambridge University Press.

—— (1995) *Germany, Hitler, and World War II*, Cambridge: Cambridge University Press.

Weltman, J. J. (1995) *World Politics and the Evolution of War*, Baltimore, MD: Johns Hopkins University Press.

Werrell, K. P. (1996) *Blankets of Fire: US Bombers over Japan during World War II*, Washington, DC: Smithsonian Institution Press.

Westad, O. A. (ed.) (2000) *Reviewing the Cold War: Approaches, Interpretations, Theory*, London: Frank Cass.

Wilkinson, S. (1991) *The French Army before Napoleon*, Aldershot: Gregg Revivals.

Williams, A. (1998) *Failed Imagination? New World Orders of the Twentieth Century*, Manchester: Manchester University Press, 1998.

Willmott, H. P. (1989) *The Great Crusade: A New Complete History of the Second World War*, New York: Free Press.

—— (1999) *The Second World War in the Far East*, London: Cassell.

Winton, H. R. and Mets, D. R. (eds) (2002) *The Challenge of Change: Military Institutions and New Realities, 1918–1941*, Lincoln, NE: University of Nebraska Press.

Wohlstetter, A. J. (1959) 'The Delicate Balance of Terror', *Foreign Affairs*, 37: 242–55.

Wylie, J. C. (1989) *Military Strategy: A General Theory of Power Control*, Annapolis, MD: Naval Institute Press.

Zabecki, D. T. (2006) *The German 1918 Offensives: A Case Study in the Operational Level of War*, London: Routledge.

Zuber, T. (2002) *Inventing the Schlieffen Plan: German War Planning, 1871–1914*, Oxford: Oxford University Press.

Zubok, V. and Pleshakov, C. (1996) *Inside the Kremlin's Cold War: From Stalin to Khrushchev*, Cambridge, MA: Harvard University Press.

Index